**Late 1800s to the 21st Century**

U.S. History Detective® products available in print or eBook form.

Book 1 • Book 2

Written by
Steven Greif

Graphic Design by
Scott Slyter
Mary O'Dell

Edited by
Joan Greif
Patricia Gray
Helen Howard

© 2016
THE CRITICAL THINKING CO.™
www.CriticalThinking.com
Phone: 800-458-4849 • Fax: 541-756-1758
1991 Sherman Ave., Suite 200 • North Bend • OR 97459
ISBN 978-1-60144-243-7

**Reproduction of This Copyrighted Material**
The intellectual material in this product is the copyrighted property of The Critical Thinking Co.™ The individual or entity who initially purchased this product from The Critical Thinking Co.™ or one of its authorized resellers is licensed to reproduce (print or duplicate on paper) each page of this product for use within one home or one classroom. Our copyright and this limited reproduction permission (user) agreement strictly prohibit the sale of any of the copyrighted material in this product. Any reproduction beyond these expressed limits is strictly prohibited without the written permission of The Critical Thinking Co.™ Please visit http://www.criticalthinking.com/copyright for more information. The Critical Thinking Co.™ retains full intellectual property rights on all its products (eBooks, books, and software).
Printed in China by Shanghai Chenxi Printing Co., Ltd. (Aug. 2020)

# Table of Contents




© 2016 The Critical Thinking Co.™ • www.CriticalThinking.com • 800-458-4849

© 2016 The Critical Thinking Co.™ • www.CriticalThinking.com • 800-458-4849 

## About the Author

Steven Greif has been named a "Distinguished Alumni" of Southwestern Oregon Community College, where he earned his Associate of Arts degree. His Bachelor of Arts degree in history came from Oregon State University, where he won several awards for student writing. He also studied colonial history at the College of William and Mary and obtained his Interdisciplinary Master's degree in history and geography at the University of Oregon. For 32 years, Greif taught leadership and civics classes, Advanced Placement® American history, and Pacific Northwest history at North Bend (Oregon) High School, and coached track and field as well. He was honored with the Oregon Education Association's "Excellence in Education Award" in 1996 and was named "Citizen of the Year" in North Bend in 2005. Greif has been a volunteer member of the Coos County Historical Society Board of Directors since 1999. Since retiring in 2010, he has taught night classes at the local community college.


© 2016 The Critical Thinking Co.™ • www.CriticalThinking.com • 800-458-4849

# Teacher Overview

*U.S. History Detective®* can be used as a stand-alone textbook, a resource of supplemental activities to enrich another textbook, or as a review course for older students. The content skills are based on common state social studies standards for Grade 8. What makes *U.S. History Detective®* different from other American history books is the integration of critical thinking into the content lessons. The questions in this book require deeper analysis and frequently ask for supporting evidence from the lesson. This in-depth analysis produces greater understanding, which results in better grades and higher test scores. Over time, students who practice critical thinking learn to apply it throughout their education and life. This book also develops reading comprehension and writing skills, and challenges students to learn new vocabulary.

## Lessons

Why study history? History, the story of mankind, helps us understand how human interaction created the culture, political situation, language, and issues that surround us today. Not knowing history is like having cultural amnesia. We should all know how the past affects our current world.

*U.S. History Detective®* Book 1 focuses on American history from the time of the first European explorers interacting with Native Americans through the Reconstruction Era following the Civil War. Book 2 focuses on the late 1800s to the 21st century. Sections covering an era (time period) are each introduced with an overview so that students can anticipate what the important events are in the section. Then the lessons provide a passage students must read, followed by a series of questions. For the most part, the questions are multiple choice or short answer, and most have short essay questions. Students are asked to identify sentence evidence from the lesson that best supports the answer. The sentences in each lesson are numbered and students will use these numbers to identify the supporting evidence. The short essay questions are excellent discussion questions. Sample answers are provided which identify key points for the essays. In addition, there are section review activities and, from time to time, other bonus activities.

## Supporting Evidence

History is full of questions. What was the most important cause of the Revolutionary War? How did American geography shape our literature and art? Historians look for evidence, and then analyze all the available evidence to see if it points to a conclusion. Sometimes evidence comes as a "primary source"—a first-hand account like a quote, a document, or a photo. Sometimes evidence is a "secondary source" such as a historian who has summarized evidence and presented conclusions about an episode of history. This textbook has both primary and secondary source information.

The more evidence and the stronger the evidence supporting a conclusion, the more likely the conclusion is to be true. However, before arriving at a conclusion, care must be taken to closely evaluate all the evidence, in order to avoid making unsupported conclusions. To illustrate: read the passage below and answer the multiple choice question on the next page.

> [21]Benjamin Franklin devoted a lot of time to making his city of Philadelphia better. [22]Since he loved learning, he started America's first lending library where citizens could check out books for free. [23]He founded a hospital and a school that became the University of Pennsylvania. [24]Franklin organized groups that installed better street lights, started a police force, cleaned the streets, and created a fire department. [25]He also ran the post office of Philadelphia for a time.
>
> [26]At age 47, he was appointed as the Postmaster General of America. [27]He made improvements to the post roads, setting up milestones alongside the roads so it would be easier for mail carriers to compute the distance traveled when figuring postal rates. [28]Communication between the colonies was vastly improved because of Franklin.

© 2016 The Critical Thinking Co.™ • www.CriticalThinking.com • 800-458-4849

QUESTION: Benjamin Franklin helped start a number of projects that bettered his adopted city. All of these are examples of this, except:

a. he founded a public library.
b. he worked for public safety.
c. he started a college.
d. he started the first post office.

Which sentences best support the answer?

______ ______ _____

The answer is "d" and sentences 22, 23, and 24 support this answer. No evidence is provided to support that Franklin created America's first post office.

## Essay Evidence

Effective writers provide the reader with evidence to support their conclusions. Supplying sentence evidence to support answers:

- encourages students to go beyond simple recall information.
- requires students to support their answers by drawing on specific information from the lesson.
- demonstrates students' understanding of the material.
- requires students to analyze the lessons in greater depth.

## Drawing Inferences and Conclusions

A conclusion is a person's decision to believe something. An inference is a conclusion based on evidence. Critical thinking teaches us to draw our conclusions based on our evaluation of the evidence. For example, if we use the fact that the Declaration of Independence was written and signed in 1776, a person may come up with the conclusion that the year 1776 was the first year of the United States of America.

## Distinguishing Between Facts and Opinions

In history, a fact is something that historians accept as truth because it is something that can be or has been proven by overwhelming evidence. It is extremely important to be able to distinguish between fact and opinion as a historian. The more factual evidence, the easier it is to form sound historical judgments.

For example: "The Declaration of Independence was written and signed in 1776."

We know this happened because we have the original document. The men who wrote and signed it wrote about the document, and observers wrote about it as well. There is no doubt in anybody's mind that the facts in this statement are true. An opinion is an expression of somebody's ideas and is debatable. Opinions that are based on facts and sound reasoning are stronger than opinions not based on facts. In history, opinions alone tend to be less persuasive than opinions supported with facts.

Which of the following sentences are facts and which are opinions?

1. _____ George Washington was the first president of the United States of America.
2. _____ George Washington was the nation's best president.
3. _____ The fact that the U.S. federal government is more powerful than state governments is what makes U.S. citizens free.
4. _____ The United States of America has 50 states.

Statements 1 and 4 are facts because both are supported by large amounts of evidence that has been verified by reliable sources. Statements 2 and 3 are opinions because they cannot be proven true. You may find evidence to support statements 2 and 3, but you will never be able to prove they are conclusively true. It is extremely important to be able to distinguish between fact and opinion as a historian. The more factual evidence, the easier it is to form sound historical judgment.


© 2016 The Critical Thinking Co.™ • www.CriticalThinking.com • 800-458-4849

## Understanding Historical Chronology, or Sequence of Events

One way to examine history is chronologically, which means in the order that events happen. Events are often related, and it is important for students to learn to analyze events to see if they show a pattern, causal relationship, or suggest something when looked at as a group. This book is organized chronologically. One lesson builds toward the next. There are several activities in *U.S. History Detective®* that ask students to place events or people in chronological order. This provides practice in the skill of analyzing history as a series of interrelated events.

## Timelines

Timelines help give us a chronological understanding of history that often shows us a big picture of what was going on when. This visual representation of historical information allows students to remember when events occurred and how events relate to each other. There are timelines at the introduction of each section in this book.

## The Use of Vocabulary in the Book

Students will sometimes come across new or unfamiliar words while reading a lesson. It is important to understand how to use the context of the word to determine its meaning. Context is the words or sentences that surround an unfamiliar word. Analyzing the other words in the sentence or surrounding sentences can often aid students in figuring out the meaning of an unfamiliar word. For example, read the sentences below and use the context clues to help identify the meaning of the word "ratification."

> The delegates at the Constitutional Convention gambled a bit when they set up a process for **ratification** of the document. It would be up to the states to decide if the Constitution would become the new law of the land. If conventions in nine of the thirteen states voted to agree to the new Constitution, the new rules would replace the old Articles of Confederation. If any states refused to agree to the Constitution, those states would remain under the old rules–the Articles.

"Ratification" would mean "the act of formally agreeing with."

Sometimes meanings of new vocabulary words have been provided by placing a more simple definition in parentheses next to a difficult word. Here is an example:

> President Jefferson sent Meriwether Lewis to Philadelphia for several months to study **zoology** (study of animals), **botany** (study of plants), and **astronomy** (star navigation) to train for the trip. Jefferson wanted this to be a scientific expedition.

## Geographical Maps

*U.S. History Detective®* lessons often contain simple maps to highlight geographical information, such as colonies, territories, routes, etc., to give students a visual understanding of important information in the lesson. Critical thinking questions about the maps test students' ability to analyze and draw information from the maps. Think of geography as the "stage" where historical events take place.

## College Level Analytical Essay Questions

*U.S. History Detective®* uses short essay questions of the type commonly found in college-level or AP classes. The questions compel the students to synthesize information in the lesson and explain it clearly and concisely in their own words. These questions develop writing skills needed in upper-level academic courses.

© 2016 The Critical Thinking Co.™ • www.CriticalThinking.com • 800-458-4849 

© 2016 The Critical Thinking Co.™ • www.CriticalThinking.com • 800-458-4849

Section 1: Introduction

# The Gilded Age: 1870-1900

After the Civil War, people were on the move. The many resources of the American West attracted cowboys, miners, and homesteaders. This increase in population brought on a conflict of cultures between the Native Americans and the settlers that climaxed at a place called Wounded Knee. By 1890, census-takers could no longer find a frontier line in America. The country had been largely settled east to west.

Back East, an age of industry was developing. It was an age with an incredible amount of new inventions that served industry and changed everyday lives. These new technologies, along with newly discovered resources, a good labor supply, and new ways of doing business all contributed to a huge growth in manufacturing. Business became "big business," and with it came issues about whether or not some companies had created situations with unfair competition. Workers formed unions and fought for a larger share of the profits and for improved working conditions.

Some businessmen rose to wealth quickly and served as examples of the "American Dream." Immigrants poured into the country at the greatest rate ever, hoping that they could materially improve their lives as well. Many immigrants crowded into the cities and lived with poor sanitation and abuses. The contrast between rich and poor was clear, causing one author to nickname the late 1800s the "Gilded Age" because the country looked shiny and bright on the outside but hid many problems on the inside.

Conditions brought forth reformers who looked for ways to make positive changes in the lives of the working class. The times also produced artists, writers, and entertainers who created ways to display the culture of the late 1800s.

## U.S. Presidents

20. James Garfield
1881-1881

21. Chester A. Authur
1881-1885

22. Grover Cleveland
1885-1889

23. Benjamin Harrison
1889-1893

24. Grover Cleveland
1893-1897

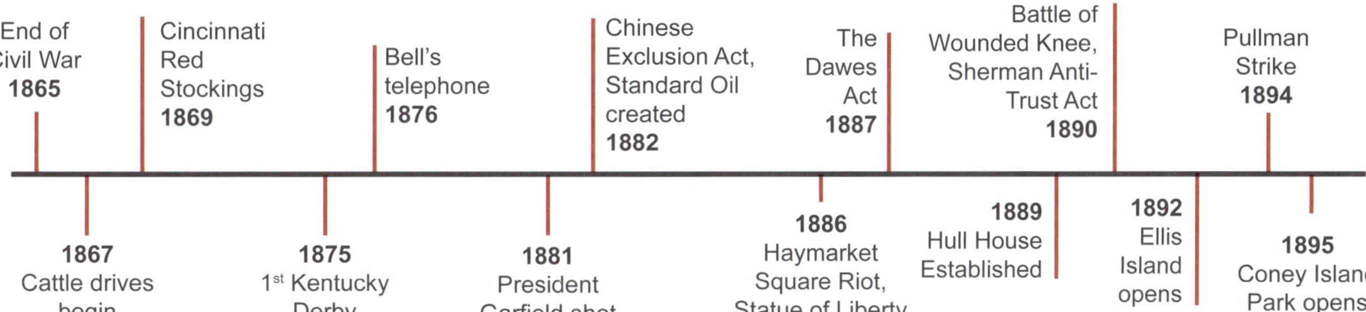

Lesson 1

# The Wild West

## A. Mining Frontier

[1]Even before the Civil War, the American West beyond the Mississippi River had been a destination for men wanting to become miners. [2]The discovery of gold in California (1848) and the silver mines of the Comstock Lode in Nevada (1853) attracted thousands of fortune seekers. [3]After the Civil War, the rush continued. [4]Silver and gold mines opened up in central Colorado and western Idaho; copper, gold, and silver mines boomed in Montana and southern Arizona; and gold rushes occurred in the Black Hills of South Dakota (1874) and Klondike, Alaska (1898), to name a few places.

Placer miners panned for gold by washing river silt through "rockers." Light-weight sand and gravel washed away while heavier gold flakes and nuggets were trapped behind wooden ridge boards in the cradle.

[5]Mining operations were generally "boom and bust." [6]When word got out about a mineral discovery, stampedes of Americans would rush to the area and quickly build towns that buzzed with excitement. [7]Many of these towns would turn into ghost towns a few years later when the easy pickings were gone and word of a new discovery in the next territory leaked out. [8]Men generally outnumbered women three to one in mining towns, which were often rough and sometimes lawless places.

[9]Mineral extraction in the 1800s was often "placer mining." [10]This meant that miners looked for easy ways to find gold in the "place" where it lay in the deposits of sand and gravel in river beds. [11]Hydraulic mining (shooting water cannons to dislodge minerals) was sometimes used as well. [12]This often caused environmental damage to the land and rivers. [13]By the late 1800s, mining companies organized to invest in expensive equipment that could dig deep shafts into the ground (hard rock mining) to follow mineral veins. [14]That made the work of mining even more dangerous. [15]In the 1870s, one out of every eighty miners was killed on the job each year, and very few of those who survived ever became rich.

## B. Chinese

[16]Thousands of Chinese immigrants, who had come to help build western railroads in the 1860s, stayed to hunt for gold as well. [17]At first, Chinese miners could file their own claims (mainly in California). [18]They worked very efficiently, often successfully finding gold in areas abandoned or worked over by other miners. [19]The Chinese lived alongside the whites in the shantytowns (hastily and crudely built villages), and some made a living selling groceries, running restaurants, or doing laundry.

Chinese miners worked alongside whites in California in the 1850s but were later banned from becoming citizens.

[20]Later, as gold became scarce, competition intensified resulting in anti-immigrant feelings in the West. [21]Many laws were passed to give whites an advantage over the Chinese, and violence against Chinese immigrants increased. [22]In 1882, the federal government passed the Chinese Exclusion Act. [23]For the first time in U.S. history, the government banned a specific ethnic group from immigrating into the country. [24]No new Chinese


© 2016 The Critical Thinking Co.™ • www.CriticalThinking.com • 800-458-4849

workers could enter the country, and those who had immigrated earlier were considered aliens–losing their chance of citizenship. [25]This law remained on the books until 1943.

### C. Western Writers and Artists

[26]The adventures of miners, bandits who robbed them, and sheriffs who tried to enforce the law made for good storytelling. [27]In the 1870s, a writer named Edward Judson penned (wrote) many dime novels about western good guys and bad guys that were inexpensively printed in paperback. [28]Selling for about ten cents, these fictionalized (often not true) adventure books were wildly popular back East. [29]Exaggerated stories about lawmen Wyatt Earp and Wild Bill Hickok chasing cattle rustlers and stage coach robbers, or tales about hunter/scout Buffalo Bill Cody, gave readers an unreal idea about how wild the West really was. [30]In many dime novels, Native Americans were portrayed as villains, women as weak, and the western United States as an area that needed to be conquered.

[31]William Cody became even more famous when he created a traveling show in the 1880s called Buffalo Bill's Wild West. [32]The circus-like show featured all the attractions that people in the East would pay to see: cowboys on horseback, gun-shooting experts, and Native Americans parading in full costume.

[33]Future U.S. President Theodore Roosevelt, a Dakota cattle rancher for a few years in the 1880s, contributed to this sensational view of the American's view of the West when he published a four-volume history in the early 1890s called *The Winning of the West*. [34]His writing glorified Westerners as independent, self-reliant heroes who tamed an uncivilized frontier inhabited by savages.

[35]Western artists also contributed to the legend of the Wild West. [36]Frederic Remington and Charles Russell painted cowboys as tough, heroic men of the plains.

"The Wagon Boss" by Charles Russell

### D. National Parks

[37]As miners and others scoured the West for mineral deposits or lands to settle, they found some amazing landscapes. [38]A Civil War veteran, John Wesley Powell, mapped the Colorado River and reported to Congress about an amazing place called the Grand Canyon. [39]Another veteran, Henry Washburn, scouted lands in northwest Colorado for a railroad company and was so impressed with the geography he saw there that he asked Congress to protect the land from sale to private companies. [40]After landscape artists such as Thomas Moran displayed popular paintings of the area, the government responded by creating the nation's first national park there—Yellowstone. [41]John Muir, a Scottish immigrant, traveled to California and was astounded by the redwood forests in the northern part of the state and a wilderness area in central California called Yosemite. [42]He became America's most famous spokesman for preserving wilderness; with his influence, Congress created Yosemite National Park in the central Sierra Nevada Mountains in 1890. [43]John Muir is sometimes known as the "Father of National Parks." [44]America was the world's first country to federally protect these unique lands for public use as national parks.

John Muir

**Fun Fact Feature**

One of the featured attractions at Buffalo Bill's Wild West show was a Native American who had fought General Custer and was perhaps the most famous Native American of his day. Can you name the performer?

1. List seven Western states where gold, silver, or copper rushes occurred.

_______________ _______________

_______________ _______________

_______________ _______________

_______________

2. Which statement below is NOT generally accurate about mining regions of the West?
   a. Towns were built quickly as miners rushed to places where minerals were discovered.
   b. Chinese immigrants often lived and worked in the mining towns.
   c. Many mining towns were abandoned when new discoveries were made in other places.
   d. Women usually outnumbered men in those regions.

   Which sentence best supports the answer?

   _____

3. Which of the following describes the mining technique of digging deep into the ground to follow mineral veins?
   a. hydraulic mining
   b. placer mining
   c. hard rock mining
   d. Chinese mining

   Which sentence best supports the answer?

   _____

4. Which of the following describes the simple mining technique of looking for gold in the place where it lay in the deposits of sands and gravel in river beds?
   a. hydraulic mining
   b. placer mining
   c. hard rock mining
   d. Chinese mining

   Which sentences best support the answer?

   _____ _____

5. One group of miners was NOT allowed to bring in more immigrant workers after 1882, and its members were denied a chance at U.S. citizenship for decades afterward. Which group was it?
   a. Chinese
   b. Indians
   c. Irish
   d. African

   Which sentence best supports the answer?

   _____

6. Who was a best-selling author of Western adventure stories called "dime novels?"
   a. Edward Judson
   b. Theodore Roosevelt
   c. John Muir
   d. Buffalo Bill Cody

   Which sentence best supports the answer?

   _____

7. What do Frederic Remington, Thomas Moran, and Charles Russell have in common?
   a. They were fictionalized Western heroes.
   b. They were important people in the mining industry.
   c. They were Western artists.
   d. They were Western politicians.

   Which sentences best support the answer?

   _____ _____

8. Some Western lands with amazing geographic features, such as Yellowstone, became America's and the world's first:
   a. Indian reservations.
   b. national parks.
   c. Western territories.
   d. settlements for European immigrants.

   Which sentences best support the answer?

   _____ _____

 © 2016 The Critical Thinking Co.™ • www.CriticalThinking.com • 800-458-4849

9. What was a bad side-effect of hydraulic mining?
   a. It yielded very little profit.
   b. It caused environmental damage.
   c. It hurt the economy of the Chinese mining community.
   d. It was the most expensive technique of mining.

   Which sentences best support the answer?

   _____ _____

## Written Response Question

10. Use complete sentences to describe what Eastern Americans thought about the American West by the late 1800s and how they formed those impressions.

______________________________________________________________________

______________________________________________________________________

______________________________________________________________________

______________________________________________________________________

______________________________________________________________________

______________________________________________________________________

______________________________________________________________________

______________________________________________________________________

______________________________________________________________________

______________________________________________________________________

### Fun Fact Finale

One of the featured attractions at Buffalo Bill's Wild West show was Sitting Bull (shown with Cody in the photo on the left), who had fought General Custer and was perhaps the most famous Native American of his day. He appeared in the show with a band of 20 of his tribesmen and performed tricks on his horse for audiences.

© 2016 The Critical Thinking Co.™ • www.CriticalThinking.com • 800-458-4849

Lesson 2

# A Culture Assaulted: Native Americans in the Late 1800s

## A. Cowboys and Native Americans

[1]In the era between 1840 and 1865, thousands of Eastern Americans moved west for various economic opportunities that included the fur trade, mining, farming, and ranching. [2]After the Civil War, Native Americans in the American West were overrun even further by the forces of business, immigration, and technology.

[3]The post Civil War westward rush started with the cowboys. [4]In 1867, Joseph McCoy built stockyards in Abilene, Kansas, and hired men to round up cattle in Texas. [5]McCoy knew that cattle could be purchased for only four dollars a head in Texas. [6]If men could drive the cattle 1,500 miles north to his stockyards, fattening them up on free grazing land along the way, McCoy could ship them by rail to Eastern markets and sell them for more than 40 dollars a head where demand for beef was growing. [7]A man named Jesse Chisholm mapped out a trail to accomplish this task. [8]Cowboys on the Chisholm Trail gathered cattle from various locations in central Texas. [9]They organized them in stockyards at Fort Worth, Texas, pushed them in large herds north through the Native American lands of Oklahoma, and finished the cattle drives at railroad towns like Abilene, Dodge City, or Ellsworth, Kansas.

Nat Love was the son of a slave who became a cowboy after the Civil War.

[10]Most cowboys were white men, but it is estimated that 15–33 percent of cowboys were Hispanic men and 15–20 percent were black Freedmen looking for work after the Civil War. [11]It was said that the only qualifications for the job of cowboy were "guts and a horse—and if you had guts you could steal a horse." [12]The cattle drives were difficult. [13]It took up to two months to push semi-wild Texas Longhorn cattle across rivers and creeks and dusty, hot Great Plains lands. [14]Trail bosses had to pay ten cents a head to compensate Native Americans so the cattle drive could cross over their land, but occasionally Native Americans attacked the cowboys because some were upset that the cattle herds were interfering with their nomadic lifestyle and competing for grazing lands with the buffalo.

[15]Business was so profitable that other cattle trails were also developed in the 1870s. [16]The Western Trail and the Goodnight-Loving Trails, for example, led from Texas to stockyard towns on the new transcontinental railroad line—Ogallala, Nebraska, and Cheyenne, Wyoming.

Cattle Trails: 1870s

© 2016 The Critical Thinking Co.™ • www.CriticalThinking.com • 800-458-4849

## B. Buffalo Culture Ruined

[17]Oregon Trail pioneers and California gold seekers basically just passed through the Great Plains on their way to lands on the Pacific Coast prior to the Civil War. [18]However, the passage of the Homestead Act in the 1860s and the advance of the transcontinental railroad with the Pacific Railway Act, encouraged Americans in the East and new European immigrants to settle on the Great Plains in large numbers. [19]The Homestead Act provided relatively cheap government land to settlers. [20]Railroad companies advertised widely to attract settlers to the West. [21]These companies had been granted thousands of square miles of land by the U.S. government to offset the cost of building western railroads. [22]Sale of their land to immigrant farmers was good business.

[23]Conditions for new farmers on the Great Plains were very difficult. [24]Extreme weather, insect infestations, drought, and the stress of living separated from urban life created much hardship. [25]Plains tribes, too, were affected by the population increase. [26]New diseases brought in by the settlers killed Native Americans. [27]Settlers plowed up the prairie grasses, put up barbed wire fences around their homesteads, and built towns. [28]Spur lines of railroads crisscrossed the plains even further. [29]All of these things decreased the migration range of the buffalo, an animal which Plains tribes greatly depended upon for their survival. [30]Demand for buffalo byproducts in the Eastern United States—hides used for robes and other clothing, buffalo horns, leather goods, and buffalo fat used in glue—created a business of hunting buffalo. [31]Whites and some Native American hunters hunted buffalo for profit. [32]Railroads encouraged the slaughter of buffalo to eliminate damage to their equipment. [33]The U.S. government encouraged the slaughter of buffalo to eliminate the major food supply of warring Native Americans that they were fighting. [34]Between 1872 and 1875 alone, more than nine million buffalo were killed. [35]By the late 1800s, only a few thousand buffalo were left from herds once numbering in the millions. [36]The nomadic lifestyle of Plains tribes, so dependent upon the buffalo, was changed forever.

Railroads made it easier for hunters to kill buffalo, and by the late 1800s they almost became extinct.

## C. Reservations and the Dawes Act

[37]After the Civil War, the U.S. government increasingly tried to settle Western Native Americans on reservation lands. [38]Treaties were negotiated but often not fulfilled by government agents. [39]As Native Americans struggled to maintain their freedom, they resisted efforts to live on the reservations and give up their free, nomadic lifestyle. [40]Conflicts between the tribes and the government often arose. [41]The Red River War (1874), Custer's Last Stand (1876), and Nez Perce War (1877) were just a few of the battles. [42]By the 1880s, many reformers convinced the government that the reservation system was not working. [43]The Dawes Act of 1887 was passed to remedy the situation. [44]This federal law tried to assimilate (the process of adapting or adjusting to the culture of a group or nation) Native Americans into white culture by training them to be farmers and individual landowners. [45]The reservations were broken up and 160 acres of land was distributed to each head of a Native American household. [46]It also tried to eliminate the recognition of tribal governments and put Native Americans on a path to gain U.S. citizenship.

[47]The Dawes Act was another crushing blow to Native American cultures. [48]Native American children were often sent to boarding schools where they were forced to give up their traditions and learn English, farming, or other trades. [49]Extra reservation land that was not divided up among the tribesmen was sold to whites. [50]Excess land in the "Native American Territory" of Oklahoma, for example, was opened up for settlers in 1889.

## D. The Ghost Dance

[51]As Native American culture faded in the American West, a visionary Native American prophet named Wovoka created a new religious movement that told of a day when there would be a peaceful end to white expansion in the West and the buffalo herds and dead relatives of Native Americans would return. [52]Wovoka thought this vision would be realized through the Ghost Dance. [53]The Ghost Dance was a variation of the traditional Native American Circle Dance. [54]The Ghost Dance became a widespread movement among tribes throughout the West by the late 1880s. [55]Although Wovoka's vision included peaceful coexistence with whites, some tribes like the Lakota Sioux preached the removal of all white Americans from their lands. [56]This view worried the whites who saw it as a counter movement to the Dawes Act. [57]To calm their fears, the government sent more troops to the Dakota Territory. As more troops arrived, the Native Americans became frightened and upset. [58]Chief Sitting Bull of the Lakota Sioux was seen as an important leader of the Ghost Dance movement, and the government demanded that he tell his people to cease the practice of the Ghost Dance. [59]He refused, and during the process of Chief Sitting Bull's arrest, a Native American shot an arresting officer who then turned and shot Sitting Bull.

[60]Two weeks later, in December of 1890, the 7th Cavalry was sent to round up weapons from a band of Sioux at a creek called Wounded Knee in modern-day South Dakota. [61]As troops gathered the cold and starving natives, a shot rang out and soldiers began shooting into the Native American crowd with repeating rifles and cannon-fire. [62]More than 150 (some historians claim as many as 300) Native Americans, mostly women and children, were killed. [63]Three days later, after a blizzard, the frozen corpses were then placed in a mass grave. [64]The massacre at Wounded Knee marked the last significant Native American/white battle in the American West.

[65]The Census Bureau of 1890 could no longer find a "frontier line"—a line on the map of the West showing how far west settlers had migrated. [66]By that time, the Great Plains had been significantly populated by whites. [67]Native Americans, however, who once numbered a quarter of a million people in that region, had lost 60 percent of their numbers.

Ghost dancers wore special clothing during ceremonial events. This ghost shirt was worn by an Arapaho native.

**Fun Fact Feature**

When the "Native American Territory" of Oklahoma was opened up to white settlement in 1889, those who rushed in to claim land on opening day, April 22, were nicknamed "Boomers." What were people called who illegally snuck in early to claim land prior to the April 22 opening date?


© 2016 The Critical Thinking Co.™ • www.CriticalThinking.com • 800-458-4849

1. Where did the cattle drives begin during the cowboy era?
   a. Kansas railheads
   b. Texas
   c. Indian Territory (Oklahoma)
   d. Colorado or Wyoming

   Which sentences best support the answer?

   ______ ______

2. Why did Native Americans object to the cattle drives like those on the Chisholm Trail?
   a. The drovers only paid ten cents a head to drive cattle through Native American territory.
   b. The cattle drives were against the philosophies in the Ghost Dance.
   c. Hispanics, Freedmen, and ex-Confederates were employed as cowboys.
   d. The cattle drives disrupted the grazing patterns of buffalo.

   Which sentence best supports the answer?

   ______

3. Complete this sentence: Cowboys in the 1870s drove cattle to towns located on new western railroads because

   ________________________________________

   ________________________________________

4. What increased on the Great Plains with the development of western rail lines and the passage of the Homestead Act?
   a. white settlement
   b. buffalo
   c. prairie grasses
   d. Indians

   Which sentence best supports the answer?

   ______

5. Name three reasons why nine million buffalo died on the Great Plains in the 1870s.

   a. ________________________________________

   ________________________________________

   b. ________________________________________

   ________________________________________

   c. ________________________________________

   ________________________________________

6. What law tried to change western Native Americans from nomadic hunters to individual land owners and farmers?
   a. Homestead Act
   b. Ghost Dance Act
   c. The Pacific Railway Act
   d. The Dawes Act

   Which sentences best support the answer?

   ______ ______

7. Which person is most closely associated with promoting the Ghost Dance?
   a. Jesse Chisholm
   b. Joseph McCoy
   c. Wovoka
   d. Chief Joseph

   Which sentences best support the answer?

   ______ ______

8. Explain why the Ghost Dance was popular among Native Americans in the late 1800s.

   ________________________________________

   ________________________________________

   ________________________________________

   ________________________________________

   ________________________________________

   ________________________________________

© 2016 The Critical Thinking Co.™ • www.CriticalThinking.com • 800-458-4849

9. The year 1890 is often given by historians as the unofficial "end of the frontier era" in the American West. Which event below contributed to that conclusion?
   a. the development of the Chisholm Trail
   b. the results of the Census of 1890
   c. the massacre at Wounded Knee
   d. the completion of the transcontinental railroad

   Which sentence best supports the answer?

   ______

## Written Response Question

10. Use complete sentences to discuss why the Native American population dropped by 60 percent in the last half of the 1800s.

______________________________________________

______________________________________________

______________________________________________

______________________________________________

______________________________________________

______________________________________________

______________________________________________

______________________________________________

______________________________________________

______________________________________________

**Fun Fact Finale**

When the "Native American Territory" of Oklahoma was opened up to white settlement in 1889, those who rushed in to claim land on opening day, April 22, were nicknamed "Boomers." Those who illegally snuck in early were called "Sooners." To this day Oklahoma is known as the "Sooner State," and the nickname of the University of Oklahoma's athletic teams is "Sooners."

 © 2016 The Critical Thinking Co.™ • www.CriticalThinking.com • 800-458-4849

# Bonus Activity
# People of the Wild West

Review Lessons 1 and 2. For each of the following people below, write one of these symbols next to their name for the Wild West category for which they are famous.

**C** = Cowboy
**N** = Native American
**WA** = Writer/Artist

_____ 1. Thomas Moran

_____ 2. Nat Love

_____ 3. Joseph McCoy

_____ 4. Wovoka

_____ 5. Edward Judson

_____ 6. Sitting Bull

_____ 7. Theodore Roosevelt

_____ 8. Charles Russell

_____ 9. Jesse Chisholm

_____ 10. Frederic Remington

Cattle Drive Around 1902.

© 2016 The Critical Thinking Co.™ • www.CriticalThinking.com • 800-458-4849

# Bonus Activity
# Land Taken From Native Americans in the West

Before Europeans started immigrating to North America and establishing territory on the continent, Native American tribes frequently fought with each other for control of land. Before, during, and after the American Revolution, European immigrants and the state and federal governments they established fought with Native Americans to acquire and hold land. The U.S. state and Federal governments also negotiated treaties with land-holding native tribes to acquire even more native lands. The map below shows how that process of giving up (ceding) land continued in the American West. Eventually the U.S. government tried to put Native Americans on reservations. Analyze the map to answer questions about Native American lands in the west.

North American Tribal Regional Lossees, 1850-1890

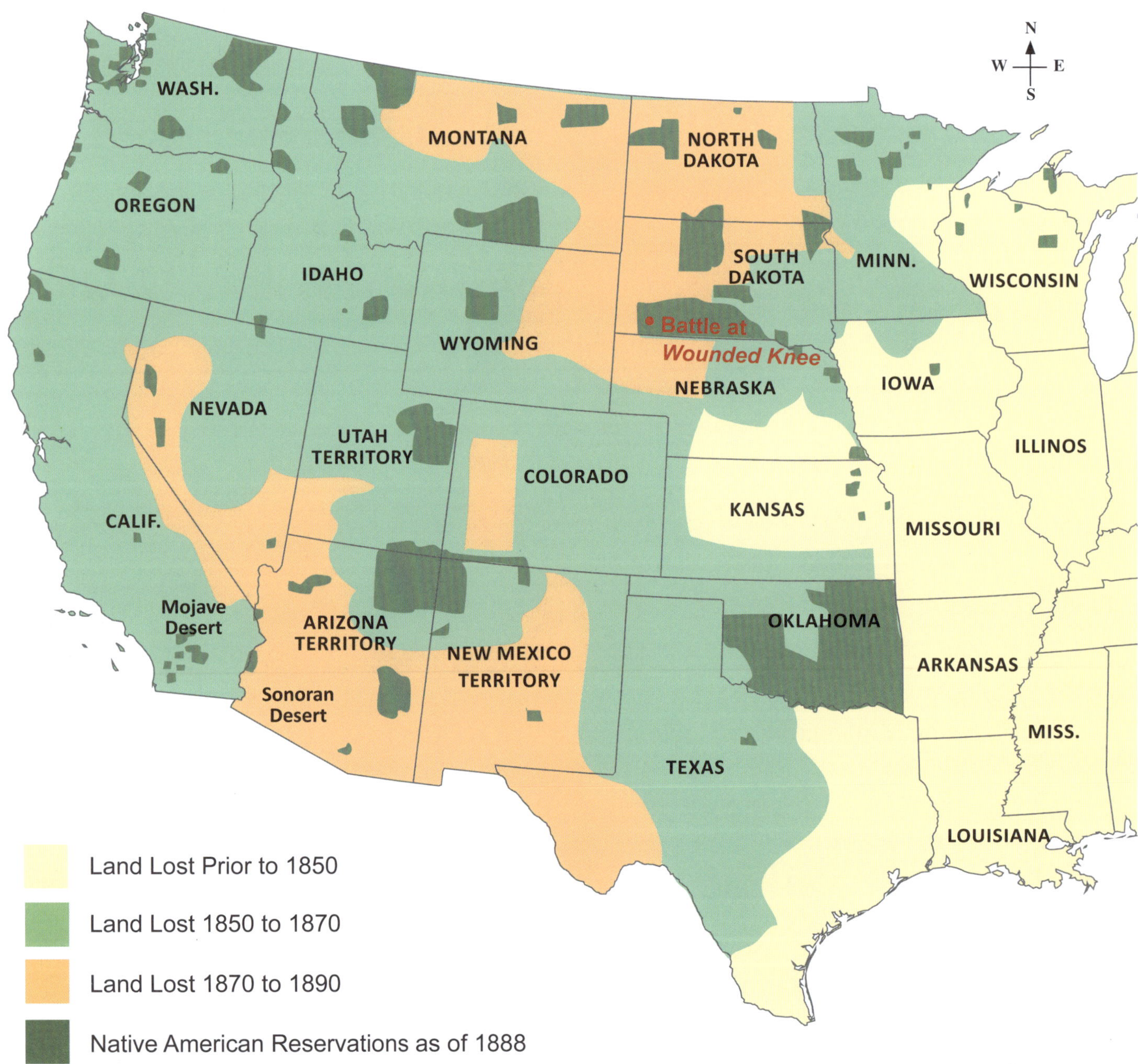



© 2016 The Critical Thinking Co.™ • www.CriticalThinking.com • 800-458-4849

_______________ 1. Native Americans had lost almost all land title east of the Mississippi River and the Midwest prior to what year?

_______________ 2. In which range of years did Native Americans cede most of their Western lands?

_______________ 3. In what period of time were most Native American lands in North Dakota and Arizona ceded?

_______________ 4. Which single state had the most Native American reservation land as of 1888?

_______________ 5. Review the text in Lesson 2. What happened to the reservation land in the state in Question 4 in 1889?

_______________ 6. Look at the Native American reservation lands in Southern California. What does their location tell you about what kind of land the government often set aside for reservations?

_______________ 7. The largest state on the map has the fewest acres of reservation land. Name that state.

_______________ 8. In which current-day state was the important Battle of Wounded Knee?

_______________ 9. Notice that a swath of land ceded by Native Americans from 1850 to 1870 cuts through the center of the map from Nebraska, through Wyoming and Idaho, and on to the Pacific states. What are two important transportation routes that went through that same zone?

10. Notice Native American lands in Nevada, Arizona, and New Mexico were among the last to cede. Explain why the climate in those regions helped that occur.

_______________________________________________

_______________________________________________

_______________________________________________

_______________________________________________

_______________________________________________

© 2016 The Critical Thinking Co.™ • www.CriticalThinking.com • 800-458-4849

Lesson 3

# The Rise of Industry

## A. Industrial Age

[1]After the Civil War a number of forces came together to bring about an age of industrial production unlike any time previously in American history. [2]The gold, silver, and copper mines of the West, large deposits of coal found in the Appalachian and Rocky Mountains, and iron ore fields located in the Great Lakes region provided manufacturers with cheap raw materials to produce goods. [3]The spread of railroads made it easier to transport materials and products long distances at lower costs. [4]New technologies, like the development of electric power, also cut manufacturing costs.

[5]This increase in manufacturing produced higher wages than jobs in Europe. [6]Some economists estimate U.S. wages increased 30 percent (for unskilled workers) to 60 percent (for skilled workers) between the Civil War and 1900. [7]As a result, a large number of European and Chinese workers immigrated to the United States in the late 1800s seeking employment or a chance to start their own business. [8]The large-scale immigration created a vast supply of labor for the new industrial age. [9]Even with wage increases, however, workers were sometimes laid off jobs during slack economic times or out of work if injured on the job. [10]This caused almost half of the unskilled work force to earn less than 500 dollars annually—the amount the government defined as the poverty line in the 1890s.

The Biltmore was the home of the George Vanderbilt family. It had more than 130,000 square feet of living space.

[11]Industrialization also produced great profits for business owners and management. [12]By the end of the century, three-quarters of the nation's wealth was held by less than 10 percent of the population. [13]In the 1800s, there was no tax on income. [14]Owners of some of the nation's very profitable businesses built lavish homes to show off their wealth. [15]Vanderbilt family members, for example, who made their money from the transportation business, had giant homes in New York, Rhode Island, and the largest private home in America—the Biltmore, in North Carolina. [16]Wealth displayed by the rich, and the large gap between the wealthy minority and the poor majority, gave rise to a nickname for the era of the late 1800s. [17]Mark Twain, a famous writer of the day, called it the "Gilded Age," and the name stuck. [18]To be gilded means something is covered with gold but is not as valuable on the inside.

## B. Rockefeller and Carnegie

[19]During the Gilded Age, several entrepreneurs (a person or persons who open a business) became America's first very wealthy citizens. [20]One example was John D. Rockefeller, a simple merchant from Cleveland, Ohio, who saw the value of oil. [21]After the Civil War, new oil drilling technology made crude petroleum abundant. [22]Rockefeller realized early on that petroleum could be refined into oil that would replace animal tallow as the major lubricant for machines. [23]Also, kerosene could be refined to become the new fuel for lighting and heating in homes and factories. [24]Rockefeller used a business strategy called "horizontal integration." [25]This is when a manufacturer tries to be the sole producer of a particular product. [26]For example, a company might not own cattle ranches, but it might control most of the meat processing plants. [27]Rockefeller established Standard Oil in 1882 by convincing dozens of small refining companies to band together to form a larger organization called a trust. [28]A trust is an organization that is created by one or more individuals or companies for the benefit of its members (creators). [29]The purpose of the Standard Oil trust was to give the trust members better

John D. Rockefeller

 © 2016 The Critical Thinking Co.™ • www.CriticalThinking.com • 800-458-4849

control of the refinery business for the purpose of earning greater profits. [30]Soon, the Standard Oil Trust controlled ninety percent of the oil refineries in the nation.

[31]Rockefeller was a careful businessman who always looked for ways to cut costs. [32]He once conducted an experiment and found that gallon cans made to hold his refined Standard Oil often leaked if sealed with only 38 drops of solder (a heated substance used to join metal objects together when cooled). [33]As a result, Rockefeller ordered that 39 drops of solder were to be used to seal the cans in each of his refineries, saving the company more than 30,000 dollars a year.

[34]Another example of a successful entrepreneur was Andrew Carnegie. [35]He used a strategy called "vertical integration of business" to improve efficiency and profitability. [36]The goal of vertical integration is for a company to control all the parts needed to manufacture its product and get it to market—typically through ownership. [37]It's often described as control from the ground up; a company owns the raw materials, its factories, and the transportation networks to get raw materials into the factory and the finished products to market.

Andrew Carnegie

[38]Carnegie started out as a poor immigrant and ended his career as one of the richest men in the country. [39]When he was twelve, his family moved from Scotland to western Pennsylvania. [40]Carnegie took a low paying job as a bobbin boy in a textile mill, moved up to a telegraph operator position for the Pennsylvania Railroad, and was eventually promoted to manager. [41]Carnegie was a good manager and saved the company a lot of money. [42]He also saved money for himself and invested it wisely. [43]By the early 1870s, he was able to build his own steel mills in Pittsburgh, Pennsylvania, and hire employees to run them.

[44]Carnegie understood that steel was a much stronger product than iron for building rails for the ever-growing railroad industry. [45]He put the latest steel production technology into his mill. [46]Using his connections with his former railroad co-workers, he negotiated lower transportation costs to bring in iron ore from mines he acquired in the Great Lakes region. [47]He also kept manufacturing costs down by using many unskilled laborers. [48]By the end of the 1800s, Carnegie Steel was the world's largest industrial corporation.

### C. Gospel of Wealth

[49]Andrew Carnegie penned an essay in 1889 called "The Gospel of Wealth," which was widely circulated. [50]He spoke for many entrepreneurs when he wrote that government should have a laissez-faire ("hands-off") approach to business. He felt that market forces (such as supply and demand) and evolutionary forces (such as competition or survival of the fittest) provided all the regulation that businesses needed. [51]He argued that the wealthy earned their status but, in return, it was their duty to use wealth wisely. [52]Unlike wealthy Europeans who generally passed on family wealth to heirs, Carnegie said a successful American should distribute his fortune to important causes before he died. [53]Carnegie practiced philanthropy (giving away surplus wealth in responsible ways to help society). [54]One of his favorite ways to do this was to donate money to create libraries throughout America. [55]If a community promised to fund a plan to employ librarians and maintain the building, Carnegie provided money to build and stock a library. [56]He liked this idea because he felt it gave the average citizen tools for self-improvement through education. [57]Carnegie eventually funded more than 2,500 libraries.

**Fun Fact Feature**

The most famous concert stage in the United States was built in 1891 in downtown New York City with donated money. Since then, many of the leading classical music and popular music artists have performed there. What is the name of this famous theater?

1. If people used the nickname of the late 1800s, "the Gilded Age," which of these would they most likely say was gilded?
   a. Carnegie libraries
   b. fabulous homes built by the wealthy
   c. immigrant workers
   d. Standard Oil cans

   Which sentences best support the answer?

   _____ _____

2. Briefly explain why Mark Twain nicknamed the late 1800s as "the Gilded Age."

   ______________________________________

   ______________________________________

   ______________________________________

   ______________________________________

3. What is the type of business integration if one sugar company owned 90 percent of the sugar refining factories in the country?
   a. vertical
   b. horizontal
   c. diagonal

   Which sentences best support the answer?

   _____ _____

4. What is the type of business integration if a coal mining company owned coal mines, railroads to transport coal to processing plants, and stores that sold coal to customers for use in home furnaces?
   a. vertical
   b. horizontal
   c. diagonal

   Which sentences best support the answer?

   _____ _____

5. Andrew Carnegie is most closely associated with development of which industry?
   a. steel
   b. railroads
   c. oil
   d. sugar

   Which sentence best supports the answer?

   _____

6. Which American businessman was associated with Standard Oil in the late 1800s?
   a. Mark Twain
   b. Samuel Gompers
   c. Mary Harris Jones
   d. John Rockefeller

   Which sentence best supports the answer?

   _____

7. What did Andrew Carnegie write about wealth?
   a. Those who acquired great wealth did not deserve it.
   b. The federal government should regulate the wealth of entrepreneurs and pass an income tax.
   c. A rich man should distribute his surplus wealth back into society before his death.
   d. Rich people became wealthy because they were lucky.

   Which sentence best supports the answer?

   _____

8. Carnegie was a philanthropist who created more than 2,500:
   a. steel mills
   b. trusts
   c. schools
   d. libraries

   Which sentences best support the answer?

   _____ _____


© 2016 The Critical Thinking Co.™ • www.CriticalThinking.com • 800-458-4849

9. Which sentence below best describes worker wages in the late 1800s?
   a. Wages fell for skilled workers but rose for unskilled workers.
   b. Wages increased so dramatically that one-third of Americans were considered to be wealthy.
   c. Wages rose for unskilled and skilled workers but many could still not escape poverty.
   d. Worker wages remained about the same as they had been prior to the Civil War.

   Which sentences best support the answer?

   _____ _____ _____

## Written Response Question

10. Use complete sentences to describe the factors that came together after the Civil War to produce the Gilded Age.

______________________________________________________________________

______________________________________________________________________

______________________________________________________________________

______________________________________________________________________

______________________________________________________________________

______________________________________________________________________

______________________________________________________________________

______________________________________________________________________

______________________________________________________________________

**Fun Fact Finale**

The most famous concert stage in the United States was built in 1891 in downtown New York City with donated money. Since then many of the leading classical music and popular music artists have performed at Carnegie Hall.

Lesson 4

# Labor Unions and Monopolies

## A. American Dream

[1]The lives of Andrew Carnegie and John Rockefeller, who gained great wealth after modest beginnings, promoted the belief that talent and hard work were the keys to success. [2]The ability to rise into a more prosperous social class and own property seemed more possible in the United States than in Europe because of the economic opportunities, lack of an established social hierarchy, and a fast growing economy. [3]This belief became known as the "American Dream." [4]Ben Franklin's life, in colonial times, was an early model. [5]In the late 1800s, a dime novelist named Horatio Alger became extremely popular by writing more than 100 books with the "rags-to-riches" theme. [6]His fictional main character was usually a youth who moved to the city to improve his poor rural family upbringing, and through hard work, honesty, and determination, wound up with a life of middle-class security. [7]In reality, many immigrants or their children improved their standard of living in the late 1800s. [8]This encouraged others that success could ultimately be found if a person had the right qualities, skills, or education, but very few persons actually went from poverty to fabulous wealth.

Horatio Alger

## B. Labor Unions

[9]The age didn't look too gilded to workers inside most factories in the last half of the 1800s. [10]Most of the work done there was by unskilled laborers. [11]Workers didn't need specialized talents or much education. [12]Blue collar jobs (jobs working with your hands) lasted twelve hours a day, six days a week for about $1.30 a day. [13]Conditions were often unhealthy and unsafe, and there was no such thing as company health insurance, sick leave, pay for workers injured on the job, or paid vacations. [14]There were also no rules outlawing child labor. [15]Youngsters aged eight or nine could be found working in cotton mills and coal mines. [16]Black Americans and women who worked the same jobs as men were paid less.

[17]After the Civil War, labor groups formed to work together for better wages, safer working conditions, and more reasonable working hours. [18]These worker groups were called unions. [19]The American Federation of Labor (AFL) was one of the most important. [20]It was led by an immigrant cigar maker named Samuel Gompers—a socialist who later came to accept capitalism. [21]Under Gompers' leadership, the AFL became a federation of skilled craft workers. [22]Gompers thought that organizing skilled workers, who were harder to replace, gave laborers more power to bargain with the corporation owners. [23]Then, if the AFL bargained for reduced work hours and/or better wages, eventually all workers, even unskilled ones, could benefit.

Samuel Gompers

[24]One tactic used by unions was the threat of a "strike." [25]A strike happened when union workers walked off their jobs in order to shut down the factory to pressure a business to bargain or accept pay raises and improved working conditions. [26]Sometimes a strike produced good results for the unions. [27]Mary Harris Jones, known by union members as Mother Jones, led a successful effort to improve wages of coal miners in Pennsylvania in 1897.

[28]However, strikes often took an ugly turn. [29]At a protest to campaign for an eight-hour workday held at the McCormick Harvester plant in 1886, policemen shot and killed four demonstrators. [30]The next day, the protest continued at nearby Haymarket Square in Chicago, Illinois. [31]When police arrived, protesters threw a bomb that killed

The Haymarket Square Riot of 1886

 © 2016 The Critical Thinking Co.™ • www.CriticalThinking.com • 800-458-4849

seven policemen. [32]Officers then fired into the crowd killing four more protesters. [33]In 1892, at Carnegie's Homestead Steel Plant in Pennsylvania, a battle broke out between striking workers and men Carnegie had hired to surround and protect his factory. [34]After seven people were killed, the governor of the state sent in the National Guard to restore order and open up the plant. [35]The union was crushed. [36]When the Pullman Company (which made fancy dining and sleeping railroad cars) cut wages after the Panic (an economic recession) of 1893, railroad union workers went on strike. [37]Federal troops were sent in to arrest strikers and a riot started that eventually led to 53 wounded and 13 dead people. [38]After Haymarket Square, Homestead, Pullman, and other instances of strike-related violence, labor unions were often portrayed as instigators of violence and had a negative public image. [39]By 1900, only five percent of America's workforce was unionized.

### C. Sherman Anti-Trust Act

[40]After the Civil War, businesses that formerly competed with each other in a market for goods joined together to form larger organizations called trusts that gave them more influence and power within the market. [41]John Rockefeller's Standard Oil Trust, for example, was an organization that united a number of oil refineries to pool resources together. [42]Besides oil trusts, trusts were formed to benefit groups of companies in the sugar, tobacco, coal, and many other markets in the late 1800s. [43]Some in government worried that these unions of companies could create unfair competition or monopolies (almost exclusive control of production of a product or service). [44]In 1890, Congress passed the Sherman Anti-Trust Act. [45]This law was intended to stop business practices designed to unfairly eliminate competition.

[46]Initial enforcement of the law in the late 1800s was problematic, because the law was too general, which made prosecution more difficult. [47]The law originally only applied to businesses that sold products or services across state lines, which meant any business that limited sales to the state in which it resided was not subject to the law. [48]By 1900, trusts controlled 40 percent of the country's manufacturing.

[49]Some writers proposed alternative plans for the industrial age economy. [50]Henry George, a California newspaper editor, wrote a proposal for government control of the economy including income taxes that would then be used to help people out of poverty. [51]This was a form of government called socialism.

[52]Capitalists are people who participate in an economic system based on earning profits and the private ownership of manufacturing, labor, and property. [53]German philosopher Karl Marx predicted that someday the impoverished working class would violently revolt against capitalists. [54]His followers, called Marxists, believed capitalism exploited workers and that the best way to stop this exploitation was for government to own all business and to have the government controlled by a single political party made up of elected workers. [55]This form of government was known as communism.

[56]Socialists and communists formed groups in America and even put up candidates for office, but most of their proposals were viewed as extreme, and they remained a small part of the overall voting public. [57]Yet, as we will see in a future lesson, their views influenced enough voters during the Progressive Era that reforms were passed in an effort to improve the condition of American workers and consumers.

**Fun Fact Feature**

In 1887, New York, New Jersey, Massachusetts, and Colorado passed laws to create a state holiday for workers. Twenty-three other states had passed similar laws by 1894. That same year Congress set aside the first Monday in September as a national legal holiday to celebrate the efforts of the working person. Can you name this holiday?

© 2016 The Critical Thinking Co.™ • www.CriticalThinking.com • 800-458-4849 

1. Define the phrase “American Dream.”

_______________________________________

_______________________________________

_______________________________________

_______________________________________

2. What were “trusts?”
   a. groups of organized workers who work together for better conditions
   b. government groups set up to regulate big business
   c. two or more businesses that form a larger organization to advance their interest
   d. the nickname given to the wealthy in the late 1800s

   Which sentence best supports the answer?

   _____

3. Who is the dime novelist closely associated with the theme “rags-to-riches”?
   a. Horatio Alger
   b. Karl Marx
   c. Samuel Gompers
   d. Henry George

   Which sentence best supports the answer?

   _____

4. Which late 1700s American was often used as an example of the “American Dream”?
   a. Benjamin Franklin
   b. Horatio Alger
   c. Mary Harris Jones
   d. Andrew Carnegie

   Which sentence best supports the answer?

   _____

5. Who used a “strike” as a tactic to pressure a business to accept higher wages or better working conditions for laborers?
   a. Marxists
   b. American Dreamers
   c. unions
   d. entrepreneurs

   Which sentence best supports the answer?

   _____

6. In the late 1800s, what were Haymarket Square, Pullman, and Homestead associated with?
   a. violence between unions and businesses
   b. scenes of successful strikes by workers
   c. important technological inventions
   d. government crackdowns using the Sherman Anti-Trust Act

   Which sentence best supports the answer?

   _____

7. The Sherman Anti-Trust Act of 1890 was a response by ________ to try to prevent monopolistic business practices by trusts that prevented fair competition in the marketplace.
   a. unions
   b. government
   c. Horatio Alger
   d. big business owners

   Which sentences best support the answer?

   _____ _____

8. Unions in the 1800s did not recruit a large percentage of the workforce, partly because unions had a bad reputation for:
   a. racism.
   b. monopolies.
   c. violence.
   d. political corruption.

   Which sentences best support the answer?

   _____ _____


© 2016 The Critical Thinking Co.™ • www.CriticalThinking.com • 800-458-4849

9. Which of the following characteristics would probably NOT be a trait of a Horatio Alger hero?
   a. truthfulness
   b. determination
   c. strong work ethic
   d. shyness

   Which sentence best supports the answer?

   ______

## Written Response Question

10. Use complete sentences to describe five issues that labor unions like the AFL worked to change so as to benefit U.S. workers in the late 1800s.

### Fun Fact Finale

In 1887, New York, New Jersey, Massachusetts, and Colorado passed laws to create a state holiday for workers. Twenty-three other states had passed similar laws by 1894. That same year Congress set aside the first Monday in September as a national legal holiday called Labor Day, which we still celebrate today.

© 2016 The Critical Thinking Co.™ • www.CriticalThinking.com • 800-458-4849

Lesson 5

# New Immigrants

## A. "Huddled Masses"

[1]In the 1870s, a French artist named Frederic Bartholdi wanted to create a gift for the upcoming 100th anniversary of American independence. [2]France, an ally of the young United States when it fought the Revolutionary War, had been inspired by the democratic experiment in America which in turn fueled the French Revolution. [3]Bartholdi's idea was to create a huge statue made of metal representing freedom and democracy. [4]When he traveled to America to discuss the idea, he found many people who agreed to help fund the project along with the French. [5]He also found a spot where he wanted the monument to stand; on an island in the harbor between Jersey City and New York City. [6]Bartholdi understood that the mouth of the Hudson River was rapidly becoming the gateway to the United States. [7]Tens of thousands of immigrants were coming through the harbor every year in the late 1800s to try to improve their lives through the economic opportunities America offered–more jobs, better pay, or the chance to start their own business.

[8]By America's centennial (100 year celebration) in 1876, only the monument's massive arm and torch were completed and displayed at an exposition in Philadelphia. [9]Ten years later the Statue of Liberty was complete, shipped to America, assembled on an island in New York City's harbor, and dedicated. [10]In the statue's uplifted right hand is a lamp lighting the way for immigrants. [11]In her left hand is a tablet inscribed with the date of America's birthday—July 4, 1776. [12]At the base of her feet, Liberty stands upon a broken chain—another symbol of liberty. [13]A poem written by the daughter of an American immigrant, Emma Lazurus, is written on a plaque on the statue's pedestal. [14]It reads in part:

Statue of Liberty

From her beacon-hand glows world-wide welcome;
Her mild eyes command the air-bridged harbor that twin cities frame. "Keep ancient lands, your storied pomp!" cries she with silent lips.
"Give me your tired, your poor,
Your huddled masses yearning to breathe free,
The wretched refuse of your teeming shore.
Send these, the homeless, tempest-tost to me,
I lift my lamp beside the golden door!"

## B. Immigration Stations

[15]In the early 1890s, so many immigrants were streaming into the country's East Coast that the federal government felt it needed a new processing center to organize the flow. [16]Near the island with the Statue of Liberty was another island in New York Harbor called Ellis Island. [17]This is where an immigration station opened in January of 1892. [18]To accommodate construction of the processing station, Ellis Island itself grew from three acres to twenty-seven acres with soil deposited there from the digging of subway tunnels under New York City.

[19]After a long voyage across the Atlantic Ocean, immigrant passengers lugged their possessions onto Ellis Island where they were tagged with information from the ship's registry. [20]Then they passed through long lines for medical and legal inspections to determine if they were healthy enough for entry into the United States. [21]Most immigrants passed through the station in a matter of hours and had their names entered into the record. [22]However, if they were found to be infected with a disease, immigrants were sent to a hospital on the island and might be detained for days or weeks. [23]If an immigrant was suspected of having a criminal background or being mentally ill, he/she could be deported (sent back to his/her country of origin). [24]In the period from 1892 to 1910, about two percent of immigrants were deported and between 5,000 to 10,000 immigrants were processed through Ellis Island every day to begin their new lives in America.

The Main Hall on Ellis Island


© 2016 The Critical Thinking Co.™ • www.CriticalThinking.com • 800-458-4849

[25]In the harbor of San Francisco, California, was another important island known as the "Ellis Island of the West." [26]Angel Island was a West Coast immigration station built in 1905. [27]It served immigrants who crossed the Pacific Ocean from China, Japan, Eastern Russia, Pacific islands, and South Asia.

### C. New Immigrants

[28]America had always been a nation of immigrants. [29]The colonies had grown quickly and the United States had expanded west partly because thousands of Northern Europeans—Brits, Irishmen, Scandinavians, and Germans—had come prior to the Civil War. [30]In the period from 1870 to 1910, the floodgates opened and millions of Europeans from all across Europe poured into the country. [31]After 1890, so-called "new immigrants" swelled the American population. [32]These were mainly people from Southern and Eastern Europe—Italians, Slavs, Poles, Greeks, Russian Jews as well as Turks and Armenians from the Middle East. [33]These new immigrants had strange languages, clothes, foods, and customs and were not as easily assimilated into American culture as the earlier immigrants. [34]They experienced discrimination from native-born Americans who knew very little about the culture and customs of some of the European countries.

[35]Fewer jobs and less pay in Europe, a chance to own your own land, along with overpopulation, famine, or religious persecution motivated many individuals and families to seek a better life in the United States. [36]Most immigrants settled in cities in the northeast or the north-central states. [37]One statistic is startling—in 1890, four out of five people living in New York City were born outside the United States or were children of foreign-born parents. [38]Immigrants tended to cluster together in city neighborhoods with people who spoke their languages and practiced familiar religions. [39]They tried to live close to their place of employment but that often meant they lived in poor, sometimes violence-ridden slum areas near noisy, smelly factories. [40]Most immigrants were packed into buildings called tenements. [41]Families living in tenements usually lived in tiny, two-room apartments that had shared bathrooms in the hallway on each floor and few windows.

Immigrants in the cities often lived in crowded tenement conditions.

[42]The crush of immigrants living in the cities convinced many wealthy and middle-class city dwellers to move outside of town. [43]The suburbs were less crowded, safer, and workers were still able to get to their places of employment because of new transportation for commuters (people who travel a distance to work) such as trolleys and subways.

### D. Tammany Hall

[44]Sometimes new immigrants were used for political purposes. [45]William M. Tweed, known as "Boss Tweed," ran a Democratic Party organization called Tammany Hall in New York City. [46]His men would meet immigrants as they arrived in the city, help them find work or a place to live, and maybe even provide a meal at Thanksgiving. [47]In return, Tweed expected voter loyalty. [48]On election day, he expected his immigrant followers to vote for Democratic candidates that Tammany Hall endorsed (supported). [49]Prior to 1900, voting was often done out-loud or publicly at a polling place. [50]Tweed's men could learn whether or not a voter was loyal to the Democratic Party's candidates. [51]If he wasn't, the voter might soon find that he was laid off work or evicted by a landlord. [52]Boss Tweed and his Tammany Hall members were very corrupt. [53]Once Tweed's men gained control of politicians at city hall, he exploited every opportunity to make money for himself and his men. [54]For example, city politicians who wanted Tweed's support would award building contracts to companies controlled by Tammany Hall. [55]Those companies, in turn, would charge the city treasury far more than construction projects actually cost.

**Fun Fact Feature**

With over 3.5 million people, what was America's largest city by 1900? What is America's largest city now?

1. The Statue of Liberty was a birthday gift to America from:
   a. Germany.
   b. France.
   c. the U.S. government.
   d. Great Britain.

   Which sentence best supports the answer?

   _____

2. Emma Lazurus is famous as the:
   a. creator of the Statue of Liberty.
   b. first person processed through Ellis Island.
   c. leader of Tammany Hall.
   d. poet celebrating immigrants at the Statue of Liberty.

   Which sentence best supports the answer?

   _____

3. What changed about the countries of origin of immigrants to America after 1890?
   a. They came from different parts of Europe than before.
   b. They most often moved to the country along the Pacific coast.
   c. They spoke English as their primary language.
   d. They assimilated into American culture more rapidly than ever before.

   Which sentences best support the answer?

   _____ _____ _____

4. Why did the creator of the Statue of Liberty site the monument where he did?

   ______________________________________

   ______________________________________

5. Ellis Island and Angel Island were both known as places where:
   a. immigrants coming across the Atlantic and Pacific were processed into America.
   b. immigrants could get an education, child care, and employment.
   c. violent immigrant criminals were arrested and locked up.
   d. corrupt city officials misused taxpayer's money.

   Which sentences best support the answer?

   _____ _____ _____ _____

6. "Boss" Tweed counted upon the loyalty of whom to support his Tammany Hall political organization?
   a. the settlement house movement
   b. reformers
   c. the French
   d. immigrant voters

   Which sentence best supports the answer?

   _____

7. Frederic Bartholdi's monument was meant to represent:
   a. an immigrant.
   b. freedom and democracy.
   c. the American worker.
   d. France.

   Which sentence best supports the answer?

   _____

8. The last line of the poem at the base of the Statue of Liberty says: "I lift my lamp beside the golden door." What might that line mean?

   ______________________________________

   ______________________________________

   ______________________________________

   ______________________________________


© 2016 The Critical Thinking Co.™ • www.CriticalThinking.com • 800-458-4849

9. Tammany Hall was a political organization known for its:
   a. effectiveness in running New York City.
   b. management of tenement housing.
   c. corruption.
   d. contributions to construction of the Statue of Liberty.

   Which sentence best supports the answer?

   ______

## Written Response Question

10. Use complete sentences to describe several hardships experienced by immigrants at the end of the 1800s.

________________________________________________________________

________________________________________________________________

________________________________________________________________

________________________________________________________________

________________________________________________________________

________________________________________________________________

________________________________________________________________

________________________________________________________________

________________________________________________________________

**Fun Fact Finale**

With over 3.5 million people, New York City was America's largest city by 1900. It had as many people as the whole country had held a half century earlier. It is still America's largest populated city today with about 8.5 million people.

© 2016 The Critical Thinking Co.™ • www.CriticalThinking.com • 800-458-4849 

# Bonus Activity
# Immigration to America

The period from the 1870s through the 1910s saw millions of people coming to live in the United States. The chart below shows the number of immigrants (in millions) from each part of the world and for each decade. Look at the chart and answer questions about the data.

| **United States Immigrants*: 1870s - 1910s** | | | | | | |
|---|---|---|---|---|---|---|
| *** immigrants in millions** | | | | | | |
| **Decade** | **NW EUROPE** | **CEN. EUROPE** | **E EUROPE** | **S EUROPE** | **AMERICAS** | **ASIA & PACIFIC IS.** |
| 1870s | 1.35 | 0.80 | 0.04 | 0.07 | 0.40 | 0.12 |
| 1880s | 2.31 | 1.85 | 0.22 | 0.05 | 0.42 | 0.06 |
| 1890s | 1.13 | 1.19 | 0.52 | 0.70 | 0.04 | 0.03 |
| 1900s | 1.56 | 2.48 | 1.76 | 2.32 | 0.36 | 0.16 |
| 1910s | 0.85 | 1.05 | 1.01 | 1.46 | 1.14 | 0.11 |
| | | | | | | |
| | *Countries* | *Countries* | *Countries* | *Countries* | *Countries* | *Countries* |
| | England | Germany (Prussia) | Russia | Italy | Canada | China |
| | Scotland | Austria-Hungary | Czechoslovakia | Greece | Mexico | Japan |
| | Ireland | Switzerland | Romania | Spain | Central America | Korea |
| | Norway | Belgium | Bulgaria | Portugal | South America | SE Asia |
| | Sweden | Netherlands | Latvia | Serbia | Carribbean Islands | India |
| | Finland | Luxemburg | Lithuania | Turkey | | Philippines |
| | Denmark | | Estonia | | | Pacific Island |
| | France | | | | | Australia |


© 2016 The Critical Thinking Co.™ • www.CriticalThinking.com • 800-458-4849

_______________ 1. On this chart, Italy and Greece are considered to be in what section of Europe?

_______________ 2. Taken as a whole, which section of the world sent the most amount of immigrants to the United States in this period: Europe, Asia, or the Americas?

_______________ 3. Taken as a whole, which section of the world sent the least amount of immigrants to the United States in this period: Europe, Asia, or the Americas?

_______________ 4. Which single section of Europe sent the most immigrants from the 1870s-1910s?

_______________ 5. In which single decade of time did most immigrants come to the United States?

_______________ 6. Northwest Europe dominated immigration through the 1880s. What area of the world sent the most immigrants to the United States after 1900?

_______________ 7. What piece of legislation that you read about in Lesson 1 might help explain the timing of the lowest number of immigrants on the chart?

_______________ 8. Does this chart tell you WHY immigrants came to the United States? (Yes/No)

_______________ 9. What do you notice about the number of immigrants in five of the six place categories when comparing 1911-1920 with 1900-1910?

_______________ 10. Find the highest number on the chart. In which decade, and from what part of the world, did this immigration occur?

© 2016 The Critical Thinking Co.™ • www.CriticalThinking.com • 800-458-4849

Lesson 6

# Reforms of the Late 1800s

## A. Social Gospel

[1]By the 1870s, a number of religious ministers began preaching that true Christians should fight social injustice wherever they found it. [2]These ministers inspired a movement called the Social Gospel which suggested that church members should take positive actions to improve society. [3]One of the major causes of this group was to improve the living conditions of the many immigrants who flooded into the United States during the industrial age.

[4]One example of the Social Gospel movement was the YMCA and YWCA—the Young Men's (or Women's) Christian Association. [5]The "Y" was a place where young urban men or women could come for temporary housing, recreation, or a meal. [6]While at the Y, a young person might also be taught Christian teachings and encouraged to lead a wholesome lifestyle. [7]Seeking a way to keep young men active indoors in the winter months, James Naismith invented the game of basketball at a YMCA in Springfield, Massachusetts, in 1891.

[8]The Salvation Army, a Protestant church organization founded in England, expanded to America in 1880 to provide food, clothing, and temporary shelter for families in need. [9]It was called an "army" because it was organized along military lines and would march through poor city neighborhoods with a band to attract attention to its cause. [10]People would follow the band to soup kitchens where they received assistance and learned virtues of temperance (drinking little or no alcohol) and self-discipline.

[11]Another member of the Social Gospel movement was Jane Addams, a leading reformer in Chicago, Illinois, who looked for ways to improve the living conditions of city immigrants. [12]She raised funds in 1889 to purchase an old mansion and turned it into a social center for immigrants. [13]Addams named her project Hull House. [14]It was a place where immigrants could find out about job openings, get legal aid or health care, take classes in English, have access to early childhood education, or even enjoy an occasional theater performance. [15]By 1895, more than fifty so-called "settlement houses" were established in cities across America. [16]Many were run by middle-class women who pressured city officials to improve sanitation and housing in their cities.

Jane Addams

## B. WCTU

[17]Another organization dedicated to improving society was the Woman's Christian Temperance Union, founded in the late 1870s. [18]The WCTU believed alcohol and tobacco were the cause of large social problems. [19]It fought for laws restricting use of those products in public and pushed for women to convince family members to abstain from (deliberately avoid) those products in their homes.

[20]One of the early leaders of the WCTU was Frances Willard. [21]She believed that women had special virtues of compassion and nurturing that could help make important improvements to society within the home and outside of it as well. [22]She convinced many other middle-class and upper-class women to join her cause. [23]These women had a presence at Ellis Island, where they tried to educate immigrants right off the boat to change habits about drinking and smoking. [24]The WCTU also fought for women's right to vote, in order to empower them to act as "citizen-mothers" and help cure the ills of society by being involved in politics. [25]Women also worked for improved public health and sanitation, prison reform, and the creation of public libraries. [26]Women's clubs organized in cities all across the country, and eventually there were about 150,000 WCTU members. [27]The WCTU became the nation's first mass organization for women.

The WCTU had a bow of white ribbon on its badge symbolizing "the purity of the home."

## C. *How the Other Half Lives*

[28]Jacob Riis was a Danish immigrant who came to America when he was 21. [29]He held several different jobs but eventually became a journalist for a New York City newspaper. [30]He wrote many stories about the poor living conditions of city immigrants. [31]By the late 1880s, Riis hit upon another way of getting out the story of tenement life. [32]The technology of


© 2016 The Critical Thinking Co.™ • www.CriticalThinking.com • 800-458-4849

flash photography had improved enough by then that Riis was able to take pictures of the inside of the tenement buildings, factories, and saloons. [33]Riis used his images, supported by his writings, in a book he published in 1890 called *How the Other Half Lives*. [34]It was one of the first books to include actual photography. [35]The photos of slum life made an immediate impression on the book's readers and many reformers joined him in an effort to improve city living conditions as a result. [36]Riis later used his camera to document evidence that city sewage was flowing directly into the drinking water supply. [37]The outrage of citizens who read his story created much needed reforms about sanitation and perhaps stopped potential disease outbreaks in the city.

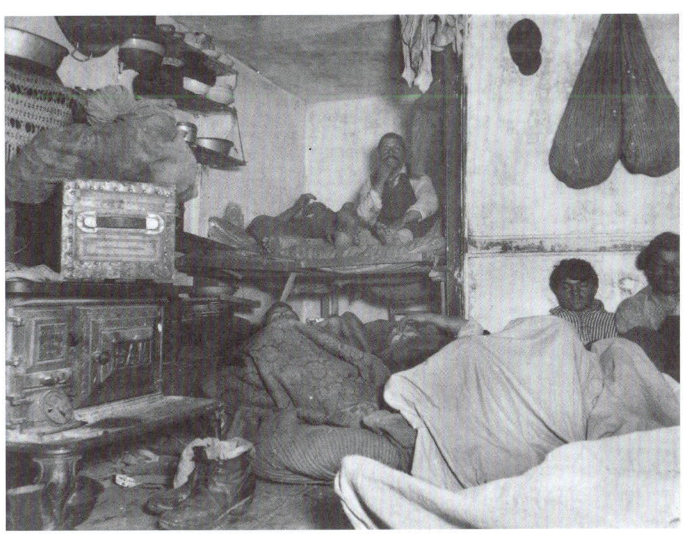

Photos like this one by Jacob Riis showing crowded tenement conditions brought much needed reforms.

**D. City Beautiful Movement**

[38]Frederick Law Olmsted is sometimes called the "American Father of Landscape Architects." [39]After the Civil War, he joined a movement called City Beautiful which attempted to clean up urban messes. [40]Cities had been growing at such an alarming rate that they were congested, dirty, and unsightly. [41]Reformers in the City Beautiful movement worked to create parks and open greenspaces where poor city dwellers could find fresh air, a bit of beauty, and a place for recreation. [42]Olmsted was a key developer of one of the country's most famous urban parks—New York City's Central Park—as well as parks in Boston, Detroit, and Chicago. [43]All across America, cities began to develop their own parks, widen their streets, and do a better job of collecting garbage.

Frederick Olmsted by artist John Singer Sargent

[44]These sanitation efforts, and the efforts of the WCTU, Jacob Riis, and those in the Social Gospel movement paid off. [45]Rates of tuberculosis, typhoid fever and other communicable diseases (ones easily capable of being transmitted), as well as death rates of young children, dropped dramatically after 1900.

**Fun Fact Feature**

Frederick Law Olmsted was also famous for designing the grounds of the largest private home in the United States. Can you name that home?

© 2016 The Critical Thinking Co.™ • www.CriticalThinking.com • 800-458-4849

1. Jane Addams is closely associated with which of these?
   a. Social Gospel movement
   b. Salvation Army
   c. Hull House
   d. YWCA

   Which sentences best support the answer?

   ______ ______

2. What was the name for the overall movement whereby church members were encouraged to take an active role in improving the conditions of American society?
   a. City Beautiful
   b. WCTU
   c. Social Gospel
   d. the "Y"

   Which sentence best supports the answer?

   ______

3. Why was the book *How the Other Half Lives* revolutionary?
   a. It was published in paperback.
   b. It showed how the wealthy lived extravagant lives.
   c. It was written by the president.
   d. It included photographs of slum conditions.

   Which sentences best support the answer?

   ______ ______

4. What is the evidence that efforts to promote public health and sanitation were somewhat successful?

   ________________________________________

   ________________________________________

   ________________________________________

   ________________________________________

5. What important recreational activity came out of the YMCA's efforts to create an indoor winter sport in the 1890s?
   a. basketball
   b. swimming
   c. wrestling
   d. indoor tennis

   Which sentence best supports the answer?

   ______

6. What was Frederick Law Olmsted closely associated with?
   a. Salvation Army
   b. Central Park in New York City
   c. *How the Other Half Lives*
   d. Ellis Island in the New York City harbor

   Which sentence best supports the answer?

   ______

7. The "settlement house movement" attempted to better the lives of:
   a. women.
   b. church members.
   c. the middle-class.
   d. immigrants.

   Which sentence best supports the answer?

   ______

8. What was the City Beautiful movement interested in developing for American cities?
   a. marching bands
   b. gymnasiums
   c. parks
   d. tenements

   Which sentence best supports the answer?

   ______

9. Which of these items was emphasized when discussing the "T" in the WCTU?
   a. alcohol and tobacco
   b. meat
   c. tenements
   d. church

   Which sentence best supports the answer?

   ______



© 2016 The Critical Thinking Co.™ • www.CriticalThinking.com • 800-458-4849

## Written Response Question

10. Use complete sentences to describe how and why women were important in the reform movements of the late 1800s.

**Fun Fact Finale**

Frederick Law Olmsted was also famous for designing the grounds of the largest private home in the United States—a home of the Vanderbilt family, "Biltmore," in Asheville, North Carolina.

© 2016 The Critical Thinking Co.™ • www.CriticalThinking.com • 800-458-4849

Lesson 7

# Arts and Entertainment

## A. The Arts

[1]Between the Civil War and the early 1900s, the United States saw a growing number of successful artists and writers. [2]The rising upper-class wanted paintings of themselves and many American painters became popular portrait artists. [3]John Singer Sargent was one of those artists who was in high demand. [4]Sargent painted portraits for several wealthy and powerful people including Frederick Law Olmsted (see Lesson 6), members of the Vanderbilt and Astor families, and presidents.

"The Child's Bath" by Mary Cassatt, 1893

[5]Mary Cassatt was another popular portrait artist of the times. [6]Her specialty was to create images of the social and family lives of ordinary women. [7]Many of Cassatt's paintings emphasize the bond between a mother and her children.

"Whistler's Mother" by James Whistler, 1871

[8]A third important portrait artist was James Whistler. [9]One of the most famous American paintings of all time was one he called "Arrangement in Gray and Black, No. 1." [10]It was a portrait of Whistler's mother who posed for the painting in London in 1871. [11]Today most people simply refer to the piece as "Whistler's Mother."

[12]Perhaps the most popular American artist of the late 1800s was Winslow Homer. [13]He started out as an illustrator for magazines. [14]During the Civil War, he drew scenes of the battlefront as well as paintings of everyday life on the home front. [15]After the war, Homer struck out on his own, painting scenes of nature and creating watercolors of American life that he sold to support his art career. [16]One of his most popular paintings showed boys at a country school playing an outdoor game called Snap-the-Whip. [17]Later in life, Homer gained fame for his many paintings of activities related to boating and the sea.

"Snap-the-Whip" by Winslow Homer, 1872

[18]In the rough times of the Industrial Age, an artistic movement started called the Ashcan School of Art. [19]Unlike the portrait artists of the day who depicted the nice lives of the rich or idealized country life, Ashcan artists were painters and photographers who wanted to portray the realities of modern city living. [20]They had subjects such as poor immigrant workers, street kids, unsanitary urban conditions, or crime.

"Cliff Dwellers" by George Bellows, 1913


© 2016 The Critical Thinking Co.™ • www.CriticalThinking.com • 800-458-4849

## B. Literature

[21]In the late 1800s, middle-class Americans were excited to read stories that involved American characters on American soil. [22]Samuel Clemens became the most popular author as he wrote and published his books in the 1870s and 1880s about country life of the pre-Civil War era. [23]Using the pen-name Mark Twain, several of his novels tell stories about people who lived along the Mississippi River. [24]The *Adventures of Tom Sawyer* and *Adventures of Huckleberry Finn* were bestsellers because they included both humorous and serious commentaries on American life. [25]He was one of the first writers to make numerous public appearances and theatrical performances about his books. [26]Clemens was also one of the first writers to have his characters speak in the vernacular (speaking like real people, using words and accents of the region). [27]Twain went out West and wrote stories about the mining frontier, such as *The Celebrated Jumping Frog of Calaveras County*.

Samuel Clemens, Also Known as Mark Twain

[28]One of Clemens' rivals was Western writer Bret Harte. [29]His fictional short stories about miners, gamblers, and outlaws also used vernacular dialogue and contributed to common—often sensationalized—visions many Americans have of the Wild West.

[30]Stephen Crane was a writer whose most famous story was about a fictional young man facing his fears of Civil War battles in *The Red Badge of Courage*. [31]Crane wrote in a new style called "realism," in which everyday subjects were discussed without romantic endings. [32]His novel explored the contrast between cowardice and heroism in war that allowed readers to feel what it was really like to be a Civil War soldier.

## C. Entertainment

[33]In the late 1800s, sports became more popular, and people started to buy tickets to watch paid athletes for the first time in America. [34]A form of baseball had been a popular game played by soldiers in the Civil War. [35]By the 1870s, professional baseball teams like the Cincinnati Red Stockings or the Washington Nationals were organized and leagues were formed. [36]By the 1890s, thousands of fans were attending baseball games in ballparks built specifically for each city. [37]Baseball was the nation's most popular sport. [38]In 1903, the first World Series was played between the winners of the American and National leagues to crown the country's championship team.

[39]Another big sport of the times was horse racing. [40]Jockeys (professional horse riders) were paid to race for prize money at tracks in many large cities. [41]In Louisville, the first Kentucky Derby took place in 1875. [42]Horse races became a popular social event for the wealthy, who could afford to own and train horses, and to bet on the outcome of the races.

[43]For working-class male Americans, boxing drew the largest crowds. [44]John L. Sullivan, "the Boston Strong Boy," was a very popular boxer among the immigrants. [45]He won the last bare-knuckles professional championship fight in 1889.

John L. Sullivan Trading Card

[46]Wealthy people were more likely to attend operas or fancy parties, but lower-class families were more likely to pay for the more affordable vaudeville shows or amusement parks for recreation. [47]Vaudeville was an inexpensive theater act with a line-up of fun individual entertainers: singers, comedians, dancers, magicians, acrobats, and animal trainers. [48]Amusement parks were places where a person could go on a carnival ride, view strange people or animals in sideshows, and eat different foods. [49]Coney Island, on the waterfront just outside of New York City, was the most famous amusement park of its day.

**Fun Fact Feature**

A new type of food became an American favorite after the Civil War. It was served up starting in 1871 at Coney Island amusement park and became a hit at baseball games in 1893 after a German-born immigrant saloonkeeper, who also owned the St. Louis Browns, sold them at his ball park. What was that food?

© 2016 The Critical Thinking Co.™ • www.CriticalThinking.com • 800-458-4849

1. Which of these American artists was, perhaps, the most popular in the late 1800s?
   a. James Whistler
   b. Mary Cassatt
   c. Winslow Homer
   d. John Singer Sargent

   Which sentence best supports the answer?

   _____

2. What made the artwork of people in the Ashcan School of Art movement different from painters like Whistler, Cassatt, Winslow, and Sargent?

   ______________________________________

   ______________________________________

   ______________________________________

3. Mary Cassatt was noted for her paintings that showed:
   a. the gritty reality of city living.
   b. the connection between a mother and child.
   c. the everyday lives of rural Americans.
   d. wealthy and famous Americans.

   Which sentence best supports the answer?

   _____

4. Who wrote about life on the Mississippi River as well as life in the western mining camps?
   a. Bret Harte
   b. Stephen Crane
   c. Tom Sawyer
   d. Samuel Clemens

   Which sentences best support the answer?

   _____ _____

5. John L. Sullivan made his mark as a:
   a. famous vaudeville act.
   b. portrait painter.
   c. boxer from Boston.
   d. western miner.

   Which sentence best supports the answer?

   _____

6. What was different about athletics in the decades right after the Civil War?
   a. Some athletes became paid professionals.
   b. Sports involved women athletes for the first time.
   c. Sports became less and less popular.
   d. Football became the country's most popular sport.

   Which sentence best supports the answer?

   _____

7. What was *The Red Badge of Courage*?
   a. a popular vaudeville act
   b. a realistic novel about the Civil War
   c. the prize won by jockeys at the Kentucky Derby
   d. the most famous book by Mark Twain

   Which sentences best support the answer?

   _____ _____

8. Name four types of entertainers one might have seen at an 1800s vaudeville show.

   a. ______________________________

   b. ______________________________

   c. ______________________________

   d. ______________________________

9. What was the most popular professional sport in America in the years after the Civil War?
   a. horseracing
   b. boxing
   c. basketball
   d. baseball

   Which sentence best supports the answer?

   _____


© 2016 The Critical Thinking Co.™ • www.CriticalThinking.com • 800-458-4849

## Written Response Question

10. Use complete sentences to discuss differences between the arts and entertainment enjoyed by the upper-class versus the middle- and lower-class Americans of the Gilded Age.

### Fun Fact Finale

A new type of food became an American favorite after the Civil War. Hot dogs, sometimes still called Coney Dogs, were served up starting in 1871 at Coney Island amusement park. They also became a hit at baseball games in 1893, after a German-born immigrant saloonkeeper, who also owned the St. Louis Browns, sold hot dogs at his ball park.

Lesson 8

# Age of Invention

## A. Thomas A. Edison

[1]The last 30 years of the 1800s saw an amazing boost to American technology. [2]Many inventions that aided industrial output and mass production were not widely seen and recognized by the general public, but had huge impacts on American lives and the country's economy. [3]These inventions included air brakes, refrigerated railroad cars, and the milling of flour, as well as innovations that dramatically improved glass making, oil refining, and lumber production.

Thomas Edison is shown here with his light bulb.

[4]The most popular inventor of the time was Thomas Edison. [5]Edison's inventions touched so many American lives that the public credited him, more than any other inventor, with bringing the country into the modern age. [6]Edison was a sickly child and had very little formal education as a youth. [7]However, he was creative and hard-working. [8]He was rewarded with a job at a telegraph office after saving the life of the child of a local railroad station operator. [9]Edison made improvements on telegraph technology and in 1868 brought forth his first invention–the stock ticker. [10]This was a machine that printed up-to-date stock market prices. [11]Using money earned from that invention, Edison created an "invention factory" in Menlo Park, New Jersey. [12]He hired university-trained scientists to form a team that, he boasted, could make "a minor invention every ten days and a big one every six months." [13]This idea of a research laboratory was an important innovation that would be copied later by other industries.

[14]Edison's team did indeed produce results. [15]In 1877, the phonograph ("phon" = sound, "graph" = writing) was introduced to the public as the first machine that could record and play back sound. [16]Two years later, the Menlo Park lab demonstrated the first commercially practical light bulb. [17]By 1882, Edison produced a complete system of electric generators, meters, storage batteries, and wiring that could be used to power entire city light systems. [18]In 1891, the next "big" invention was the motion picture camera (a device he called the kinetograph). [19]Edison's team is also credited with inventing the microphone, an X-ray machine, and an early copy machine (mimeograph). [20]By the time he died, he and his research team patented more than 1,000 inventions, and Edison was nicknamed the "Wizard of Menlo Park."

## B. Alexander G. Bell

[21]Another important inventor of the age was Alexander Graham Bell. [22]He was born in Scotland, immigrated to Canada, and, in his twenties, immigrated to America. [23]Bell followed in his father's footsteps as a teacher of the deaf and started a school for deaf students in Boston, Massachusetts, in 1872. [24]To help his students, he experimented with a means of transmitting several telegraph messages simultaneously over a single wire and also with various devices to help the deaf learn to speak.

Alexander G. Bell

[25]Bell's breakthrough came when he invented a device to send the human voice over an electric wire. [26]In his first test of the machine in 1876, Bell spoke this sentence into the machine to his laboratory assistant: "Mr. Watson, come here; I want you." [27]Bell called his invention the telephone ("tele" = across, "phon" = sound). [28]He gave a public demonstration at the Centennial Celebration in Philadelphia in the summer of 1876; in the fall, Bell and Watson demonstrated that a conversation could be electronically transmitted over two miles. [29]The Bell Telephone Company was established the next year.

[30]By 1892, telephone lines extended from New York City to Chicago, but it took until 1914 before telephone technology had improved enough to make the first cross-continent long-distance phone call. [31]Bell later conducted experiments that aided flight technology. [32]He also developed an electrical bullet probe to aid surgeons in locating the bullet after hearing President Garfield was shot in 1881. [33]Despite Bell's and the surgeon's efforts, Garfield died from the assassin's shot, but Bell's invention did help save the lives of wounded soldiers in later wars.


© 2016 The Critical Thinking Co.™ • www.CriticalThinking.com • 800-458-4849

## C. Other Inventors

[34]George Eastman left school at age 14 to go to work after his father died. [35]Eastman took a banking job but eventually he improved equipment for his hobby of photography and started his own photography company in Rochester, New York. [36]In 1884, he patented rollable film as an alternative to glass plate negatives. [37]By 1888, the Eastman Kodak Company created small, easy-to-use cameras for people of all ages. [38]The slogan for his cameras said it all: "You push the button, we do the rest." [39]Amateur photographers could snap 100 pictures on the rollable film inside the camera body for only 15 cents a roll and then send the film to Eastman Kodak to make prints from it. [40]Eastman also worked with Edison to create special film used in the new motion picture cameras to create films for movie theaters.

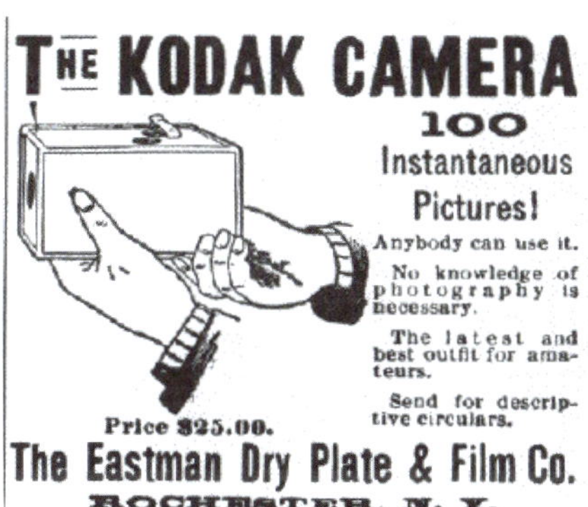


This advertisement for Eastman's camera emphasized that "anyone can use it."

[41]Other notable inventors of the late 1800s included Christopher Sholes, who created the first practical typewriter. [42]Samuel Clemens was one of the first authors to use the machine to produce a manuscript for one of his novels.

[43]James Ritty patented the mechanical cash register in 1883. [44]It came with a familiar ring that came to be known as the "Bell Heard Round the World."

[45]Joseph Glidden lived in the Midwest and, in 1874, created a process for twisting wire barbs with wire fencing. [46]His invention became in such high demand by ranchers in the West that, by the time of Glidden's death in 1906, he was one of America's richest men.

[47]Two ways of moving people were invented in the 1800s. [48]Elisha Otis created a special mechanism in 1853 to lock elevator cars in place if the hoisting ropes failed. [49]Elevators, along with better steel, electric lights, and telephones hastened the development of tall buildings. [50]The term "skyscraper" was first used in the 1880s, after buildings of more than ten stories in height were constructed. [51]Jesse Reno created the first version of the escalator as an entertainment ride at Coney Island, New York, in 1891. [52]His version of the inclined moving stairway climbed only seven steps at a speed of about one foot per second. [53]In 1899, the Otis Elevator Company and Reno joined forces to create commercial escalators to move people in buildings.

**Fun Fact Feature**

AT&T is a large telecommunications company still in business today, which was associated with Bell Telephone and had its start in 1885. The first three characters of the company's name stand for "American Telephone and …" What does the last "T" stand for?

© 2016 The Critical Thinking Co.™ • www.CriticalThinking.com • 800-458-4849

1. Of all the inventors of the late 1800s, which one got a nickname of "Wizard"?
   a. Alexander Graham Bell
   b. George Eastman
   c. Joseph Glidden
   d. Thomas Edison

   Which sentence best supports the answer?

   ______

2. Inventors Eastman and Edison teamed together

   to produce the ______________________________.

   Inventors Otis and Reno teamed together to

   produce the ______________________________.

3. Alexander Graham Bell's breakthrough invention in 1876 was intended to help:
   a. telephone operators.
   b. telegraph operators.
   c. the deaf.
   d. the stock market.

   Which sentence best supports the answer?

   ______

4. "You push the button, we do the rest" was a slogan intended to make which product appeal to amateurs?
   a. phonograph
   b. mechanical cash register
   c. Kodak camera
   d. typewriter

   Which sentence best supports the answer?

   ______

5. What did both Elisha Otis and Jesse Reno inventions do?
   a. moved people in buildings
   b. improved communication
   c. made innovations in entertainment
   d. failed miserably

   Which sentence best supports the answer?

   ______

6. What was an important difference between Edison's inventions and those inventions for industrial technologies after the Civil War?

   ______________________________________________

   ______________________________________________

   ______________________________________________

   ______________________________________________

   ______________________________________________

   ______________________________________________

7. Thomas Edison's genius and popularity was not only that he produced hundreds of inventions; it was the way that he did it. Explain.

   ______________________________________________

   ______________________________________________

   ______________________________________________

   ______________________________________________

   ______________________________________________

   ______________________________________________

8. Which Christopher Sholes invention did Mark Twain use?
   a. phonograph
   b. typewriter
   c. telephone
   d. camera

   Which sentence best supports the answer?

   ______


© 2016 The Critical Thinking Co.™ • www.CriticalThinking.com • 800-458-4849

9. "Phone" and "phono" were used in the names of several inventions of the age (phonograph, microphone, telephone). What does the Greek root "phon" mean?
   a. across
   b. write
   c. new
   d. sound

   Which sentences best support the answer?

   _____ _____

## Written Response Question

10. Out of all the inventions listed in this lesson, choose one and use complete sentences to defend it as the most important of the era.

______________________________________________________________________

______________________________________________________________________

______________________________________________________________________

______________________________________________________________________

______________________________________________________________________

______________________________________________________________________

______________________________________________________________________

______________________________________________________________________

______________________________________________________________________

**Fun Fact Finale**

AT&T is a large telecommunications company still in business today, which was associated with Bell Telephone. The company's name stands for "American Telephone and Telegraph." When it was started in 1885, it was unclear whether or not the telephone would make the telegraph go out of business, so the company kept both machines in their name.

© 2016 The Critical Thinking Co.™ • www.CriticalThinking.com • 800-458-4849 

# Review: Lessons 1 – 8
# Gilded Age Vocabulary

Write the letter of the definition of each vocabulary word. The number following each vocabulary word is the number of the lesson (1–8) where the word was used. All definitions are used once.

_____ 1. hydraulic (1)

_____ 2. fictional (1)

_____ 3. shantytown (1)

_____ 4. assimilate (2)

_____ 5. stockyard (2)

_____ 6. entrepreneur (3)

_____ 7. philanthropy (3)

_____ 8. laissez-faire (3)

_____ 9. blue collar jobs (4)

_____ 10. union (4)

_____ 11. monopoly (4)

_____ 12. centennial (5)

_____ 13. commuter (5)

_____ 14. endorse (5)

_____ 15. deport (5)

_____ 16. communicable (6)

_____ 17. temperance (6)

_____ 18. vernacular (7)

_____ 19. jockey (7)

_____ 20. mimeograph (8)

a. words and accents of the region

b. diseases easily transmitted

c. a business with almost exclusive control of a product or service

d. a professional horse race rider

e. laborers who work together to improve wages and working conditions.

f. one hundred year anniversary

g. using water power

h. the process of adapting or adjusting to the culture of a group or nation

i. an early copy machine

j. a temporary place to store cattle

k. giving away surplus wealth in responsible ways to help society

l. person who runs a business

m. drinking little or no alcohol

n. a hastily and crudely built village

o. manual labor

p. stories that are not entirely factual

q. someone who travels a distance to work

r. support a candidate for election

s. very little governmental interference

t. send back to one's original country


© 2016 The Critical Thinking Co.™ • www.CriticalThinking.com • 800-458-4849

Section 2: Introduction

# Imperialism and Progressives: 1890s-1910s

In the last decade of the 1800s, as the American frontier was disappearing, some leaders began calling for expansion of United States territory. The desire to extend America's rule by acquiring and controlling foreign colonies was called imperialism. There were economic, military, political, and religious reasons for obtaining new U.S. lands. Soon the government owned many islands in the Pacific Ocean region. Then a war with Spain in 1898 resulted in new U.S. territories in the Caribbean Sea.

After the assassination of President William McKinley, Republican Theodore Roosevelt, who was a hero of the Spanish-American War, became the new chief executive. He was an imperialist and soon acquired more U.S. land to construct a canal linking the Atlantic and Pacific Oceans through the Isthmus of Panama. To demonstrate America's growing naval strength, Roosevelt sent the Navy on a world cruise during his second term of office.

Roosevelt was also a Progressive—a group of politicians who pushed reforms to fix political and business corruption, advance women's rights, change unsafe working conditions, and improve the lives of working class Americans. Roosevelt was one of the country's most active presidents and led a number of national improvements, especially in the area of land conservation.

When Roosevelt decided not to seek reelection after seven years in office, he endorsed William Howard Taft as the next president. However, Roosevelt became unsatisfied with Taft's administration and challenged him to regain the presidency in 1912. That election divided the Republican Party and brought a Democrat into office.

## U.S. Presidents

25. William McKinley
1897-1901

26. Theodore Roosevelt
1901-1909

27. William H. Taft
1909-1913

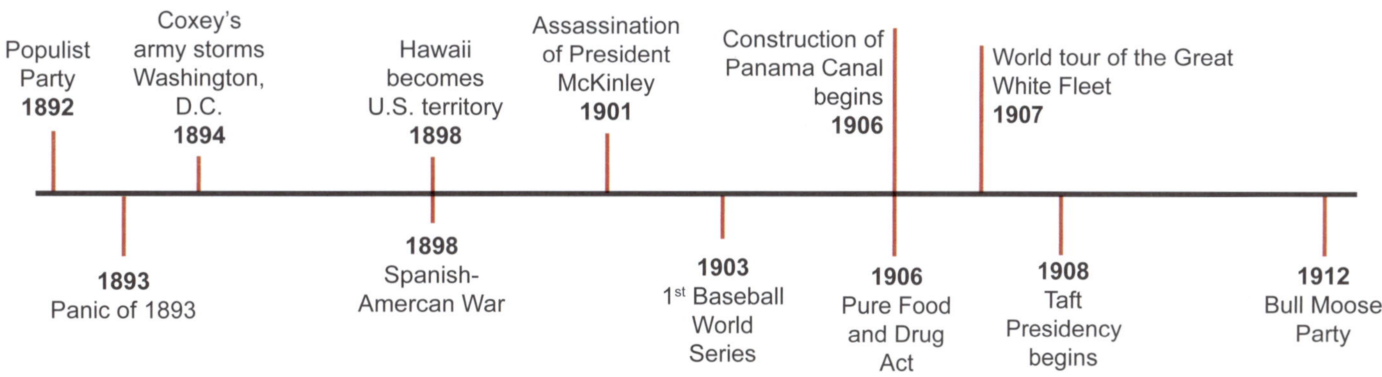

Lesson 9

# Pacific Expansion

## A. Imperialism

[1]By the late 1800s, Great Britain, France, Italy, Germany, Spain, Japan, and other nations were heavily involved in imperialism—a policy of extending a country's rule by acquiring and controlling foreign colonies. [2]Their empires now reached into Asia, Africa, the Caribbean Sea, and the Pacific Islands. [3]The United States, which had once been a colony of Great Britain itself, had been busy establishing its own independent government and settling the American West in the 19th century. [4]However, the end of the Civil War solidified (strengthened) the power of the federal government and the census of 1890 seemed to show that there no longer was a western frontier line. [5]Some Americans wondered whether the United States ought to seek overseas colonies as well, before it was too late to get into the game.

[6]Some business and political leaders argued that the expanded industrial production of the late 1800s demanded that the United States partake (to join with others) in imperialism. [7]They said America must continue to look for raw materials for its industries and find new markets for its products to keep a healthy economy. [8]Some religious leaders stated that establishing overseas colonies made moral sense. [9]The Reverend Josiah Strong, in his 1885 book *Our Country*, said that it was the mission of church-going Americans to take over islands with native cultures in order to bring civilization and the Christian religion to the world's "weaker races."

[10]Military leaders added to the expansionist argument. [11]Alfred Thayer Mahan argued in his 1890 book, *The Influence of Sea Power Upon History*, that all great nations must have a strong navy. [12]It was important that the United States acquire good ports in the Atlantic and Pacific Oceans to safeguard the country's coastline. [13]Navies required access to good harbors. [14]"The United States Navy was now a fleet of steam ships that needed refueling stations around the globe," Mahan wrote. [15]Senator Henry Cabot Lodge of Massachusetts argued that the rush for overseas colonies was similar to Darwin's new theory of "survival of the fittest"—it was a contest between nations that the United States must join if it hoped to compete in future wars.

Alfred Thayer Mahan

## B. Alaska

[16]America had actually expanded into new Pacific territory just after the Civil War. [17]In 1867, Secretary of State William Seward arranged a deal with Russia to purchase Alaska for the United States. [18]In exchange for 7.2 million dollars, Russia gave up any claims to a region which it had used primarily to gather furs in the early 1800s.

[19]It took Congress about a year to agree to sign off on the deal. [20]Many people felt the land, which stretches far north of the Arctic Circle, was just a frozen wasteland with few resources and no market for goods. [21]They derided (made fun of, mocked) the idea as "Seward's Icebox" or "Seward's Folly." [22]By the 20th century, no one was laughing. [23]Alaskan gold discoveries, oil deposits, and seafood resources provided valuable products to the nation. [24]Alaska provided important military base locations during World War II and, in early 1959, became the country's 49th state.

This map compares how Alaska, with more than 663,000 square miles, is the largest state in the Union by far.

## C. Pacific Islands

[25]Starting in the late 1850s, the United States began taking possession of uninhabited, unclaimed islands in the Pacific Ocean that had large deposits of guano (seabird manure). [26]Dried guano has high quantities of nitrogen, phosphate, potassium, and other minerals and was mined to make fertilizer and used as a key ingredient in the production of gunpowder. [27]The Guano Act of 1856 allowed


© 2016 The Critical Thinking Co.™ • www.CriticalThinking.com • 800-458-4849

Howland, Jarvis, Palmyra, Johnston, Kingman, and Baker (all small islands in the Pacific Ocean) to be used by guano mining companies. [28]Some eventually housed military installations and all remain as U.S. territories today.

[29]Samoa is a chain of islands in the central Pacific, south of the equator, long inhabited by native peoples. [30]Missionaries and marine traders from Europe and the United States began arriving there in the mid-1800s. [31]The islands provided a safe ocean harbor and had important crops such as cocoa beans, coconut products, and root crops. [32]In 1889, the German navy invaded Samoa and destroyed property of some Americans living there. [33]The United States government responded by sending in the U.S. Navy and a war between Germany and the United States nearly broke out over the incident. [34]Eventually a treaty between the two countries was signed and the territory split between the two nations. [35]American Samoa, a series of five islands totaling about 80 square miles, soon became an important naval base.

### D. Hawaii

[36]Another important chain of islands in the Pacific were the Hawaiian Islands. [37]King Kamehameha was a Hawaiian tribal chief who was the first to conquer all of the Hawaiian Islands (1798) with the help of arms bought from American and British traders. [38]During his rule, the United States and British governments became increasingly interested in controlling the islands and securing Hawaiian resources such as whale oil, pineapple, and sugarcane. [39]Hawaii's ports, including Pearl Harbor near the city of Honolulu, were also eyed as valuable ports for trade with Asian countries. [40]Worried about retaining control of their islands, the Hawaiian monarchy imposed legislation to prevent foreigners from owning Hawaiian land. [41]Nearly all Hawaiian property was owned by Hawaiian royalty and chiefs, with only a very small percentage of land owned by the average Hawaiian. [42]As the sugarcane trade became more profitable, the upper-class Hawaiian land owners started selling more and more property to American businessmen to create pineapple and sugar cane plantations (large farms).

Queen Liliuokalani

[43]By the early 1890s, the kingdom of Hawaii was governed by Queen Liliuokalani. [44]She was not supportive of the American companies that now controlled much of the country's land. [45]Threatened by the views of Queen Liliuokalani, American planters staged a revolt in January 1893 to overthrow the queen in order to maintain control of their economic interests. [46]Even though President Benjamin Harrison had not approved the use of U.S. military forces, American Marines landed on the island to protect Americans and American interests. [47]The queen was forced to resign. Sanford Dole, a member of a powerful American planter family on the island, claimed the presidency of a new Hawaiian republic.

[48]U.S. President Grover Cleveland was inaugurated shortly after the uprising and felt Americans had acted wrongfully in Hawaii. [49]He was an anti-imperialist (someone against U.S. foreign expansion) and tried to restore Liliuokalani to her throne. [50]However, he was unsuccessful. [51]Most Americans were in favor of keeping Hawaii as a territory for a naval base in the Pacific, especially after war broke out between the United States and Spain in the Philippines later in the decade (see Lesson 10). [52]Eventually the next U.S. president, William McKinley, who supported imperialists, signed legislation annexing Hawaii as a U.S. territory in 1898. [53]It would eventually become America's 50th state in 1959.

**Fun Fact Feature**

Of all the places mentioned in this lesson, which territory governed by the United States is the farthest south?

1. What is odd about the United States becoming an imperialistic nation in the late 1800s?
   a. America was the first nation to become imperialistic.
   b. America had once been a colony of another imperialistic nation.
   c. By 1890, America had still not explored all the land within its own borders.
   d. Imperialism was against the U.S. Constitution.

   Which sentence best supports the answer?

   _____

2. What are the reasons Alfred Thayer Mahan argued for American imperialism?
   a. military
   b. religious
   c. economic
   d. educational

   Which sentences best support the answer?

   _____ _____

3. The United States acquired Alaska from which nation?
   a. Germany
   b. Great Britain
   c. Spain
   d. Russia

   Which sentence best supports the answer?

   _____

4. Originally, the United States was attracted to several uninhabited islands in the Pacific Ocean because they:
   a. gave American missionaries a chance to spread Christianity.
   b. offered some businesses a chance to mine seabird manure.
   c. made good army bases.
   d. provided a good market for American-made products.

   Which sentences best support the answer?

   _____ _____

5. Which area was once an independent republic ruled by a monarchy (king/queen) before annexation to the United States in 1898?
   a. Alaska
   b. Samoa
   c. Hawaii
   d. Midway

   Which sentences best support the answer?

   _____ _____

6. Explain why Alaska was nicknamed "Seward's Icebox" or "Seward's Folly" in the 1860s.

   ______________________________

   ______________________________

7. What are the reasons Josiah Strong argued for American imperialism?
   a. military
   b. religious
   c. economic
   d. educational

   Which sentence best supports the answer?

   _____

8. Name two important products that can be produced from dried seabird manure called guano.

   ______________________________

   ______________________________

9. Which anti-imperialist U.S. President was unsuccessful in restoring Queen Liliuokalani to the throne of her government in Hawaii in the 1890s?
   a. Sanford Dole
   b. William McKinley
   c. Benjamin Harrison
   d. Grover Cleveland

   Which sentences best support the answer?

   _____ _____

 © 2016 The Critical Thinking Co.™ • www.CriticalThinking.com • 800-458-4849

## Written Response Question

10. Use complete sentences to explain the major reasons why some Americans pushed for expansionism.

___

___

___

___

___

___

___

___

___

### Fun Fact Finale

American Samoa is the territory governed by the United States that is the farthest south. American Samoa and Jarvis Island are the only two territories controlled by the United States government that are south of the equator.

© 2016 The Critical Thinking Co.™ • www.CriticalThinking.com • 800-458-4849 

Lesson 10

# Spanish-American War

## A. Cuba

[1]Spain was one of the first European nations to claim land in the New World in the 1500s. [2]At one time, Spain had colonies stretching from California, Texas, and Florida through South America. [3]Over time, however, revolutions and wars had taken place in most of those colonies and Spain became a weak imperialistic power. [4]One of the few overseas colonies still possessed by Spain in the 1890s was the island of Cuba in the Caribbean Sea. [5]In 1895, rebels there launched a revolution for independence as well. [6]The Spanish government sent military officials to Cuba to put down the revolution and violence escalated (increased in intensity). [7]A huge number of Cubans suspected of supporting independence were rounded up and put in poorly-run concentration camps where an estimated 200,000 people died from disease, malnutrition, or poor sanitation.

[8]The federal government of the United States was concerned. [9]Cuba lay only about 90 miles south of Florida. [10]America still believed in the Monroe Doctrine of 1823 which stated that the United States would not tolerate interference from European powers in nations in North and South America. [11]Also, Cuba was a good source of sugar cane and other products used by the United States.

## B. Yellow Journalism

[12]The revolts in Cuba made good copy for newspapers, and two publishers in New York City competed to feed the public's curiosity about those events. [13]William Randolph Hearst printed the *Journal*. [14]He was the first to use color print in his paper (a tinted comic strip was called "The Yellow Kid") and soon his sensational stories about death, disease, battles, and violence in Cuba were nicknamed "yellow journalism." [15]Hearst's competitor, Joseph Pulitzer of the *New York World*, also stooped down to sensationalize the news out of Cuba. [16]Both newspapers increased their circulation by printing front page yellow journalism stories about bloody atrocities committed in the war. [17]Sometimes rumors were headlined as facts to capture reader interest to increase paper sales. [18]Pulitzer wrote in one editorial, "Blood on the roadsides, blood in the fields, blood on the doorsteps: blood, blood, blood! [19]The old, the young, the weak, the crippled: all are butchered without mercy in Cuba .... [20]Is there no nation wise enough, brave enough, and strong enough to restore peace in this bloodsmitten land?" [21]Hearst

This 1898 political cartoon shows newspaper publishers Joseph Pulitzer (left) and William Randolph Hearst (right).

sent a reporter to Cuba who wired back that things were not as bad as he had thought. [22]Hearst reportedly replied, "You furnish the pictures and I'll furnish the war." [23]Another Hearst reporter actually helped a female Cuban rebel escape from jail so he could write another story.

## C. "Remember the *Maine*"

[24]President William McKinley was for imperialism but moved slowly on the Cuban crisis. [25]He wasn't convinced America had a solid reason for interfering in the situation. [26]However, he was embarrassed in early February 1898, when Hearst's *Journal* printed an intercepted message from the Spanish ambassador, who wrote that "McKinley is weak, and a bidder for the admiration of the crowd besides being a would-be politician." [27]The president responded by sending a U.S. Navy warship, the *U.S.S. Maine*, to the harbor in Havana, Cuba, to show some support of the rebel cause.

[28]On the night of February 15, 1898, a mysterious explosion rocked the *Maine*, sinking the

Wreckage of the *USS Maine* in the Harbor of Havana, Cuba, 1898

 © 2016 The Critical Thinking Co.™ • www.CriticalThinking.com • 800-458-4849

battleship, and killing 266 crewmen. [29]Newspaper headlines screamed "Remember the *Maine*!" and immediately blamed Spanish authorities for the American deaths. [30]The outraged Assistant Secretary of the Navy, Theodore Roosevelt, claimed that the *Maine* "was sunk by an act of dirty treachery on the part of the Spaniards," even before an investigation was completed. [31]Roosevelt also stated that if the president did not respond to the attack, he had "no more backbone than a chocolate éclair." [32]Roosevelt ordered the naval commander of the U.S. Pacific Fleet, Admiral George Dewey, to sail toward the Spanish colonies of the Philippine Islands in case war broke out between Spain and the United States.

## D. Spanish-American War

[33]After the *Maine* disaster, public opinion was strong for revenge and President McKinley could stall no longer. [34]Despite Spanish offers to close Cuban concentration camps and agree to a truce with the rebels, Congress agreed to President McKinley's request on April 11, 1898, to declare war against Spain.

[35]On May 1st, Admiral Dewey steamed his U.S. fleet into the Philippines and easily took the capital of Manila. [36]A few weeks later, American troops landed on the island of Cuba and advanced toward a Spanish stronghold at Santiago. [37]Leading one group of U.S. troops was Theodore Roosevelt. [38]He had resigned his position with the naval office in Washington, D.C., to lead a cavalry regiment (an army unit of soldiers on horseback) nicknamed the "Rough Riders." [39]The regiment was a mix of ex-military men, western cowboys, miners, hunters, and Native Americans. [40]All of the Rough Riders were skilled horsemen. [41]On July 1st, Roosevelt led his men on a charge up San Juan Hill and several other higher places above the city of Santiago. [42]Alongside the Rough Riders were troops of the 24th Infantry and the 9th and 10th Calvary, which were regiments primarily made up of black soldiers. [43]Victory in battle by the Americans secured the eastern end of Cuba and propelled Roosevelt into the headlines as a major hero of the war. [44]A few days later, the Spanish navy was destroyed in a battle off the Cuban coast and the Spanish-American War was over. [45]Less than 400 American soldiers died in battle during the war, although several thousand others died of disease. [46]Spain lost more than 50,000 soldiers.

Colonel Theodore Roosevelt led the "Rough Riders"

## E. After the War

[47]Spain signed a peace treaty with the United States soon after the last battles of the war. [48]Both sides agreed to Cuban independence, but America insisted on the right to locate a naval base on the east end of the island at Guantanamo Bay. [49]The United States still operates that military base today. [50]Investments by U.S. companies in Cuban businesses soared from fifty million dollars in 1898 to a half-billion dollars over the next twenty years. [51]Spain also turned over three of its colonial islands to the United States. [52]The United States took control of Puerto Rico in the Caribbean Sea and Guam and the Philippines in the Pacific. [53]U.S. Naval bases were soon established on all these new possessions, as well.

[54]The United States was now an imperial power with territories in the Atlantic and Pacific. [55]The U.S. Secretary of State, John Hay, noted that this short, successful war had reaped great prizes for America. [56]He wrote Roosevelt shortly after the treaty signing that it had been "a splendid little war." [57]The nickname stuck.

[58]U.S. business leaders were very happy that the United States took the Philippine Islands. [59]They saw the islands as an important base of business operations for the nearby Chinese market. [60]President McKinley felt the five million Filipinos were not ready for self-rule and that U.S. missionaries should "educate the Filipinos, and uplift, civilize, and Christianize them." [61]McKinley did not understand that, in fact, most Filipino people were already Catholic (having lived under Spanish rule for centuries) and were bitterly disappointed that they were not given independence like Cuba. [62]The "splendid little war" soon had an aftermath that was not so splendid. [63]In 1899, Emilio Aguinaldo led rebels, who had been fighting against Spanish rule, on an all-out attack on the United States military personnel still on the islands to establish independence for the Philippines. [64]During the next four years, more than four thousand U.S. troops and twenty-thousand Filipino independence fighters were killed in battle. [65]Villages were destroyed and civilian casualties mounted into the tens of thousands. [66]By 1902, an uneasy peace was restored and the U.S. government appointed a governor-general to rule the Philippines along with an elected Filipino congress. [67]After World War II, the United States finally granted the Philippines complete independence.

© 2016 The Critical Thinking Co.™ • www.CriticalThinking.com • 800-458-4849

**Fun Fact Feature**

An American who died in 1904 put in his will that he wanted his inheritance used as prize money for awards for excellent writing. Today those prizes annually honor the country's best poets, biographers, novelists, historians, musicians, playwrights, and journalists. Can you tell the name of that prize?

1. At the start of the 1890s, Cuba was still a colonial possession of:
   a. the United States.
   b. Great Britain.
   c. Spain.
   d. the Caribbean Sea.

   Which sentence best supports the answer?

   _____

2. "*Blood on the roadsides, blood in the fields, blood on the doorsteps: blood, blood, blood!*" What is this style of newspaper writing called?
   a. imperialism
   b. yellow journalism
   c. comic journalism
   d. investigative journalism

   Which sentences best support the answer?

   _____ _____ _____

3. What event, in February of 1898, sparked President McKinley to ask Congress to declare war on Spain?
   a. A Hearst reporter rescued a jailed female Cuban rebel.
   b. The Rough Rider's charged up San Juan Hill.
   c. There was a mysterious explosion on the *USS Maine*.
   d. Spain sent military officials to Cuba to put down the rebels.

   Which sentences best support the answer?

   _____ _____ _____

4. In the eyes of many Americans, who was the hero of the Spanish-American War?
   a. Theodore Roosevelt
   b. George Dewey
   c. William McKinley
   d. William Randolph Hearst

   Which sentence best supports the answer?

   _____

5. Why did the U.S. Secretary of State call the Spanish-American War "a splendid little war"?

   ______________________________

   ______________________________

   ______________________________

   ______________________________

6. What became of Cuba after the Spanish-American War?
   a. Cuba remained a colonial possession of Spain.
   b. Cuba became a U.S. territory.
   c. Cuba suffered the same fate as the Philippines.
   d. Cuba became an independent country with a U.S. Naval base.

   Which sentence best supports the answer?

   _____

7. Who led rebels in an attempt to secure Filipino independence after the Spanish-American War?
   a. George Dewey
   b. Emilio Aguinaldo
   c. Joseph Pulitzer
   d. William McKinley

   Which sentence best supports the answer?

   _____


© 2016 The Critical Thinking Co.™ • www.CriticalThinking.com • 800-458-4849

8. What was not well thought-out about President McKinley's plan to "uplift, civilize, and Christianize" the people of the Philippines after the Spanish-American War?
    a. Many were already Christian.
    b. No American missionaries were willing to go to the Philippines.
    c. Filipino people had no churches.
    d. The Philippines were still a Spanish colony after the war

    Which sentence best supports the answer?

    _____

9. Which Caribbean Island did the United States gain as a territory after the Spanish-American War?
    a. Puerto Rico
    b. Guam
    c. Cuba
    d. The Philippines

    Which sentence best supports the answer?

    _____

## Written Response Question

10. Look at the political cartoon in this lesson. a. Explain as many symbols as you can. Who are the people? Why are they wearing that clothing? What might the objects behind the men, and in-between them, represent? b. Explain the message of the cartoonist.

a. ______________________________________________________________

______________________________________________________________

______________________________________________________________

______________________________________________________________

______________________________________________________________

b. ______________________________________________________________

______________________________________________________________

______________________________________________________________

______________________________________________________________

______________________________________________________________

**Fun Fact Finale**

Ironically, Joseph Pulitzer, a newspaper publisher who had stooped to "yellow journalism," put in his will that he wanted his inheritance used as prize money for awards for excellent writing. Today the Pulitzer Prize annually honors the country's best poets, biographers, novelists, historians, musicians, playwrights, and journalists.

© 2016 The Critical Thinking Co.™ • www.CriticalThinking.com • 800-458-4849

Lesson 11

# Theodore Roosevelt

## A. Roosevelt's Background

[1]Theodore Roosevelt's heroics in the Spanish-American War propelled him to a victorious election as governor of New York in 1898. [2]However, he was not the first famous Roosevelt. [3]He had been born into a prominent Dutch family in New York City just before the Civil War. [4]His father, Theodore, Sr., had run a profitable glass import business and helped start the New York City Children's Aid Society, the Metropolitan Museum of Art, the American Museum of Natural History, and the New York Children's Orthopedic Hospital. [5]The Roosevelt family took an extended trip to the Middle East and Europe when young Theodore ("Teddy") was a teenager. [6]There he gained valuable cultural experiences and a strong education and was able to start his studies of biology at Harvard at the age of 18.

Roosevelt was only 24 when he won election to the New York state assembly in 1882.

[7]Theodore, Sr. was nominated for an important New York customs house job while Teddy was in college. [8]However, political bosses kept Theodore, Sr. from getting the position. [9]Teddy was saddened by the corruption found in the politics of his day. [10]When his father died shortly after his political appointment was not granted, Teddy entered Columbia Law School and decided to go into politics himself. [11]Upon graduation, Roosevelt married Alice Lee and was soon elected as one of the youngest men ever to serve in the state legislature in Albany, New York. [12]He fought for many reforms while in office, which upset some of his older political foes.

## B. Heading West

[13]While working on a government reform bill at the statehouse in early 1884, Roosevelt received an urgent message to come home to New York City. [14]His pregnant wife was very ill and so was his mother. [15]On February 14th, Roosevelt suffered a double tragedy when his mother died of typhoid fever and his wife died in childbirth on the same day in the same house. [16]His baby, Alice, survived but Roosevelt was devastated. [17]Within months, Roosevelt decided to quit the legislature, leave his young daughter with his sister, and head out West.

[18]A few years prior to this, Roosevelt had invested in a cattle ranch called Elkhorn in the Badlands region of the Dakota Territory. [19]After the 1884 tragedy, it provided him with a place to clear his head, earn a different kind of living, and meet new people. [20]He also enjoyed the idea of hunting for big game in the American West. [21]He had been a sickly child, and his father had always insisted that young Theodore take part in vigorous physical activity to improve his health. [22]Following that advice, he had taken up boxing, hiking, fishing, and hunting and had grown to love the outdoors. [23]Roosevelt looked forward to the life of a rancher in the West.

Roosevelt posed as a western hunter in 1885.

[24]In the Badlands, Roosevelt learned to ride a horse and run a cattle business, and he made friends with many different types of people with whom he had normally not associated in the urban East. [25]He also was able to hunt deer, elk, and buffalo and explore various regions of the West. [26]In his spare time, he wrote several books. [27]Roosevelt started a hunting club whose purpose was to protect the habitat of large game animals. [28]Once he even chased after, and arrested, cattle thieves. [29]Unfortunately, a harsh winter decimated (wiped out) his cattle herd, and Roosevelt was forced to end his career as a rancher [30]After two years in Dakota Territory, Roosevelt returned to New York City. [31]He brought Alice back under his care and started a large family with his new wife, Edith, in 1886.

## C. Back East

[32]Only a few years earlier, President James Garfield had been assassinated by a disappointed office seeker. [33]In 1883, Congress reacted by passing the Pendleton Civil Service Act. [34]This law provided selection of government employees by competitive exams instead of the "spoils system,"


© 2016 The Critical Thinking Co.™ • www.CriticalThinking.com • 800-458-4849

which allowed appointments to people who were merely friends of politicians or members of a certain political party. [35]In the presidential election of 1888, Roosevelt worked hard to support the successful Republican candidate, Benjamin Harrison. [36]When Harrison won, he encouraged Roosevelt to take a position as Civil Service Commissioner, and Congress granted him that position. [37]For the next seven years, Roosevelt lived in Washington, D.C., vigorously enforcing civil service laws and earning much praise as a government official.

[38]In 1895, the Roosevelt family moved back to New York City when Theodore became the head of the police department. [39]The city had a reputation for having the most corrupt police department in the nation but, over the next two years, Roosevelt totally reformed the department. [40]He standardized recruitment, training, and equipment, and made a few more political enemies in doing so. [41]After reading Jacob Riis' book, *How the Other Half Lives*, Roosevelt worked with Riis to rid the poorest neighborhoods in the city of crime and corruption.

## D. A National Figure

[42]Roosevelt was back in Washington, D.C., in 1897, after he was appointed to the job of Assistant Secretary of the Navy. [43]Roosevelt had always loved sailing and had once written a book, *The Naval War of 1812*, which was so well respected it became a textbook at the naval college. [44]After the *U.S.S. Maine* blew up in Havana, Cuba, Roosevelt hurriedly gave orders that prepared the United States Navy for war against Spain. [45]When war broke out, he resigned his job to take an active role with his Rough Riders regiment on the ground in Cuba.

Roosevelt used his popularity as a war hero, shown here on a campaign button, to win the governorship of New York in 1898.

[46]When Roosevelt served as governor of New York after the Spanish-American War, he developed a program he called the "Square Deal." [47]A square is equal on all sides, and Governor Roosevelt worked hard to bring an equal playing field to small businesses, large corporations, the middle-class, and the lower economic class. [48]He was strongly in favor of laws that set aside natural resources and laws to protect consumers from business trusts.

[49]In the course of creating a number of reforms, Roosevelt upset some powerful politicians who had previously held control of New York state and city affairs, like those in Tammany Hall, as well as some big business owners. [50]Roosevelt was so popular, however, that he did not need the support of corrupt politicians. [51]In 1900, some of Roosevelt's enemies pushed hard to get him out of New York by nominating him for vice president. [52]Some of his friends also supported the idea, so Roosevelt reluctantly agreed to run with President McKinley, knowing full well that the vice president had very little real power in office. [53]Roosevelt campaigned with his usual energy, and Republican McKinley easily won reelection. [54]Roosevelt was back in Washington, D.C., for a third time in his career.

[55]During the first half of 1901, Vice President Roosevelt was a forgotten man. [56]There was little real responsibility in his job, other than occasionally presiding over the Senate. [57]Often the position seemed only ceremonial. [58]However, that all changed on September 6, 1901, when President McKinley was shot by a lone socialist (someone who wants equal distribution of wealth) and anarchist (a person who wants government rule replaced with self-rule) during an event in Buffalo, New York. [59]McKinley died eight days later, and Theodore Roosevelt was soon sworn in as the 24th President. [60]One of his political enemies, Senator Mark Hanna of Ohio, expressed the shock of many when he exclaimed: "Now look! That damned cowboy is President of the United States!"

**Fun Fact Feature**

Theodore Roosevelt was 42 years old when he succeeded William McKinley as U.S. President in 1901. What was significant about that fact?

© 2016 The Critical Thinking Co.™ • www.CriticalThinking.com • 800-458-4849 

1. Which New Yorker helped to start both the Metropolitan Museum of Art and the American Museum of Natural History?
   a. Theodore Roosevelt
   b. William McKinley
   c. Theodore Roosevelt, Sr.
   d. Benjamin Harrison

   Which sentence best supports the answer?

   _____

2. Explain the double tragedy Theodore Roosevelt suffered on Valentine's Day, 1884.

   ______________________________

   ______________________________

   ______________________________

   ______________________________

3. What job did Theodore Roosevelt take right after the double tragedy of 1884?
   a. rancher
   b. police commissioner
   c. civil service commissioner
   d. soldier

   Which sentence best supports the answer?

   _____

4. Theodore Roosevelt made a decision to go into politics rather than the field of biology after:
   a. the explosion of the *U.S.S. Maine*.
   b. returning from an extended trip to Europe and the Middle East with his family.
   c. becoming a hero in the Spanish-American War.
   d. the death of his father.

   Which sentence best supports the answer?

   _____

5. Upon the assassination of President Garfield by a disappointed office seeker, which of these called for the creation of a system of exams for jobs in government?
   a. the spoils system
   b. the Pendleton Civil Service Act
   c. the Square Deal
   d. the assassination of President McKinley

   Which sentences best support the answer?

   _____ _____ _____

6. Which job did Theodore Roosevelt reluctantly take after the urging of his friends and enemies in 1900?
   a. governor of New York
   b. head of the New York City police department
   c. vice president of the United States
   d. Assistant Secretary of the Navy

   Which sentences best support the answer?

   _____ _____

7. Which event immediately propelled Theodore Roosevelt to become the U.S. President in 1901?
   a. his heroics during the Spanish-American War
   b. the success of his adventures at Elkhorn Ranch in the Dakota Territory
   c. the assassination of President McKinley
   d. the explosion of the *U.S.S. Maine*

   Which sentences best support the answer?

   _____ _____

8. With whom did Theodore Roosevelt work while fighting crime in New York City in the 1890s?
   a. Benjamin Harrison
   b. cowboys from the Dakota Territory
   c. Rough Riders
   d. author Jacob Riis

   Which sentence best supports the answer?

   _____


© 2016 The Critical Thinking Co.™ • www.CriticalThinking.com • 800-458-4849

9. What event prompted Roosevelt to abandon his life as a western rancher?
   a. his nomination as vice president
   b. a terrible winter that killed many of his cattle
   c. his marriage to Alice Lee
   d. his appointment as U.S. Civil Service commissioner

   Which sentence best supports the answer?

   ______

## Written Response Question

10. Use complete sentences to explain why Theodore Roosevelt made a number of political enemies during his career prior to becoming president.

_______________________________________________

_______________________________________________

_______________________________________________

_______________________________________________

_______________________________________________

_______________________________________________

_______________________________________________

_______________________________________________

_______________________________________________

**Fun Fact Finale**

Theodore Roosevelt was 42 years old when he succeeded William McKinley as U.S. President in 1901, thereby becoming the youngest person to ever serve in that office.

# Bonus Activity
# Theodore Roosevelt — Which Came First?

Review Lessons 10 and 11. The events below are connected to the Revolutionary War. Put these events in chronological order (1, 2, 3).

Examples

| | | | |
|---|---|---|---|
| 3 | December | 2 | Wednesday |
| 1 | April | 3 | Friday |
| 2 | July | 1 | Monday |

a. _____ head of New York City police department
_____ governor of New York state
_____ hero of Battle of San Juan Hill in the Spanish American War

b. _____ a rancher in Dakota Territory
_____ attended Harvard College
_____ traveled to the Middle East and Europe with his family

c. _____ elected vice president of the United States
_____ attended Columbia Law School after father died
_____ his mother and wife died on same day

d. _____ chased after, and arrested, western cattle thieves
_____ served in New York state legislature
_____ Assistant Secretary of the Navy

e. _____ married Alice Lee
_____ Civil Service Commissioner in Washington, D.C.
_____ moved to the Badlands but a harsh winter decimated his cattle herd

f. _____ resigned as Assistant Secretary of the Navy to form the Rough Riders
_____ became President of the United States
_____ took up boxing, hiking, fishing, and hunting to improve his health


© 2016 The Critical Thinking Co.™ • www.CriticalThinking.com • 800-458-4849

Lesson 12

# Populists and Progressives

## A. Populist Party

[1]In the late 1800s, there was a lot of dissatisfaction among farmers in the country, especially Southern cotton farmers and wheat farmers in the Plains states. [2]Crop failures could be blamed on Mother Nature, but farmers held politicians, banks, trusts, and railroad operators at fault for problems like lack of credit, high transportation and marketing costs, and falling prices. [3]Groups such as the Grange and the National Farmer's Alliance formed to look after the interests of rural folks and, in 1892, the People's Party of the United States, usually referred to as the Populist Party, was born. [4]The Populist Party was a political organization created to help rural farmers by supporting candidates for election against Republicans and Democrats. [5]Populists campaigned for reforms to help farmers get tighter control over railroads and improved tax and banking regulations. [6]Populists also wanted the government to mint silver coins. [7]Gold coins were viewed as the money of the upper class. [8]Three Populist Party state governors, five senators, and ten representatives were, in fact, elected in 1892.

[9]The next year, a financial crisis—called the Panic of 1893—caused a full scale economic depression. [10]One of the major causes of the panic was the over-investing (investing more than it is worth) in railroads by U.S. citizens, businesses, and the government. [11]The railroads then used the money to expand beyond what their profits could support. [12]This resulted in several railroad companies collapsing, which caused the financial ruin of many individuals and businesses that had invested in them. [13]Fearful investors began to withdraw their money from the stock market, which in turn caused more financial ruin in other business markets. [14]The other major cause of the Panic of 1893 was a shortage of U.S. gold reserves, which was the result of legislation to have the U.S. government buy silver.

[15]After the Panic of 1893, farmers were hit hard by farm prices that dropped more than 20 percent over the next four years. [16]In reaction to the falling prices, thousands of desperate farmers and unemployed factory workers, led by Ohioan Populist Jacob Coxey, marched to Washington, D.C., in 1894. [17]Protesters in "Coxey's Army" demanded help from the federal government, but Congress and President Cleveland did little. [18]Most politicians at the time believed that boom-and-bust economic cycles were natural consequences of capitalism, and thus were matters out of the control of the government. [19]In the 1896 presidential election, the Populist Party decided to back Democrat William Jennings Bryan instead of having their own Populist candidate. [20]This blow to their claim of independence, the overwhelming defeat of Bryan in the election, and an improving economy brought an end to the Populist Party. [21]However, other reformers continued pushing forward the idea that government should take a more active role in the lives of American citizens.

Protesters from Coxey's Army, the first-ever march on the nation's capital, reached the steps of Congress in 1894.

## B. Progressive Movement

[22]By the time that Theodore Roosevelt became president in 1901, the "Progressive Movement" was well underway. [23]This was a spirit of reform to fix political and business corruption; advance the status of women, blacks, and immigrants; change unsafe working conditions; and improve the lives of middle-class Americans. [24]It was urban, educated, middle-class reformers, academics, and journalists who led the Progressive Movement. [25]Unlike the Populists who fought for the farmers, Progressives worked mainly on reforms that affected cities. [26]Also, Progressives didn't start a political party until later, in 1912. [27]Instead, they believed that most social, economic, and political problems could be fixed by getting scientific and technical data into the hands of supportive Republican or Democratic politicians, who would then create reform legislation. [28]For example, Progressives formed the National Child Labor

© 2016 The Critical Thinking Co.™ • www.CriticalThinking.com • 800-458-4849

Committee, an organization dedicated to the abolition of all child labor, in 1904. [29]By publishing statistics on the lives and working conditions of young workers, it helped to mobilize popular support for child labor laws in various states.

[30]Lesson 6 introduced many of the Progressive reformers such as Jane Addams, Frances Willard, Jacob Riis, and Frederick Law Olmsted. [31]Other Progressives of the time included Lincoln Steffens (who wrote of shameful conditions of the urban poor), John Spargo (child labor in the mines), and Ida Tarbell (corruption in big business). [32]These were three of the many magazine authors who exposed bad social or economic conditions. [33]President Roosevelt labeled these investigative reporters "muckrakers" and the nickname became a badge of honor.

[34]Governor Robert La Follette of Wisconsin and state legislator William S. U'Ren of Oregon were Progressives who brought many reforms to the political process in the early 1900s. [35]The "Wisconsin Idea" championed the idea of direct primaries (where voters chose candidates for the general election), women's suffrage (right to vote), and the direct election of U.S. Senators (instead of election by state legislatures). [36]The "Oregon System" gave citizens the option of recall (to vote corrupt officials out of office), referendum (to approve ideas submitted by state lawmakers), initiative (to vote on ideas submitted by petition of citizens), and the secret ballot (to vote in private). [37]Many other states eventually enacted the same ideas as Wisconsin and Oregon.

William S. U'Ren helped create a number of political reforms known as the "Oregon System."

[38]Progressives also worked to pass Congressional laws such as the Elkins Act (1903) and the Hepburn Act (1906) that regulated railroads. [39]The Mann Act (1910) attempted to cut down on prostitution by making it illegal to "transport women across state lines for immoral purposes." [40]The Federal Reserve Act (1913) created banks to stabilize the economy. [41]The Harrison Act (1914) banned the use of heroin, cocaine, and other addictive drugs.

[42]New amendments to the Constitution were also passed in response to pressure from Progressives. [43]To provide a stable base of income for the federal government, the 16th Amendment, created an income tax that was graduated (the higher a person's income, the higher the rate of tax). [44]The power of political bosses was weakened with the passage of the 17th Amendment which allowed state citizens to directly elect their U.S. Senators. [45]The temperance movement was bolstered with the passage of the 18th Amendment banning the use, sale, or manufacture of alcoholic drinks. [46]The 19th Amendment guaranteed that women had the right to vote.

[47]U.S. Progressives widely supported the theory of eugenics. [48]The theory of eugenics claimed that certain races and classes of people (Western Europeans) commonly had better traits than other races and classes of people (Africans, Asians, Jews, and criminals), so eugenics could improve the human race and society by encouraging some races and classes to have children while discouraging or preventing others. [49]Eugenics will be covered in more detail in Lesson 14.

### C. A Progressive President

[50]Even though Theodore Roosevelt was a Republican, a party generally considered to be conservative, he turned out to be a person who greatly supported the Progressive cause. [51]Within months of succeeding the assassinated McKinley as U.S. President, Roosevelt took action that defended the right of unions to organize. [52]Roosevelt forced coal mine owners to meet with union representatives at the White House, which soon ended the five-month strike and gave miners a small pay raise. [53]No president had ever negotiated a strike settlement before.

[54]At Roosevelt's first State of the Union address in 1902, he used the term "trustbusting" and called for breaking up business monopolies (exclusive control of a commodity or service). [55]Soon thereafter, he directed his attorney general


© 2016 The Critical Thinking Co.™ • www.CriticalThinking.com • 800-458-4849

President Roosevelt was depicted as a "trustbuster" in this political cartoon.

to pursue the breakup of the Northern Securities Company, a huge Northwest railroad company that Roosevelt felt violated the Sherman Anti-Trust Act. [56]"We don't wish to destroy corporations," President Roosevelt said, "but we do wish to make them serve the public good." [57]The Roosevelt administration eventually took more than 40 companies to court, and large monopolies such as Standard Oil and the American Tobacco Company were forced to breakup.

## D. Pure Food

[58]In 1906, President Roosevelt read a popular book by Upton Sinclair called *The Jungle*. [59]Sinclair had written his novel after disguising himself as an employee at a Chicago meat factory. [60]A Progressive muckraker, Sinclair had intended to show readers the plight (unfavorable conditions) of immigrant workers. [61]However, Sinclair's graphic (stirring, vivid) description of the unsanitary way that meat was processed became the most memorable passages of the book. [62]"I aimed at the nation's heart," Sinclair later said, "but hit it in the stomach." [63]The morning after President Roosevelt finished reading *The Jungle*, he was too disgusted to eat breakfast. [64]He rushed to Congress and demanded that the federal government pass legislation to clean up the nation's food. [65]As a result, two Progressive laws were created. [66]The Pure Food and Drug Act (1906) and the Meat Inspection Act (1906) outlawed the sale of foods that had been substantially altered, required that food be labeled, and set up strict standards for sanitation in food preparation plants. [67]Today the Food and Drug Administration (FDA) still watches over one-quarter of the nation's products in an effort to protect the consumer.

This novel by Upton Sinclair in 1906 led to Progressive legislation.

**Fun Fact Feature**

What substance (now illegal) found in the original recipe for the soft-drink Coca-Cola helped give the product its name?

1. The Populist Party generally tried to help which group of Americans?
   a. rural farmers
   b. black Americans
   c. urban workers
   d. women

   Which sentence best supports the answer?
   _____

2. What event helped spur the protest movement known as "Coxey's Army"?
   a. publication of the book The Jungle by Upton Sinclair
   b. the start of the Progressive Movement
   c. the Panic of 1893
   d. the reelection of President William McKinley in 1900

   Which sentences best support the answer?
   _____ _____

3. The Progressive Movement was generally led by:
   a. farmers.
   b. Republicans.
   c. educated, urban middle-class leaders and writers.
   d. leaders of big corporations.

   Which sentence best supports the answer?
   _____

4. People who got the nickname "muckrakers" were employed as:
   a. politicians.
   b. mine or railroad operators.
   c. farmers.
   d. investigative journalists.

   Which sentence best supports the answer?
   _____

5. The "Wisconsin Idea" and the "Oregon System" both created a set of laws that reformed what area of American life?
   a. political
   b. economic
   c. social
   d. religious

   Which sentences best support the answer?
   _____ _____

6. Give one example from the lesson that shows President Theodore Roosevelt acted as a "Progressive."

   ______________________________

   ______________________________

7. In their efforts to create reforms, Progressives often relied on:
   a. violence.
   b. scientific and technical data.
   c. the U.S. court system.
   d. the churches.

   Which sentence best supports the answer?
   _____

8. Look at the political cartoon in this lesson. Explain the symbols in the cartoon. Then explain the cartoon's message.

   a. Symbols: ______________________

   ______________________________

   ______________________________

   b. Message: ______________________

   ______________________________

   ______________________________


© 2016 The Critical Thinking Co.™ • www.CriticalThinking.com • 800-458-4849

9. Upton Sinclair's book, *The Jungle*, exposed the poor sanitation in:
   a. the White House.
   b. the medical industry.
   c. coal mines.
   d. meat processing plants.

   Which sentence best supports the answer?

   _____

**Written Response Question**

10. Choose five pieces of Progressive legislation, and use complete sentences to explain why you find them important improvements to the lives of Americans.

a. ____________________

____________________

b. ____________________

____________________

c. ____________________

____________________

d. ____________________

____________________

e. ____________________

____________________

**Fun Fact Finale**

One ingredient of the soft drink Coca-Cola was cocaine, an extract from coca leaves, as seen in this early newspaper advertisement. It stopped being added to the drink in 1900. Cocaine, an addictive stimulant, was made illegal by the Harrison Act of 1914.

**Coca Cola**

The Great Headache Specific. Delicious, refreshing, exhilerating, invigorating. The new and popular soda fountain drink, containing the tonic p.operties of the wonderful Coca Plant and the famous Cola Nuts. EVANS & HOWARD, at the Central Drug Store, furnish it fresh from their Soda Fount. ap26 6m

# Bonus Activity
# Progressive People

Review Lessons 6 and 12. Then write the letter of the name of the person next to his/her most famous Progressive Reform.

_____ 1. pure foods and drugs

_____ 2. "Oregon System" of political reforms

_____ 3. settlement house movement

_____ 4. trustbusting president

_____ 5. Women's Christian Temperance Union

_____ 6. Urban slums: *How the Other Half Lives*

_____ 7. publicized corruption in big business

_____ 8. beautiful city parks

_____ 9. "Wisconsin Idea" of political reforms

_____ 10. healthy winter games at the YMCA

a. Jane Addams

b. Robert La Follette

c. Frederick Law Olmsted

d. William S. U'Ren

e. Ida Tarbell

f. Upton Sinclair

g. Frances Willard

h. Theodore Roosevelt

i. James Naismith

j. Jacob Riis

Reformer, Photographer, Writer: Jacob Riis


© 2016 The Critical Thinking Co.™ • www.CriticalThinking.com • 800-458-4849

# Bonus Activity
# The Wonderful Wizard of Oz

Stories are sometimes written as "allegories," which are representations of real situations in symbolic terms. *The Wonderful Wizard of Oz* could be one of these. Some say it represents the political, economic, and social issues of the late 1800s and early 1900s.

L. Frank Baum, the author, had lived in South Dakota for a number of years where he had been a marginally successful businessman and newspaper editor. He moved to Chicago, but the Panic of 1893 nearly ruined him. His wife encouraged him to write down some of the fanciful tales he loved to tell children (especially his ill niece Dorothy). When he published *The Wonderful Wizard of Oz* in April of 1900, he finally achieved financial success. Many sequels to *The Wonderful Wizard of Oz* were later published and Baum's stories remain popular even today. A 1939 movie starring Judy Garland as Dorothy was spectacularly successful.

Could the Land of Oz be used as an allegory for the late 1800s and early 1900s? What follows is a summary of Baum's famous story; one many of you are very familiar with. As you read, keep in mind what you have learned about the times that Baum lived in.

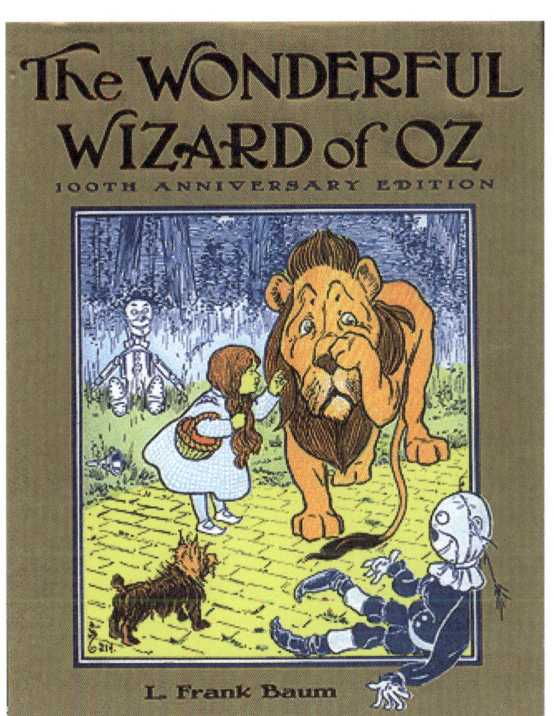


Answer the questions that follow each paragraph of the summary.

A. A little orphan girl named Dorothy Gale lived in the midst of the great Kansas prairies with her Uncle Henry, a poor farmer, and Auntie Em. Dorothy is a good, levelheaded girl who constantly thinks of others. Yet, "when Dorothy looked around, she could see nothing but the great gray prairie on every side. The sun had baked the plowed land into a gray mass, with little cracks running through it. Even the grass was not green, for the sun had burned the tops of the long blades until they were the same gray color to be seen everywhere. Once the family house had been painted, but the sun blistered the paint and the rains washed it away, and now the house was as dull and gray as everything else. When Auntie Em came there to live she was a young, pretty wife. The sun and wind had changed her, too. They had taken the sparkle from her eyes and left them a sober gray; they had taken the red from her cheeks and lips, and they were gray also. Uncle Henry never laughed. He worked hard from morning till night. He was gray also, from his long beard to his rough boots."

1. What kind of people might the family of Uncle Henry, Auntie Em, and Dorothy symbolize?

_______________________________________________

2. What might the color "gray" suggest in the introduction?

_______________________________________________

© 2016 The Critical Thinking Co.™ • www.CriticalThinking.com • 800-458-4849

B. One day a cyclone generated from the climate of the prairie, lifted Dorothy, her dog, and their farm house and deposited them in a new place: a country of marvelous beauty called the Land of Oz. When Dorothy's house landed, it crushed the Wicked Witch of the East, killing her. The Wicked Witch of the East had kept all the little citizens of Oz, Munchkins, in "bondage for many years, making them slave for her night and day." The local people were grateful that the Wicked Witch had been killed. They danced and sang with new freedom! They wanted to help Dorothy. They told her that to get back home she must contact a Wizard who lived in a far away capitol.

3. What new political party (discussed in Lesson 12) from the 1890s might be represented by the cyclone in this story? Explain your choice.

______________________________________________

______________________________________________

4. Think about the large trusts and big corporations that fought the unions in the late 1800s. What character might symbolize them in Baum's book?

______________________________________________

C. Dorothy was told to follow the yellow brick road, a dangerous path, to find the Wizard of Oz and must be careful of other wicked witches. To safeguard her on the trip, however, Glinda, the Good Witch, appeared and gave Dorothy magical silver slippers. The slippers had great powers, Glinda explained, but Dorothy didn't realize the power of these silver slippers until later in the story.

5. Think about what Populists wanted to do about currency (Lesson 12). What symbols might be used for currency in this story? (Hint: What did Dorothy have to follow, and what did the Good Witch give her for protection?)

______________________________________________

D. Off to see the Wizard, Dorothy comes to a farm and meets a talking Scarecrow. The Scarecrow begged Dorothy to rescue him from his lonely perch. After Dorothy saved him, the Scarecrow told her that he felt inferior in his corn field because he had only common straw in his head—no brain. Dorothy suggested that the Wizard could help him too, so he joined her on the trip to see the Wizard. Soon they met a Tin Woodsman. He was once a hardworking human being but had been put under a curse by the Witch of the East. Each of his body parts had been replaced with metal. Work had become scarce and, when the Tin Woodsman had stood in the same position for several years, he rusted. After being oiled again by Dorothy, he told her he felt a void within his chest. He was convinced he needed a heart. Dorothy suggested that perhaps the Wizard could help the Tin Woodsman too. Finally, Dorothy met the Cowardly Lion who tried to scare the group. Dorothy scolded him and asked why he was so loud. The Lion explained, "I learned that if I roared very loudly, every living thing was frightened and got out of my way." But he admitted that he was a coward who rarely had much power. The Lion sobbed, but when he learned about the powerful Wizard, he immediately sought to join the group and ask him for courage.

6. The Scarecrow stood in corn fields all day and didn't feel very smart. Which group of people might he represent in Baum's story? Explain your answer.

______________________________________________

7. The Tin Woodsman was a hard worker put under a curse of the Witch of the East. Who might he represent? Explain your answer.

______________________________________________

 © 2016 The Critical Thinking Co.™ • www.CriticalThinking.com • 800-458-4849

8. What economic event in 1893 might have caused workers, symbolized by the Tin Woodsman, to stand in the same place for several years and rust?

______________________________________________________________________

9. What kind of person, such as the Cowardly Lion, roared very loudly (Hint: at election time) but often didn't have much power to interfere with American economics?

______________________________________________________________________

E. Dorothy and her new friends were now a group marching to the capital city of Oz. Emerald City is the place where a wonderful Wizard ruled the Land of Oz. The group asked him for help, but he said they must fend for themselves. He suggested that if they could slay another wicked witch, he might be able to help them. So courageously, they set forth. The Wicked Witch of the West sent wolves, crows, a great swarm of black bees, and flying monkeys against them. Yet Dorothy managed to conquer the Witch of the West by dissolving her with a bucket of water. The Monkey King was grateful for Dorothy's actions and turned out to be kind and grateful. He sadly admitted to Dorothy: "Once we were a free people, living happily…flying from tree to tree, eating nuts and fruit, and doing just as we please without calling anybody master." Dorothy invited the monkeys to come back with her to the Emerald City, but the Monkey King declined, saying: "We belong to this country alone, and cannot leave it."

10. Who might the group marching to the capitol city symbolize? (see Lesson 12)

______________________________________________________________________

11. Who might the flying monkeys of the West represent?

______________________________________________________________________

F. When the group returned to the capitol city to report on their accomplishments, they discovered that the Wizard of Oz was only a common man behind a curtain whose power rested on myth and illusion! "I am just a humbug," he admitted. "I have been making believe." Yet the shrewd Wizard was able to convince the Scarecrow, Woodsman, and Lion that they got what they came for by presenting them with a university degree, a ticking heart clock, and a bravery medal. Dorothy knew there was no material thing in the Wizard's bag that could help her. For of all the characters, she was the only character who had a wish that was selfless: to be back with her loved ones. Luckily, Glinda the Good Witch reappeared to show Dorothy how to use the power of the silver slippers. By clicking her heels together and repeating "There's no place like home", she was transported back to Kansas. Dorothy's laughter, love, and hard work were no small addition to that gray Kansas land and her return cured some of the misery and heartache of her uncle and aunt. The farm started to prosper. Dorothy's friends had also found happiness and justice. Dorothy wondered if it had all been a dream.

12. What position in the American government might the Wizard represent? Explain your answer.

______________________________________________________________________

13. After all these adventures, life on the Kansas farm improves. What famous "dream" might symbolize this ending?

______________________________________________________________________

Lesson 13

# Roosevelt Takes Control

## A. Forest Conservation

[1]Theodore (Teddy) Roosevelt—a Progressive member of the Republican Party—ascended to the presidency upon the assassination of William McKinley in 1901. [2]In 1904, Roosevelt ran for reelection. [3]Roosevelt won 57 percent of the popular vote, which was the largest presidential election victory up to that time. [4]Clearly popular, and with the support of a Republican majority in Congress, Roosevelt was now ready to act on other Progressive measures that he deemed (considered) important.

[5]The president had spent a few days before the election in California with wilderness advocate John Muir. [6]Muir gave the president a personal tour of the wonders of Yosemite National Park. [7]Roosevelt had always enjoyed hiking and hunting in the outdoors and thoroughly enjoyed the visit. [8]After the election, he decided to take action to conserve even more of the American environment. [9]President Roosevelt created a new agency in 1905 called the U.S. Forest Service and appointed Gifford Pinchot to head it. [10]Both the president and Pinchot agreed that the purpose of the new agency was to halt the exploitation (selfish overuse) of the nation's forests and do a better job of managing the public and commercial use of public forests.

[11]Before 1900, about 35 million acres of forest land had been set aside for public use. [12]Now in his second term, Roosevelt set aside an additional 200 million acres of forest to be managed by the U.S. Forest Service. [13]Some land would be wilderness while other parts could be used for lumber production, mineral development, and waterpower sites. [14]Congressmen in six Western states received opposition to this plan from corporate interests, so they helped passed a law banning the president from creating more national forests. [15]Roosevelt, however, created an additional 16 million acres of national forests in those same six Western states just prior to the midnight hour when that law took effect. [16]During his presidency, Roosevelt also used his executive powers to create 53 wildlife preserves (many of them for birds) and 16 national monuments. [17]In addition, his recommendations to Congress that five new national parks be created were passed. [18]By 1916, Congress established the National Park Service to manage all the parks and monuments.

Crater Lake in Oregon became a national park in 1902 during Theodore Roosevelt's presidency.

## B. Panama Canal

[19]During the Spanish-American War, when Roosevelt was the Assistant Secretary of the Navy, a battleship called the *U.S.S. Oregon* was ordered to sail from her port in San Francisco, California, to join the war effort in the Caribbean Sea. [20]The *Oregon* had to travel around the southern tip of South American to make the trip and by the time it reached Cuba, sixty-six days later, the war was almost over.

[21]As president, Roosevelt decided that the United States must do something to create a better naval defense of both American coasts in time of war. [22]He directed his Secretary of State, John M. Hay, to negotiate a deal to construct a canal across property Columbia owned in Central America. [23]When the Colombian government held out for a better deal with the United States, Roosevelt and Hay were incensed (very upset). [24]They decided to work with revolutionaries on the Isthmus of Panama to spur development of the canal instead. [25]On November 3, 1903, a revolution on the isthmus was supported by an American warship. [26]Within days, the new country of Panama declared itself independent from Colombia. [27]The U.S. Secretary of State then quickly signed a treaty with the new Panamanian government which gave America a ten-mile-wide strip of land through Panama, connecting the Atlantic and Pacific shorelines, so that a canal could be built. [28]Many Americans were shocked by the imperialist methods of the president, but Roosevelt later boasted, "I took the Canal Zone, and let Congress debate, and while the debate goes on, the canal does also."

[29]Construction of the Panama Canal began in 1906 during Roosevelt's second term. [30]A team of doctors led by Walter Reed of the U.S.



© 2016 The Critical Thinking Co.™ • www.CriticalThinking.com • 800-458-4849

The Panama Canal greatly decreased the travel distance for American naval and commercial vessels between the country's two coasts.

Army Medical Corps solved a major roadblock to construction. 31They discovered that the cause of yellow fever, a disease that crippled workers in Panama, was carried by mosquitoes breeding in swampy water. 32By creating a large-scale drainage project around construction sites and protecting workers with netting around their sleeping and eating quarters, Reed's team successfully eradicated (removed or utterly destroyed) the cause of the disease.

33Roosevelt became the first U.S. President to travel away from United States soil when he visited the Panama Canal construction site in 1906. 34The canal was completed in 1914 and owned by the United States until full control was given over to Panama in 2000. 35In 1921, a few years after Roosevelt's death, the U.S. Congress voted to give Colombia a payment of 25 million dollars for its loss of territory.

### C. Great White Fleet

36Now that the United States governed islands in the Caribbean Sea and the Pacific Ocean and was building a major canal, President Roosevelt wanted to demonstrate to other world powers that the United States Navy was capable of defending its territories. 37In 1907, Roosevelt (as America's commander-in-chief) ordered 16 battleships and numerous escort vessels on a trip around the world. 38The battleships were new steel vessels, painted white, which had been built during Theodore Roosevelt's administration. 39Starting at Chesapeake Bay in Virginia, the Great White Fleet, as it was nicknamed, sailed around South America and up the Pacific Coast to California. 40From there the fleet steamed to Australia and on to the Philippines and Japan.

The Great White Fleet of 1907

41Roosevelt was particularly interested in displaying his naval power to Japan. 42The Japanese had recently become a new Pacific naval power, after a short war with Russia. 43Roosevelt had called Russian and Japanese ambassadors to the United States and forced a negotiated settlement to end to that war. 44The president received the Nobel Peace Prize for his efforts to end the Russo-Japanese War, but the Japanese government was displeased with the treaty. 45Even though Japan had clearly won victories over the Russian army and navy, the settlement did not give Japan any new territory nor did it force Russia to pay Japan for war costs.

46After leaving Japan, the American fleet then sailed across the Indian Ocean, traveled through the Suez Canal and the Mediterranean Sea, and back to the East Coast of the United States. 47The voyage had succeeded in demonstrating America's naval power in the age of imperialism and also benefited U.S. military officials planning future battle strategies and ship designs.

48President Roosevelt once used this phrase in a speech he made about foreign policy: "Speak softly and carry a big stick and you will go far." 49By this he meant that a country should use diplomacy whenever possible but should always have a strong military to back up the country's interests. 50His use of the military in the Panama Canal and Great White Fleet episodes are two examples of his "big stick" policy.

© 2016 The Critical Thinking Co.™ • www.CriticalThinking.com • 800-458-4849

**Fun Fact Feature**

Theodore Roosevelt was a president with many firsts. Among them—he was the first president to go "up" in some machine and the first to go "down under" in some other machine. Can you guess the machines?

1. What was significant about the presidential election of 1904? Theodore Roosevelt:
   a. changed to the Democratic Political Party and still won.
   b. won the election with the largest percentage of the popular vote ever to that time.
   c. lost his bid for reelection.
   d. won the election but was assassinated shortly thereafter.

   Which sentence best supports the answer?

   _____

2. Which of these governmental agencies did President Theodore Roosevelt create?
   a. U.S. Forest Service
   b. National Park Service
   c. U.S. Navy
   d. U.S. Army Medical Corp

   Which sentence best supports the answer?

   _____

3. Explain the role of the *U.S.S. Oregon* in the desire of the American government to build the Panama Canal.

   ______________________________________

   ______________________________________

   ______________________________________

   ______________________________________

   ______________________________________

   ______________________________________

4. Prior to it becoming an independent country in 1903, which country was the territorial ruler of Panama?
   a. Colombia
   b. Japan
   c. Russia
   d. United States

   Which sentence best supports the answer?

   _____

5. What was the major problem with construction of the Panama Canal that Walter Reed solved?
   a. canal water quality
   b. food poisoning
   c. lead poisoning
   d. yellow fever

   Which sentence best supports the answer?

   _____

6. Which nation did President Roosevelt most want to impress with his round-the-world tour of the Great White Fleet in 1907?
   a. Colombia
   b. Australia
   c. Russia
   d. Japan

   Which sentence best supports the answer?

   _____

7. How many years did it take the United States to construct the Panama Canal?
   a. 3
   b. 5
   c. 8
   d. 14

   Which sentences best support the answer?

   _____ _____


© 2016 The Critical Thinking Co.™ • www.CriticalThinking.com • 800-458-4849

8. President Roosevelt won the Nobel Peace Prize for negotiating an end to what war?
   a. Spanish-American War
   b. World War I
   c. Russo-Japanese War
   d. Panama Revolution

   Which sentence best supports the answer?
   ______

9. President Roosevelt's foreign policy was sometimes labeled "Big Stick Diplomacy." What was his "big stick"?
   a. the U.S. military
   b. the Panama Canal
   c. the Constitution
   d. the Nobel Prize

   Which sentence best supports the answer?
   ______

## Written Response Question

10. Theodore Roosevelt was a "take-charge" style of president who used his powers as the Chief Executive fully. Use complete sentences to describe at least three examples from this lesson which illustrate this conclusion.

______________________________________________________________________

______________________________________________________________________

______________________________________________________________________

______________________________________________________________________

______________________________________________________________________

______________________________________________________________________

______________________________________________________________________

______________________________________________________________________

### Fun Fact Finale

Theodore Roosevelt was a president with many firsts. He was the first president to go "up" in an airplane on October 11, 1910, went he took a ride while visiting Missouri (see photo on right). Airplanes had only been invented seven years earlier. He was also the first president to go "down under" the sea in a submarine on August 26, 1905, when given the opportunity to explore the Long Island Sound off his home at Sagamore Hill, New York.

© 2016 The Critical Thinking Co.™ • www.CriticalThinking.com • 800-458-4849

# Bonus Activity

## Panama Canal

Look at the map and diagrams on this page. Then answer questions about how the canal operates.

**Map A**

**Diagram B**

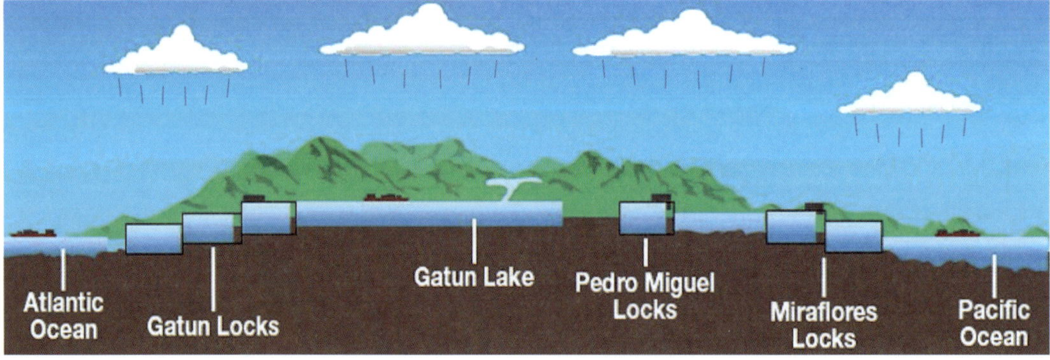


**Diagram C**

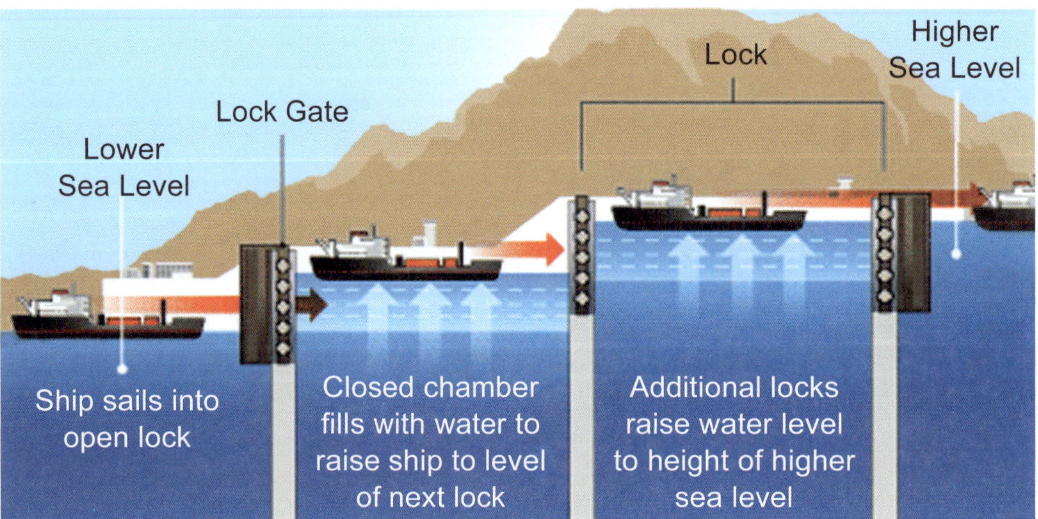



© 2016 The Critical Thinking Co.™ • www.CriticalThinking.com • 800-458-4849

# Questions About the Panama Canal

## Map A

_______________ 1. The Panama Canal provides a waterway between which two continents?

_______________

_______________ 2. Which two oceans does the Panama Canal connect?

_______________ 3. Which direction does the Panama Canal mainly run: north–south OR east–west ?

_______________ 4. Besides the canal, what other form of transportation connects Colon with Panama City?

_______________ 5. A high ridge of land runs through the country of Panama. Name the place where most of the hard digging of the canal probably took place.

_______________ 6. Approximately how long (in miles) is the Panama Canal?

## Map A and Diagram B

_______________ 7. What water source is used to fill the locks in the canal?

_______________ 8. How does that water source continually get replenished?

_______________ 9. What is the name of the lock system at the Atlantic entrance of the canal?

_______________ 10. What is the name of the lock system at the Pacific entrance of the canal?

## Diagram C

_______________ 11. What are like stair steps in a canal?

_______________ 12. Locks systems are needed in order to do what to ships?

_______________ 13. Locks have what on both ends of a chamber?

_______________ 14. What is used to raise or lower ships within the chamber of a lock?

Theodore Roosevelt became the first President of the United States to leave the country when he went to Panama and actually spent time on one of the machines used to dig it.

© 2016 The Critical Thinking Co.™ • www.CriticalThinking.com • 800-458-4849 

Lesson 14

# Questions of Race in the Early 1900s

## A. Plessy v. Ferguson

[1]In 1892, a man named Homer Plessy bought a train ticket in New Orleans, Louisiana. [2]Plessy was a man of mixed race: 7/8ths European and 1/8th African. [3]Passenger trains in his state were segregated (separated by race). [4]When Plessy took a seat in the rail car for white passengers, he was asked to move to the "blacks-only" rail car, and when Plessy refused to move, he was arrested and fined. [5]Lawyers for Plessy appealed his case to the U.S. Supreme Court, arguing that his right of equal treatment guaranteed by the 14th Amendment had been violated. [6]In 1896, in a landmark decision called *Plessy v. Ferguson*, the court ruled that segregation of races was legal as long as black citizens had equal access to public facilities available to whites. [7]In other words, since there was a rail car for Plessy to sit in, the railroad company could indeed separate the races. [8]After the *Plessy v. Ferguson* decision, many other segregation laws (sometimes called Jim Crow laws) were passed based on the concept of "separate but equal." [9]By the early 1900s, schools, theaters, restaurants, restrooms, churches, and even graveyards (especially in Southern states) were often separated by race. [10]Unfortunately, segregated facilities were often not very equal. [11]Black schools, for example, rarely received equal funding from districts that were dominated by white school board members.

After *Plessy v. Ferguson*, signs of segregation, like this one at a train station, grew more commonplace.

## B. Booker T. Washington

[12]In the 1890s, the most noted black leader in America was a man named Booker T. Washington. [13]Born a Virginia slave before the Civil War, Washington, like other Freedmen, had been made a citizen by the 13th, 14th, and 15th Amendments. [14]He gained an education and then founded a college in Alabama for other black men, called Tuskegee University. [15]Tuskegee was a vocational school—a place that trained men to be skilled laborers such as carpenters and farmers. [16]About the time of the Plessy decision, Washington made a speech called the "Atlanta Compromise," in which he urged black men to be patient about equality. [17]He did not challenge segregation. [18]He said black men would earn respect and eventual equality with whites only by accommodation (if they fit into American society by proving to have useful skills). [19]Washington published a book about his life called *Up From Slavery* that showed how, through hard work, he had obtained success as a black man in this country.

Booker T. Washington

[20]Washington proudly pointed out Tuskegee graduate George W. Carver as another example of a successful black man who "fit in." [21]Carver had studied farming and concluded that much more productive use could be made of agricultural lands by using crops in new ways. [22]He discovered hundreds of new uses for sweet potatoes, pecans, and peanuts. [23]Peanut butter was one such example. [24]Washington saw a future in Carver's type of agriculture, which could raise the economic status of African Americans who took up farming.

## C. W.E.B. Du Bois

[25]William Edward Burghardt (W.E.B.) Du Bois was a Massachusetts black man who was born free after the Civil War. [26]Like Washington, Du Bois had earned a college education and was, in fact, the first black to receive a doctorate degree from Harvard. [27]However, when it came to civil rights, Du Bois condemned Washington's focus on vocational skills for blacks. [28]Du Bois wrote a book called *The Souls of Black Folk* that argued against accommodation. [29]He was very critical of the Plessy decision and said blacks should demand an immediate end to segregation. [30]He felt that many blacks could seek a classical education (training the mind) and develop leadership skills in law, politics, business, and other professions.

W.E.B. Du Bois

 © 2016 The Critical Thinking Co.™ • www.CriticalThinking.com • 800-458-4849

[31]By 1909, W.E.B. Du Bois and other black and white leaders had formed an organization called the National Association for the Advancement of Colored People. [32]The NAACP, which still exists today, works for the national equality of all races, fights discrimination, and tries to improve the self-image of African Americans. [33]For more than 20 years, Du Bois was the editor of the NAACP's publication, *The Crisis*, which took positions on political issues facing blacks while also publishing poetry by black authors and stories about progress for black Americans.

**D. Eugenics**

[34]White Progressives did not have a very good record when it came to black civil rights. [35]Generally, they rarely spoke out against segregation or the suppression of black voting rights. [36]About 75 lynchings (the hanging of black Americans, without trial, by white mobs) took place in America every year during the first two decades of the 1900s, and Progressives did little to protest it. [37]White Progressives—and even a few prominent black Progressives such as W.E.B. Du Bois—generally supported the idea of using "eugenics" to improve society. [38]In the early 1900s, many books were written on the subject, and hundreds of colleges had courses on eugenics. [39]Eugenicists believed they could improve the human race and society by promoting certain races and classes to have children while discouraging or preventing other less desirable races and classes from reproducing. [40]The theory of eugenics was popular in the United States and Europe in the early and mid-1900s, and Progressives claimed it was based on science. [41]Eugenicists believed they had scientific data that showed Nordic, Germanic, and Anglo-Saxons typically had more desirable human traits than other races and classes of people such as Africans, Asians, Italians, Jews, "the feeble minded," poor people, and criminals. [42]Eugenicists also urged the passage of anti-immigration laws to slow certain populations (like Asians, Jews, Italians, or Eastern Europeans) from coming to the United States in order to prevent them from lowering the quality of the U.S. population and gene pool. [43]They praised the most popular movie of the day, *Birth of a Nation*, which glorified the Ku Klux Klan (racist organization), and they also supported the policy of separate but equal laws—segregation of blacks from white society. [44]The theory of eugenics also influenced the philosophy Germany's Nazi Party. [45]After the horrors of WWII were exposed, eugenics was considered a racist concept and lost its popularity.

**Fun Fact Feature**

President Theodore Roosevelt shocked many Southerners and reporters when, during his first year in office, he invited a black American to eat dinner with him and his family at the White House. Who do you think Roosevelt invited to dinner: Plessy, Washington, Carver, or Du Bois?

© 2016 The Critical Thinking Co.™ • www.CriticalThinking.com • 800-458-4849 

1. What was one result of the *Plessy v. Ferguson* case?
   a. Plessy got to ride wherever he desired on the next train out of New Orleans.
   b. Segregation became a common way to treat black citizens.
   c. Jim Crow laws were abolished.
   d. Black Americans gained more equal civil rights.

   Which sentence best supports the answer?

   _____

2. In your own words, what did the concept of "separate but equal" mean?

   ________________________________________

   ________________________________________

   ________________________________________

   ________________________________________

3. Which of these famous black Americans invented new uses for Southern crops?
   a. George W. Carver
   b. Booker T. Washington
   c. W.E.B. Du Bois
   d. Homer Plessy

   Which sentences best support the answer?

   _____ _____

4. Which of these famous black Americans wrote the book, *Souls of Black Folk*, and started the NAACP to support black causes?
   a. George W. Carver
   b. Booker T. Washington
   c. W.E.B. Du Bois
   d. Homer Plessy

   Which sentences best support the answer?

   _____ _____

5. Which of these famous black Americans established a college for black men to gain a vocational education?
   a. George W. Carver
   b. Booker T. Washington
   c. W.E.B. Du Bois
   d. Homer Plessy

   Which sentence best supports the answer?

   _____

6. Which of these was a racist movie shown in the early 1900s that supported the Ku Klux Klan?
   a. *Up From Slavery*
   b. *The Crisis*
   c. *Souls of Black Folk*
   d. *Birth of a Nation*

   Which sentence best supports the answer?

   _____

7. Write a sentence from the lesson that shows "eugenics" was very popular in the early 1900s.

   ________________________________________

   ________________________________________

8. Which of these ideas would have gotten support from people who believed in eugenics in the early 1900s?
   a. mixed-race marriages
   b. ideas of W.E.B. Du Bois
   c. anti-lynching laws
   d. anti-immigration laws

   Which sentence best supports the answer?

   _____

 © 2016 The Critical Thinking Co.™ • www.CriticalThinking.com • 800-458-4849

9. Look at this photograph to the right which shows a result of the *Plessy v. Ferguson* Supreme Court decision.
   a. What concept does the photo illustrate?
   b. What is ironic (odd or unintended) about what the image shows?

a. ______________________________________

______________________________________

______________________________________

b. ______________________________________

______________________________________

______________________________________

## Written Response Question

10. Use complete sentences to describe the different philosophies of Booker T. Washington and W.E.B. Du Bois regarding black Americans.

______________________________________

______________________________________

______________________________________

______________________________________

______________________________________

______________________________________

______________________________________

______________________________________

______________________________________

### Fun Fact Finale

President Theodore Roosevelt shocked many Southerners and reporters when, during his first year in office, he invited Booker T. Washington to eat dinner with him and his family at the White House. As an illustration of the times, look at what a newspaper editor from Tennessee wrote about the event: "It was the most damnable outrage which has ever been perpetrated by any citizen of the United States." There would not be another black guest invited to the White House by a U.S. President for the next 30 years.

© 2016 The Critical Thinking Co.™ • www.CriticalThinking.com • 800-458-4849 

# Bonus Activity
# Important Black Americans of the Early 1900s

Review Lesson 14. Then use the Venn diagram below to show the similarities and differences between the two men: Booker T. Washington and W.E.B. Du Bois. All items in the choice box should be placed on the Venn diagram.

| | | | |
|---|---|---|---|
| *Souls of Black Folk* | improve conditions for blacks | | 1st black Harvard PhD |
| Tuskegee University | once a slave | highly educated | Atlanta Compromise |
| focus on vocational skills | civil rights immediately | | *Up From Slavery* |
| NAACP | accommodation | black leader | *The Crisis* editor |

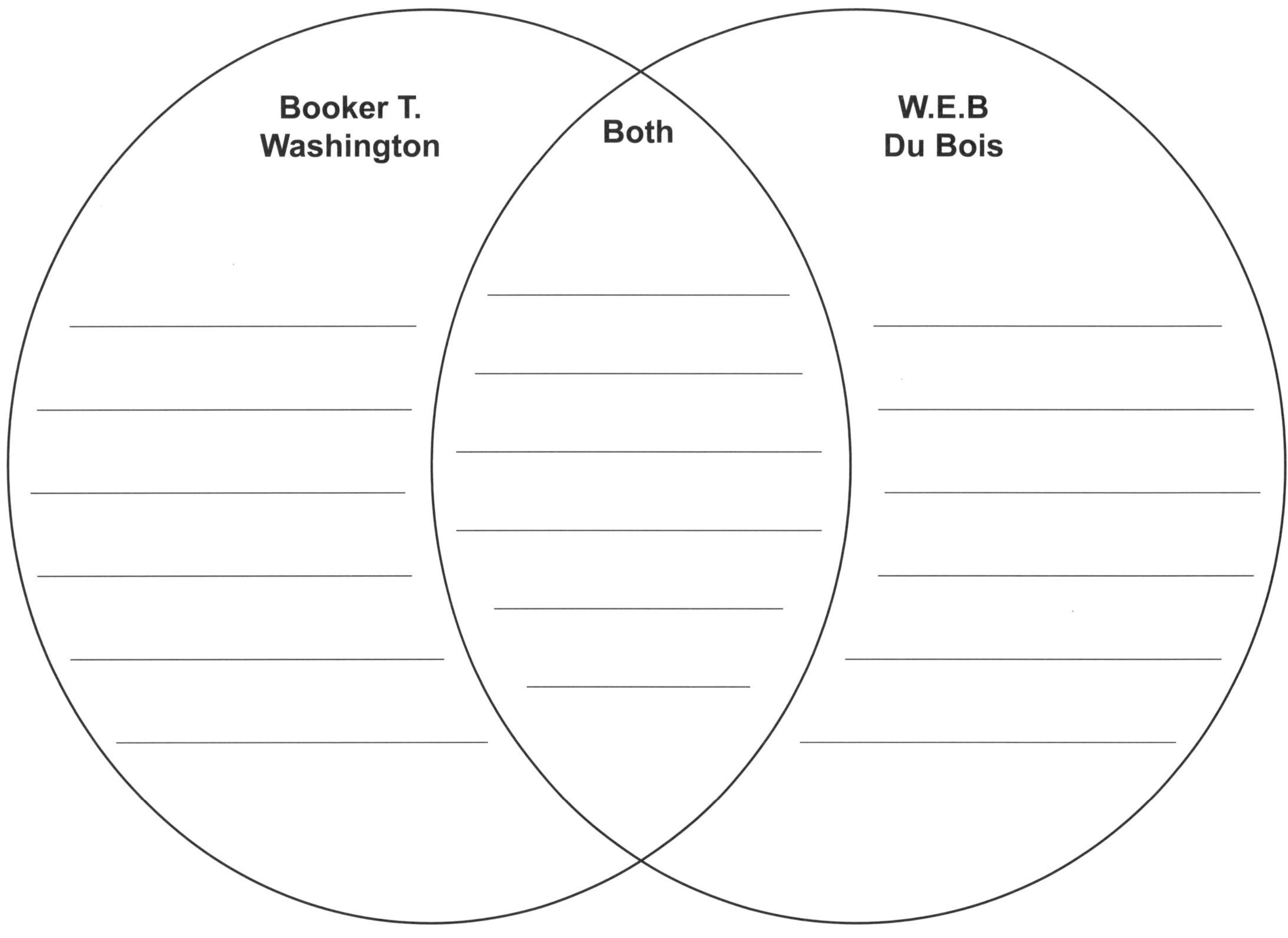



© 2016 The Critical Thinking Co.™ • www.CriticalThinking.com • 800-458-4849

Lesson 15

# President Taft

## A. Roosevelt Chooses a Successor

[1]Early in his second term as president, Theodore (Teddy) Roosevelt promised not to run for reelection in 1908. [2]Although he could have sought another term legally, he felt the tradition of a self-imposed two-term limit, established by George Washington, should be honored. [3]Therefore, as Roosevelt's administration wound down, he endorsed (approved, supported) William Howard Taft as the Republican nominee for president. [4]Taft had served as the governor of the Philippine Territory, then as Roosevelt's Secretary of War. [5]Roosevelt and Taft were good friends. [6]Roosevelt thought Taft would carry on his Progressive policies. [7]With Roosevelt's support, Taft easily won the 1908 presidential election.

[8]In many ways, the two men were very different. [9]Roosevelt was out-going, bold, physically active, and a talented politician. [10]Taft was shy, didn't share all of Roosevelt's Progressive views, and most importantly was not a talented politician. [11]Taft's wife once said he did not know or care to play the game of politics. [12]He was only 5 feet 11 inches tall, but weighed more than 350 pounds. [13]His White House servants claimed he once got stuck in the mansion's bathtub. [14]When Taft once sent a telegram to his Secretary of War saying, "Took a long horseback ride today; feeling fine," his cabinet secretary replied: "How is the horse?"

President William Taft was our nation's largest president.

## B. Taft Administration

[15]When Roosevelt retired from the presidency, he traveled to Africa with his son and several other men to collect animal specimens for some American museums. [16]He spent more than a year hunting in Africa, and the expedition gathered so much material that it took Smithsonian Museum naturalists the next eight years to catalog it all. [17]When a U.S. Senator, one of Roosevelt's enemies, was asked to comment on Roosevelt's upcoming hunting trip, he remarked: "Let every lion do its duty."

After his presidency, Theodore Roosevelt went on a big game expedition in Africa.

[18]While Roosevelt was away, Taft started showing he was neither as progressive nor as politically talented as his predecessor (the person who held office just before him). [19]Taft appointed a man to the post of Secretary of the Interior who was later accused by Progressives of abandoning Progressive conservationist policies by favoring big business over public interest. [20]Taft also disagreed with Progressives who wanted lower taxes on imports and signed a bill that raised those tariffs.

[21]However, Taft did continue to prosecute anti-trust cases. [22]He also signed a bill creating an eight-hour workday for federal employees, and he supported the 16$^{th}$ Amendment that created a federal income tax. [23]Despite this, Taft lost favor with Progressives in Congress and divided the Republican Party into two groups: Progressive Republicans and Conservative Republicans. [24]During his term in office, Taft also lost some his popularity with the American voting public.

© 2016 The Critical Thinking Co.™ • www.CriticalThinking.com • 800-458-4849

### C. Election of 1912

[25]Almost as soon as Roosevelt returned from his African expedition, he started making speeches that criticized Taft's administration. [26]Roosevelt, too, had decided that Taft had been a poor choice to carry on his goals of Progressive reform. [27]By 1912, Roosevelt openly expressed his desire to run for president again. [28]Taft wanted to run for reelection as well. [29]At the Republican convention in 1912, conservative Republicans selected Taft as their candidate. [30]Roosevelt's supporters bolted (left quickly, broke away) from the Republican convention and quickly formed their own political party—the Progressive Party. [31]When one reporter asked Roosevelt if he was physically fit to run again for office, Teddy replied, "I feel fit as a bull moose!" [32]After that, the Progressive Party was almost always referred to as the Bull Moose Party. [33]The Democrats named Woodrow Wilson as their candidate for president. [34]A fourth candidate, Eugene Debs, ran as a Socialist and campaigned for an end to capitalism. [35]Four candidates would now divide the American vote.

This cartoon from the 1912 election makes fun of the Bull Moose Party. The Democratic Party (donkey) and Republican Party (elephant) symbols are watching from beyond a fence.

[36]Roosevelt gave a name to his ideas for reform in 1912—"New Nationalism." [37]These were Roosevelt's ideas: a minimum wage, a workers' compensation act, more land conservation, a child labor law, a government pension for retirees, government funds to assist Americans with their health care costs, a woman's right to vote, and the creation of a federal agency to keep a watchful eye on unfair business practices. [38]He campaigned vigorously across the country. [39]Taft disagreed with almost all of Roosevelt's ideas but did not mount a very active campaign for reelection. [40]Woodrow Wilson called his plan "New Freedom" and discussed ways of making government smaller and more limited. [41]He also came out strongly against the banks and big business.

[42]During the campaign, an angry saloon keeper shot at Roosevelt just before a speech he planned to make in Wisconsin. [43]Luckily for Roosevelt, the bullet was slowed down when it penetrated his metal eyeglasses' case and thick (50 pages) folded speech, which were both in his chest pocket. [44]Despite blood seeping through his shirt, he concluded that the wound was not life-threatening and went on to make a 90-minute speech, telling the Milwaukee crowd, "It takes more than a shot to kill a Bull Moose!" [45]Roosevelt only spent a few days in the hospital after the speech, and survived, but carried the bullet in his chest for the remainder of his life.

[46]Roosevelt received more votes than President Taft in the election. [47]However, with Republican votes split between Roosevelt and Taft, Woodrow Wilson—the Democrat—easily won. [48]Roosevelt stayed out of politics for the remainder of his life and died in 1919. [49]Taft went on to teach law and, in 1921, was nominated to fill the job of Chief Justice on the Supreme Court, a position he held until his death in 1930. [50]He is the only American to have held the two most important positions in the federal Executive and Judicial branches.

**Fun Fact Feature**

In April of 1910, President William Taft started a presidential tradition at the first professional baseball game of that season. What is that tradition?


© 2016 The Critical Thinking Co.™ • www.CriticalThinking.com • 800-458-4849

1. Which of these facts about Taft is NOT true? Taft was:
   a. a personal friend of Roosevelt and had served in his cabinet.
   b. a former governor of the U.S. territory of the Philippines.
   c. noted for his unusual height.
   d. elected president in 1908 following Theodore Roosevelt.

   Which sentence best supports the answer?

   ______

2. Taft eventually held high office in which of the three branches of government below? Circle all that apply:
   a. Legislative
   b. Executive
   c. Judicial

   Which sentence best supports the answer?

   ______

3. Which of these events is true about Theodore Roosevelt when his term of office ended in 1909?
   a. He went on an expedition to Africa to hunt museum specimens.
   b. He ran for reelection for a 2nd term in office.
   c. He ran for election for a 3rd term from the Progressive Party.
   d. He was killed by an assassin.

   Which sentence best supports the answer?

   ______

4. What did the U.S. Senator who remarked in 1909, "Let every lion do its duty," mean by that statement?

   ______________________________________

   ______________________________________

5. True or False? Taft was not popular after his first term as president?

   ____________________

   Which sentence best supports the answer?

   ______

6. Why did Theodore Roosevelt, who had originally supported Taft as his successor in 1908, run against him in the 1912 presidential election?
   a. Taft had become more popular and Roosevelt was jealous.
   b. Taft had made fun of Roosevelt's African expedition.
   c. Taft had joined the Democratic party.
   d. Roosevelt did not think Taft was a true Progressive.

   Which sentence best supports the answer?

   ______

7. Theodore Roosevelt's Progressive Party was split off from the:
   a. Democratic Party.
   b. Socialist Party.
   c. Republican Party.
   d. Bull Moose Party.

   Which sentence best supports the answer?

   ______

8. Look at the cartoon of the Bull Moose Party in this lesson. Who does the moose symbolize?
   a. William Taft
   b. Theodore Roosevelt
   c. Woodrow Wilson
   d. Eugene Debs

   Explain how you decided on your answer?

   ______________________________________

   ______________________________________

   ______________________________________

© 2016 The Critical Thinking Co.™ • www.CriticalThinking.com • 800-458-4849

9. What amazing event took place during the presidential campaign of 1912?
   a. Roosevelt won fewer votes than the seemingly unpopular Taft, yet still won the election.
   b. Roosevelt survived an assassin's bullet and continued a campaign speech.
   c. Taft quit the campaign and took the job of Chief Justice of the Supreme Court.
   d. Roosevelt was nearly killed by a lion while on his African expedition.

   Which sentence best supports the answer? _____

## Written Response Question

10. Use complete sentences to analyze this political cartoon below. Explain the symbols in the cartoon and explain the message of the cartoonist.

    a. Symbols

    ______________________________________________

    ______________________________________________

    ______________________________________________

    ______________________________________________

    b. Message

    ______________________________________________

    ______________________________________________

    ______________________________________________

    ______________________________________________

**Fun Fact Finale**

In April of 1910, President William Taft started a presidential tradition at the first professional baseball game of the season when he threw out a ceremonial first pitch. Since then, every president has kept up that tradition at least once during his term of office.

© 2016 The Critical Thinking Co.™ • www.CriticalThinking.com • 800-458-4849

# Bonus Activity
# Political Cartoons

Answer the questions about the symbols and the message of each of the political cartoons below. These cartoons are related to topics discussed in lessons 9 through 15.

1. **Symbols**

a. Who is riding in the boat?______________________

b. What symbols in the cartoon might represent the military?

______________________

**Message**

c. Notice where the boat is headed. What event (discussed in lesson 13) is the cartoonist portraying?

______________________

______________________

d. Why does the cartoonist draw the "big stick" and the person so large?

______________________

______________________

2. **Symbols**

a. The man observing the action in the background is Uncle Sam. Who might he represent?

______________________

b. The two characters wrestling are subjects mentioned in lesson 12. Who might they represent?

______________________

**Message**

c. Explain how this cartoon is similar to the message in the cartoon in lesson 12.

______________________

______________________

3. **Symbols**
   a. Review lesson 15. Who do these two characters represent?

   ______________________________________________

**Message**

   b. Notice the years in each cartoon frame. What event in each of those years is the cartoonist showing?

   ______________________________________________

   ______________________________________________

   ______________________________________________

   c. Why does the cartoonist put a gun in Teddys hand in the second frame?

   ______________________________________________

   ______________________________________________

***The Only Way to Handle It*** *(Library of Congress.)*

4. **Symbols**
   a. Uncle Sam is the largest figure. Look where he stands. What does he represent?

   ______________________________________________

   b. Who do all the people at the large end of the funnel represent?

   ______________________________________________

**Message**

   c. Review lesson 14. The caption of this cartoon says "The Only Way to Handle It." What is "It"?

   ______________________________________________

   d. What is the cartoonist saying America should do about this issue?

   ______________________________________________

   ______________________________________________


© 2016 The Critical Thinking Co.™ • www.CriticalThinking.com • 800-458-4849

5. **Symbols**

a. The man in this cartoon is a "big business" or a "trust." Why is he drawn so large?

________________________________________

b. Who might the small girl on the ladder, who feeds profits to the trust, represent?

________________________________________

________________________________________

**Message**

c. What point is the cartoonist trying to make about child labor?

________________________________________

________________________________________

d. Review lesson 12. This cartoonist could be classified as being in favor of what reform movement?

________________________________________

6. **Symbols**

a. Who is the person in this cartoon? ________________

b. Review lesson 12. People who exposed bad social conditions in the Progressive Era had a nickname (and the cartoonist has given you a clue about it). What was that nickname?

________________________________________

**Message**

c. What event is being shown? ____________________

________________________________________

# Review: Lessons 9–15
# Imperialism and Progressives Vocabulary

Write the letter of the definition that matches each vocabulary word. The number following each vocabulary word is the number of the lesson (9–15) where the word was used. All definitions are used once.

_____ 1. imperialism (9)

_____ 2. deride (9)

_____ 3. guano (9)

_____ 4. escalate (10)

_____ 5. cavalry (10)

_____ 6. anarchist (11)

_____ 7. decimate (11)

_____ 8. graphic (12)

_____ 9. progressive (12)

_____ 10. allegory (review: "OZ")

_____ 11. exploit (13)

_____ 12. eradicate (13)

_____ 13. segregation (14)

_____ 14. accommodation (14)

_____ 15. eugenics (14)

_____ 16. Jim Crow laws (14)

_____ 17. endorse (15)

_____ 18. predecessor (15)

_____ 19. tariff (15)

_____ 20. bolt (15)

a. the act of overusing something selfishly

b. a person who seeks to overturn government with violence to achieve self-rule

c. writing that represents real situations in symbolic terms

d. fitting in with American society

e. to wipe out

f. soldiers on horseback

g. to leave quickly, break away

h. careful selection of mates to produce superior human offspring

i. holding foreign colonies

j. make fun of, mock

k. person who comes just before another

l. to utterly destroy, remove

m. writing that is vivid and stirring

n. a nickname for segregation

o. seabird manure

p. a tax on imports

q. support or approve

r. to increase in intensity

s. a person in the early 1900s who worked for social, political, or economic reform

t. separation of the races


© 2016 The Critical Thinking Co.™ • www.CriticalThinking.com • 800-458-4849

Section 3: Introduction

# The Great War: 1914-1919

A war broke out in Europe in the summer of 1914 that came to be called the Great War (later World War I) because it was the largest war in world history to that time. The spark of the war was an assassination of a leader from Austria-Hungary. His death set off a chain reaction that drew a number of other nations into a conflict which involved one set of alliances (the Central Powers) against a rival group (the Allied Powers). The war became known as "the first modern war" because of a number of technological advances. For the next few years, however, the war bogged down into a bloody stalemate (a situation in which further action is blocked) on several battle fronts in Europe.

The United States, under the leadership of President Woodrow Wilson, attempted to stay out of the war. Wilson asked the government and the American people to remain neutral. However, a series of aggressive actions by the Central Powers eventually drew America into the war on the side of the Allied Powers in 1917.

Once the United States declared war, a massive national effort was made to support the American military, which was not prepared for a large scale war. Several governmental agencies were created to shift America from a neutral nation to a nation at war. These agencies recruited soldiers, produced war-related materials, and raised money. After about a year of preparation, the United States sent the A.E.F. (American Expeditionary Force) to Europe. The arrival of U.S. troops helped break the stalemate on the Western Front, and the Allied Powers claimed victory by November of 1918.

Near the end of the Great War a disastrous spread of disease killed millions of people worldwide. Americans, tired of war, disease, and fearful of the spread of communism at home and abroad, increasingly supported government efforts to stay out of European affairs.

**U.S. President**

28. Woodrow Wilson
1913-1921

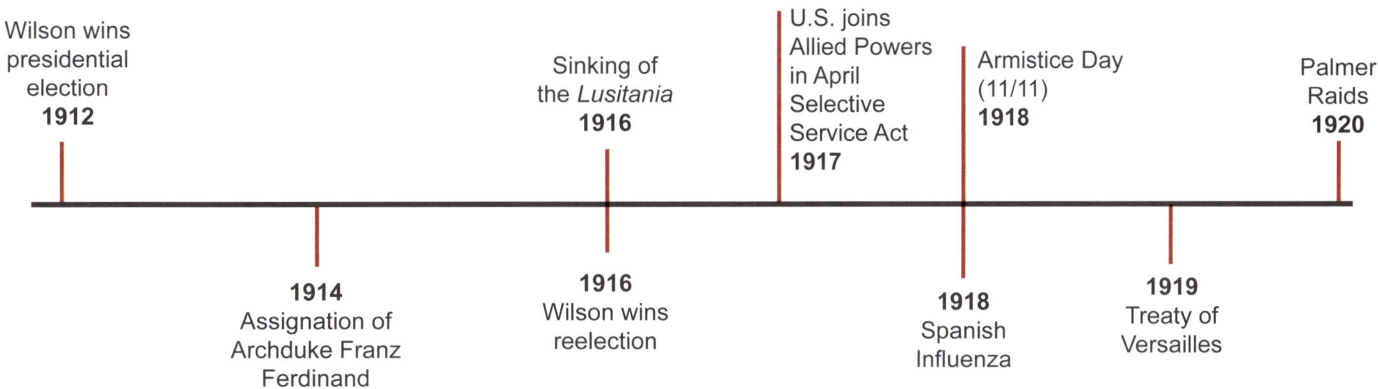

Lesson 16

# The Great War Begins (World War I)

## A. The Spark

[1]In June of 1914, Archduke Franz Ferdinand and his wife were assassinated (murdered for political reasons) while visiting a small Eastern European country in a region called the Balkans. [2]This event proved to be a spark that set off a chain reaction leading to the Great War (or World War I). [3]The Great War eventually involved dozens of countries in Europe, Asia, the Middle East, and North America –including the United States. [4]Eight to ten million soldiers were killed, and seven to twelve million civilians (non-soldiers) also died of disease and famine during the conflict.

Archduke Franz Ferdinand

[5]The war had several causes. [6]One was militarism. [7]At the turn of the century, several European countries had greatly increased the size of their armies and navies, and military leaders had gained more influence in the affairs of their governments. [8]In an effort to protect themselves, some nations joined mutual defense alliances that called for them to join a war if any one of the alliance members was attacked. [9]Military leaders also promoted another cause of the war—imperialism. [10]European powers were rivaling one another to increase the size of their territories, both in Europe and overseas, to improve their economies. [11]A third cause was nationalism—an excessive feeling of loyalty to your country that puts the interests of your nation ahead of the common interests of neighboring nations. [12]Some nationalists wanted to enlarge their governmental influence, while others tried to gain independence for their own culture groups.

[13]By 1914, this climate of aggression came to a head in the Balkan region controlled by Austria-Hungary. [14]Archduke Ferdinand was a member of the royal family of the empire of Austria-Hungary. [15]He was shot by a Serbian nationalist who wanted independence for the South Slavic countries which were controlled by Austria-Hungary. [16]After the assassination, the network of military alliances in Europe turned the death of one leader into a world conflict. [17]When Austria-Hungary declared war on Serbia in revenge for the assassination, the Serbians appealed to Russia for help. [18]Germany, concerned that Russia would use the conflict to gain more control in Europe, joined their ally, Austria-Hungary, in response. [19]By August of 1914, all of Europe was at war as nations took sides in the conflict in order to protect their national interests. [20]The Ottoman Empire (Turkey) joined Germany and Austria-Hungary in a partnership called the Central Powers. [21]Opposing them were Russia, France, and Great Britain, which fought together as the Triple Allied (or Alliance Powers). [22]Other small European nations also took sides with either the Central Powers or the Allied Powers.

## B. An Attempt at Neutrality

[23]In his Farewell Address of 1796, President George Washington had asked Americans to avoid "entangling alliances" with European countries. [24]Over the next century, the United States tried to follow Washington's advice. [25]When various small conflicts between European nations developed, the United States did not take sides and did not send troops in support of foreign wars. [26]President Woodrow Wilson, elected in 1912, wanted to continue this policy of neutrality as the Great War broke out. [27]He asked the American government and citizens to "be neutral in name and action." [28]In reality, the United States was a nation of immigrants. [29]Although Britain had been America's Mother Country, there were many German-American citizens and recent immigrants from Austria-Hungary living in the country, as well. [30]When the war started, Americans found it difficult to choose who to support.

Woodrow Wilson was the U.S. President during the Great War.

[31]Another reason for neutrality involved the American economy. [32]American businesses had strong ties to both the Allied Powers and the Central Powers. [33]If the United States took one side, it would mean not sending supplies to the other. [34]Many leaders felt an embargo (not trading goods with a country) would severely hurt the American economy.


© 2016 The Critical Thinking Co.™ • www.CriticalThinking.com • 800-458-4849

### C. Submarine Warfare

[35]Both the Allied Powers (Triple Alliance and the Central Powers) took actions that hindered American neutrality. [36]The British had the world's strongest navy and, soon after the war began, their war ships blockaded the coastlines of the Central Powers. [37]The Allies forced merchant ships to turn away from trading with the Central Powers. [38]Within a year, American trade with countries of the Central Powers dropped by 90 percent. [39]Not wanting to lose all business with European nations, American trade with the Allied Powers tripled instead.

[40]Germany responded with a tactic of its own. [41]The German navy developed a new kind of powerful submarine they called the "Unterseeboot" or "U-boat." [42]They began to target merchant ships in the Atlantic Ocean that were bringing supplies to Britain or France. [43]Germany hoped this would make it harder for the Allies to continue the war. [44]It was practically impossible to spot and defend against German U-boats as they approached merchant ships and launched torpedoes (underwater missiles) to sink those ships carrying goods to the Allies. [45]President Wilson and leaders of other neutral countries protested the sinking of merchant ships that sailed on international waters.

[46]U-boat attacks continued despite the protests. [47]Then, without warning, in May 1915 a U-boat attacked a British passenger ship that was sailing from the United States to Great Britain. [48]Germany was aware that the *Lusitania* was also carrying small arms and some other military cargo. [49]When the *Lusitania* went down, nearly 1,200 passengers drowned, including 128 Americans. [50]Americans vigorously protested the attack, and it was all President Wilson could do to hold back Congress from immediately declaring war on the Central Powers. [51]After sinking another passenger vessel, the *Sussex*, in early 1916, Germany—under great international pressure—issued a promise, called the Sussex Pledge, to halt its unrestricted submarine warfare against passenger vessels in neutral waters.

"All the News That's Fit to Print."

The New York Times.

THE WEATHER

LUSITANIA SUNK BY A SUBMARINE, PROBABLY 1,000 DEAD; TWICE TORPEDOED OFF IRISH COAST; SINKS IN 15 MINUTES; AMERICANS ABOARD INCLUDED VANDERBILT AND FROHMAN; WASHINGTON BELIEVES THAT A GRAVE CRISIS IS AT HAND

SHOCKS THE PRESIDENT

Washington Deeply Stirred by Disaster and Fears a Crisis.

SOME DEAD TAKEN ASHORE

Several Hundred Survivors at Queenstown and Kinsale.

DEATH OF FROHMAN IS FEARED IN LONDON

THE LOST CUNARD STEAMSHIP LUSITANIA

Cunard Office Here Besieged for News; Fate of 1,918 on Lusitania Long in Doubt

Loss of the Lusitania Fills London With Horror and Utter Amazement

### D. Americans Begin to Take Sides

[52]When U-boats began killing neutral citizens sailing on international waters, American attitudes about which side to support in the Great War started to change. [53]Another reason Americans started to favor the Allied Powers was that early in the war the Central Powers had also opened up a battle-line, called the Western Front, against America's oldest ally. [54]France had come to the aid of the United States during the Revolutionary War, and it was hard for Americans to remain neutral as the French suffered huge losses on the Western Front. [55]The Central Powers had invaded neutral Belgium on their way to attack France, and the brutal tactics used there—the killing of civilians, the destruction of cities—had also upset Americans.

[56]Some people in the United States started calling the Central Powers the "Huns." [57]Americans began to make fun of the leader of Germany, Kaiser Wilhelm II. [58]They compared him to Attila the Hun who, with his tribesmen, had been ruthless invaders from Central Asia in the early centuries. [59]The Huns had broken the Roman Empire and had a reputation for barbaric (uncivilized, crude) warfare tactics.

[60]President Wilson felt that by obtaining the Sussex Pledge from Germany, he had again secured American neutrality. [61]He ran for reelection in 1916 using the slogan: "He Has Kept Us Out of War." [62]Most Americans were glad that Wilson had not resorted to intervention (joining in the affairs of other countries) in Europe. [63]He was elected to serve a second term.

1916 presidential campaign button.

**Fun Fact Feature**

The Great War is now often referred to as World War I. Why didn't it have the name of World War I originally?

© 2016 The Critical Thinking Co.™ • www.CriticalThinking.com • 800-458-4849 

1. What did the assassination of Archduke Franz Ferdinand spark?
   a. U-boat warfare
   b. the Great War
   c. the reelection of President Woodrow Wilson
   d. World War II

   Which sentences best support the answer?

   _____ _____

2. Which three major European countries were known as the Allied Powers (or Triple Alliance) during the Great War?

   a.________________

   b.________________

   c.________________

3. President Wilson is steering a boat in this political cartoon.

   What might the ship represent?
   a. American merchant ships
   b. the British navy and blockade
   c. American attempts at neutrality
   d. the Sussex Pledge

4. What did Germany do to stop the spread of supplies to the Allied Powers during the Great War?
   a. remained neutral
   b. used their navy to blockade the Central Powers
   c. invaded Belgium
   d. sank merchant ships with their U-boats

   What sentence best supports the answer?

   _____

5. Why were Americans very upset with the sinking of the *Lusitania*?
   a. The ship was carrying medical supplies to the Central Powers.
   b. The ship had no military cargo.
   c. The sinking of the ship caused the United States to immediately join the Great War.
   d. There were many American passengers on board who drowned.

   What sentences best support the answer?

   _____ _____

6. During the Great War, the term "Huns" was used to describe:
   a. the Central Powers.
   b. the victims of the sinking of the *Sussex*.
   c. the victims of the sinking of the *Lusitania*.
   d. President Wilson's advisors.

   What sentence best supports the answer?

   _____

7. What evidence can you give that shows most Americans were pleased with President Wilson's policy of neutrality by 1916?

   ________________________________________

   ________________________________________

 © 2016 The Critical Thinking Co.™ • www.CriticalThinking.com • 800-458-4849

8. What did Germany promise when it made the Sussex Pledge in early 1916?
   a. end submarine warfare against passenger vessels
   b. end the Great War
   c. stop building "Unterseeboots"
   d. campaign for the reelection of President Woodrow Wilson

   What sentence best supports the answer?

   ______

9. Kaiser Wilhelm II was the leader of which nation during the Great War?
   a. Austria-Hungary
   b. Serbia
   c. Germany
   d. Great Britain

   What sentence best supports the answer?

   ______

## Written Response Question

10. Use complete sentences to answer these questions:
    a. Why did President Wilson want a policy of American neutrality at the start of the Great War?
    b. Why did Americans eventually reject that policy?

______________________________________________________________________

______________________________________________________________________

______________________________________________________________________

______________________________________________________________________

______________________________________________________________________

______________________________________________________________________

______________________________________________________________________

______________________________________________________________________

______________________________________________________________________

**Fun Fact Finale**

The Great War did not have the name World War I in 1914 because no one anticipated that another large war, World War II—involving many of the same nations—would start 25 years later.

# Bonus Activity
# Geography of the Great War

Look at the map below of Europe during the Great War. Then follow directions to fill in the map and answer questions about the geography of the Great War.

The Great War, 1914-1918

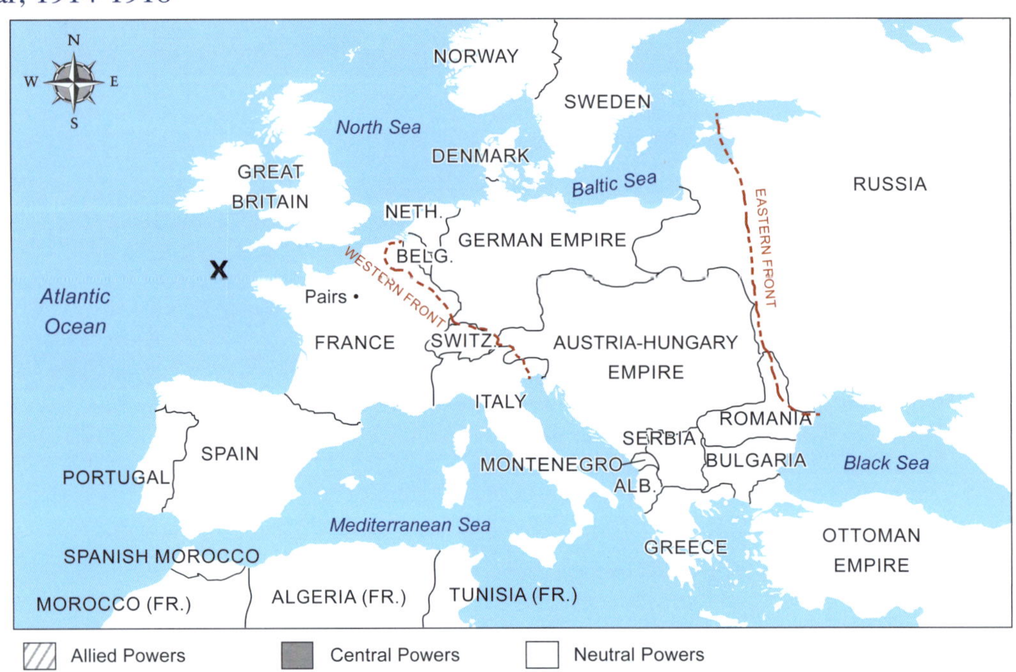


1. Shade completely (like the key) all the Central Powers: German Empire, Austria-Hungary Empire, Ottoman Empire, and Bulgaria. Why do you think the Central Powers got their name?

   ______________________________________________________________

2. Shade with diagonal lines (like the key) all the Allied Powers: Russia, France, Great Britain, Portugal, Italy, Serbia, Montenegro, Albania, Greece, Romania, and the northern African territories of Morocco, Algeria, and Tunisia. Why do you think these northern Africa territories were on the side of the Allied Powers? (Hint: look carefully at their labels on the map).

   ______________________________________________________________

3. Notice the lines marked Western Front and Eastern Front. A "front" in wartime refers to the area where enemies are meeting to fight. What problem would a "two-front" war create for the Central Powers? ______________________________________________

   What problem would a two-front war create for the Allied Powers?

   ______________________________________________________________

4. Look at the "X" in the Atlantic Ocean. Write the name of the ship that was sunk by German U-boats in May of 1915. ______________________

5. Draw an arrow going west from Germany through the neutral country that Germany invaded on the way to attack France at the start of the war. What is the name of the neutral country?

   ______________________

6. What large nation (on the west side of the Atlantic Ocean and not shown on this map) tried to stay neutral for the first years of the Great War? ______________________


© 2016 The Critical Thinking Co.™ • www.CriticalThinking.com • 800-458-4849

Lesson 17

# The Great War: Over Here

## A. America Joins the Great War

[1]Despite President Wilson's campaign slogan of 1916, "He kept us out of war," the United States became actively involved in the Great War (World War 1) by the spring of 1917. [2]Two events early that year turned Wilson and Americans away from a policy of neutrality. [3]First, the Sussex Pledge was broken. [4]German U-boats again started to torpedo all ships trading or shipping supplies to the Allied Powers (Great Britain, France, or Russia). [5]Secondly, British spies intercepted a message from Germany to Mexico and gave it to President Wilson. [6]Known as the Zimmermann Note (named for the German foreign minister who sent it), the Germans asked Mexico to join the war on their side and attack the United States. [7]In return, Germany promised to return the states of Texas, New Mexico, Arizona, and California to Mexico if the Central Powers won the war.

[8]Wilson had the Zimmermann Note published in U.S. newspapers and the news caused an uproar. [9]President Wilson asked Congress to declare war against the Central Powers in early April. [10]In his speech to Congress, Wilson pointed out that most of the Central Powers were governed by monarchs (inherited royalty, kings). [11]Wilson said that the United States military should help "make the world safe for democracy." [12]He also said that, by helping the Allied Powers crush the empires of the old monarchial governments of the Central Powers, the Great War could be "the war to end all wars." [13]Congress agreed with the president and voted to join the Allied Powers by a wide margin. [14]In the Senate, only two members voted against going to war. [15]One of those "nay" votes came from the first female senator in U.S. history: Montana's Jeannette Rankin.

Jeannette Rankin voted against the U.S. entering the Great War.

## B. Unprepared for War

[16]George M. Cohan was inspired to write a song to convince Americans to join the new war effort. [17]His tune *Over There* became so popular that it later was awarded the Congressional Medal of Honor. [18]His lyrics promoted the war effort.

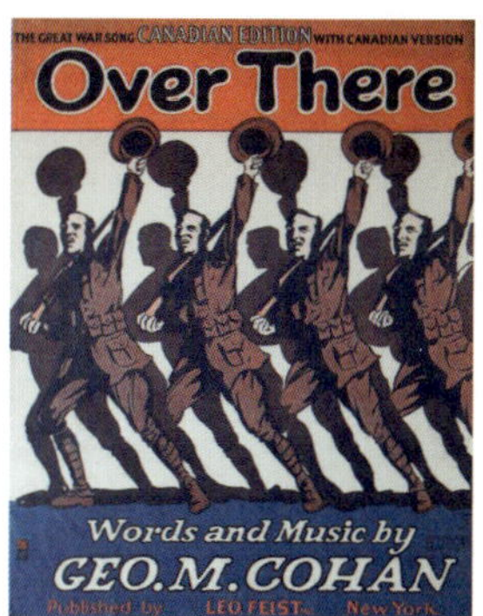


Johnny, get your gun, get
your gun, get your gun.
Johnny show the Hun,
you're a son-of-a-gun.
Hoist the flag and let her
fly. Yankee Doodle, do or
die…

Hurry right away, no
delay, go today.
Make your Daddy glad,
to have had such a lad.
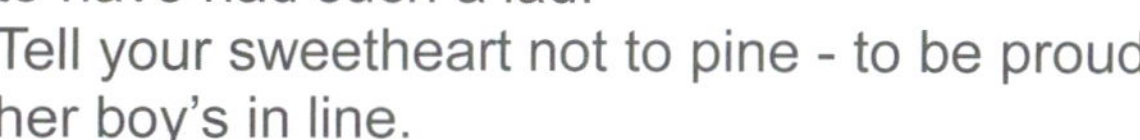
Tell your sweetheart not to pine - to be proud
her boy's in line.

(chorus) Over there, over there. Send the word,
send the word over there.
That the Yanks are coming, the Yanks are
coming,
The drums rum-tumming everywhere.
So prepare. Say a prayer.
Send the word, send the word to beware.
We'll be over, we're coming over,
And we won't come back, till it's over, over there.

[19]"Over there" in the song meant Europe, of course. [20]However, over here, in the United States, the military was unprepared to send any Yanks (American soldiers) into battle against the Huns. [21]The army was segregated (separated by race), was not very large, and had only enough bullets to last for two days of battle. [22]There would have to be a massive effort to raise more food, produce more uniforms and weapons, and train the soldiers. [23]Then there was the problem of how to transport the troops "over there" through ocean waters infested with enemy U-boats. [24]It was clear elected officials would have to pass new war-time laws and raise money to build up and fund a larger and more effective American military.

## C. War Measures

[25]One of the first requirements of the government was to recruit more soldiers. [26]At first the government relied on volunteers. [27]Wilson appointed George Creel to head a new agency, called the Committee on Public Information, to get the word out that men should volunteer for service. [28]The CPI organized parades, produced short patriotic movies, designed posters, and made speeches.

[29]Many volunteers responded out of a sense of patriotic duty. [30]Even Theodore Roosevelt, now nearly 60 years old, volunteered to fight, but President Wilson said "no." [31]When the military needed even more soldiers, however, the Selective Service Act was passed. [32]All males between the ages of 21 and 30 were required to register for military service. [33]Then a "draft" was conducted by random lottery (soldiers were called into service by a chance drawing). [34]By the end of the war, more than 4.5 million American men and 11,000 American women served in the armed forces. [35]Half of them saw active duty in Europe.

[36]Another government agency, the War Industries Board, was created to produce more war supplies. [37]This department could order that certain raw materials, such as steel or wood, be used for war supplies instead of consumer goods. [38]The WIB could also give government contracts to private businesses to produce war goods. [39]The WIB encouraged women to take manufacturing jobs in order to replace the thousands of men who left the factories to join the military.

A poster from the Great War encouraging citizens to loan money to the government.

[40]Herbert Hoover led the Food Administration. [41]His task was to raise enough food to not only feed the American military, but the soldiers of the Allied Powers, as well. [42]By 1917, the Allies had been fighting for three years and their food supplies were extremely low. [43]Hoover asked Americans to honor "Wheatless Wednesdays" (not to eat bread products on that day of the week) and "Meatless Mondays," in order to have more of those products to share with the Allies. [44]Hoover also encouraged American families to grow "victory gardens," which were small patches of vegetables in backyards, parks, or in window boxes. [45]Thousands of Americans joined in. [46]Woodrow Wilson allowed a flock of sheep to graze on the White House lawn in order to donate wool to the war effort, and to show the American public that even the president was joining the war effort.

[47]Finally, millions of dollars were raised for the war effort when the Liberty Loan Act was passed. [48]This law asked Americans to loan the government money for the war by buying a document called a liberty bond. [49]In return, the federal government promised to return the money to bond holders, with interest, after the war was won.

[50]The most controversial war measures were the Espionage and Sedition Acts. [51]Congress passed these laws to punish those who interfered with the war effort. [52]Americans caught aiding the enemy or who used "any disloyal, profane, scurrilous (crude or gross), or abusive language about the form of government of the United States ... or the flag of the United States, or the uniform of the Army or Navy" were arrested. [53]As patriotism for the war effort grew, many anti-war protesters and immigrants were unfairly targeted for punishment by U.S government officials. [54]Free speech was severely curtailed (cut short, reduced). [55]More than 4,000 suspected German-Americans were jailed in 1917-1918, with very few of those ever convicted of a criminal offense. [56]One suspected German-American was taken from his jail cell by a mob and hanged. [57]German-sounding street or city names were often replaced with English or American sounding labels. [58]German language classes were removed from schools, and German language books were removed from libraries. [59]The Red Cross would not allow volunteers with German last names to serve. [60]Even some vocabulary changed. [60]Sauerkraut was changed in America to "liberty cabbage" and German measles became "liberty measles."

Political Cartoon About the Espionage and Sedition Acts of 1917

**Fun Fact Feature**

What did the government order all Americans to do with their clocks each spring during the Great War? (Hint: Americans still do this today.)


© 2016 The Critical Thinking Co.™ • www.CriticalThinking.com • 800-458-4849

1. The Zimmermann Note asked which nation to attack the United States during the Great War?
   a. Germany
   b. Great Britain
   c. France
   d. Mexico

   Which sentence best supports the answer?

   _____

2. What did President Wilson think America's entry into the Great War would do?
   a. gain more territory for the United States
   b. be the war to end all wars
   c. make the world safe for monarchies
   d. create more freedom of speech

   Which sentence best supports the answer?

   _____

3. Besides being one of the few members of Congress to cast a "no" vote for U.S. entry into the Great War, what else is Senator Jeannette Rankin noted for?

   ________________________________________

   ________________________________________

4. The line, "Show the Hun you're a son-of-a-gun," in the song *Over There* shows the song was:
   a. anti-German.
   b. against the war.
   c. support for the Allied Powers.
   d. anti-American.

   Explain why you chose this answer.

   ________________________________________

   ________________________________________

5. What new Great War law drafted young American men into military service?
   a. War Industries Board
   b. Selective Service Act
   c. Committee on Public Information
   d. Espionage and Sedition Act

   Which sentences best support the answer?

   _____ _____

6. Who was appointed to raise large amounts of food for American soldiers and the Allied Powers during the Great War by heading the Food Administration?
   a. George Creel
   b. George M. Cohan
   c. Herbert Hoover
   d. Woodrow Wilson

   Which sentences best support the answer?

   _____ _____

7. Look at the political cartoon in this lesson. Who does the tall man in the middle of the cartoon represent?

   ________________________________________

8. A "Victory Garden" was a volunteer effort aimed at:
   a. recruiting more men for the military.
   b. raising money for the U.S. government to buy war supplies.
   c. raising more food for the war effort.
   d. erasing German sounding names from the map and from the American vocabulary.

   Which sentences best support the answer?

   _____ _____

9. What federal law raised millions of dollars for the American military effort in the Great War?
   a. The Liberty Loan Act
   b. The Selective Service Act
   c. The Committee on Public Information
   d. The War Industries Board

   Which sentence best supports the answer?

   _____

© 2016 The Critical Thinking Co.™ • www.CriticalThinking.com • 800-458-4849

## Written Response Question

10. Use complete sentences to explain why the Espionage and Sedition Acts wound up being laws that unfairly punished a class of Americans.

### Fun Fact Finale

During the Great War, the U.S. government ordered Daylight Savings Time. Each spring Americans were to adjust their clocks one hour ahead. This was an effort to create longer periods of daylight in the early evening allowing for a longer work day and more productivity for the war effort. Clocks were adjusted back one hour each fall.

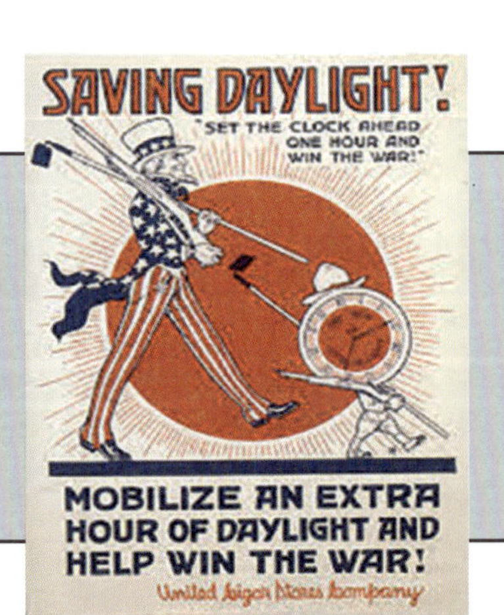



© 2016 The Critical Thinking Co.™ • www.CriticalThinking.com • 800-458-4849

# Bonus Activity
# Great War Posters

Look at each of these posters produced by the Committee on Public Information during the Great War and answer the questions.

1. This poster, by James Montgomery Flagg, was one of the most popular of the Great War.

a. What does the man, named Uncle Sam, in the poster represent?

______________________________________________

b. Move your head from side to side and watch the eyes of Uncle Sam and the tip of the finger that points at you. What do you notice?

______________________________________________

c. What do you notice about the three main colors used for this poster?

______________________________________________

2.

a. What do you think the "mad brute," shown here as a wild animal, represents?

______________________________________________

b. The "mad brute" seems to be stepping onto America's shores. What region of the world do you think the mad brute came from? How can you tell?

______________________________________________

______________________________________________

c. What does the artist want a young man in 1917 to do next after looking at this poster?

______________________________________________

© 2016 The Critical Thinking Co.™ • www.CriticalThinking.com • 800-458-4849

3.

a. What might the woman dressed in the flag in this poster represent? What evidence supports your answer?

______________________________________________

______________________________________________

______________________________________________

b. The uniform of the young boy, and the motto on the sword, indicate who the young boy symbolizes. Who does the boy represent?

______________________________________________

c. What does the artist want a person in 1917 to do next after looking at this poster?

______________________________________________

4.

a. What might the female figure in this poster represent? What evidence supports your answer?

______________________________________________

______________________________________________

b. Look back at Lesson 17. What government agency, headed by Herbert Hoover, might this poster be promoting? What did Hoover want Americans to create (as in this poster)?

______________________________________________

______________________________________________

c. "Munitions" are materials (such as weapons or ammunition) used in war. Explain what the slogan at the bottom of the poster, "Every Garden a Munitions Plant" means.

______________________________________________

______________________________________________


© 2016 The Critical Thinking Co.™ • www.CriticalThinking.com • 800-458-4849

Lesson 18

# New War Technology

## A. War in the Air

[1]The Great War was fought with many kinds of new technology. [2]This was the first war where airplanes were used, for example. [3]American inventors, brothers Orville and Wilbur Wright, demonstrated the first successful motorized, piloted airplane in December 1903. [4]For the next ten years, their plane was an oddity mainly used in public demonstrations, flying contests, or message delivery. [5]Airplanes of the era were biplanes (they had double wings), were made of canvas and wood, and carried a pilot and only one passenger at most. [6]By the time the Great War broke out in 1914, some leaders realized the airplane could be used for military purposes. [7]At first, airplanes were used for reconnaissance (a search for useful military information in the field). [8]Pilots took photographs of enemy positions and tracked enemy movements.

[9]Next came the idea to use airplanes as offensive weapons. [10]High-flying planes were used to drop bombs on enemy soldiers, who often hid in trenches (ditches dug for protection). [11]Soon after that, machine guns were added so that enemy planes could be shot down. [12]Enemy pilots began shooting at one another, and aerial battles became headline news. [13]The hero for the Central Powers was Manfred von Richthofen, a German pilot better known as the Red Baron, who shot down 80 planes in air-to-air combat. [14]The American ace (most skilled fighter pilot) was Captain Eddie Rickenbacker. [15]He destroyed 26 enemy planes in 1918 and was awarded the Congressional Medal of Honor. [16]Many pilots were killed in the war. [17]Parachutes had not been invented yet, and a hit from an aerial opponent was often fatal. [18]One famous U.S. pilot who died in action was Quentin Roosevelt, Theodore (Teddy) Roosevelt's son. [19]By the end of the war, the British had built the first aircraft carrier for its navy. [20]Planes could now take off and land on a ship at sea.

Great War Ace
Eddie Rickenbacker

## B. War on the Ground

[21]Prior to 1900, horses were critically important to move men and military equipment. [22]However, during the Great War, armies used a new technology—a self-propelled vehicle called the automobile. [23]German engineer Karl Benz created the first car when he mounted an improved gasoline-powered engine onto a four-wheeled vehicle in 1891. [24]America's first gasoline-powered commercial car manufacturers were Charles and Frank Duryea. [25]The brothers had been bicycle makers but built their first motor vehicle in Springfield, Massachusetts, in 1893. [26]In 1901, Ransome E. Olds moved to Detroit, Michigan, and began producing gasoline-powered cars for sale to the American public.

Henry Ford

[27]Henry Ford was another Michigan resident who was fascinated with automobile technology. [28]Ford had built his first car, called the "Quadricycle," in 1896 and formed his own company to compete with Olds in 1903. [29]Five years later, Ford unveiled the Model T. [30]The Model T was the first successful attempt to design a simple automobile that was affordable to the middle-class. [31]The Model T soon became the most popular car in the United States. [32]By the start of the Great War, orders for the Model T were so great that Ford created America's first assembly line so that he could speed up production. [33]Each laborer at a Ford plant worked at a station, adding specific parts to a Model T as it moved through each station on a mechanical conveyor belt. [34]Instead of working on one car at a time, workers were producing many cars simultaneously (at the same time). [35]His assembly line produced a new automobile every 90 minutes and Henry Ford soon became the world's leading manufacturer. [36]Automobiles were put to use immediately in the Great War. [37]They were used as ambulances

Henry Ford's Assembly Line
Production in Michigan

and to transport troops, equipment, and messages to and from the front.

[38]The land between two opposing armies' trenches was called No Man's Land. [39]Most trench warfare battles were fought in No Man's Land. [40]Trench warfare often resulted in long, drawn-out battles. [41]In an effort to end these stalemates, both sides produced armored vehicles known as "tanks." [42]Tanks were protected from enemy fire with shields of metal. [43]They ran on tracks rather than wheels and could plow over barbed wire and through mud. [44]Both the Central Powers and Allied Powers used European-built tanks. [45]American tank production came only at the end of the war.

These Americans stand by one of their tanks during the Great War.

### C. Other Technologies

[46]Several other types of technologies contributed to the reputation of the Great War as the first modern war. [47]To counter the effectiveness of the first submarines, the British developed sonar, which was a device used underwater that could detect the sound of nearby enemy vessels. [48]When an enemy submarine was located with sonar, another new invention, the depth charge, could be launched from the back of a ship. [49]A depth charge was basically an underwater bomb that was activated by water pressure once it reached a preset depth beneath the sea.

[50]Another advancement of technology was the radio. [51]A practical radio had been invented by Italian Guglielmo Marconi in 1896, just a few years before the start of the war, but it was improved and used for communication in the Great War. [52]Rapid-fire weapons were invented during the Civil War but not mass produced. [53]During the Great War, machine (rapid fire) guns were mass produced and commonly used by both sides on the Western Front. [54]Germany first used poison gas as its army advanced through Belgium and continued to use gas to try and break the stalemate of trench warfare. [55]France and Great Britain soon followed with poison gas attacks as well. [56]To defend against gas attacks, the gas mask was developed. [57]Germans also invented a flamethrower to try to advance troops across No Man's Land. [58]Since the flames only had a short range, however, flame thrower operators were often exposed to enemy rifle fire.

Allied soldiers are shown in this photo using gas masks while in trenches on the Western Front.

**Fun Fact Feature**

American men had smoked tobacco in pipes and in cigars ever since colonial days. What new form of tobacco was used by soldiers as a result of trench warfare on the Western Front?


© 2016 The Critical Thinking Co.™ • www.CriticalThinking.com • 800-458-4849

1. Who was the most famous American fighter ace in the Great War?
   a. the Red Baron
   b. Karl Benz
   c. Eddie Rickenbacker
   d. Quentin Roosevelt

   Which sentence best supports the answer?

   ______

2. Orville and Wilbur Wright were American brothers credited with:
   a. building the first piloted, powered airplane.
   b. starting the nation's first automobile company.
   c. perfecting the radio.
   d. creating the tank.

   Which sentence best supports the answer?

   ______

3. What was Henry Ford's claim to automobile fame?
   a. He mass produced the first affordable automobile.
   b. He invented the first car.
   c. He started the first automobile company in the United States.
   d. He developed the first gasoline powered engine.

   Which sentences best support the answer?

   ______ ______

4. Why were military tanks called "armored" vehicles?
   a. had armaments (guns) installed on them.
   b. used poisoned gas.
   c. were used for the armistice (peace treaty).
   d. used protective metal for shielding.

   Which sentence best supports the answer?

   ______

5. Why did military leaders use the airplane, tank, poison gas, and flamethrowers on the Western Front?

   ______________________________________

   ______________________________________

   ______________________________________

6. Who built the Quadricycle and the Model T?
   a. Charles and Frank Duryea
   b. Ransome E. Olds
   c. Henry Ford
   d. Karl Benz

   Which sentences best support the answer?

   ______ ______

7. "Sonar" and the "depth charge" were two wartime inventions created to fight the:
   a. airplane.
   b. machine gun.
   c. submarine.
   d. tank.

   Which sentences best support the answer?

   ______ ______

8. Which nation first used poison gas as a weapon of war?
   a. Great Britain
   b. Germany
   c. Belgium
   d. Russia

   Which sentence best supports the answer?

   ______

9. What invention by Guglielmo Marconi greatly improved military communications during the Great War?
   a. television
   b. telegraph
   c. radio
   d. sonar

   Which sentence best supports the answer?

   ______

## Written Response Question

10. The Great War has been called "the first modern war." List ten examples of evidence from this lesson that supports that title.

a. ____________________

b. ____________________

c. ____________________

d. ____________________

e. ____________________

f. ____________________

g. ____________________

h. ____________________

i. ____________________

j. ____________________

### Fun Fact Finale

American men had smoked tobacco in pipes and in cigars ever since colonial days. During the Great War, cigarettes ("small cigar") became very popular. The pack was easy to carry in a uniform pocket, it wasn't constantly going out like a pipe or subject to getting soggy like a cigar. Also, a cigarette could be snuffed out on a moment's notice and saved for later. The American Red Cross and YMCA even put forth efforts to supply them to American soldiers as a form of relaxation for the soldiers while they were in the trenches. The link between smoking and lung cancer would not be known for several decades.


© 2016 The Critical Thinking Co.™ • www.CriticalThinking.com • 800-458-4849

Lesson 19

# The Great War: Over There

## A. Doughboys Head to the Western Front

[1]After declaring war against the Central Powers (Austria-Hungary, Germany, and the Ottoman Empire) in April of 1917, it took almost an entire year for the American military to recruit, supply, train, and transport the bulk of its troops across the Atlantic Ocean to join the fighting on the Western Front of the Great War. [2]The British and U.S. navies worked together to ship the American forces overseas in convoys (groups of vessels traveling together) protected by escort ships, to discourage attacks by German U-boats. [3]The overall commander of U.S. forces was General John J. Pershing.

U.S. General John J. Pershing

[4]The United States called its troops the A.E.F. (the American Expeditionary Forces). [5]When Americans landed in France in early 1918, Pershing exclaimed, "Lafayette, we are here!" [6]He was reminding the French that they had sent military assistance to the United States under the command of the Marquis de Lafayette during the Revolutionary War and that the United States was now returning the favor. [7]At first, the French were not impressed with the quality of the American army. [8]Thinking the Yanks soft, the French jokingly nicknamed the American soldiers "Doughboys." [9]Allied governments wanted the Americans to quickly join the fight on the Western Front under French commanders, but Pershing insisted that U.S. troops needed more training first and would fight only under his command when ready.

## B. Western Front

[10]One reason France and Great Britain needed immediate help from the United States was that both countries were nearly worn out. [11]For three years, fighting on the Western Front had become a brutal stalemate. [12]The war had bogged down into a situation where no progress had been made. [13]Enemies had dug hundreds of miles of defensive trenches along the front outside of Paris and reinforced them with land mines, barbed wire, and machine guns. [14]The area between the trenches was called "No Man's Land." [15]Occasionally, Allied or Central Powers troops might charge "over the top" into No Man's Land to try and drive their enemies out of their trenches. [16]But poison gas, heavy artillery, and modern weapons took a deadly toll, and millions of soldiers were killed.

American troops look out over No Man's Land from a trench in France during the Great War.

[17]Another reason that France and Great Britain were desperate for American reinforcements was that one of their allies, Russia, had quit the war. [18]The Russian Revolution of October 1917 had overthrown the government of Tsar Nicholas II, a monarchy, and replaced it with a communist government under leader Vladimir Lenin. [19]Devastated by the war and the internal revolution, Lenin's new government negotiated a peace agreement with the Central Powers just prior to the arrival of the Americans. [20]Now the Central Powers could take all their military power from the Eastern Front, along the Russian border, and launch one final assault on the Western Front in Belgium and France to try to win the war.

[21]The "Spring Offensive" of the Central Powers did indeed open in March 1918. [22]The additional troops from the Eastern Front allowed Germany to break through No Man's Land and push the Allies west to within 75 miles of Paris, France. [23]American troops were quickly rushed from training camps to the front, where their numbers and vitality made an immediate difference in the war. [24]Soon the Central Powers were stopped and then driven to the east. [25]By July, the Central Powers had been backed up to their original spring position, and their spirit was broken. [26]Throughout the rest of the summer and fall, British, French, and American troops took the offensive and drove the enemy further and further to the German border.

© 2016 The Critical Thinking Co.™ • www.CriticalThinking.com • 800-458-4849

[27]By late fall, the military of the Central Powers was in shambles. [28]The Ottoman Empire surrendered on October 30. [29]Austria-Hungary quit on November 2. [30]Germans replaced their king with a democratic government and asked for peace soon thereafter. [31]On November 11, 1918, at 11 a.m., a document to end the war was signed by German representatives. [32]Thereafter, that day was celebrated as Armistice Day (an armistice is a truce, an end to the fighting). [33]In the United States, November 11th is still celebrated as a federal holiday, called Veterans Day.

### D. Influenza

[34]One of the reasons Germany was forced to abandon the war was that thousands of its soldiers were unfit for duty due to a disease called the Spanish Influenza. [35]Its name came from early reports—later proven wrong—that indicated Spain was hit harder by the disease than other parts of Europe. [36]Those infected with the disease often died quickly from attacks from their own immune system (the body's natural disease fighting system) that resulted in lung failure or a secondary bacterial infection. [37]The flu virus that caused the disease was believed to have started in birds and then mutated (evolved) and was spread to pigs and then to humans.

[38]It is widely believed that the Spanish Influenza started in France. [39]It became a pandemic (a disease that spreads over a large region) when it spread over Europe. [40]The fact that so many soldiers lived close to one another and moved to various locations throughout the war, hastened the spread of the flu throughout Europe. [41]After infecting much of Europe, Spanish Influenza spread through human travel to other parts of the world. [42]It has been estimated that one-third of the world's population came down with the flu and between 50 and 100 million people died from it. [43]Some historians have called that pandemic the worst medical disaster in world history.

[44]The disease spread to the United States in the summer and fall of 1918 and eventually caused the deaths of more than a half-million civilians. [45]Government officials took drastic measures to prevent its spread. [46]Schools, churches, and places of entertainment were closed to avoid gathering people together in groups. [47]Those who did venture out into public places often wore face masks. [48]A popular American short novel by Katherine Anne Porter about the episode, called *Pale Horse, Pale Rider*, was published in 1939.

Masked nurses from the American Red Cross remove patients in St. Louis during the outbreak of the 1918 influenza pandemic.

**Fun Fact Feature**

After the Great War, a special burial took place at Arlington National Cemetery in Washington, D.C. Although the person buried there was not famous, the grave of this Great War soldier is one of the most famous in the country. Can you name this special tomb?


© 2016 The Critical Thinking Co.™ • www.CriticalThinking.com • 800-458-4849

1. What was John J. Pershing's role in the Great War?
   a. commander of U.S. military forces
   b. leading medical officer in the fight against the Spanish flu
   c. a political leader in the Wilson administration
   d. leader of the French forces on the Western Front

   Which sentence best supports the answer?

   _____

2. The official name of the U.S. military in the Great

   War was ________________________, but

   their nickname was ____________________.

3. John J. Pershing fought the desire of Allied leaders to immediately:
   a. join Russian troops on the Eastern Front.
   b. sign a peace treaty with the Central Powers.
   c. send American troops back to the United States for more training.
   d. join battles on the Western Front under French commanders.

   Which sentence best supports the answer?

   _____

4. What was the area between enemy trenches on the Western Front called?
   a. the Eastern Front
   b. Doughboys
   c. the Armistice
   d. No Man's Land

   Which sentence best supports the answer?

   _____

5. What caused American churches, schools, and places of entertainment to temporarily close in the summer and fall of 1918?
   a. a shortage of food
   b. the Spring Offensive of the Central Powers
   c. outbreak of the Spanish Influenza
   d. Armistice Day

   Which sentences best supports the answer?

   _____ _____

6. Describe what allowed Germany to move all its military force from the Eastern Front and focus on fighting France in the Western Front in the spring of 1918.

   ______________________________________

   ______________________________________

   ______________________________________

   ______________________________________

7. Which Central Power nation was the first to surrender in the Great War?
   a. Austria-Hungary
   b. Russia
   c. Ottoman Empire
   d. Germany

   Which sentence best supports the answer?

   _____

8. What has sometimes been labeled as the worst medical disaster in world history?
   a. the poison gas attacks in No Man's Land
   b. the Spanish flu pandemic
   c. the Spring Offensive of 1918
   d. the Russian Revolution of 1917

   Which sentence best supports the answer?

   _____

© 2016 The Critical Thinking Co.™ • www.CriticalThinking.com • 800-458-4849

9. Why is November 11th celebrated in America?
   a. Memorial Day
   b. Veterans Day
   c. Thanksgiving Day
   d. Labor Day

   Which sentence best supports the answer?

   ______

## Written Response Question

10. Use complete sentences to explain why the American Expeditionary Forces made a difference in the outcome of the Great War.

_______________________________________________

_______________________________________________

_______________________________________________

_______________________________________________

_______________________________________________

_______________________________________________

_______________________________________________

_______________________________________________

_______________________________________________

### Fun Fact Finale

An unidentified American soldier killed in the Great War was buried at Arlington National Cemetery in Washington, D.C. several years after the war. His burial was in remembrance of all soldiers who died or were missing in action during war. Today the Tomb of the Unknown Soldier also contains the remains of an unknown American soldier from WWII and from the Korean War as well.

© 2016 The Critical Thinking Co.™ • www.CriticalThinking.com • 800-458-4849

Lesson 20

# Aftermath of the Great War

## A. Wilson's 14 Point Plan

[1]Even before the Great War ended, President Woodrow Wilson put forth a plan that he hoped would stop future world wars from happening. [2]Wilson's 14 Point Plan proposed steps to achieve peace. [3]These steps included:

(1) Countries should not make secret deals with one another, because secret alliances (formal agreements) had drawn so many nations into the war.
(2) Ships should be able to sail anywhere in both peacetime and war (freedom of the seas) because U-boats had caused so much loss of life.
(3) Trade barriers, like high tariffs, should be reduced.
(4) Each nation should reduce the size of its military.
(5) European empires should be broken up because the Great War had started with a shot by a nationalist Serbian assassin.
(6) Several borderlines should be adjusted.
(7-13) There should be independence for some colonies, so that groups of people with the same culture and heritage could form their own independent countries if desired.
(14) An international organization called the League of Nations should be formed to enforce these new rules.

## B. Treaty of Versailles

[4]The President of the United States, however, was considered an outsider who had come late to the war by the other Allied leaders. [5]When the peace talks started in January of 1919, the rulers of France, Great Britain, and Italy rejected Wilson's call for "a just peace," as outlined in his 14 Point Plan. [6]The European victors wanted retribution—punishment for the Central Powers for the destruction they had caused.

The British Prime Minister (left), French leader, and President Wilson arrive at the Versailles peace talks.

[7]Many Allied nations attended the peace conference at the historic Palace of Versailles outside of Paris, France, but representatives of the Central Powers were not even invited. [8]Neither was Russia, which had already signed a treaty with the Central Powers.

[9]After a half year of discussion, the final document, the Treaty of Versailles, ignored most of Wilson's suggestions and took a harsh attitude toward the defeated nations. [10]No language in the treaty discussed the end of secret alliances or freedom of the seas. [11]The treaty put most of the blame for the war on Germany. [12]Germany was told to admit responsibility for most of the damage and pay billions in reparations (money for repairs). [13]The German empire was broken up, and parts of German territory were given to France and Poland. [14]German colonies overseas were taken away and given to Allied Powers. [15]The German military was reduced to the level of a state police force. [16]Austria-Hungary was split into two countries and parts of the former empire were used to create Czechoslovakia, Yugoslavia, and to enlarge Romania. [17]Finland and other nations were carved out of former Russian territory.

## C. League of Nations

[18]One of the few parts of Wilson's 14 Point Plan that did survive the peace talks was his idea for a League of Nations. [19]The Treaty of Versailles did include language that formed the international peace organization. [20]Wilson, therefore, returned to the United States to convince the U.S. Senate to ratify (approve) the language of the treaty.

[21]Wilson was a Democrat, but the Senate was controlled by the Republican Party and its leader, Henry Cabot Lodge. [22]Republicans were in opposition of the treaty for many reasons. [23]Some German-Americans were upset about the harsh punishment of their former homeland, while French and Italian-Americans thought Allied victors should have received even more territory from the Central Powers. [24]Remembering George Washington's warnings, Lodge and the Republicans did not want to join an international organization. [25]They feared the United States might someday be required to send troops or impose economic sanctions (penalties) somewhere in the world if such actions were passed by the League of Nations.

[26]Wilson decided to put pressure on the Senate by convincing the American public that joining the League was a good idea. [27]In September 1919, he went on a month-long railroad tour speaking in states all across America and traveling more than 8,000 miles. [28]The effort was physically harsh and, in early October, Wilson suffered a severe stroke (the blockage of a blood vessel in the brain). [29]The president was paralyzed on his left side and his vision was weakened.

© 2016 The Critical Thinking Co.™ • www.CriticalThinking.com • 800-458-4849

[30]For the remaining year and a half of his second term, President Wilson could no longer speak or perform many other presidential duties. [31]The First Lady, Edith Wilson, tried to shield her husband from more stress. [32]While the president recovered in bed, Edith insisted that she screen all of Wilson's paperwork and allowed very few visitors—even the vice president—to meet with him. [33]In some cases, it is thought that Edith even signed Wilson's name to documents without consulting him. [34]As a result, some historians label Edith as "the first female U.S. President." [35]With Wilson unable to defend his plan for a lasting peace, and the election of a Republican president (Warren Harding) in 1920, who was also against the League, the United States Senate voted not to join the League of Nations.

Edith Wilson: 1st female U.S. president?

## D. Xenophobia (fear of strangers)

[36]After fighting a deadly war (World War I) on foreign soil and observing the communist revolution in Russia, Americans became more and more xenophobic (fearful of strangers) and isolationist (setting apart one's country from the affairs of foreign nations). [37]Soon after the war, Russia became known as the Soviet Union (USSR or Union of Soviet Socialist Republics), and a small Communist Labor Party was founded in the United States. [38]Many leftist (communist, anarchist, and socialist) leaders were recent immigrants to the United States, and Americans now worried that communists and socialists might try to overthrow democracy and capitalism in the U.S. [39]American concern grew when the Communist Labor Party supported many union strikes against companies after the war. [40]Other events that contributed to American fear of foreigners were the deadly anarchist (a person who believes that government and laws are not necessary) bombings in the United States by the followers of leftist Luigi Galleani. [41]In the spring of 1919, several bombings linked to Gallenists and other radical groups occurred that targeted political and business leaders in the United States. [42]One bomb even damaged the home of Wilson's Attorney General, Mitchell Palmer, in Washington, D.C. [43]Another contributing factor was the well-publicized murder trial of two Italian-American immigrants who were self-declared socialists—Nicola Sacco and Bartolomeo Vanzetti.

[44]As a result, a wave of fear called the "Red Scare," swept through the United States. [45]The "red" part in the label came from the fact that Moscow, the capital of the USSR, had a large brick plaza called Red Square, and the flag of the USSR was dominated by the color red. [46]Mitchell Palmer decided to take action. [47]He created a new agency within the Department of Justice, called the Federal Bureau of Investigation (FBI), and named young Edgar J. Hoover to head it. [48]The Attorney General then used the FBI to investigate and arrest suspected socialist and communist radicals in a series of attacks called the Palmer Raids. [49]Thousands were arrested, and hundreds of recent immigrants, mainly Russians, were deported (expelled or sent out of the country).

THE LOWELL SUN 7 O'CLOCK

Comb City For Alleged Radicals

Federal and Lowell Police Take Forty Men and Women to the Police Station

"Perfect Cases" Against 2613 of 4500 Persons Arrested in Nation-Wide Radical Raids

[50]Palmer was later heavily criticized for violating the civil rights of many Americans, and the deportations ceased. [51]Congress, however, still worried about foreigners, and passed the Emergency Immigration Act, which for the first time put a quota (an amount limit) on the number of Europeans who could come to live in the United States. [52]The law set the quotas in a way that heavily favored immigrants from the Allied Powers of Western Europe while making it difficult for Southern and Eastern Europeans and Russians to immigrate.

[53]Xenophobia also caused a rebirth of the Ku Klux Klan. [54]The KKK of the Reconstruction days following the Civil War had been prejudiced against blacks. [55]The new Klan now also opposed Jews and Catholics, since many immigrants from those religious groups came from war-torn Europe. [56]Ku Klux Klan members opposed communism, supported the theory of eugenics, and praised the new immigration restrictions. [57]Within a few years of the end of the Great War, KKK membership increased nationally to between three and eight million Americans.

**Fun Fact Feature**

Which U.S. President was the first to travel to Europe during his term of office?


© 2016 The Critical Thinking Co.™ • www.CriticalThinking.com • 800-458-4849

1. What new international organization for world peace did President Wilson suggest in his 14 Point Plan?
    a. United Nations
    b. Allied Powers
    c. International World Court
    d. League of Nations

    Which sentence best supports the answer?

    _____

2. Generally, how did European leaders view Wilson's 14 Point Plan for world peace?
    a. They agreed with almost every point.
    b. They agreed with every point except that of the League of Nations.
    c. They rejected every single one of Wilson's ideas, except that of the League of Nations.
    d. They ignored most of his ideas.

    Which sentence best supports the answer?

    _____

3. Look at the two maps below showing Europe before and after the Great War. Then list six countries that were created after the war.

    a. ________________________________

    b. ________________________________

    c. ________________________________

    d. ________________________________

    e. ________________________________

    f. ________________________________

Source: *Regional Extensions*, 1999

© 2016 The Critical Thinking Co.™ • www.CriticalThinking.com • 800-458-4849 

4. The Red Scare, the Palmer Raids, and the rise of the Ku Klux Klan are all examples of what following the Great War?
   a. 14 Point Plan
   b. communism
   c. xenophobia
   d. retribution

   Which sentences best support the answer?

   _____ _____ _____

5. What was the main reason that Republicans in the Senate voted against the ratification of the Treaty of Versailles?
   a. America wanted a share of German territory and received none in the treaty.
   b. They didn't want America to be controlled by the League of Nations.
   c. The Palmer Raids uncovered thousands of European terrorists in America.
   d. Henry Cabot Lodge, a Democrat, was for the idea of the League.

   Which sentences best support the answer?

   _____ _____

6. What happened to President Woodrow Wilson during his efforts to convince the Senate that the United States should join the League of Nations?
   a. Wilson was not reelected as president.
   b. Wilson joined the Republicans in his opposition against the United States joining the League.
   c. Wilson was injured when a radical socialist bombed Washington, D.C.
   d. Wilson suffered a stroke.

   Which sentence best supports the answer?

   _____

7. Why would some historians refer to Edith Wilson as the "first female president"?

   ________________________________________

   ________________________________________

   ________________________________________

   ________________________________________

8. Who became the head of the new Federal Bureau of Investigation (FBI) shortly after the Great War?
   a. Mitchell Palmer
   b. J. Edgar Hoover
   c. Henry Cabot Lodge
   d. Nicola Sacco

   Which sentence best supports the answer?

   _____

9. What did the Emergency Immigration Act do?
   a. limited the number of European immigrants to America
   b. opened the door to European immigrants torn by the Great War
   c. rejected all immigration from the USSR
   d. allowed more immigrants from Eastern and Southern Europe than Western Europe

   Which sentence best supports the answer?

   _____


© 2016 The Critical Thinking Co.™ • www.CriticalThinking.com • 800-458-4849

## Written Response Question

10. Review the section on the League of Nations in this lesson. Then look at the political cartoon below. Use complete sentences to describe what the bridge represents. Who helped to build the bridge? Who does the man in the cartoon represent? What is the message of the cartoonist?

THE GAP IN THE BRIDGE.

### Fun Fact Finale

Woodrow Wilson became the first U.S. President to travel to Europe during his term of office when he attended peace talks at Versailles, France, in 1919. Theodore Roosevelt had been the first U.S. President to travel anywhere outside the United States when he visited the Panama Canal construction zone, in 1906.

© 2016 The Critical Thinking Co.™ • www.CriticalThinking.com • 800-458-4849

# Review: Lessons 16–20
# The Great War Vocabulary

Write the letter of the definition that matches each vocabulary word. The number following each vocabulary word is the number of the lesson (16–20) where the word was used. All definitions are used once.

_____ 1. assassinated (16)

_____ 2. civilians (16)

_____ 3. embargo (16)

_____ 4. torpedo (16)

_____ 5. barbaric (16)

_____ 6. intervention (16)

_____ 7. monarchy (17)

_____ 8. drafted (17)

_____ 9. scurrilous (17)

_____ 10. curtail (17)

_____ 11. convoy (18)

_____ 12. armistice (18)

_____ 13. stalemate (18)

_____ 14. pandemic (18)

_____ 15. reconnaissance (19)

_____ 16. ace (19)

_____ 17. simultaneously (19)

_____ 18. reparations (20)

_____ 19. xenophobia (20)

_____ 20. deport (20)

a. a government run by inherited royalty/kings

b. money for repairs

c. crude or gross language

d. a group of vessels traveling together

e. when a country will not allow trade with another country

f. to expel or send out of the country

g. fear of foreigners or strangers

h. searching for military information

i. uncivilized or crude behavior

j. a spreading of disease over a large region

k. an underwater missile from a submarine

l. nickname for a skilled fighter pilot

m. murdered for political reasons

n. to cut short, reduce

o. to be assigned to military service through a random lottery

p. a truce or end to wartime hostilities

q. when a country joins in the affairs of another country

r. non-soldiers in time of war

s. a situation where no progress is made

t. at the same time


© 2016 The Critical Thinking Co.™ • www.CriticalThinking.com • 800-458-4849

Section 4: Introduction

# The Roaring Twenties: 1920-1929

Many aspects of America that we recognize today got their start in the 1920s. The decade following the Great War brought an amazing set of technological, cultural, and social changes. It was the decade in which the automobile became the common mode of transportation, electrical appliances served the home, movies added sound, and radio revolutionized communication. Americans became fascinated with sports stars, actors, authors, and other celebrities. Women's fashions changed dramatically, and young ladies began going to college and working outside the home in greater numbers. Blacks experienced a revival of culture in the arts. The economy hummed along at a record pace.

However, beneath the excitement of the Jazz Age, there were issues that made the decade a time of tension. The quick pace of change divided the country between those who embraced the "New Era," and those who struggled to preserve pre-war American values. Enforcement of national laws against alcohol, the rise of organized crime, a backlash (a strong reaction) against a new wave of immigrants, and the ongoing debates about the teaching of the theory of evolution were only a few of the events that made the 1920s "roar." The nickname "Lost Generation" began to be applied to the young people of the 1920s, who were confused about how to live their postwar lives.

Three Republican presidents ruled the country with a conservative philosophy during the era. At the beginning of the decade, Harding was plagued with scandal. His successor, Coolidge, tried to restore faith in the executive office and supported business growth. The economy of the Twenties did roar until 1929, but what happened in 1929 saddled Herbert Hoover with a worldwide economic downturn and the worst economic period in American history.

## U.S. Presidents

29. Warren Harding
1921-1923

30. Calvin Coolidge
1923-1929

31. Herbert Hoover
1929-1933

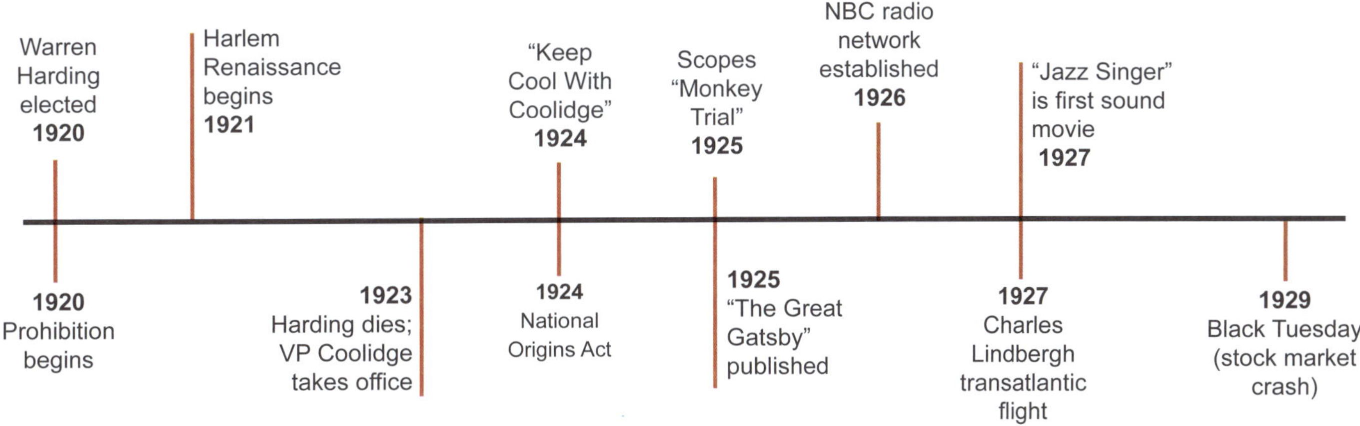


© 2016 The Critical Thinking Co.™ • www.CriticalThinking.com • 800-458-4849 

Lesson 21

# National Prohibition

## A. Progressives Win a Battle

[1]During the Great War, Americans were encouraged by the government to conserve food for the war effort. [2]Throughout this conservation campaign, Protestant churches, Progressives, and women's groups promoted one of their long standing goals: to prohibit (to forbid by law) the consumption of alcohol. [3]Ever since the temperance movement of the early 1800s, reformers had pointed to alcohol abuse as one of America's biggest problems. [4]During the war, reformers argued that it was a waste to use valuable agricultural land for grapes and grains to make wine and beer. [5]Many of the large breweries were run by German families and some Americans, fearful of the Central Powers, wondered if beer was a plot to reduce manufacturing productivity in this country. [6]Saloons seemed to be gathering places for immigrants in urban neighborhoods, and in the xenophobic atmosphere of the times, it seemed appropriate to many native-born Americans to shut them down. [7]Even the Ku Klux Klan supported the law, because of its dislike of immigrants. [8]"Save the women and children from the evils of drink!" became the battle cry of the era.

[9]Within a half-year of America's war declaration in 1917, Congress passed the 18th Amendment and forwarded it to the states. [10]It was ratified in 1919, and national prohibition went into effect January 1, 1920. [11]The manufacture, transportation, or sale of alcoholic beverages was now outlawed in the entire country. [11]It was the first amendment that restricted, rather than increased, the rights of Americans.

Poster Promoting National Prohibition

[12]"Drys"—people who supported Prohibition—were excited. [13]In the early 1920s, the law seemed to be making a positive difference. [14]It was estimated that alcohol consumption levels dropped by two-thirds and alcohol-related diseases steeply declined, while productivity and family wages increased. [15]Henry Ford supported Prohibition. [16]He increased wages if company inspectors found no alcohol in workers' homes.

[16]"Wets"—people who opposed the 18th Amendment—found it fairly easy, however, to obtain alcoholic drinks. [17]By the mid-1920s, the law was widely abused. [18]Prohibition was not in effect in America's neighboring regions of Canada, Mexico, and the Caribbean Islands. [19]"Rum runners" or "bootleggers"—people who smuggled alcoholic drinks—easily broke the law, and enforcement officers, who were underfunded, could not keep up. [20]Criminals who manufactured and sold illegal alcohol commonly enjoyed healthy profits. [21]Practically every town had "speakeasies," which were illegal saloons or nightclubs where patrons gained access with secret passwords. [22]"Moonshiners"—people who made their own liquor—began to flourish. [23]Unregulated alcoholic drinks were often much stronger, and sometimes so strong they were actually poisonous.

[24]Soon gangs of criminals started to control the illegal alcohol business. [25]Al Capone, a Chicago gangster, made millions of dollars in illegal sales, by bribing enforcement officers, importing booze (liquor) from Canada, and violently eliminating rival gang members. [26]For example, on February 14, 1929, Capone's mobsters brutally killed seven members of a rival gang. [27]The crime was called the St. Valentine's Day Massacre and was only a small part of the estimated 550 gang-related murders in Chicago, Illinois, in the 1920s.

Mug Shot of Gangster Al Capone

## B. President Warren Harding

[28]The Republican candidate from Ohio, Warren G. Harding, easily won the 1920 presidential election. [29]It was the first national election in which women voted. [30]That right was given to women with the passage of the 19th Amendment, which had become law during the war. [31]Senator Harding had been a strong supporter of women's rights. [32]Harding was publicly supported by Henry Ford, Thomas Edison, and several Hollywood movie celebrities. [33]In the 1920 campaign, sensing American's weariness from the Great War, Harding had used the slogan "Return to


© 2016 The Critical Thinking Co.™ • www.CriticalThinking.com • 800-458-4849

Normalcy." [34]He spoke out against the League of Nations and promised a return to old-fashioned American values.

[35]Despite his public support of Prohibition, however, even Harding himself broke the law. [36]It became known that Harding shared drinks with his friends in the White House and in a house on nearby K Street during Wednesday night poker parties.

Harding Campaign Poster

[37]Harding was 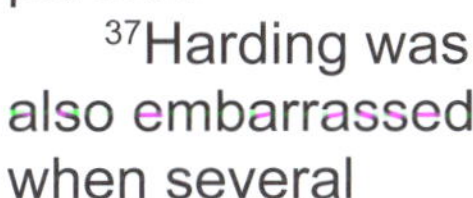also embarrassed when several members of his administration were later convicted of crimes. [38]Officials in the Department of Justice kept thousands of cases of illegal alcohol that was confiscated in raids, and then sold the alcohol to bootleggers. [39]The head of the Veterans' Bureau, Charles Forbes, took money intended to build hospitals for wounded American soldiers. [40]Albert Fall, the Secretary of the Interior, gave drilling rights to government oil reserves, like the Teapot Dome reserve in Wyoming, to private companies in exchange for cash. [41]The head of the U.S. Shipping Board made personal profits by selling surplus war ships at discounted prices. [42]Altogether, journalists called Harding and his associates "The Ohio Gang."

[43]President Harding, embarrassed by the revelation of these scandals, set out on a tour of the American West in 1923 to explain his policies and start a campaign for reelection. [44]After speeches in Missouri, Kansas, and Colorado, he became the first president to visit Canada and Alaska. [45]Harding then headed south by train through Washington, Oregon, and California. [46]Harding died of a heart attack in San Francisco, California, in August. [47]Vice President Calvin Coolidge finished Harding's remaining year in office and won the presidential election of 1924.

### C. The Booze War Is Lost

[48]The great "social experiment" of Prohibition, designed to improve public morality, had backfired by the mid-1920s. [49]Average citizens became law-breakers as they made moonshine for home consumption. [50]Organized crime had developed. [51]School-age children delivered booze for gangs. [52]Pharmacies (drugstores) provided medical prescriptions for alcohol. [53]Women had often been vocal leaders of the temperance movement before the war, but young women of the 1920s found it exciting to sneak into speakeasies with their dates, and drink and smoke in public.

Patrons of a 1920 "speakeasy" openly made fun of the 18th Amendment. Notice that women are also violating the law.

[54]When hard economic times came in the 1930s, some government officials decided it was wrong to spend money on a law that was so unenforceable. [55]Also, it seemed important to again regulate the quality of alcoholic beverages and to help the country's legitimate economy by re-opening breweries, wineries, and saloons. [56]Following the election of a Democratic president in 1932, the 21st Amendment repealing the 18th was passed and Prohibition ended.

**Fun Fact Feature**

What famous American sport today has its roots in the Prohibition era?

© 2016 The Critical Thinking Co.™ • www.CriticalThinking.com • 800-458-4849 

1. What was one of the reasons Prohibition legislation passed in the late 1910s?
   a. "Wets" said it made great economic sense.
   b. It supported the war effort.
   c. Alcohol was found to contain many poisonous ingredients.
   d. Organized crime gangs knew it would make great profits.

   Which sentence best supports the answer?

   _____

2. Which group did NOT favor national Prohibition?
   a. Protestant church
   b. Ku Klux Klan
   c. Progressives
   d. "wets"

   Which sentence best supports the answer?

   _____

3. In your own words, describe how the poster in this lesson, "Wet or Dry?" tried to influence how a person should vote about Prohibition?

   ______________________________________

   ______________________________________

   ______________________________________

   ______________________________________

4. One of the failures of the 18th Amendment can be traced to what cause?
   a. It reduced alcohol related diseases.
   b. The Great War ended in Europe.
   c. Agencies set up to enforce the law were inadequately staffed and under-funded.
   d. President Warren Harding died of a heart attack.

   Which sentence best supports the answer?

   _____

5. Which group initially in support of Prohibition, often became drawn into the culture of publicly drinking and smoking in the "speakeasies" of the 1920s?
   a. Protestant ministers
   b. immigrants
   c. women
   d. "wets"

   Which sentence best supports the answer?

   _____

6. Who was a major figure in organized crime in the 1920s and was responsible for the St. Valentine's Day Massacre?
   a. Al Capone
   b. Albert Fall
   c. Charles Forbes
   d. Warren Harding

   Which sentences best support the answer?

   _____ _____

7. What was the nickname given to the scandalous criminals in President Harding's administration?
   a. Ohio Gang
   b. wets
   c. bootleggers
   d. moonshiners

   Which sentence best supports the answer?

   _____

8. While in office, Harding was the first U.S. president to visit:
   a. Mexico and the Caribbean Islands.
   b. Canada and Alaska.
   c. Europe.
   d. Ohio.

   Which sentence best supports the answer?

   _____


© 2016 The Critical Thinking Co.™ • www.CriticalThinking.com • 800-458-4849

9. Explain why Calvin Coolidge became president in 1923?

______________________________________

______________________________________

______________________________________

______________________________________

## Written Response Question

10. Use complete sentences to discuss the political cartoon shown above. What symbols are used in the cartoon and what is the message of the cartoonist?

______________________________________

______________________________________

______________________________________

______________________________________

______________________________________

______________________________________

______________________________________

______________________________________

______________________________________

**Fun Fact Finale**

In the days of Prohibition, many Southern bootleggers learned how to drive their cars quickly to avoid capture as they transported illegal moonshine. Eventually they held race contests to see who was the fastest driver. This amateur sport eventually grew into today's professional NASCAR: the National Association for Stock Car Auto Racing.

© 2016 The Critical Thinking Co.™ • www.CriticalThinking.com • 800-458-4849

Lesson 22

# 1920s Economics and Technology

## A. Strong Consumer Economy

[1]The decade after the Great War is often referred to as "the Roaring 20s," because the economy boomed and technology blossomed. [2]The decade became known for its strong financial growth powered by mass production and industrial growth. [3]After a short postwar recession (economic downturn), unemployment fell to only three percent, production grew by forty-three percent, the national debt decreased, wages increased, and prices remained steady through 1929. [4]The value of stocks on Wall Street grew and grew, and more people started "playing the market" in an attempt to cash in on corporate growth. [5]In the mid-1920s, President Calvin Coolidge summed it up by remarking: "The business of America is business." [6]The president easily won reelection in 1924 with a campaign slogan—"Keep Cool With Coolidge"—that suggested voters should stick with a leader in charge of such a strong economy.

[7]One group that did not experience the economic prosperity, however, was farmers. [8]Prices for farm products dropped dramatically when the government stopped wartime purchases, and farm exports dropped as European nations started their postwar agricultural recovery.

[9]The automobile industry was the leader of the American economy in the 1920s. [10]Before the war, automobiles were considered luxury items. [11]By 1930, almost two-thirds of Americans owned cars. [12]Although Ford Motors remained the giant of the industry, General Motors and other auto manufacturers also profited. [13]About nine percent of all the country's manufacturing wages came directly from the auto industry. [14]The growth of auto sales also indirectly produced huge increases in road construction, oil and gas production, tire production, leather production, and advertising.

[15]Henry Ford's success with the assembly-line influenced many other companies to mass produce goods such as electric appliances, furniture, and clothing. [16]These companies also advertised like never before. [17]Using the new mediums of radio, magazines, and roadside billboards, advertising agencies pumped billions of dollars into convincing Americans that they needed all the new products arriving on the market each year. [18]The use of celebrities such as movie actors, authors, and sport figures to sell products became popular. [19]Companies made it easier to purchase these items, too. [20]Prior to the Great War, consumers (buyers of products or services) paid cash in full for items or borrowed money from a bank to make an expensive purchase. [21]Now companies themselves offered the chance to buy on credit: pay a small down-payment, with an agreement to pay the remainder of the bill over time. [22]More than half of all automobile sales were sold on credit.

Sports celebrities were popular stars of 1920s advertising efforts.

[23]Besides mass-production, advertising, and easy credit, another reason consumer sales boomed was because of new ways of distributing goods. [24]The increased production of automobiles and delivery trucks meant that companies could supply goods to chain stores throughout the country. [25]Chain stores were retail outlets owned by a company that sold similar merchandise. [26]The A&P Grocery chain, for example, had more than 17,000 markets. [27]Woolworth's lured consumers into its department store chains across the nation by using a new 1920s invention—air-conditioning.

## B. 1920s Technology

[28]Air-conditioning was just one way that Americans felt the influence of a wave of technology that affected their lives in the 1920s. [29]There were so many advances in technology and medicine that the decade received another nickname—"The New Era." [30]Most American homes, for example, now had radios. [31]More than 600 new radio stations were created in the first years after the Great War. [32]By the mid-20s, NBC (National Broadcasting Company) was one of five networks linking radio stations across the country. [33]Citizens of Oregon and Florida could now listen to the same programing at the same time. [34]By 1929, radios were installed in cars. [35]As Americans listened

This 1923 magazine ad promoted radio.


© 2016 The Critical Thinking Co.™ • www.CriticalThinking.com • 800-458-4849

to the same radio broadcasts of baseball games, political speeches, advertising, and news events, a national culture started to develop, while regional differences slowly started to melt away.

[36]Life in the home saw many advances in time-saving technology, most of them involving electronics. [37]Electric refrigerators and freezers replaced the old ice-box as a way to store foods. [38]Electric washing machines and dryers made doing laundry much easier. [39]Rugs no longer had to be rolled up and beaten clean outside, once the electric home vacuum was introduced. [40]The first electric dishwashers were marketed. [41]Men could shave with an electric razor by 1928. [42]Indoor plumbing became commonplace, and more and more people sought store-bought clothes instead of sewing their own.

[43]Lives were improved by medical advances as well. [44]The common Band-Aid® was introduced in 1921. [45]Insulin, to help with the symptoms of diabetes, was available by 1922. [46]Also, the age of antibiotics to combat many bacterial diseases started in 1928.

### C. Automobile Culture

[47]The automobile had the most influence on American culture in the 1920s. [48]All the labor saving technology and increased wages allowed families to vacation away from home more often than before. [49]As a result, roadside diners started to dot the landscape. [50]The first fast-food chain, A&W Root Beer, developed as a result of the auto as well. [51]Vacationers needed a place to stay on the road. [52]In the early 1920s, tourist auto-camps or cabins provided accommodations (lodging; a place to stay for the night). [53]By mid-decade, the word "motel" was coined to designate a place with many rooms under one roof, usually on one roadside level, with easy parking access. [54]The word came from the combination of "motor" and "hotel."

[55]The car allowed some families to have jobs in the city while living outside of town in the suburbs. [56]Women who learned to drive had more independence than before to visit friends or go places that were not necessarily in their neighborhoods. [57]Teenagers, too, had more freedom, which sometimes led to a lessening of parental control. [58]Farm families experienced less isolation. [59]The tractor, the cousin of the automobile, revolutionized farm life. [60]Yet, while the tractor allowed farmers to plow more land faster, the increase in production ironically helped to keep the price of agricultural products low, due to an increase in crops without an increase in demand.

[61]The rise of the automobile and highways meant the decline (decrease) of passenger railroads. [62]Railroad travel involved more expense, with fixed schedules and routes. [63]The automobile brought greater convenience, but also traffic jams, more pollution, more fatalities, and more roads. [64]It also created a decline in the ironworks and blacksmith shops that had prospered in the age of the horse. [65]During Prohibition, the automobile provided a convenient way to transport moonshine or elude law enforcement.

Notice that women are featured in this Chevrolet ad of the late 1920s.

**Fun Fact Feature**

So much automobile traffic crowded American roads after the Great War that a device to control traffic had to be introduced at critical intersections in 1923. Can you name it?

1. The economy of the 1920s was generally strong EXCEPT in which area?
   a. car manufacturing
   b. advertising
   c. electric appliances
   d. farming

   Which sentence best supports the answer?

   ______

2. What industry lead all others in manufacturing in the 1920s?
   a. radio
   b. alcohol
   c. refrigerators
   d. automobiles

   Which sentence best supports the answer?

   ______

3. Mass-production, renewed industrialization, advertising, easy credit, and chain stores all contributed to a boom in what in the 1920s?
   a. religion
   b. women's' rights movement
   c. a strong economy
   d. the rise of the Progressive movement

   Which sentence best supports the answer?

   ______

4. Which of the following contributed most to the development of a national American culture in the 1920s?
   a. farming
   b. radio
   c. easy credit
   d. stock market

   Which sentence best supports the answer?

   ______

5. Who was Calvin Coolidge?
   a. a leading businessman of the 1920s
   b. a leader in the 1920s advertising business
   c. the U.S. president who won reelection in 1924
   d. an American inventor in the 1920s

   Which sentence best supports the answer?

   ______

6. Many of the new consumer products for the home in the 1920s:
   a. ran on steam power.
   b. were too expensive to purchase.
   c. used electricity.
   d. were unpopular with the public.

   Which sentence best supports the answer?

   ______

7. Name two major innovations in medicine in the 1920s.

   a. ______________________________

   b. ______________________________

8. What word describes a new type of accommodation that was developed for vacationers in the 1920s?
   a. motel
   b. hotel
   c. resort
   d. diner

   Which sentence best supports the answer?

   ______

9. What was NBC in the 1920s?
   a. a television network
   b. a radio network
   c. a network of chain stores
   d. an automobile company

   Which sentence best supports the answer?

   ______

 © 2016 The Critical Thinking Co.™ • www.CriticalThinking.com • 800-458-4849

## Written Response Question

10. List five "positive" things about the 1920s automobile industry and five "negative" things.

Positives

a. ______________________________

b. ______________________________

c. ______________________________

d. ______________________________

e. ______________________________

Negatives

f. ______________________________

g. ______________________________

h. ______________________________

i. ______________________________

j. ______________________________

**Fun Fact Finale**

So much automobile traffic crowded American roads after the Great War that the electric traffic signal, with its red, yellow, and green lights to control traffic, had to be introduced at critical intersections in 1923.

© 2016 The Critical Thinking Co.™ • www.CriticalThinking.com • 800-458-4849

Lesson 23

# Cultural Changes in the 1920s

## A. Women

[1]During the Great War, many women entered the workplace when men went off to the battlefields. [2]With the strong economy of the 1920s, women continued to work outside the home in larger numbers. [3]Most employed women held office jobs such as telephone operators, typists, clerks, secretaries, or they worked in sales in the department stores or became teachers. [4]Women were usually paid less, however, than their male counterparts. [5]Young women went to college in greater numbers than ever before. [6]There were three times the number of women in college in 1930 than there were ten years earlier.

[7]Educated, single young women, with jobs in Northern cities, set the fashion trends of the 1920s. [8]They "bobbed" their hair (cut it short); put away their corsets and petticoats; wore high heels, jewelry, and makeup; and shortened the length of their dresses. [9]These women were known as "flappers." [10]They openly went to speakeasies, smoked in public, and dated without chaperones (an adult who supervises a young person in public). [11]Shedding the days of pre-war modesty, young women openly displayed their bodies in beauty contests such as the Miss America Pageant, which started in 1921 in Atlantic City, New Jersey. [12]With their new voting rights and fashion trends, these young women sought independence and a greater level of equality. [13]Clara Bow, a famous movie star of the day, captured the flapper look and was nicknamed the "It Girl."

This film, starring Clara Bow, won the very first Academy Award for "Best Picture" in 1927.

## B. Celebrity Culture

[14]The growth of the movie industry in the 1920s was one of the factors that brought about a popularity of celebrities (a famous, well-known person) like never before. [15]Film stars such as Clara Bow, Mary Pickford (nicknamed "America's Sweetheart"), and Rudolph Valentino ("the Latin Lover") had mass followings. [16]Audiences were thrilled in 1927, when the addition of sound came to the silent movies with Al Jolson's *The Jazz Singer*. [17]A year later, Walt Disney introduced the first animation (cartoon) with sound that was successfully timed to the animation on the screen. [18]Disney's Mickey Mouse was the first successful cartoon character of the era. [19]By the decade's end, more than 80 million moviegoers attended the theater each week.

[20]With the increasing ease of communication, fads (temporary trends followed by many persons) swept the nation in the 1920s. [21]Crossword puzzle books became popular. [22]Goldfish swallowing was a brief craze. [23]A Chinese board game using tiles, called Mah Jongg, became a hit. [24]Stuntman Avon Foreman was an overnight sensation when he set a record for sitting atop a flagpole for ten days, ten hours, ten minutes, and ten seconds.

[25]Sports heroes were another new kind of celebrity. [26]With contests being broadcast on radio, and photographs published in weekly magazines such as *Life* or *Time*, professional sports became more popular than ever before, and athletes became famous to all. [27]Sports stars such as baseball's home run king, Babe Ruth; prizefighter, Jack Dempsey; golfer, Bobby Jones; swimmer, Gertrude Ederle; football players, Jim Thorpe and Red Grange; and tennis stars, Bill Tilden and Helen Wills became national heroes and advertisers' darlings.

[28]Perhaps the greatest celebrity of all was pilot Charles Lindbergh. [29]Responding to a prize offer from a New York City hotel operator, Lindbergh became the first to successfully fly a plane on his

Charles Lindbergh and his plane.


© 2016 The Critical Thinking Co.™ • www.CriticalThinking.com • 800-458-4849

own across the Atlantic Ocean, from New York to Paris, France, in a plane he called *The Spirit of St. Louis*. [30]Millions cheered his 1927 accomplishment as a triumph of American technology and the spirit of individualism.

### C. Jazz Age

[31]Yet another nickname of the 1920s came from the popular music of the day. [32]Jazz was born in New Orleans, Louisiana, as a cross between African American and European rhythms. [33]The new form of music received national attention with the growth of radio, and the Jazz Age began. [34]Flappers in the cities danced the wild "Charleston" to jazz. [35]Music celebrities such as trumpet player Louis Armstrong, band leader Duke Ellington, and jazz singer Bessie Smith became stars of black culture that were appreciated by white audiences as well.

Flappers of the Jazz Age dance to the "Charleston."

[36]During the Great War, thousands of black Americans from the South moved to Northern cities to seek jobs in manufacturing—an event known as the Great Migration. [37]Blacks still found prejudice in the North, however, and tended to live together in common neighborhoods. [38]In New York City, the largest black part of town was a district called Harlem. [39]In the 1920s, a rebirth of pride in African American culture flowered there in a movement that became known as the Harlem Renaissance. [40]Besides popular jazz nightclubs, Harlem featured theaters that produced all-black musicals, with actors such as Paul Robeson, authors such as Claude McKay and Zora Hurston who wrote about African American topics, and dancers such as Josephine Baker.

[41]Harlem resident and writer Langston Hughes wrote insightful poetry about black life in America. [42]One of his most popular poems was called *The Weary Blues*.

Poet Langston Hughes

The Weary Blues

Droning a drowsy syncopated tune,
Rocking back and forth to a mellow croon,
I heard a Negro play.
Down on Lenox Avenue the other night
By the pale dull pallor of an old gas light
He did a lazy sway . . . He did a lazy sway . . .
To the tune o' those Weary Blues.
With his ebony hands on each ivory key
He made that poor piano moan with melody. O Blues!
Swaying to and fro on his rickety stool
He played that sad raggy tune like a musical fool.
Sweet Blues!
Coming from a black man's soul. O Blues!
In a deep song voice with a melancholy tone
I heard that Negro sing, that old piano moan.
"Ain't got nobody in all this world,
Ain't got nobody but ma self.
I's gwine to quit ma frownin'
And put ma troubles on the shelf."
Thump, thump, thump, went his foot on the floor.
He played a few chords then he sang some more—
"I got the Weary Blues
And I can't be satisfied.
Got the Weary Blues
And can't be satisfied—
I ain't happy no mo'
And I wish that I had died."
And far into the night he crooned that tune.
The stars went out and so did the moon.
The singer stopped playing and went to bed
While the Weary Blues echoed through his head.
He slept like a rock or a man that's dead.

### D. Marcus Garvey

[43]Another famous Harlem resident of the 1920s was Marcus Garvey, a Jamaican who had traveled internationally before coming to New York. [44]Saddened by the discrimination he found in many parts of the world he had traveled, Garvey started the Universal Negro Improvement Association (UNIA) in Jamaica in 1914, and held an international convention in New York in 1921. [45]The UNIA is considered to be one of the first mass movements to promote black culture in America. [46]"He taught his followers that black is beautiful," wrote a reporter in one African American newspaper. [47]Garvey tried to start black-owned companies and promote black culture. [48]He also promoted a "Back to Africa" movement. [49]Recalling that the American Colonization Society had established the country of Liberia in the early 1820s as a homeland for free blacks, Garvey urged black Americans of the 1920s to move to Liberia, as well, to enjoy the full richness of African culture and have better opportunities to prosper.

[50]Not all African Americans supported Garvey's ideas. [51]W.E.B. Du Bois—another popular black leader and the co-founder of the NAACP—was highly critical of Garvey, even referring to him as "a little, fat black man, ugly … with a big head." [52]Du Bois argued that the future of American blacks was in America, not overseas. [53]Undeterred by Du Bois' attacks, Garvey attempted to raise funds to build a steamship to help transport blacks to Liberia. [54]In 1927, Garvey was charged and convicted of soliciting funds for the steamship through the mail but never building the boat. [55]Garvey and his supporters claimed he hadn't raised enough money and that the charges were politically motivated. [56]During his imprisonment, President Calvin Coolidge pardoned Garvey, but had him deported back to Jamaica. [57]The UNIA movement fell apart.

Marcus Garvey

**Fun Fact Feature**

What 1925 event set in motion a craze in America for everything Egyptian?


© 2016 The Critical Thinking Co.™ • www.CriticalThinking.com • 800-458-4849

1. Which of the following is generally true of women in the 1920s?
   a. Women finally received equal pay with men at the workplace.
   b. More women went to college than ever before.
   c. Women dressed more modestly than they did before the Great War.
   d. Women rarely worked outside the home.

   Which sentences best support the answer?

   _____ _____

2. What were young urban women with short hair, short dresses, make-up, and jewelry known as in the 1920s?
   a. flappers
   b. jazz singers
   c. celebrities
   d. chaperones

   Which sentences best supports the answer?

   _____ _____

3. Name three "fads" of the 1920s.

   a. ______________________________

   b. ______________________________

   c. ______________________________

4. What helped drive America's fascination with fads, professional sports, and jazz in the 1920s?
   a. women's right to vote
   b. national means of communication
   c. flappers
   d. Prohibition

   Which sentences best support the answer?

   _____ _____ _____

5. What were two important changes to movies in the 1920s?

   a. ______________________________

   b. ______________________________

6. Who was involved in the Great Migration?
   a. women looking to be urban flappers
   b. blacks looking for work in Northern cities
   c. blacks moving back to the "Motherland" of Africa
   d. Charles Lindbergh.

   Which sentence best supports the answer?

   _____

7. The Harlem Renaissance was located in:
   a. Hollywood, California.
   b. New Orleans, Louisiana.
   c. Paris, France.
   d. New York City, New York.

   Which sentences best support the answer?

   _____ _____

8. The Harlem Renaissance was a 1920s rebirth of:
   a. celebrity culture.
   b. the women's rights movement.
   c. pride in African American culture.
   d. the rise of professional athletics.

   Which sentence best supports the answer?

   _____

9. Who started one of the first mass movements to promote black culture in America and also promoted a "Back to Africa" movement in the 1920s?
   a. Louis Armstrong
   b. Langston Hughes
   c. Marcus Garvey
   d. W.E.B. Du Bois

   Which sentences best support the answer?

   _____ _____ _____

## Written Response Question

10. Look at the Langston Hughes poem *Weary Blues* to answer these questions.

a. Who is the poem about?

______________________________________________

b. Briefly describe what the poem is about.

______________________________________________

______________________________________________

c. Where does the poem take place?

______________________________________________

d. List six adjectives (description words) that Hughes used to create a mood.

____________________ ____________________

____________________ ____________________

____________________ ____________________

Cover of Sheet Music From the 1920s With Egyptian Fashion and Makeup

### Fun Fact Finale

In 1925, the tomb of Egyptian King Tutankhamen—nicknamed "King Tut"—was opened after 3,200 years. The nation was gripped with curiosity about this exotic discovery. Fashion designers created Egyptian dresses, movie houses were designed with Egyptian themes, and women started to use eye shadow, lipstick, and other beauty products marketed by advertisers as being descended from Egyptian traditions. The craze spread quickly with the advent of national radio, movies, and magazines.


© 2016 The Critical Thinking Co.™ • www.CriticalThinking.com • 800-458-4849

# Bonus Activity
# 1920's Slang

Throughout time, new words and phrases are created in every culture. In the 1920s, with all the changes in society, this was particularly true. Read the fictional story below. Words that are in bold are actual 1920s slang vocabulary. Using the context clues around each word or phrase, match them to their meanings on the next page.

## The Blind Date

Gertrude was set up on a **blind date** by a friend of hers in July of 1922. She didn't know who she would meet but when her date, John, drove up to her home in his Model T, she was excited to see that he was a handsome young man. As they introduced themselves to one another, Gertrude could tell that John had a great personality as well as good looks. "He's **the cat's meow**," she thought and blushed. Soon she was **in a sweat** and couldn't wait for the date. John thought Gertrude was nice looking as well. John thought she really showed off her nice **gams** with the short, flapper-style dress she was wearing.

John suggested they go to a speakeasy and get some **giggle water**. Gertrude nervously agreed even though she had never been to a **gin mill** before. Her heart was racing and her hands shook a bit. She hoped her **heebie jeebies** weren't obvious to her date. She and John **tossed the bull** around as they drove to the speakeasy, and Gertrude calmed down. However, she embarrassed herself when she told John to slow down and take a different route to downtown. "Don't be such a **back-seat driver**," John admonished her.

Gertrude's nervousness came back when they got to the door of the speakeasy. John noticed, and he began to **razz** her a bit when she showed her fright. "Quit teasing me," she pleaded. "This is all new to me. I'm not usually a **night owl**," she claimed. "This is late for me. What do we do to get in?"

Suddenly a man with a gray beard, **father time** himself, opened a sliding slot in the door and asked for a code word. John provided it, and he and his date were allowed through the door. After walking down a dark hallway, John and Gertrude entered the bar. The place was fabulously decorated and the patrons were well-dressed. "Wow, this place is **the nuts**," whispered Gertrude to John. "It's much classier than I thought it would be." There was a small band in the corner playing jazz. "They can really **jam**," John declared of the band. "I love their sound."

John sat Gertrude at a table and approached the bar. "Are you the **big cheese**, here?" he asked the bartender. "No," came the response. "The boss is in the back setting up a deal with the local **bootlegger** to get more supplies for the speakeasy." John laid down a few **smackers** on the bar and ordered drinks for himself and his date.

While John was at the bar, a **snake charmer** approached Gertrude and tried to start a conversation with her. "You here alone tonight?" the man smoothly inquired in a low voice. "**Go fly a kite**!" Gertrude responded. "My date's at the bar. Go find someone else to hassle," she said smartly as she dismissed him. The man left quickly.

John noticed the exchange as he came back to Gertrude's table with their drinks. He also noticed that the man had gone to another table where he apparently already had a date. "Who was that **two-timer**?" John asked, slightly annoyed.

"Oh, just some **lounge lizard** who thinks he can date any girl," Gertrude replied. "Don't worry about him. He's **all wet**. Hey, the band is playing the Charleston. Let's dance!"

Write the letter of the meaning that matches the 1920's slang.

| 1920's Slang | Meaning |
|---|---|
| ______ 1. blind date | a. a person who stays out late |
| ______ 2. cat's meow | b. to play music together |
| ______ 3. in a sweat | c. make fun of someone, tease |
| ______ 4. gams | d. a ladies man who hangs around a bar |
| ______ 5. giggle water | e. alcohol |
| ______ 6. gin mill | f. very important person |
| ______ 7. heebie jeebies | g. anxious, nervous, worried |
| ______ 8. toss the bull | h. an old man |
| ______ 9. back seat driver | i. female legs |
| ______ 10. razz | j. completely mistaken, wrong |
| ______ 11. night owl | k. go on a date with a person not previously met |
| ______ 12. father time | l. an illegal drinking establishment |
| ______ 13. the nuts | m. make small talk, gossip |
| ______ 14. jam | n. get out of here, get lost |
| ______ 15. big cheese | o. a smooth talker |
| ______ 16. bootlegger | p. one who offers unwanted advice |
| ______ 17. smackers | q. having more than one boy/girl friend at a time |
| ______ 18. snake charmer | r. very nice, highly sought after |
| ______ 19. go fly a kite | s. something fantastic, very cool |
| ______ 20. two-timer | t. excited |
| ______ 21. lounge lizard | u. dollars |
| ______ 22. all wet | v. a supplier or transporter of illegal alcohol |


© 2016 The Critical Thinking Co.™ • www.CriticalThinking.com • 800-458-4849

Lesson 24

# Twenties Tensions

## A. Liberty's Light Is Dimmed

[1]The quickened pace of life and the changes in so many areas of U.S. culture after the Great War (World War I) were not embraced by all Americans. [2]Tensions grew during the decade between those Americans who welcomed the modern life and those who held more conservative values. [3]As previously noted in Lesson 20, the federal government reacted to Americans' negative attitudes toward foreigners by passing new laws that restricted immigration from Southern and Eastern European nations. [4]Asian immigration was banned completely. [5]More than 1.2 million immigrants had come to the United States the year before the war started. [6]By the end of the 1920s, total immigration had fallen by 75 percent.

Mexican immigrants faced discrimination from businesses in America, as seen in this store sign from the 1920s.

[7]Most of the immigrants who did come to the United States in the 1920s were from Mexico. [8]They mainly traveled to California and the American southwest in search of jobs in agriculture. [9]They often worked at the lowest paying jobs, but often experienced discrimination in churches, housing, schooling, and the workplace. [10]By 1929, Congress passed laws to close the door to immigration along the Mexican border, too.

[11]The 1920s was also a time with much anti-Semitism (religious prejudice against Jews). [12]Some of the governments of the former Central Powers, such as the new Nazi Party of Adolph Hitler in Germany, falsely blamed Jews as the source of trouble in the defeated countries. [13]Jews were increasingly discriminated against in America as thousands came to the United States after the war. [14]Newspapers and magazines printed anti-Semitic articles stereotyping (an unfair belief that all people of the same color or race are all the same) Jews as anti-democratic or radical. [15]American Jews were commonly excluded from jobs, social clubs, or certain neighborhoods. [16]In 1922, Harvard put a quota (limited number) on how many Jews would be accepted to its college. [17]Many other colleges in the East followed Harvard's example.

## B. Ku Klux Klan Comeback

[18]In 1915, a silent movie called *The Birth of a Nation* became a national sensation when it showed a fictional story of the Civil War era. [19]The movie glorified the actions of the Ku Klux Klan by casting the Klan as protectors of white society fighting against sexually aggressive, unintelligent, criminal-minded blacks. [20]Using the film's popularity, and the growing fear of foreigners, some business leaders in Atlanta, Georgia, sponsored a re-birth of the KKK and profited from the sale of white robes, masks, books, and other Klan-related gear. [21]The new Klan preached "100 percent Americanism" and patriotism. [22]It was not only anti-black but against Jews, Catholics, immigrants, flapper-style women, and those who violated Prohibition. [23]The Klan grew from a small 5,000 member group in the South at the end of the Great War to become a national organization of about five million members in the early 1920s. [24]It helped to elect leaders to government positions in several states, such as Oregon Governor Walter Pierce, in the mid-20s. [25]With Pierce's support and the backing of the Ku Klux Klan and some other Protestant organizations, an Oregon law called the Compulsory Education Act was passed by the state legislature. [26]This law banned private schools for children ages 8 to 16. [27]Supporters of the law targeted Catholic schools because they felt those religious schools were not holding true to American values. [28]The Supreme Court disagreed and struck down the law in 1926 in a case called *Society of Sisters of the Holy Names v. Walter Pierce*. [29]After that defeat in court, and the revelation that several national Klan leaders had been convicted on charges of corruption and other crimes, the KKK faded again.

The Ku Klux Klan marched in the nation's capital in 1926.

## C. Religious Reaction

[30]Some religious groups found the scientific theories of the 1920s threatening. [31]A movement known as fundamentalism, in particular, protested biologists' explanations of the development of

© 2016 The Critical Thinking Co.™ • www.CriticalThinking.com • 800-458-4849 

human life. [32]In 1859, British naturalist Charles Darwin had proposed his theory of evolution. [33]Darwin suggested that all species of human life have descended over time from common ancestors and that gradual changes in the characteristics of a population occur over generations through a process called natural selection.

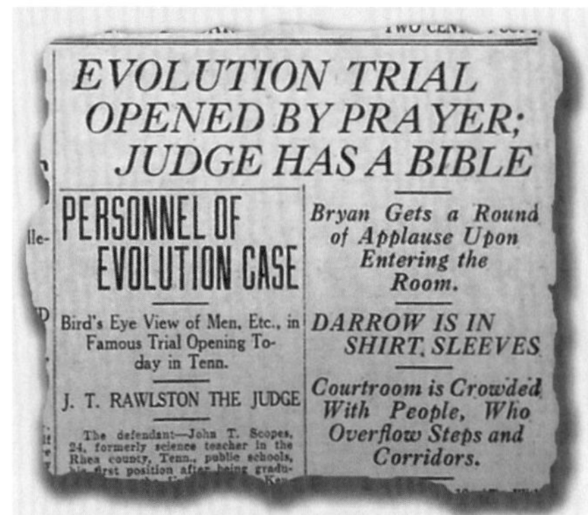
EVOLUTION TRIAL OPENED BY PRAYER; JUDGE HAS A BIBLE

PERSONNEL OF EVOLUTION CASE

Bird's Eye View of Men, Etc., in Famous Trial Opening Today in Tenn.

J. T. RAWLSTON THE JUDGE

The defendant—John T. Scopes, 24, formerly science teacher in the Rhea county, Tenn., public schools,

Bryan Gets a Round of Applause Upon Entering the Room.

DARROW IS IN SHIRT SLEEVES

Courtroom is Crowded With People, Who Overflow Steps and Corridors.

The trial of John Scopes became a sensational national event, and debate, between conservatives and liberals in the 1920s.

[34]Fundamentalists believed that the account of man's creation told in the Bible was the literal (strict word-for-word interpretation) truth: God created man separately from all other animals. [35]Fundamentalists convinced several states to pass laws barring the teaching of evolution. [36]Tennessee was one such state. [37]When biology teacher John Scopes summarized Charles Darwin's theory of evolution in his Dayton, Tennessee, high school classroom in 1925, he was arrested.

[38]Big-name lawyers for both the prosecution and defense signed on to argue for or against the teacher's actions and the Tennessee law. [39]The resulting Scopes Trial became a national sensation, and a national debate, when it became the first court case ever broadcast on radio. [40]The event was nicknamed by some as the "Monkey Trial," because the lawyer for Tennessee stated during the trial that he was saddened that school children would be taught that humans had evolved from monkeys and "not even from American monkeys, but from old world monkeys." [41]At the trial, Scopes' lawyers argued that the theory of evolution and the biblical account of creation were not in conflict with each other, but the judge ruled against them and the law remained on the books. [42]Scopes was found guilty of breaking the law and was fined 100 dollars. [43]For the next three decades, the theory of evolution was downplayed in American schools, and textbook publishers avoided the discussion of evolution in their lessons.

[44]Religious conservatives found a leader in the 1920s and, surprisingly for that era, it was a woman. [45]Aimee Semple McPherson was an evangelical preacher—a person who believes that their religious faith should influence all parts of their life, and that they have a responsibility to spread the message of the Bible while trying to convert listeners to Christianity. [46]She spoke at revival meetings, attended by many, and was the first woman to preach a sermon using radio broadcasts. [47]In an era of vast change, McPherson's message against the "modernist" culture of the Roaring Twenties struck a strong chord among conservative Americans, and she had a huge following. [48]McPherson conducted many faith healing sessions and founded the International Church of the Foursquare Gospel in 1923. [49]She claimed the United States was a nation founded and sustained by divine inspiration and worked especially hard to reform women's roles in Christianity.

Aimee Semple McPherson

## D. Lost Generation

[50]A nickname was given to the young Americans who grew up in the age of the Great War and the Roaring Twenties—the "Lost Generation." [51]"Lost" in this case meant that, in the years after the war, people lacked direction and were confused about how to live their lives. [52]Some were disheartened about the horror and bloodshed of the war; others saw a loss of morality in the "Jazz Age" and quickly changing society.

[53]American authors, in particular, spoke out about their generation through their stories. [54]Many of them moved away from America to live and write in Paris. [55]Ernest Hemingway eventually won a Nobel Prize for literature for his 1920's books, *The Sun Also Rises* and *A Farewell to Arms*, which portrayed the uselessness of war and the emptiness of political efforts for peace. [56]Sinclair Lewis was another American Nobel Prize winner, for his novels *Main Street* and *Babbitt*, which took critical aim at small town, middle-class life in America. [57]Perhaps the greatest novel to depict (describe or show) the Jazz Age was F. Scott Fitzgerald's *The Great Gatsby*. [58]His novel, set in the rich suburbs of New York City, best captured his view of the Roaring Twenties: selfish attitudes, fixation with wealth, decay of social values, acceptance of organized crime, and the general corruption of the American Dream in the 1920s.


© 2016 The Critical Thinking Co.™ • www.CriticalThinking.com • 800-458-4849

**Fun Fact Feature**

Which president made the first radio broadcast from the White House and was the first to be recorded on film with sound?

1. In the 1920s, tensions in America most often centered on:
   a. art and literature.
   b. the use of radio.
   c. the changes and pace of modern life.
   d. rulings made by the Supreme Court.

   Which sentences best support the answer?

   _____ _____

2. U.S. laws of the 1920s restricted immigration by each of these groups of people, EXCEPT.
   a. French
   b. Asians
   c. Mexicans
   d. Southern and Eastern Europeans

   Which sentences best support the answer?

   _____ _____ _____

3. Which religious group experienced strong discrimination in both Germany and the United States in the 1920s?
   a. Church of the Foursquare Gospel
   b. fundamentalists
   c. Jews
   d. Protestants

   Which sentences best support the answer?

   _____ _____

4. The movie *Birth of a Nation* helped spark a rise in what organization in America in the 1920s?
   a. Nazi party
   b. groups supporting the theory of evolution
   c. Lost Generation
   d. Ku Klux Klan

   Which sentences best support the answer?

   _____ _____

5. Would fundamentalists have been for OR against what John Scopes did in his classroom in 1925?
   a. for
   b. against

   Which sentence best supports the answer?

   _____

6. Oregon's Compulsory Education Act was supported by the Ku Klux Klan as a way to protest:
   a. black civil rights movement.
   b. Catholic schools.
   c. women's rights movement.
   d. fundamentalism.

   Which sentence best supports the answer?

   _____

7. The "Monkey Trial" was centered around the debate over:
   a. evolution.
   b. immigration.
   c. the Ku Klux Klan.
   d. radio.

   Which sentence best supports the answer?

   _____

8. Aimee Semple McPherson was known as a:
   a. leading writer of the 1920s.
   b. political leader of the Roaring Twenties.
   c. Jazz age musician and film star.
   d. religious leader of the 1920s.

   Which sentences best support the answer?

   _____ _____

© 2016 The Critical Thinking Co.™ • www.CriticalThinking.com • 800-458-4849

9. Who were some of the more famous members of the "Lost Generation"?
   a. radio stars
   b. scientists
   c. writers
   d. military officers

   Give three examples: ____________________

   ____________________ ____________________

## Written Response Question

10. Use complete sentences to summarize why this lesson was titled "Twenties Tensions."

______________________________________________________________________

______________________________________________________________________

______________________________________________________________________

______________________________________________________________________

______________________________________________________________________

______________________________________________________________________

______________________________________________________________________

______________________________________________________________________

______________________________________________________________________

### Fun Fact Finale

The inaugural speech of President Calvin Coolidge, in 1924, was the first ever broadcast on radio. Coolidge also made the first radio broadcast from the White House on March 4, 1925. It is estimated that 23 million Americans listened to that speech. You can hear a recording of his speech at: http://www.whitehousehistory.org/whha_classroom/images/06.html. He also recorded a speech on film, with sound, in 1924; he was the first president to do so. You can watch this film at: https://archive.org/details/coolidge_1924.


© 2016 The Critical Thinking Co.™ • www.CriticalThinking.com • 800-458-4849

Lesson 25

# Coolidge, Hoover, and Black Tuesday

## A. President Coolidge Administration

[1]Calvin Coolidge was born on the 4th of July, 1872 and lived most of his life in New England. [2]He served as governor of Massachusetts during the Great War (World War I). [3]In 1920, Warren Harding was elected president and Coolidge was elected vice president. [4]Coolidge was visiting family in Vermont on August 3, 1923, when he received word of President Harding's sudden death. [5]Coolidge famously took his oath of office for president from his father, a storekeeper and notary public, early the next morning under the light of a kerosene lamp with his hand on the family Bible.

[6]Unlike Harding, whose administration was full of scandals, President Coolidge restored a conservative morality to the executive branch. [7]His actions showed the public that he was an honest, quiet, and frugal (thrifty) man. [8]He even cooked his own meals in the White House. [9]Coolidge rarely granted interviews. [10]He became known as "Silent Cal" after a dinner party during which a young woman seated next to the president told him she had bet she could get at least three words of conversation from him. [11]Without looking up, Coolidge answered, "You lose." [12]Coolidge was not comfortable with the multitude of social changes taking place in the American culture of the 1920s, once even admitting: "I feel I no longer fit in with these times."

[13]As president, Coolidge tried to rein in what he believed was out of control federal spending and growing federal deficits. [14]During his years in office, the United States experienced the rapid economic growth which characterized the Roaring Twenties. [15]Coolidge promoted and signed the Revenue Act of 1924, which cut income tax rates. [16]He pushed Congress to raise tariffs on foreign imports to give American goods an advantage over foreign goods sold in the United States, and he also reduced the size of the military. [17]Farmers asked for help from the federal government, but Coolidge vetoed two farm bills. [18]He refused to add more regulations on the stock market or businesses. [19]He made no changes to Prohibition policy even though it seemed unenforceable and out of control. [20]Some members of Congress wanted to create a large hydro-electric project on the Tennessee River, but Coolidge refused to use federal money on the idea. [21]When the Great Mississippi Flood of 1927 caused the worst natural disaster of the first half of the 20th Century, Coolidge did not visit the affected area, nor did he provide governmental flood relief. [22]He did not believe that the federal government had a role in disaster relief. [23]Under Coolidge's economic policies, the federal budget was balanced, and the national debt reduced by 25 percent.

[24]Coolidge promoted civil rights by making a speech against Ku Klux Klan policy, saying that the rights of African Americans and Catholics "were just as sacred as any other citizen's." [25]Coolidge noted, "Race hatred, religious intolerance, and disregard of equal rights" only hurt the nation. [26]In 1924, the president signed the Indian Citizenship Act granting United States citizenship to all Native Americans while allowing them to keep their tribal lands.

[27]Coolidge agreed with his fellow Republicans that America should not join the League of Nations. [28]Also, during Coolidge's administration, his Secretary of State and the foreign minister of France crafted the Kellogg-Briand Pact of 1928. [29]This was eventually approved by Congress, resulting in the governments of more than 60 nations renouncing (giving up, putting aside) war "as an instrument of national policy." [30]Although isolationists praised the treaty, it did little practical good. [31]World War II would break out within the next decade.

President Coolidge wore a Native American headdress when he visited a tribe in South Dakota in 1927.

[32]Coolidge enjoyed tremendous popularity as the economy soared in the mid-20s. [33]Yet, when he had the chance to run for another term of office, he turned it down in typically brief Coolidge style. [34]"I do not choose to run for president in 1928," was his entire statement.

## B. President Hoover's Administration

[35]Herbert Hoover also had a humble beginning. [36]He was born in Iowa to parents who both died at a young age. [37]Young Herbert went to live with an aunt and uncle in Oregon and eventually qualified to attend Stanford University in California. [38]He had a successful career as a mining engineer and supported the Progressive Party of Theodore Roosevelt. [39]When the Great War broke out, President Wilson asked Hoover to lead the Food Administration. [40]Hoover's program was very successful at supplying food, not only to the U.S. military, but to war-torn allies as well. [41]He was nominated for a Nobel Peace Prize for his efforts. [42]Continuing those peace efforts, Hoover generously contributed money to start the Hoover Institution on War, Revolution, and Peace at the Stanford campus in 1919.

A 1928 presidential campaign poster for Herbert Hoover promised prosperity.

[43]During the 1920s, both President Harding and President Coolidge appointed Hoover to their cabinets as Secretary of Commerce. [44]In that role, Hoover is considered to be one of the most successful cabinet members in U.S. history. [45]He standardized numerous products and services —everything from radio station call-letters and frequencies to airplane flight patterns. [46]He led efforts that saw the start of the construction of Boulder Dam (now Hoover Dam) in Nevada and the St. Lawrence Seaway along the Canadian border.

[47]In 1928, when Coolidge chose not to run for another term as president, the obvious choice for Americans was Herbert Hoover. [48]The economy was booming and Hoover used that to his political advantage. [49]One campaign slogan he used was: "A chicken in every pot, two cars in every garage." [50]During one speech he predicted: "We are nearer today to the ideal of the abolition of poverty and fear from the lives of men and women than ever before in any land."

## C. Stock Market Crash

[51]Hoover easily won the 1928 presidential election. [52]However, six months into his term of office, an event known as "Black Tuesday" occurred. [53]In late October of 1929, the value of stocks at the New York Stock Exchange fell rapidly. [54]Between 1929 and 1932, stock values continued to drop until they were worth only about 20 percent of what they had been before Black Tuesday. [56]This large drop in stock values led or contributed to a nearly worldwide economic depression—known as the Great Depression—and became the worst economic period in U.S. history.

[57]After the late 1929 stock market panic (Black Tuesday), other weaknesses developed in United States and world economies. [58]Historical economists list several reasons why the economy of the 1930s fell into a deep and long lasting depression (a long period of time when business activity is weak and in decline). [59]The booming economy of the 1920s had set record after record. This led many Americans to invest more and more in the stock market. [60]Many people even borrowed money to do so, especially in early 1929. [61]People also purchased expensive items in the 1920s—cars, home appliances, radios—often using credit and piling up more debt. [62]The loss of income and large debt caused people to cut back on their spending, which deepened the recession. [63]With fewer people buying their products, businesses collapsed or slowed down production, laid employees off, and paid remaining workers smaller wages—all of which, in turn, further contributed to the economic decline. [64]The high tariffs on imports imposed by Congress and supported by Coolidge and Hoover backfired when foreign nations retaliated (returning an action like for like) by imposing high tariffs on American goods. [65]The high tariffs reduced trade between European nations, resulting in further damage to the economies of the United States and European countries.

[66]Many American farmers were dealt a crushing blow in the summer of 1929, when wheat prices dropped tremendously. [67]Low prices, followed by a multi-year drought in the mid-1930s, made life even harder for struggling farmers and crippled a key part of the economy. [68]The final—and many economists argue, the major—cause of the Great Depression was the banking crisis. [69]After the U.S. economy began to struggle, the U.S. Federal Reserve, which controls the cost of money banks borrow and then loan to businesses and consumers, did not lower the cost of borrowing for the banks. [70]This caused nearly a third of all U.S. banks to collapse, causing further economic pain and panic. [71]With fewer banks able to loan money—and loans costing more money—businesses and consumers borrowed less money, which led to even less spending. [71]This deepened and significantly lengthened the Great Depression.

[72]Hoover had been highly successful as an engineer, Food Administrator, and Secretary of Commerce. [73]However, as president, Hoover took


© 2016 The Critical Thinking Co.™ • www.CriticalThinking.com • 800-458-4849

the brunt of the blame for the failing economy after the stock market crash. [74]Hoover and the Federal Reserve were reluctant to have the nation go beyond a balanced budget to provide relief for individuals and businesses. [75]In the first months after the crash, Hoover relied mainly upon churches, charities, or states to provide relief, and he asked businesses to voluntarily halt layoffs and wage decreases. [76]As the depression deepened, Hoover, a philanthropist and Progressive, yielded to growing cries for greater government spending and support. [77]He did try some limited government-funded work projects, which were paid for by significantly raising the amount of taxes paid by the wealthy from 25 percent to 63 percent and raising taxes paid by corporations, but the economy continued to decline.

[78]Hoover initially predicted that the depression would be over by the end of 1929 and once told businessmen that "Prosperity is just around the corner." [79]However, the depression got deeper and deeper each year of his presidency. [80]Soon, one out of every four employees was out of work. [81]Banks started to close as money they had lent to consumers, before the stock market crash, was not repaid. [82]Some people who could no longer make their house payments moved to temporary shack villages they nicknamed "Hoovervilles." [83]Instead of an end to poverty, as Hoover had predicted, the country was in one of the worst poverty-stricken eras in American history. [84]Hoover faced a steep uphill battle when he ran for reelection in 1932.

"Look, it seems there wasn't any depression at all!"

**Fun Fact Feature**

Herbert Hoover was the 30th President. Look again at the lesson to find Hoover's birthplace. What do you think was unusual about his birthplace?

© 2016 The Critical Thinking Co.™ • www.CriticalThinking.com • 800-458-4849

1. When did Calvin Coolidge became president?
   a. When President Harding died in office.
   b. When Coolidge easily won the 1924 election.
   c. After Coolidge's successful job as Food Administrator in the Great War.
   d. When Herbert Hoover decided not to run for president.

   Which sentences best support the answer?

   ______ ______

2. Which of these adjectives does NOT fit the image of President Calvin Coolidge?
   a. quiet
   b. honest
   c. frugal
   d. scandalous

   Which sentences best support the answer?

   ______ ______

3. President Coolidge is remembered for:
   a. promoting civil rights for blacks, Catholics, and Native Americans.
   b. supporting federal relief for farmers.
   c. providing funds for victims of the 1927 Great Mississippi River flood.
   d. his regulation of the stock market.

   Which sentences best support the answer?

   ______ ______ ______

4. Which law, supported by President Coolidge, tried to outlaw war?
   a. Immigration Act of 1924
   b. Revenue Act of 1924
   c. Kellogg-Briand Pact of 1928
   d. Indian Citizenship Act of 1924

   Which sentences best support the answer?

   ______ ______

5. What was surprising about Coolidge's not running for reelection as president in 1928?
   a. He wanted to run but was not nominated by his political party.
   b. He decided to go into a career in radio broadcasting instead.
   c. He was popular and the economy was booming.
   d. Many scandals in his administration were revealed.

   Which sentence best supports the answer?

   ______

6. Look at the political cartoon in the lesson. Which numbered sentence in the lesson best explains the irony of the cartoon (a meaning opposite to what the characters are saying)?

   ______

7. In your words, explain the Hoover campaign slogan: "A chicken in every pot, two cars in every garage."

   ________________________________________

   ________________________________________

   ________________________________________

   ________________________________________

8. "Black Tuesday" is known as the day when:
   a. the U.S. stock market crashed.
   b. Herbert Hoover announced he would run for reelection.
   c. the first Hooverville was established.
   d. the stock market got out of the "red" (debt) and into the "black" (profit).

   Which sentences best support the answer?

   ______ ______


© 2016 The Critical Thinking Co.™ • www.CriticalThinking.com • 800-458-4849

9. Before his years as president, Herbert Hoover was considered to be:
   a. a failure who could not fix the national economy.
   b. a person with a highly successful career.
   c. an unknown politician.
   d. a scandalous member of Harding's "Ohio Gang."

   Which sentences best support the answer?

   _____ _____ _____

## Written Response Question

10. Use complete sentences to describe some of the reasons why the Great Depression occurred?

________________________________________

________________________________________

________________________________________

________________________________________

________________________________________

________________________________________

________________________________________

________________________________________

**Fun Fact Finale**

Herbert Hoover was the 30th President and the first to be born west of the Mississippi River. He was also the first, and only, president born in Iowa.

© 2016 The Critical Thinking Co.™ • www.CriticalThinking.com • 800-458-4849

# Review: Lessons 21–25
# 1920s Vocabulary

Write the letter of the definition of each vocabulary word. The number following each vocabulary word is the number of the lesson (21–25) where the word was used. All definitions are used once.

_____ 1. prohibit (21)

_____ 2. bootlegger (21)

_____ 3. speakeasy (21)

_____ 4. recession (22)

_____ 5. consumer (22)

_____ 6. accommodations (22)

_____ 7. decline (22)

_____ 8. billboard (22)

_____ 9. chaperone (23)

_____ 10. celebrity (23)

_____ 11. fad (23)

_____ 12. anti-Semitism (24)

_____ 13. quota (24)

_____ 14. literal (24)

_____ 15. evangelical (24)

_____ 16. depict (24)

_____ 17. frugal (25)

_____ 18. renounce (25)

_____ 19. retaliate (25)

_____ 20. depression (25)

a. roadside advertising

b. a long period of economic decline

c. lodging

d. limited number

e. religious prejudice against Jews

f. secret, illegal saloon or nightclub

g. thrifty

h. to forbid an activity by law

i. to describe or show

j. strict word-for-word interpretation

k. person who smuggled illegal alcoholic drinks during Prohibition

l. person who buys a product or service

m. give up, put aside

n. well-known; famous person

o. to return an action like for like

p. an adult who supervises a young person in public

q. decrease

r. short economic downturn

s. enthusiastically following Bible teachings

t. temporary conduct followed by many persons



© 2016 The Critical Thinking Co.™ • www.CriticalThinking.com • 800-458-4849

Section 5: Introduction

# The Great Depression: 1929-1939

In the first year of his presidency, Republican Herbert Hoover faced one of the worst economic crises in American history. The Great Depression set in after the crash of the stock market in 1929. The economy of America continued to slide over the next few years, with low manufacturing, low consumer sales, and high unemployment. To add to the problem, a multi-year severe drought settled over the Great Plains creating a natural disaster for farmers, called the Dust Bowl. In 1932, a presidential election year, Hoover's bid for a second term was hampered further when his administration mismanaged a protest by veterans of the Great War in the nation's capital just prior to the vote.

Franklin Delano Roosevelt (FDR) was swept into office along with a Democratic Congress in the spring of 1933. FDR, partially paralyzed from polio in mid-life, had to find ways to lead his administration despite his disability. The president put together a team he considered experts and nicknamed them his Brain Trust. FDR and his Brain Trust recommended a vast program of government agencies and work projects, called the New Deal. These agencies were designed to provide immediate relief to those suffering from the depression, bring about an economic recovery, and create reforms. This new approach of massive government spending and regulations affecting the lives of its citizens and businesses was controversial. FDR faced criticism from conservatives, who said his spending and regulation was too much, but also from a few critics from his liberal base, who said the government was still not doing enough. FDR's New Deal did not pull the country out of the depression, but it did ease the pain of the depression for enough Americans that Roosevelt was easily reelected in 1936. More New Deal programs were implemented. Franklin's wife, Eleanor, took on a large role in assisting the president.

The Great Depression had a huge impact on society and culture as well as on government and economics. Family lives and the world of entertainment would undergo vast changes.

## U.S. President

32. Franklin D. Roosevelt
1933-1945

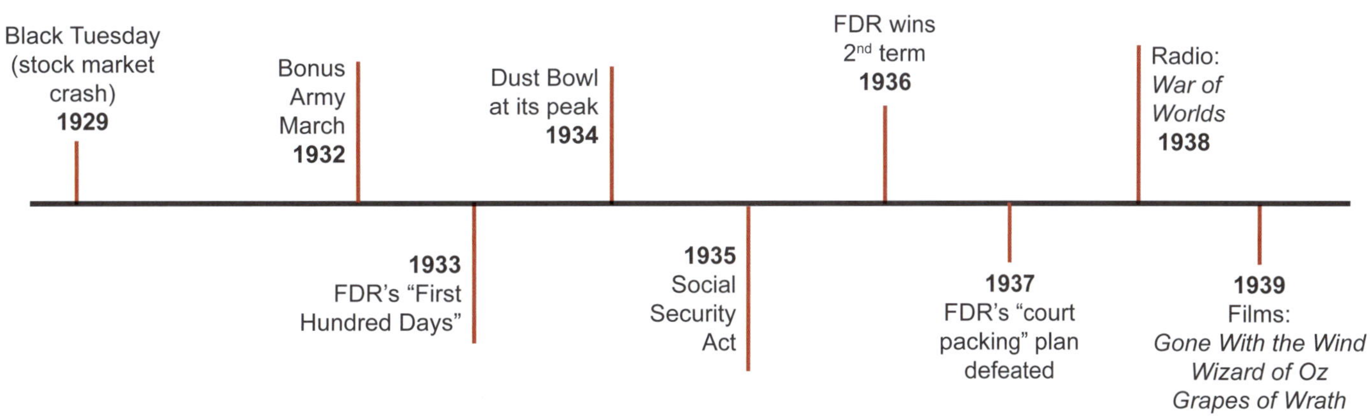


© 2016 The Critical Thinking Co.™ • www.CriticalThinking.com • 800-458-4849 

Lesson 26

# The Great Depression Begins

## A. Bonus Army March

[1]To fight the Great Depression, President Hoover marginally increased federal spending, set up the Emergency Committee for Employment to coordinate voluntary relief efforts, increased taxes on the wealthy, and increased tariffs (import taxes) on foreign goods. [2]In 1932, he convinced Congress to create the Reconstruction Finance Corporation (RFC) to make federal loans to banks and help states create some public works programs. [3]In spite of these efforts, nothing seemed to stem the tide of a worsening economy. [4]Now he faced an uphill battle as he ran for reelection in 1932. [5]In that year alone, there were 32,000 business failures and more than 2,200 bank closures. [6]Thousands of farmers in the Midwest lost their lands because they could not pay their mortgages and taxes after a long drought and low crop prices. [7]Stock values had fallen by 85 percent since 1929, and one out of every four job-seekers was unemployed.

[8]In the early 1920s, Congress had passed a law to provide Great War veterans with benefits spread out over a twenty-year period. [9]However, in 1932, many veterans who were jobless or homeless marched to Washington, D.C., to ask Congress for immediate payment of their bonuses in full. [10]Congress denied the request of the "Bonus Army Marchers." [11]Thousands of former soldiers refused to leave the city, however, and built makeshift (temporary) shelters just outside of town, planning to continue their protest. [12]President Hoover fearfully called in the army to evict (expel, remove) the Bonus Army Marchers. [13]Using tanks, bayonets, and tear gas, the military drove the veterans out of their camp and burned their shacks. [14]As a result, many Americans viewed Hoover as uncaring as well as unsuccessful.

Under orders from President Hoover, the U.S. Army forced thousands of Great War veterans out of the nation's capital during the Bonus Army March.

## B. FDR Wins the Presidency

[15]The Democratic Party put forth a candidate for the 1932 presidential election who promised bold steps by the federal government to turn around the American economy. [16]Like his famous Republican cousin, Theodore Roosevelt, Franklin Delano Roosevelt (FDR) had been born to a wealthy family, graduated from Harvard, attended Columbia Law School, and served as Assistant Secretary of the Navy. [17]Franklin had been an unsuccessful vice presidential candidate in 1920, but seemed like a young politician with a promising future. [18]Then in 1921, FDR contracted a viral infection called poliomyelitis (polio) which left both his legs paralyzed. [19]He spent the rest of the 1920s in therapy, often swimming at Warm Springs, Georgia, but was never able to walk again without braces and crutches.

[20]Franklin's wife, Eleanor Roosevelt, encouraged him to return to politics despite his disability. [21]She assisted him in 1928 when he campaigned and won the governorship of New York. [22]During the first years of the Great Depression, Governor Roosevelt created a model agency for the relief of unemployed workers in his state, ushered in new labor laws, and created an old-age pension plan.

[23]When he ran for the presidency against Hoover in 1932, Roosevelt promised "a new deal for the American people." [24]He said his fight against polio had given him compassion for "the forgotten man," and he promised "bold, persistent experimentation" on the part of the federal government to end the depression, if elected. [25]The American people responded and overwhelmingly elected him to become the next president.

[26]FDR's ideas were heavily influenced by a new theory of that era called Keynesian Economics. [27]John Maynard Keynes was a British economist who wrote that government spending—even deficit spending (spending more money than it collects in taxes)—would stimulate an economy during a depression and lower unemployment. [28]Any debts created in the process, Keynes reasoned, could be repaid after the economy recovered.

[29]When Roosevelt took the oath of office in March of 1933, the Great Depression was at its deepest. [30]On inauguration day, he told the American people: "The only thing we have to fear is, fear itself—nameless, unreasoning, unjustified terror which paralyzes needed efforts to convert


© 2016 The Critical Thinking Co.™ • www.CriticalThinking.com • 800-458-4849

retreat into advance." [31]More than a half-million letters from citizens requesting help or offering support soon arrived at the White House.

### C. "First Hundred Days"

FDR Campaign Button

[32]FDR quickly appointed a diverse cabinet and a large circle of experts from colleges and businesses to try to find creative solutions to America's economic problems. [33]Over the course of the first three months of the Roosevelt administration, three law professors from Columbia University (nicknamed the "Brain Trust"), who had advised him during his campaign, suggested dozens of ideas in an effort to stimulate the economy and ease the pain of the average American. [34]Congress, now controlled by FDR's Democratic Party majority, responded quickly to his requests. [35]To emphasize the need for immediate action, one FDR advisor said, "People don't eat in the long run, they eat every day." [36]More than a dozen key pieces of legislation were passed in FDR's so-called "First Hundred Days" in office, which was one of the busiest periods in Congressional history. [37]These new government agencies and programs became known as "The New Deal." [38]Although Herbert Hoover, his predecessor (a person coming just before), had also tried to stimulate the economy with limited federal spending, President Roosevelt, applying Keynesian economic theory, took national government spending to new heights never seen before in U.S. history.

[39]In his efforts to sell his economic program to the American public, FDR used an analogy (a story of comparison) of a man who once fell off a broken sidewalk and was injured: [40]First, medical personnel provided him with immediate care to stop the bleeding [relief]. [41]Next, the accident victim received therapy so he could walk again [recovery]. [42]Finally, measures were taken to fix the sidewalk so there wouldn't be other accident victims [reform]. [43]Under the New Deal, Roosevelt saw the national government as the medical personnel in his analogy who provided immediate care for the injured economy. [44]Roosevelt called Relief, Recovery, and Reform the "Three R's of the New Deal." [45]Legislation passed in his first hundred days fell into one of these three categories.

[46]During the early years of the Great Depression, many banks failed (went out of business when their loans were not repaid). [47]If a bank closed, it took the savings of its customers with it, leaving many of those people without their money. [48]This caused many Americans to fear banks and to withdraw their money. [49]Since banks had less money to loan, it made it harder for individuals and businesses to borrow money which, in turn, meant consumers made fewer purchases, and businesses slowed production. [50]This cycle slowed the economy even further and was at a crisis point when FDR became president in the spring of 1933.

[51]The day after taking the oath of office, FDR ordered a temporary "bank holiday"—closing all banks while federal inspectors looked over their books. [51]FDR did this to try to prevent more bank failures and restore the confidence of citizens in their local banks. [52]The move worked. [53]When government inspectors allowed "healthy banks" to reopen a few days later, the rush by citizens to withdraw their deposits slowed.

orter

Snow or rain; ...
Temp.—Max. 36; Min. 28

PRICE—THREE CENTS

BANKS OF ENTIRE NATION ARE CLOSED FOR BRIEF HOLIDAY

*Federal Government To Provide Temporary Medium of Exchange*

Washington, March 6.—(U.P.)—The nation began a four-day emergency bank holiday today with assurance from the federal government that a ...change for payrolls and other essential needs would be pro- ... Thursday for corrective

[54]Soon thereafter, FDR proposed the Federal Emergency Relief Act (FERA), funneling millions of dollars to state and local relief agencies to provide food, clothing, and shelter to the poor. [55]People who couldn't make house payments took advantage of another new relief agency, called the Home Owners Loan Corporation (HOLC), to refinance their homes and avoid eviction.

[56]Recovery legislation came in the form of the Civilian Conservation Corps (CCC), which put thousands of young men to work in conservation and public works projects. [57]The Tennessee Valley Authority (TVA) created even more jobs by building dams on the Tennessee River to provide power generation, flood control, and recreation. [58]Businesses benefited when the National Recovery Administration (NRA) provided 3.3 billion

A New Deal poster used to recruit young men for the Civilian Conservation Corps.

© 2016 The Critical Thinking Co.™ • www.CriticalThinking.com • 800-458-4849 

dollars to stimulate job growth. [59]Farmers were helped by the Agricultural Adjustment Act (AAA). [60]This law gave payments, called subsidies, to farmers of basic crops such as corn, wheat, cotton, and dairy products, if they would cut production. [61]Although this act paid farmers not to grow certain crops, the supply reduction was intended to increase demand and put money into the hands of struggling farmers.

[62]Reform laws came next. The Emergency Banking Act set up reforms to better manage failing banks. [63]Then the Federal Deposit Insurance Corporation (FDIC) provided a guarantee that savings accounts would be protected in the future. [64]The Federal Securities Act, with a Securities Exchange Commission, was created to reform stock market practices. [65]Labor department head Francis Perkins—the first woman cabinet member—ordered an end to child labor in the textile industry.

[66]The day FDR took the oath of office, he had noted: "This nation asks for action, and action now!" [67]He was true to his word and created many new government programs and record federal debt (Keynesian economic theory) to try and pull the U.S. economy out of the Great Depression and ease the suffering of the poor. [68]His programs were very popular with the American people, and slowed the decline of the economy.

Francis Perkins

**Fun Fact Feature**

President Franklin Roosevelt did something many Sunday evenings to let Americans know about his progress on the New Deal. How did millions of Americans get this information?


© 2016 The Critical Thinking Co.™ • www.CriticalThinking.com • 800-458-4849

1. List four pieces of evidence showing that the nation's economy was in very bad shape in 1932.

   a. ______________________________

   b. ______________________________

   c. ______________________________

   d. ______________________________

2. Who were the Bonus Army Marchers?
   a. landless farmers
   b. Great War veterans
   c. unemployed steel workers
   d. Democratic politicians

   Which sentence best supports the answer?

   _____

3. Franklin Roosevelt was a lot like his older cousin Theodore Roosevelt; in which of the following ways were they NOT alike?
   a. attended the same universities.
   b. had been elected governor of New York.
   c. were members of the same political party.
   d. came from wealthy backgrounds.

   Which sentences best support the answer?

   _____ _____

4. What were President Roosevelt's handpicked economic policy advisors called?
   a. Brain Trust
   b. Bonus Army
   c. New Deal
   d. Three R's

   Which sentence best supports the answer?

   _____

5. Why did Franklin Roosevelt often visit Warm Springs, Georgia, during the 1920s?
   a. therapy for his polio
   b. to campaign for political office
   c. to create the New Deal
   d. to become "the forgotten man"

   Which sentence best supports the answer?

   _____

6. In his first inaugural address as president, what did Roosevelt say that Americans should fear?

   ______________________________

7. Who convinced Franklin Roosevelt to return to politics after suffering his paralyzing polio attack and helped him campaign for office?
   a. Herbert Hoover
   b. Theodore Roosevelt
   c. Francis Perkins
   d. Eleanor Roosevelt

   Which sentence best supports the answer?

   _____

8. What was the first action that Franklin Roosevelt took after becoming president in 1933?
   a. reformed the stock market
   b. ordered temporary closure of all U.S. banks
   c. ordered payment of a bonus to U.S. war veterans
   d. created the Agricultural Adjustment Act to help farmers.

   Which sentence best supports the answer?

   _____

9. What was the busiest legislative period in American history called?
   a. Federal Emergency Relief Act
   b. Bank Holiday
   c. First Hundred Days
   d. Bonus Army March

   Which sentence best supports the answer?

   _____

© 2016 The Critical Thinking Co.™ • www.CriticalThinking.com • 800-458-4849

## Written Response Question

10. Use complete sentences to describe the "Three R's" of Roosevelt's New Deal program and give one example of each.

________________________________________

________________________________________

________________________________________

________________________________________

________________________________________

________________________________________

________________________________________

________________________________________

### Fun Fact Finale

President Franklin Roosevelt did something many Sunday evenings to inform Americans about progress for the New Deal. About 90 percent of Americans had radios in 1933 and FDR gave regular radio speeches that became known as "Fireside Chats."

He began many of the chats with the greeting "My friends," and referred to himself as "I" and the American people as "you," as if addressing his listeners directly and personally. Following each broadcast, the national anthem was played. The radio broadcasts greatly increased FDR's popularity and inspired confidence in Americans that the Great Depression (and later, World War II) could be successfully conquered.

 © 2016 The Critical Thinking Co.™ • www.CriticalThinking.com • 800-458-4849

Lesson 27

# New Deal Critics and the Dust Bowl

## A. Critics on the Right

[1]Franklin Roosevelt called himself a pragmatist (someone who is practical). [2]As he continued to apply Keynesian economic principles to try to end the depression, he told the public he was willing to listen to any advisor who could suggest practical, flexible, and workable solutions. [3]During his campaign, FDR had once said: "The country needs … bold, persistent experimentation. [4]It is common sense to take a method and try it. [5]If it fails, admit it frankly and try another. [6]But above all, try something." [7]Programs and agencies continued to unfold in his administration after the First Hundred Days. [8]In the fall of 1933, the Civil Works Administration (CWA) was unveiled as a plan to provide relief to the unemployed during the depth of the Great Depression. [9]Paid with federal funds, several million workers built parks, schools, athletic facilities, roads, airports, and other facilities across America. [10]The temporary CWA agency was soon replaced with a more permanent, and expanded, work program called the Works Progress Administration (WPA). [11]In addition to building bridges, water systems, and other public projects, the WPA had an arts program that employed thousands of writers, musicians, actors, photographers, and artists. [12]The Rural Electrification Administration (REA) gave low cost loans to farm cooperatives to bring electric power to rural communities.

A WPA Road Project in North Carolina in the 1930s.

[13]While FDR called himself a pragmatist, conservative critics labeled him a socialist. [14]Socialism is a way of organizing a society in which businesses are owned and controlled by the government rather than by individual people. [16]Many Republicans and even some conservative Democrats were critical of FDR's higher taxes, government regulations, and the growing national debt. [17] Regardless of their criticism, many of FDR's reforms were very popular with the American people.

[18]Conservative critics in particular were alarmed with the large increase in the size and cost of the federal government. [19]There had been 600,000 federal employees the last year of Hoover's administration. [20]By the mid-1930s there were more than one million. [21]The creation of so many governmental agencies seemed to be replacing services that families, churches, and other social organizations had provided prior to the 1930s. [22]Most historians agree that the foundations of a welfare state, where the government takes on much of the responsibility of providing for the health and financial stability of its citizens, was established by the New Deal. [23]And those agencies cost more money than the government took in—a situation called deficit spending.

[24]Regardless of their criticism, FDR and his Democratic Party, who controlled Congress, remained steadfast in their Keynesian-based economic plan and continued FDR's government spending and regulation of businesses, labor, and banking. [25]FDR's advisors labeled this government deficit spending "pump priming." [26]In order to operate a hand pump, sometimes fluids need to be introduced to seal the pump to get it started. [27]FDR and his supporters claimed that an injection of government dollars was necessary to get the economy going again. [28]Once the economy recovered, Keynesian theory called for repayment of the debt and a balanced budget. [29]That was the theory, but in reality, while the economy improved slightly under the New Deal, it never truly recovered until the start of World War II. [30]The deficits from the New Deal were never repaid and the national debt continued to grow.

[31]Some business leaders, fearful of over-regulation, formed an anti-New Deal organization called the Liberty League in united protest in 1934. [32]Critics also felt that much of the employment created by the government were "make-work" jobs —jobs that cost more to complete than their value while providing little practical training or experience to the employee. [33]The initials of the WPA, for

© 2016 The Critical Thinking Co.™ • www.CriticalThinking.com • 800-458-4849

example, were mocked (jokingly attacked) as "We Poke Along," because projects seemed to take so long to complete with workers having little incentive to finish a project quickly. [34]Dozens and dozens of new governmental agencies—all with acronyms (a set of initials for an organization)—were springing up to implement (put into action) and regulate the New Deal. [35]Those in opposition to Roosevelt nicknamed the myriad (great number) of agencies "alphabet soup."

### B. Critics on the Left

[36] Although most of FDR's critics were conservatives, a few of FDR's fellow liberal Democrats were also critical of the New Deal, claiming it did not go far enough to provide for the welfare of citizens. [37]Many of these critics were initially supporters of the New Deal, such as Father Charles Coughlin, a priest who became a popular radio announcer with 40 million weekly listeners. [38]Coughlin later called on the government to run all the banks and spend more money on the poor. [39]A broke, retired California doctor named Francis Townsend wanted the government to do more for the elderly. [40]His "Townsend Plan" called for the federal government to pay all retired citizens 200 dollars a month which, he said, would encourage more people to retire early, thus opening up jobs for the unemployed while also stimulating spending by the elderly. [41]Another supporter of FDR in his 1932 election, Senator Huey Long, a Democrat from Louisiana, dropped his support for FDR in 1933 and pushed a plan he called "Share Our Wealth." [42]He wanted a 100 percent tax on all income more than one million dollars and a distribution of those funds, with a guaranteed annual income, to all working class families. [43]Long made a serious bid for the presidency, but was assassinated in 1935. [44]FDR would propose a 100 percent tax on incomes of more than 25,000 dollars in 1942 during World War II, but rejected Long's idea in 1933.

Huey Long

[45]In spite of FDR's huge popularity with labor unions, the Communist Party in America clamored for Roosevelt to do more. [46]The party pointed out that crop reductions in the Agricultural Adjustment Act severely hurt tenant farmers, sharecroppers, and migrant laborers. [47]The Communist party grew as dissatisfaction with the economy mounted. [48]Many Americans were so desperate for work that they actually left the country to live in the communist Soviet Union. [49]In fact, the decade of the 1930s is the only one in American history in which more people left the United States than immigrated to it.

[50]The Supreme Court overturned some New Deal programs, most notably the National Recovery Act. [51]The court ruled the NRA to be unconstitutional because it gave power to the executive branch that actually belonged to the legislative branch. [52]It also said the program went beyond the limits of the federal government to regulate commerce.

### C. Dust Bowl

[53]A strong drought, lasting eight years in some areas of the country, along with deep plowing of topsoil with the new gasoline-powered tractors and strong seasonal plains winds, created huge dust storms of dry soil in the center of the country in the 1930s. [54]As the drought continued year after year, the Great Plains, from North Dakota through Texas, became known as the Dust Bowl. [55]When, in 1934, a two-mile high cloud of soil actually blew over the nation's capital in the District of Columbia, hundreds of miles to the east, one Congressman commented: "There goes Oklahoma." [56]A school teacher wrote this about living in the Dust Bowl:

> [57]The air is just full of dirt. It sifts into everything. [58]After we wash the dishes and put them away, so much dust sifts into the cupboard we must wash them again before the next meal. [59]Clothes in the closets are covered with dust... The dust tortures animals... and ruins machinery. [60]The crops are long since ruined.

[61]Over 3.5 million people left the Dust Bowl area—about one-fourth of the residents—in one of the largest migrations in American history. [62]Many farmers packed up and moved to cities, leaving farm life forever, while others looked to hire out as laborers on farms along the Pacific Coast. [63]In an effort to use the federal government to help farmers

 © 2016 The Critical Thinking Co.™ • www.CriticalThinking.com • 800-458-4849

during the drought, FDR's administration created New Deal programs to plant vegetation to stabilize (maintain, hold firm) the soil and educate farmers on how to conserve water resources.

64Although these programs had some benefit, the area did not recover until the Great Plains finally received normal rainfall in the fall of 1939.

**Fun Fact Feature**

Coughing spasms, shortness of breath, asthma, bronchitis, and pneumonia were a few of the symptoms caused by a 1930s event called the "Brown Plague." Hundreds were killed—especially infants, children and the elderly. Sometimes static electricity in the air would generate a spark and knock people to the ground if they shook hands. What caused these issues?

© 2016 The Critical Thinking Co.™ • www.CriticalThinking.com • 800-458-4849

1. What did critics label as "alphabet soup"?
   a. the Dust Bowl
   b. the Communist Party
   c. the Great Plains
   d. New Deal agencies

   Which sentence best supports the answer?

   ______

2. True or False? New Deal programs ceased to be created after the "First Hundred Days."

   ______________

   Which sentence best supports the answer?

   ______

3. What did the conservatives who thought the New Deal added too much federal regulation and debt call President Roosevelt?
   a. a pragmatist
   b. a capitalist
   c. a socialist
   d. a Republican

   Which sentence best supports the answer?

   ______

4. The New Deal practiced deficit spending. What did FDR and the New Dealers call it?
   a. pump priming
   b. alphabet soup
   c. communism
   d. "Share Our Wealth" plan

   Which sentence best supports the answer?

   ______

5. Who called for the federal government to take over and run all the banks?
   a. John Steinbeck
   b. Francis Townsend
   c. Huey Long
   d. Father Charles Coughlin

   Which sentence best supports the answer?

   ______

6. Look at this political cartoon. Who is the patient? Who is the doctor? What would some people call all the labeled medicine?

   a. patient __________________________

   b. doctor __________________________

   c. medicines __________________________

7. What were the series of droughts on the Great Plains in the 1930s called?
   a. Dust Bowl
   b. Great Migration
   c. Townsend Plan
   d. Liberty League

   Which sentence best supports the answer?

   ______

8. Democratic senator Huey Long of Louisiana supported a plan called "Share Our Wealth." This plan called for:
   a. the public to pool their money
   b. churches to care for the poor
   c. taxing the wealthy and distributing those funds
   d. paying retired citizens 200 dollars a month

   Which sentence best supports the answer?

   ______



© 2016 The Critical Thinking Co.™ • www.CriticalThinking.com • 800-458-4849

9. The Great Depression was the only time in U.S. history when more people:
   a. moved to the Great Plains than left the region.
   b. left the country than immigrated to it.
   c. become Republicans than Democrats.
   d. quit jobs in the federal government than took jobs with it.

   Which sentence best supports the answer?

   ______

## Written Response Question

10. Use complete sentences to describe at least three reasons why some people criticized the New Deal of the 1930s.

______________________________________________

______________________________________________

______________________________________________

______________________________________________

______________________________________________

______________________________________________

______________________________________________

______________________________________________

**Fun Fact Finale**

The dust storms of the Dust Bowl, sometimes called the "Brown Plague," caused coughing spasms, shortness of breath, asthma, bronchitis, and pneumonia. Hundreds were killed—especially infants, children, and the elderly. Sometimes a spark could knock people to the ground if they shook hands with one another because of the static electricity in the air from the dust storms.

Lesson 28

# Society and Culture in the 1930s

## A. Depression Era Demography

[1]Demography is the science of studying the vital statistics of a population. [2]In the era of the Great Depression, demographers noted many changes in the characteristics of Americans. [3]Beer, wine, and liquor were available when Prohibition ended with the passage of the 21st Amendment in December of 1933. [4]That fact and the despair of the poor economy led to an increase in alcoholism. [5]Crime and suicide rates also grew.

[6]Young Americans delayed getting married because of their concern about their ability to support a family. [7]As a result, marriage rates declined, and the number of children born fell by 20 percent from 1929 through 1935. [8]For those couples who did marry, the birth rate also declined. [9]More couples were learning about birth control and having fewer children because of concerns about the added expense of unexpected pregnancies. [10]The low birth rate, coupled with low numbers of immigrants, created the only time in American history when the U.S. population actually dropped. [11]Divorces became rarer as couples in troubled marriages avoided legal fees and the effort to support two separate households. [12]However, many husbands—some demographers say 1.5 million—simply abandoned their wives by walking out when they could not provide an income for their families. [13]Traditionally, married women had rarely sought employment outside their home. [14]However, in the desperation of the Great Depression, many wives found jobs to help support their families.

One of the most famous images from the 1930s was this photograph taken by Dorothea Lange, showing the despair of Mrs. Florence Thompson and her children.

[15]Since job prospects were so dim, many young males stayed in public schools longer than they had previously. [16]This increased the size of many American high schools. [17]However, fewer students could afford a college education. [18]For most of the 1930s, the population at American universities shrank. [19]Perhaps two million men and women started "riding the rails." [20]They became hoboes—illegally hopping on a freight train in search of work and begging for food along the way.

## B. 1930s Entertainment

[21]Americans sought ways to escape the hard times of the Great Depression in a number of ways. [22]Radio comedians such as Jack Benny, Bob Hope, and George Burns became popular as depressed Americans looked for a bit of humor. [23]Even as some families sold their possessions to make ends meet, they held on to their radios to hear free news, music, drama, and FDR's Fireside Chats—used by the president to promote his policies.

[24]One radio broadcast that became famous was a fictional story called *War of the Worlds*, aired on Halloween night in 1938. [25]Directed by Orson Welles, the drama simulated a realistic hour-long news broadcast about aliens from Mars who had landed on Earth and were battling authorities. [26]Some listeners who tuned in at mid-broadcast did not understand that they were hearing a fictional drama.

[27]The introduction of color and animation to movies in the 1930s, along with the improvement of sound, enabled the film industry to thrive, despite the Great Depression. [28]About half of all Americans went to the theaters at least once a week by the late 1930s. [29]Ticket prices were low, and movies provided a cheap source of entertainment. [30]Double-features—two movies back-to-back for the price of one—drew large audiences after they were introduced in 1931. [31]With the increased use of the automobile, drive-in theaters (an outdoor movie screen viewed by people in automobiles) became popular as early as 1933.

The comedy *Modern Times*, which debuted in 1936, showed a common man who struggled to survive.

[32]Some movies tried to show the impact of the Great Depression on American lives. [33]One such movie was John Steinbeck's *Grapes of Wrath*—a


© 2016 The Critical Thinking Co.™ • www.CriticalThinking.com • 800-458-4849

fictional work that depicted (showed) the plight of an Oklahoma farm family forced from their farm during the Dust Bowl (severe dust storms that damaged ecology and agriculture during the 1930s). [34]Steinbeck said the story was written to shame the greedy people he blamed for the Great Depression—a view not shared by economists. [35]Other movies of the era showed lawmen who battled gangsters, politicians who fought for the average citizen, striking coal miners, and liberated women. [36]After several scandals in the movie industry in the 1920s and 1930s, the movie industry's reputation was tarnished (damaged) in the public eye. [37]In an effort to improve its reputation with the public and fend off a growing number of state laws governing films, the industry attempted to reform itself by hiring a conservative politician to regulate it. [38]By 1934, Hollywood producers developed their own codes, with stricter rules about what could not be spoken or shown in the movies.

[39]Musicals, on the other hand, provided dancing, music, and light-hearted fun. [40]Comedies by the Marx brothers and Charlie Chaplin kept Americans laughing. [41]Shirley Temple became a major child movie star. [42]The giant ape, King Kong, made his film appearance in 1933. [43]In 1937, Walt Disney Studios became the king of animated films when it produced a full-length cartoon, *Snow White and the Seven Dwarfs*.

[44]Two films shown in 1939 made movie history. [45]The children's fantasy *Wizard of Oz* is still considered to be one of America's best known films and an important part of the country's culture. [46]It was also one of the first movies to use color, as was *Gone With the Wind*, a Civil War-era romance that won ten Academy Awards and still holds the record as the most successful box-office film of all time.

[47]The golden age of comic books started with the publication of the first *Superman* series in 1938. [48]Within the next three years, comic book heroes such as Batman, Wonder Woman, the Green Lantern, and Aquaman also became extremely popular.

A football game in 1930 tried to raise money to help unemployed New Yorkers.

[49]Athletics also provided an inexpensive form of entertainment. [50]In 1932, the Winter Olympics came to Lake Placid, New York, and the Summer Olympics were held in Los Angeles, California. [50]Fans still attended professional sports, but in fewer numbers. [51]Baseball parks developed "cheap seats" beyond the outfield for low-income families to watch players such as Babe Ruth and Lou Gehrig. [52]In 1935, night games were started in Cincinnati, Ohio, allowing workers to see games after their day shift. [53]The National Football League (NFL) made a rule change—allowing the forward pass—in order to make the game more exciting on offense, to attract more fans. [54]Although the National Basketball Association (NBA) would not get started until the 1940s, the Harlem Globetrotters, a traveling basketball team/comedy act, toured the country to large audiences. [55]College basketball started its first national championship tournament in 1937 and soon grew in popularity. [56]Despite the weak economy, horse racing experienced a revival in the 1930s when legalized betting on races was allowed and visitors to the track streamed (moved continuously) in for what some hoped was a potential poverty-ending payoff. [57]The racehorse Seabiscuit became extremely popular. [58]He was an underdog (someone expected to lose) who became a champion and a symbol of hope to many Americans during the depression.

### Fun Fact Feature

Soap and detergent companies began to advertise on short, fifteen-minute radio domestic dramas in the 1930s. Housewives, in particular, became a regular audience, temporarily escaping their own difficulties. What was the nickname given to these shows?

1. Which of the following statistics increased during the Great Depression era?
   a. marriage rates
   b. divorce rates
   c. birth rates
   d. crime rates

   Which sentence best supports the answer?
   _____

2. Who were the two million people "riding the rails" in the 1930s?
   a. Hoboes looking for work and a handout.
   b. Military troops headed for war training.
   c. Professional sports teams traveling to different towns in America.
   d. Sports fans going to baseball games.

   Which sentences best support the answer?
   _____ _____

3. Which of the following statistics decreased during the Great Depression era?
   a. suicide rates
   b. college attendance
   c. alcoholism
   d. fathers abandoning their families

   Which sentence best supports the answer?
   _____

4. What was the name of the fictional 1938 Halloween radio drama about aliens from outer space that frightened some Americans?
   a. *War of the Worlds*
   b. *Gone With the Wind*
   c. *Modern Times*
   d. *King Kong*

   Which sentences best support the answer?
   _____ _____

5. Despite the poor economy, what was one thing most Americans had in their homes during the 1930s to provide entertainment?

   ______________________________

6. What is something that professional baseball teams started to do in the 1930s to increase fan attendance?
   a. make major rule changes
   b. increase seating prices
   c. introduce night baseball
   d. allowed betting on games

   Which sentence best supports the answer?
   _____

7. What did Los Angeles, California, and Lake Placid, New York, host in 1932.
   a. the first world's fair held in the United States
   b. the first games of the National Basketball Association (NBA)
   c. the Olympic Games
   d. the Academy Awards

   Which sentence best supports the answer?
   _____

8. In the 1930s, who were George Burns, Bob Hope, and Jack Benny?
   a. comic book characters
   b. television hosts
   c. sports stars
   d. radio comedians

   Which sentence best supports the answer?
   _____

9. Seabiscuit was the star attraction who helped revive the:
   a. movie industry.
   b. sport of horseracing.
   c. radio industry.
   d. era of comic book heroes.

   Which sentences best support the answer?
   _____ _____

 © 2016 The Critical Thinking Co.™ • www.CriticalThinking.com • 800-458-4849

## Written Response Question

10. Use complete sentences to describe at least five things that allowed the movie industry to thrive during the Great Depression.

### Fun Fact Finale

Soap and detergent companies began to advertise on short, fifteen-minute radio domestic dramas in the 1930s. Housewives, in particular, became a regular audience, temporarily escaping their own difficulties. Known as "soap operas," they continued even as radio programing declined and television audiences increased in the 1950s and beyond.

© 2016 The Critical Thinking Co.™ • www.CriticalThinking.com • 800-458-4849

Lesson 29

# FDR's Second New Deal

## A. Second New Deal

[1]After the initial rush of New Deal programs in the first years of FDR's presidency, the U.S. economy experienced some improvement. [2]Unemployment had dropped from 23 percent to 17 percent but was nowhere near the 4-5 percent unemployment levels prior to the stock market crash of 1929. [3]In an effort to achieve the economic recovery he had promised the public, FDR continued the policy of more government spending programs in spite of the growing federal deficits. [4]When FDR first entered office, the U.S. national debt was 16 billion dollars. [5]By the end of FDR's first term, his spending programs had increased the U.S. national debt to 28 billion dollars.

[6]The growing deficits and continuing economic struggles created critics. [7]FDR's critics on the left were fellow liberal Democrats—former New Deal supporters—who wanted government seizure of big businesses and banks, government guaranteed incomes, and the seizure of income greater than a million dollars. [8]FDR's conservative critics were conservative Republicans and Democrats who thought his deficit spending was irresponsible because they believed large deficits, increased taxes, and excessive government regulations prevented economic recovery.

[9]In response to these critics, FDR, with the help of his fellow Democrats in Congress who controlled both houses, passed major acts and reforms sometimes called the Second New Deal. [10]Many historians believe the legislation passed in the second New Deal was influenced by FDR's liberal critics. [11]The 1935 Revenue Act increased taxes on the wealthiest citizens' income from 63 percent to 79 percent. [12]The Social Security Act (1935) collected taxes from workers to provide unemployment insurance and to help fund benefits to retired workers. [13]The Farm Security Administration (1935) aided small farmers and tenant farmers. [14]The National Youth Administration (1935) provided job training and part-time jobs to high school and college students. [15]The Fair Labor Standards Act (1938) established the first minimum wage at 25 cents an hour, banned child labor in dangerous professions, and established a 44 hour work week for many businesses.

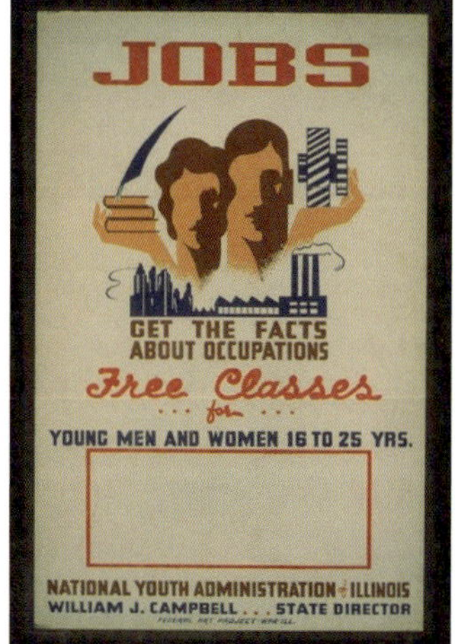

An NYA Poster

## B. Second Term

[16]U.S. citizens ignored the growing national debt and embraced the government benefits they received from the Second New Deal. [17]They reelected Franklin Roosevelt to his second term as president in 1936. [18]Roosevelt won by the largest margin since 1820. [19]His opponent, Alfred Landon, didn't even win the vote of his home state of Kansas.

[20]The election of 1936 brought a new coalition (an alliance, union, or combination) to the Democratic Party. [21]Since the Civil War, Democrats had usually won the votes of white Southerners, immigrants, Catholics, and Jews in the cities. [22]Urban minority groups still voted Democratic, but now black Americans, who earlier had supported the party of Abraham Lincoln, switched to the Democratic Party in large numbers. [23]FDR's policies had improved their economic status, and FDR had appointed more than one hundred blacks to important, high-level government positions. [24]One appointment was a black woman, Mary McLeod Bethune, to head the National Youth Administration. [25]FDR relied on her and other black leaders—nicknamed Roosevelt's "black cabinet"—for advice on racial issues.

[26]Democrats also won the vote of many women. [27]FDR had appointed the first woman—Francis Perkins—to a presidential cabinet, the first female ambassador (a diplomat sent to another country to represent his/her nation), and a number of female lower court justices. [28]Also, his wife, Eleanor, was extremely popular and active, and the first-ever First Lady to hold her own press conferences. [29]To provide equal time to women—who were traditionally barred from presidential press conferences—Eleanor allowed only female reporters to attend.

[30]FDR's New Deal programs encountered both legal and economic setbacks. [31]The legal setback occurred when the U.S. Supreme Court ruled that several programs, such as the National Recovery Act and the Agricultural Adjustment Act, were unconstitutional. [32]At the start of his second term, Roosevelt was concerned that other key pieces



© 2016 The Critical Thinking Co.™ • www.CriticalThinking.com • 800-458-4849

of his relief, recovery, and reform programs would be cancelled. [33]He asked Congress to pass a law allowing him to appoint additional Supreme Court justices for each current justice more than 70 years old. [34]This would ease the heavy workload of the aging justices, FDR declared. [35]The public, along with Congressional Republicans and Democrats alike, saw the request for its true political motives—the opportunity for the president to appoint more justices in an effort to control the court. [36]Critics labeled FDR's plan as "court packing," and the law was never passed. [37]The Supreme Court remained with nine justices but over the next few years, four justices retired, and Roosevelt was able to replace them with justices who would rule that his policies were constitutional.

FDR wanted the Supreme Court to go along with his New Deal programs, as Congress had done.

[38]An economic setback began the first year of Roosevelt's second term in 1937. [39]Economists disagree on the cause of that recession. [40]Some blame FDR's cutbacks in some of his New Deal relief programs, some blame additional taxes put on businesses, and others point to the cost of borrowing money. [41]Regardless of the cause, the U.S. economy shrunk again, and unemployment rose to 20 percent. [42]In contrast to a worsening U.S. economy, FDR's conservative critics pointed out that most European countries that had been devastated during the Great Depression were experiencing a quicker recovery without deep deficit spending and higher taxes. [43]In 1938, the average European unemployment was 12 percent, which was significantly lower than U.S. unemployment. [44]The Second World War (World War II), which began in Europe in 1939, further added to the U.S. debt as the federal government began spending money to mobilize for war. [45]However, the war effort did improve U.S. unemployment numbers when many young men entered the military and stopped looking for jobs.

### C. The Politics of Polio

[46]By the end of the 1930s, Franklin Roosevelt had been in office for nearly eight years. [47]He had appeared before millions of Americans in person and in newsreels (short news films shown before the main feature in movie theaters), and millions had listened to his fireside chats. [48]During all this time, FDR still lived with the paralyzing effects of his polio. [49]He was forced to move about in a wheelchair, use a cane as a crutch when slowly walking with long leg braces, or steady himself on the arms of a strong man when he stood. [50]He had to be pulled to a standing position and lifted in and out of cars and up and down stairways. Yet very few Americans thought, or even realized, that their president was disabled. [51]Orson Welles, the director who had deceived radio listeners with his War of the World's broadcast, once visited FDR. [52]President Roosevelt remarked on that occasion, "Orson, you and I are the two best actors in America!" [53]FDR felt it was important for Americans to see their president as strong, healthy, and optimistic (having a favorable, hopeful view of conditions) during the troubling times of the Great Depression. [54]As a result, the president set up deliberate deceptions designed to make him appear to be fully able-bodied to the public.

[55]The Secret Service had to engage in careful planning prior to every trip Roosevelt made outside the White House. [56]They lifted the president out of his wheelchair or car seat at the back entrances of buildings, out of public view. [57]Ramps were installed where needed. [58]The Secret Service even practiced gripping FDR by his elbows to lift him up a few inches in a standing position as he "moved" in a crowd. [58]Lecterns were bolted to the floor so FDR would have a stable base to grip during speeches. [59]Every chair for the president needed armrests. [60]Sometimes, if he needed to use a cane in public, other politicians would use a cane as well, so that FDR would not appear as a unique person on stage.

FDR, 4th from the left, used several methods to disguise his paralysis from polio.

[61]FDR always wore dark pants and socks with his black leg braces so that they would be more concealed. [62]When he needed to tour a New Deal project—a dam site, CCC camp, or factory yard for example—he did so sitting down in the back seat of an open touring car. [63]Occasionally Roosevelt even drove a car himself, which was an auto that had been specially outfitted with hand controls for the accelerator and brake.

[64]Most importantly, the White House press corps never reported on his polio. [65]In the 1930s, the private lives of public officials were still considered to be private. [66]Roosevelt had an unspoken agreement with the press that he would provide at least two press conferences a week, with photo opportunities once he was seated, in exchange for the press not reporting on his paralysis. [67]The agreement held. [68]During Roosevelt's entire presidency, there was never a story written about his disability. [69]Even though FDR used a wheelchair after age 39 for the rest of his life, there are only two known photographs of him in it, and both of those photos were taken by his family members.

[70]Roosevelt's wife, Eleanor, described herself as the "eyes, ears, and legs" of the president. [71]She traveled all over the country to inspect New Deal projects and the living conditions of Americans and reported her observations to FDR upon her return to Washington, D.C. [72]She wrote a daily newspaper column called "My Day," starting in 1935, and relayed important information to FDR from the hundreds of letters she received daily at the White House. [73]Regarding her husband's polio, Eleanor once wrote: "Franklin's illness proved a blessing in disguise; for it gave him strength and courage he had not had before. [74]He had to think out the fundamentals of living and learn the greatest of all lessons—infinite patience and never-ending persistence."

Eleanor Roosevelt

**Fun Fact Feature**

Since 1946, Franklin Roosevelt's image has been placed on a U.S. coin. Which coin bears FDR's image, and why was that coin chosen for it?

 © 2016 The Critical Thinking Co.™ • www.CriticalThinking.com • 800-458-4849

1. Which political party controlled Congress during FDR's administration?

   ______________________________

   Which sentence best supports the answer?

   _____

2. What law, passed during FDR's second term, established a minimum wage and maximum work hours?
   a. Farm Security Administration
   b. Social Security
   c. Revenue Act of 1935
   d. Fair Labor Standards Act

   Which sentence best supports the answer?

   _____

3. What two pieces of evidence in this lesson showed that FDR won the 1936 presidential election in a landslide?

   a. ______________________________

   ______________________________

   b. ______________________________

   ______________________________

4. Which of the following groups switched to the Democratic Party in the 1936 election?
   a. women
   b. blacks
   c. wealthy class
   d. urban minorities

   Which sentence best supports the answer?

   _____

5. Who was Mary McLeod Bethune?
   a. the first female presidential cabinet member
   b. the first female U.S. ambassador
   c. the first female Supreme Court justice
   d. a member of Roosevelt's black cabinet

   Which sentences best support the answer?

   _____ _____

6. FDR once compared himself with Orson Welles as two of the:
   a. most important law-makers in the United States.
   b. country's best actors.
   c. greatest military leaders in America.
   d. nation's best magicians.

   Which sentence best supports the answer?

   _____

7. What was the primary reason President Roosevelt took measures to hide his disabilities from polio?
   a. He wanted to win reelection in 1936.
   b. He was embarrassed by it.
   c. The press continually wanted to write stories about it.
   d. He felt it was important for Americans to see their president as strong and healthy.

   Which sentence best supports the answer?

   _____

8. Explain why FDR's critics called his idea to appoint extra Supreme Court justices a "court packing plan."

   ______________________________

   ______________________________

   ______________________________

   ______________________________

9. Who probably took this photograph of President Roosevelt?
   a. a Roosevelt family member
   b. newspaper photographers
   c. a television crew
   d. the Secret Service

   Which sentence best supports the answer?

   ______

## Written Response Question

10. Use complete sentences to describe why Eleanor Roosevelt is often considered to be one of the most active First Ladies in U.S. history.

________________________________________

________________________________________

________________________________________

________________________________________

________________________________________

________________________________________

________________________________________

________________________________________

### Fun Fact Finale

After Franklin Roosevelt's death in 1945, his image was placed on the U.S. dime. It was placed there partly because of his role in founding the March of Dimes—a fundraising effort to find a cure for polio. Polio vaccines were finally developed by the 1950s.

© 2016 The Critical Thinking Co.™ • www.CriticalThinking.com • 800-458-4849

# Review: Lessons 26-29
# 1930s Vocabulary

Write the letter of the definition of each vocabulary word. The number following each vocabulary word is the number of the lesson (26-29) where the word was used. All definitions are used once.

_____ 1. makeshift (26)

_____ 2. evict (26)

_____ 3. analogy (26)

_____ 4. subsidy (26)

_____ 5. pragmatist (27)

_____ 6. make-work jobs (27)

_____ 7. mock (27)

_____ 8. acronyms (27)

_____ 9. myriad (27)

_____ 10. deficit (27)

_____ 11. stabilize (27)

_____ 12. demography (28)

_____ 13. hobo (28)

_____ 14. double-feature (28)

_____ 15. censor (28)

_____ 16. underdog (28)

_____ 17. coalition (29)

_____ 18. ambassador (29)

_____ 19. newsreel (29)

_____ 20. optimist (29)

a. to maintain, hold firm

b. person who is practical, flexible, and believes in workable solutions

c. short news film shown before a movie

d. two movies back-to-back for the price of one

e. someone expected to lose

f. an alliance, union, or combination

g. when a sum of money falls short of the required amount

h. to jokingly attack

i. to delete parts of media on moral ground

j. diplomat sent to another country to represent his/her nation

k. temporary

l. story of comparison

m. person with a favorable, hopeful view

n. to expel, remove

o. set of initials for an organization

p. money paid by the government for support

q. employment that cost more to complete than their value while providing little practical training

r. great number

s. the science of studying the vital statistics of a population

t. person who has no home, a tramp

© 2016 The Critical Thinking Co.™ • www.CriticalThinking.com • 800-458-4849

# Bonus Activity
# New Deal Cartoons

Answer the questions about the symbols and the message of each of the political cartoons below. These cartoons are related to topics discussed in lessons 26 through 29.

1. **Symbols**
a. Who is the person dressed as a magician?

_______________________________________________

b. What does the rabbit represent?

_______________________________________________

**Message**
c. Why does the cartoonist have the caption "Old Reliable"?

_______________________________________________

_______________________________________________

2. **Symbols**
a. FDR is in the lead. Who does the other man in the cartoon represent?

_______________________________________________

b. What is in the 2nd man's left arm?

_______________________________________________

**Message**
c. Look carefully at the 2nd man's face and the words he is speaking. What is the message of the cartoonist?

_______________________________________________

_______________________________________________

 © 2016 The Critical Thinking Co.™ • www.CriticalThinking.com • 800-458-4849

3. **Symbols**

a. Who is the man at the fence?

_______________________________________

b. What might the donkey represent?

_______________________________________

**Message**

c. What is the New Deal event being shown here?

_______________________________________

d. Look at the man's face and what he is saying. What is the message of the cartoonist?

_______________________________________

_______________________________________

4. **Symbols**

a. Who is the man dealing the cards?

_______________________________________

b. What do all the cards represent on the table?

_______________________________________

**Message**

c. The title of this cartoon is "New Deal Lexicon." A lexicon is "a dictionary of the vocabulary of the times." Can you recall (lesson 26) what critics called the New Deal lexicon?

_______________________________________

© 2016 The Critical Thinking Co.™ • www.CriticalThinking.com • 800-458-4849

5. **Symbols**
a. Who is the smiling man on the right?

______________________________

b. Who are the old couple in the buggy?

______________________________

______________________________

c. Compare the mode of transportation on the left with the poster on the right.

______________________________

______________________________

**Message**
d. What does this cartoon imply about the New Deal?

______________________________

______________________________

6. Notice how FDR is drawn in cartoons 1, 2, 3, and 5. How does this relate to the "Politics of Polio" section of Lesson 29?

______________________________

______________________________

______________________________


© 2016 The Critical Thinking Co.™ • www.CriticalThinking.com • 800-458-4849

Section 6: Introduction

# World War II: 1939-1945

During the worldwide depression in the 1930s known as the Great Depression, Germany, Italy, and Japan (Axis Powers) used aggressive tactics to claim more land and resources. Their neighbors, England, France, Russia, and China, tried to compromise with the Axis Powers to avoid war, but failed. The United States tried to remain neutral and out of the war for as long as possible, while President Roosevelt focused his second term on his New Deal program in hopes of reviving the suffering U.S. economy. In spite of the efforts of the United States to avoid entering the war, Germany's 1939 invasion of Poland and later invasion of France (1940), along with the aggressive moves in the Pacific by Japan, convinced FDR and the American public that the Axis Powers also threatened American interests.

After FDR was elected for a third term, he faced open warfare when the Japanese bombed Pearl Harbor on December 7, 1941, and Italy/Germany also declared war on America. The U.S. strategy was to use most of its resources to push back the European Axis first while building a defensive front against further Japanese expansion. While the Russians battled Germans in Russia, the United States and Britain attacked Italy in North Africa and the Mediterranean Sea region.

On the U.S. home front, everything was focused on war production. Culture in America was vastly altered in many ways because of the war. Unemployment nearly vanished as men and women joined the military or worked in war-related industries. Minority groups such as blacks, Native Americans, and Hispanics experienced tremendous changes as the war began to alter the climate of racism in America.

After immense military efforts in both Europe and the Pacific, the tide of war began to change for the Allies. In 1944, FDR was elected to a fourth term. By the spring of 1945, the Axis Powers were on their heels when President Roosevelt died in office, and his vice president, Harry Truman, took over the U.S. presidency. Truman was not well known, but as he became the top commanding officer of the United States, he learned that the U.S. had an amazing and powerful new secret weapon. Would he use it to end the war?

## U.S. Presidents

32. Franklin D. Roosevelt
1933-1945

33. Harry S. Truman
1945-1953

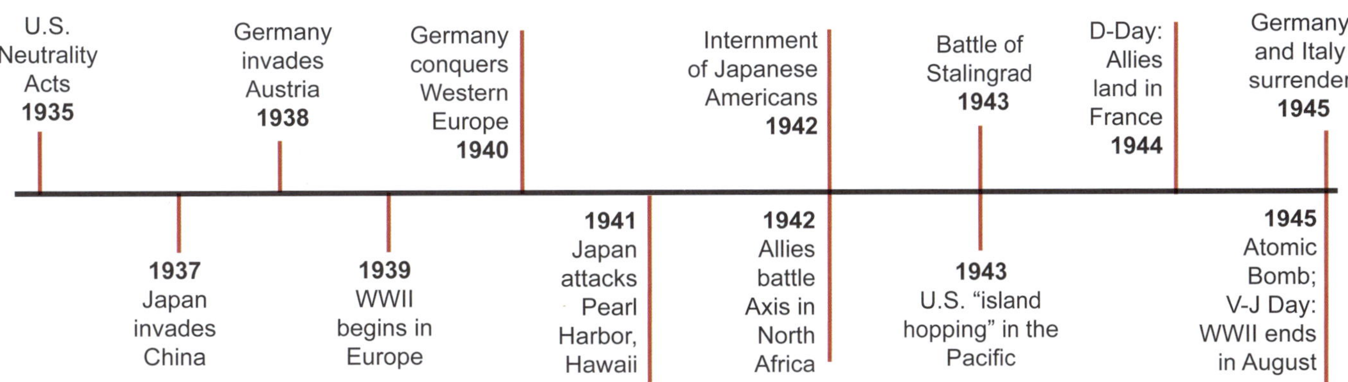

Lesson 30

# A World in Crisis

## A. Rise of Dictatorships

[1]The Great Depression was not only an American economic crisis; it was a worldwide event. [2]Economic and social unrest led a number of nations in Europe and Asia to turn to strong leaders who looked for military solutions to their problems. [3]In 1933, the same year that FDR became president of the United States and started the New Deal, Adolf Hitler and his National Socialist Party (Nazi) gained control of Germany—formerly part of the Austria-Hungary Empire—by crushing all their opponents. [4]Hitler was a Great War (World War I) veteran and blamed the defeat of the Central Powers in WWI and the resulting poor economy on the Jews, whom he considered an inferior race to the Aryan (of Northern European ancestry) people. [5]His government passed a series of laws in the 1930s that stripped German Jews of their rights as citizens in an effort to "purify the fatherland" and create a "master race" of Germans/Aryans. [6]Hitler also started to rebuild the German military, even though the Treaty of Versailles that ended the Great War forbade Germany from doing so. [7]German troops moved west into a region near France called the Rhineland in 1936, and two years later marched south to take control of neighboring Austria. [8]Meeting little resistance, Hitler's troops next took a section of neighboring Czechoslovakia to the east, on the pretext (misleading statement, an excuse) that many German-speaking people lived in that region.

Benito Mussolini and Adolf Hitler

[9]During these same years, Italian dictator Benito Mussolini also showed military aggression. [10]In an effort to recreate a new Roman Empire, he also imposed anti-Semitic laws, created a one-party government, and sent his troops across the Mediterranean Sea to occupy Libya and Ethiopia. [11]In the early 1930s, Japanese military leaders gained control of their government and convinced young Emperor Hirohito to expand into neighboring Manchuria, north of mainland China. [12]By the late 1930s, Germany and Italy had agreed to join forces and support one another. [13]This union soon included Japan and became known as the Axis Powers when the three nations signed the Tripartite Pact in 1940.

## B. Appeasement

[14]President Roosevelt, as well as the leaders of Britain, France, and the Soviet Union, made feeble (weak, lacking force) verbal protests against the actions of Germany, Italy, and Japan. [15]They hoped that allowing the Axis Powers to expand into a few neighboring territories would satisfy or relieve the demands of those aggressors enough that they would no longer have further territorial ambitions. [16]This policy of avoiding a large war by yielding on smaller demands was known as "appeasement." [17]Occupied by the crises of their own economic depressions, leaders of the former Allied nations were not willing to involve their countries in another disastrous war such as the Great War fought twenty years earlier. [18]The United States, in particular, was in an isolationist mood—unwilling to get heavily involved in foreign affairs. [19]A poll in 1937 revealed that 70 percent of Americans thought that entering the Great War had been a mistake because it a failed to "make the world safe for democracy," and because many businesses had made improper financial gains. [20]A powerful organization called the America First Committee was formed to oppose the U.S. entry into a future war. [21]More than 800,000 citizens joined, including 1920s aviation hero Charles Lindbergh.

[22]Likewise, President Roosevelt put most of his energy into his New Deal programs in the first years of his presidency, rather than concentrate on foreign policy. [23]He did, however, try to improve relations with nations in the Western Hemisphere by declaring a "Good Neighbor Policy." [24]In an effort to contrast America with Germany's aggression, FDR stated that the United States had no intention of interfering in the affairs of its neighbors. [25]He hoped to improve relations by pulling U.S. troops out of the Caribbean who had

A 1930s WPA Poster


© 2016 The Critical Thinking Co.™ • www.CriticalThinking.com • 800-458-4849

remained there after the Spanish-American War. [26]In addition, he did not use the U.S. military when issues arose within other Latin American nations.

[27]At the start of FDR's second term, Congress passed a series of neutrality acts outlawing sales of weapons to foreign nations. [28]The laws even banned Americans from traveling on German, Italian, and Japanese ships. [29]When tens of thousands of European-Jewish refugees (people fleeing their country for safety) fled persecution (hostility and ill-treatment) in Europe, many wanted to come to the United States. [30]However, Congress refused to change the quotas on immigration that had been established in the 1920s, and many Jews were turned away from entering the U.S. [31]Some who did immigrate made significant contributions to America in the fields of economics, social science, and technology. [32]Jewish scientists feared that Hitler and Mussolini were developing a super-bomb. [33]Some of those scientists escaped Europe and later led the development of the nuclear reactors and atomic bomb for America.

[34]One way Americans did show their contempt for the Axis Powers was by cheering American athletes who entered international contests. [35]At the 1936 Summer Olympics held in Berlin, Germany, Americans celebrated the success of African American track star Jesse Owens. [36]He set world records on his way to earning four gold medals—embarrassing Hitler—at an event that Hitler thought would showcase the athletic superiority of his Germanic "master race." [37]They also heartily supported African American boxer Joe Louis, who knocked out German fighter Max Schmeling in a world heavyweight championship fight in 1938.

Poster portraying U.S. Olympian Jesse Owens on a track lane bordered by the Nazi symbol—the swastika.

## C. World War II Begins

[38]Appeasement failed in 1937, when Japan invaded China. [39]This was followed, in 1939, by Nazi troops overrunning the rest of Czechoslovakia in the spring and then attacking the country of Poland in late summer. [40]Britain and France declared war on the Axis Powers on September 1, 1939. [41]World War II in Europe was officially on.

[42]President Roosevelt had to navigate public opinion between the strong sense of neutrality and the emergency of military defense. [43]He began to take a number of actions short of declaring war. [44]First, he asked Congress for a much larger military budget and began to order increased production of warplanes, tanks, and weapons. [45]As the Axis Powers conquered Belgium, Denmark, Netherlands, Norway, and then most of France in 1940, and Japanese troops plunged deeper into China, the president convinced Congress to order the first peacetime military draft in U.S. history —the Selective Service and Training Act. [46]U.S. merchant ships were armed. [47]When Germany began to bomb Great Britain in 1941, Winston Churchill, the country's leader, pleaded for U.S. aid, and Roosevelt and Congress responded with the Lend-Lease Act. [48]This allowed the United States to loan or lease—not sell—war material to any nation that was important to American security interests. [49]Even though the U.S. government hated the communist government of the Soviet Union, when the U.S.S.R was invaded by Axis Powers in June of 1941, America allowed Lend-Lease war materials to go to that country as well. [50]"To defeat Hitler," Roosevelt remarked, "I would hold hands with the Devil."

## D. Third Term

[51]1940 was a presidential election year. [52]Although there was no Constitutional ban against it, no U.S. president had ever run for a third term in office out of respect for George Washington's decision to step down in 1800, after eight years in office. [53][Note: in 1951, the 22nd Amendment was passed, formally limiting a president to two terms]. [54]With the crisis of world war threatening the nation, FDR let it be known just prior to the 1940 election that he would accept a nomination for a third term if the Democratic Party "drafted" him to run at its convention in the summer. [55]His opponent, Wendell Willkie, campaigned against FDR by claiming Roosevelt had failed to end the depression and was too eager to enter the war. [56]During the election, a few major economic events worked in FDR's favor. [57]The U.S. military buildup leading up to the war dramatically increased factory

orders for military supplies, creating more U.S. factory jobs. 58At the same time, a large number of young men signed up for military service. 59Both of these economic events helped lower the number of unemployed workers, which gave many Americans the sense the Great Depression was easing. 60Finally, normal rainfall returned to the Dust Bowl, and farmers once again enjoyed healthy harvests. 61All of these events helped FDR remain very popular with the American public, and they elected him to a third term—the only president to have been elected more than twice.

A campaign poster for FDR in 1940.

**Fun Fact Feature**

One famous scientist was visiting the United States in 1933 when Adolf Hitler gained control. Being Jewish, he decided not to return to his native country of Germany. Said to be the most brilliant scientist of the 1900s, he had won the Nobel Prize for physics in 1921 and had developed the famous theory of relativity ($E = MC^2$). In the late 1930s, he recommended to President Roosevelt that the United States should develop an atomic bomb before the Axis Powers did. Who was this famous scientist?

---

## Bonus Activity
## Political Cartoon

Do you recognize the art of this cartoonist? In the lead up to World War II, Theodor Geisel drew political cartoons such as the one to the left. After the war, he wrote and illustrated many famous children's books under his pen name: "Dr. Seuss." Let's analyze this cartoon:

1. Look at sentence 20 in the lesson. What group opposed the United States going to war in the 1930s?

______________________________

2. Who does the man on the platform on the right represent? Give Evidence.

______________________________

______________________________

3. "Uncle Sam," a symbol of the U.S. government, is the announcer at this carnival "side show." Why does he use the words "perplexing" and "mystifies"?

______________________________

______________________________

______________________________


© 2016 The Critical Thinking Co.™ • www.CriticalThinking.com • 800-458-4849

1. Write the name of the dictator for each of these countries in the 1930s.

   a. Italy ______________________________

   b. Japan ______________________________

   c. Germany ______________________________

2. Which group of people did the governments of Germany and Italy target with laws that stripped them of their rights in the 1930s?
   a. Nazis
   b. scientists
   c. Jews
   d. immigrants

   Which sentences best support the answer?

   _____ _____

3. Which European nation took control of bordering countries Austria, the Rhineland, and Czechoslovakia in the 1930s?
   a. Japan
   b. Great Britain
   c. Germany
   d. Italy

   Which sentences best support the answer?

   _____ _____

4. What evidence can you cite showing that the policy of "appeasement" did not work in the 1930s with regard to the Axis Powers?

   ______________________________________

   ______________________________________

5. President Franklin Roosevelt's "Good Neighbor Policy" applied to:
   a. nations in the Western Hemisphere.
   b. Great Britain, France, and the Soviet Union.
   c. the Axis Powers.
   d. the Democratic Party.

   Which sentence best supports the answer?

   _____

6. What was ironic (an unexpected consequence) about the German and Italian governments' policies that forced many Jews to immigrate to the United States?
   a. The policies used millions of dollars from the German and Italian budget.
   b. Jews became the military leaders of the U.S. military.
   c. Jews decided they did not want to live in the United States.
   d. Jews became leading American scientists, economists, and social scientists.

   Which sentences best support the answer?

   _____ _____

7. Which African American athlete made a mockery of Hitler's claims of racial superiority of the Germanic/Aryan people by winning four gold medals at the Berlin Olympics of 1936?
   a. Jesse Owens
   b. Max Schmeling
   c. Joe Louis
   d. Enrico Fermi

   Which sentences best support the answer?

   _____ _____

8. Name three ways that President Roosevelt and Congress prepared for WWII, or aided their allies, while not directly entering the war by 1940.

   a. ______________________________________

   ______________________________________

   b. ______________________________________

   ______________________________________

   c. ______________________________________

   ______________________________________

© 2016 The Critical Thinking Co.™ • www.CriticalThinking.com • 800-458-4849

9. What was unusual about the 1940 presidential election?
    a. Roosevelt's victory margin was the greatest in U.S. history.
    b. Roosevelt won a third term in office.
    c. Americans voted in a Republican for the first time in eight years.
    d. Roosevelt lost his an election for the first time.

   Which sentence best supports the answer?

   ______

## Written Response Question

10. Use complete sentences to explain why President Roosevelt and Congress were reluctant to involve the U.S. in the war against the Axis Powers in the late 1930s.

________________________________________

________________________________________

________________________________________

________________________________________

________________________________________

________________________________________

________________________________________

________________________________________

**Fun Fact Finale**

Albert Einstein, a Jewish German refugee, stayed in America after a visit in 1933 and eventually helped the United States develop the atomic bomb that ended World War II.

© 2016 The Critical Thinking Co.™ • www.CriticalThinking.com • 800-458-4849

Lesson 31

# The United States Enters WW II

## A. Inching Toward War

[1]As the 1930s ended, Americans were still hoping to stay out of a war that seemed increasingly threatening. [2]For example, in December of 1937, a Japanese plane bombed an American naval vessel, the *USS Panay*, which was stationed near the coast of China. [3]Even though three Americans were killed, public opinion was only mildly stirred once Japan apologized and paid compensation (making up for damage with a payment) for the loss. [4]It was quite a different response than the one in 1898 when an explosion had sunk the *USS Maine* in Cuba, and Americans rushed into the Spanish-American War.

[5]After the German's invaded Poland in 1939 and seized control of France in 1940, U.S. public opinion began to shift away from neutrality and toward fighting with the Allies against the Axis Powers (German, Japanese, and Italians). [6]After listening to pleas for American aid from allies such as Britain and France, and observing the changing public opinion away from neutrality, FDR inched the country closer to war. [7]In 1939, he convinced Congress to pass a change to the neutrality act that would allow American allies to buy U.S. weapons on a "cash and carry" basis. [8]That meant, for example, that Great Britain could buy American guns if Britain shipped them across the Atlantic on her own vessels. [9]In 1940, Congress ended a trade agreement with Japan and banned the sale of airplane fuel and scrap metal to that nation. [10]After Japan continued to occupy Eastern China and then moved south into the French colony of Indochina (today's Vietnam) in July 1941, Roosevelt ordered that all Japanese bank deposits in the United States be frozen and all trade with Japan suspended.

FDR met with Britain's Winston Churchill (right) in 1941 and issued the Atlantic Charter.

[11]In August 1941, Roosevelt met with Britain's Prime Minister, Winston Churchill, on a British warship off the eastern coast of Canada. [12]The two leaders issued a statement, later known as the Atlantic Charter, while on the ship. [13]They condemned the aggression of the Axis Powers, agreed to work with each other on national security issues, and called for freedom of the seas and for all nations to scale back on military weaponry. [14]Soon thereafter, a German submarine fired upon an American naval vessel in the Atlantic, and FDR ordered the American Navy to shoot at any Axis vessels operating off the eastern coast of the United States. [15]America was now fighting a limited war.

## B. Pearl Harbor

[16]The end of U.S. trade with Japan put a strain on the Japanese war effort. [17]In the fall of 1941, the Japanese Prime Minister, General Hideki Tojo, decided that his country must attack the United States in order to defend its newly conquered territories in Asia. [18]Tojo ordered a bold move—to attack America's largest fleet, located in the central Pacific Ocean. [19]U.S. intelligence sources (government agencies that gather secret information on its enemies) had learned that Japan was planning an attack, but did not know where. [20]The government was taken by surprise when, on December 7, 1941, Japanese planes, launched from undetected aircraft carriers in the North Pacific, bombed Pearl Harbor, Hawaii.

[21]The Japanese attack caused the destruction of eighteen naval vessels anchored in rows along the harbor. [22]More than 360 American aircraft, parked wing-to-wing on nearby Honolulu airbases, were also destroyed or heavily damaged. [23]There were more than 2,500 Americans killed in the two-hour battle. [24]Despite the extent of the tragedy, the naval repair yards at Pearl Harbor were spared and the United States recovered from the attack far faster than Japan anticipated.

[25]President Roosevelt immediately addressed the nation, calling December 7$^{th}$ "a date which will live in infamy" (known for a shameful, criminal

A U.S. battleship sinks during the Japanese attack on Pearl Harbor, Hawaii in 1941.

act), because the Japanese attack came before a declaration of war and without justification. [26]Congress declared war on Japan the very next day and then passed the War Powers Act, granting President Roosevelt full use of his authority as Commander-in-Chief. [27]A few days later, Adolf Hitler and Benito Mussolini declared war on the United States, and Congress responded with a war declaration on Germany and Italy. [28]Ready or not—and America was definitely unprepared—the United States was now fully involved in World War II. [29]Isolationism and neutrality were things of the past.

### C. Mobilizing for War

[30]Roosevelt soon said he was changing from "Dr. New Deal" to "Dr. Win the War." [31]His focus was now on defeating the Axis Powers rather than concentrating on domestic issues. [32]FDR organized the Joint Chiefs of Staff (leaders from the Army, Navy, Marine, and Army Air Force) to direct the U.S. military strategy. [33]He asked Congress for funds to build the largest military building in the world, the Pentagon, in Washington, D.C. [34]Roosevelt ordered the creation of the Office of Strategic Services (OSS), later to become the spy bureau known as the Central Intelligence Agency (CIA), to conduct covert (secret) foreign operations.

[35]Perhaps the most important action taken by the federal government was the establishment of the War Production Board. [36]This agency was tasked with directing resources used for consumer goods into the manufacturing of wartime material. [37]President Roosevelt called for America to be the "arsenal of democracy," and soon it was. [38]A year after Pearl Harbor, one-third of all U.S. factories were manufacturing military goods for the country and her allies. [39]Two years after Pearl Harbor, the United States alone was making more war equipment than Germany, Italy, Japan, and their Axis partners combined. [40]By 1944, the United States was producing two-thirds of all the military gear used by the Allies.

The Pentagon, headquarters for the U.S. military, was built in Washington, D.C. during WWII.

[41]From early 1942 through the duration (entire length) of the war, no commercial cars or trucks were made for Americans. [42]Instead, companies such as Ford Motor quickly re-tooled car assembly lines to produce war transportation. [43]They were part of a national effort that built more than 80,000 tanks and 300,000 planes during the next four years. [44]Henry Kaiser, nicknamed "Sir Launchalot," constructed a ship-building plant in Portland, Oregon, that could turn out a cargo ship every day by the end of the war. [45]Needing rubber for tires since U.S. plants could no longer count on imports of crude rubber from Asia, government scientists invented synthetic rubber. [46]By the end of the war, the United States was so successful at producing a man-made rubber substitute, it became the world's largest exporter of rubber. [47]American scientists at the Office of Scientific Research and Development (OSRD), another Roosevelt alphabet agency, improved devices for detecting planes (radar) and submarines (sonar). [48]They built America's first rockets and produced new drugs, like penicillin, to stop the spread of disease. [49]They also constructed the first computer–the Mark I–a five-ton machine used to calculate equations for the military.

**Fun Fact Feature**

During World War II, copper was in short supply and needed for ammunition and other war materials. As a result, U.S. money underwent a change. Can you guess which coin was affected?


© 2016 The Critical Thinking Co.™ • www.CriticalThinking.com • 800-458-4849

1. The reaction of the bombing of the *USS Panay* in 1937 compared with the explosion of the *USS Maine* in 1898 in what way?
    a. Both attacks prompted the United States to immediately declare war.
    b. Neither attack prompted Americans to immediately declare war.
    c. In both attacks, the United States immediately declared neutrality.
    d. Americans had little reaction to the *Panay* incident in contrast to the *Maine* incident.

    Which sentence best supports the answer?

    _____

2. The Atlantic Charter was an agreement of support between what two countries?
    a. Great Britain and the United States
    b. Japan and the United States
    c. France and Great Britain
    d. the United States and Germany

    Which sentences best support the answer?

    _____ _____

3. In the 1930s, in response to Japan's military expansion in China and Southeast Asia, the United States tried economic tactics, rather than military action. Give two examples:

    a. ______________________________

    ______________________________

    b. ______________________________

    ______________________________

4. What event finally caused Congress to officially enter WWII?
    a. the bombing of the *USS Panay*
    b. the German submarine attack on a U.S. naval vessel in the Atlantic
    c. the Japanese bombing of Pearl Harbor, Hawaii
    d. the fact that Hitler and Mussolini declared war on the United States

    Which sentences best support the answer?

    _____ _____ _____

5. When Congress passed "cash and carry" legislation in 1939, why do you think the "carry" part was included in the law?

    ______________________________

    ______________________________

6. When it was created, what was the job of the C.I.A.?
    a. to gather secret information on U.S. enemies
    b. to convince more men to join the military
    c. to produce smart scientific inventions to aid the military
    d. to stop the United States involvement in WWII

    Which sentence best supports the answer?

    _____

7. What is the Pentagon?
    a. a building used for Congressional hearings
    b. the U.S. military headquarters
    c. a place to produce wartime equipment.
    d. the home of the U.S. spy agency—the C.I.A.

    Which sentence best supports the answer?

    _____

8. Why do you think Henry Kaiser earned the nickname "Sir Launchalot"?

    ______________________________

    ______________________________

© 2016 The Critical Thinking Co.™ • www.CriticalThinking.com • 800-458-4849

9. What was the name of the U.S. agency in charge of getting consumer resources turned into military equipment?
   a. Office of Strategic Services (OSS)
   b. Central Intelligence Agency (CIA)
   c. Office of Scientific Research and Development (OSRD)
   d. War Production Board (WPB)

   Which sentences best support the answer?

   _____ _____

## Written Response Question

10. An "arsenal" is a collection of weapons and war supplies. Use complete sentences to cite evidence from the lesson that shows America did become, as President Roosevelt urged, the "arsenal of democracy."

________________________________________

________________________________________

________________________________________

________________________________________

________________________________________

________________________________________

________________________________________

________________________________________

**Fun Fact Finale**

During World War II, copper was in short supply and needed for ammunition and other war materials. As a result, the U.S. penny (one cent piece) was changed from copper to steel in 1943 and 1944.

© 2016 The Critical Thinking Co.™ • www.CriticalThinking.com • 800-458-4849

Lesson 32

# A Two-Front War

## A. Soft Underbelly

[1]After the attack on Pearl Harbor, Americans wanted revenge against Japan. [2]However, America was faced with war on two fronts. [3]Besides the war in the Pacific, Germany and Italy had declared war on the United States as well. [4]It was truly going to be a world war. [5]President Roosevelt, as commander-in-chief, and his military leaders had to develop a strategy to use American resources wisely. [6]U.S. allies (Britain, France, and the Soviet Union) were in grave danger of collapse from the German and Italian attacks. [7]By the beginning of 1942, American officials agreed that the Axis Powers in Europe must be defeated first. [8]If Nazi troops gained total control of Europe, they would be difficult to dislodge (remove or force out). [9]Efforts in the Pacific, meanwhile, would center on controlling further Japanese expansion until America was ready to go on the offensive.

[10]In Western Europe (see map, pg 174), most of France had been overrun by Germany and was well defended. [11]In 1942, the German army invaded the Soviet Union and drove deep into the USSR. [12]Russia's communist leader, Josef Stalin, demanded that the Allies open an attack in Western Europe to force Hitler to transfer his troops west, thus relieving pressure on the Soviet front. [13]The Allies agreed, but British Prime Minister Winston Churchill argued against a direct Western European invasion across the English Channel. [14]Churchill feared that an Allied invasion of northern France would drain British resources and end in defeat, with a tremendous loss of life. [15]For the time being, Allied vessels blockaded (closed off) Germany in the North Sea, and planes launched from Britain dropped bombs on German cities.

[16]Churchill recommended, and FDR agreed, that British and American troops should instead open a front at what he called the "soft underbelly of Europe," the Mediterranean Sea area. [17]Although the Axis Powers controlled lands on both the northern and southern shores of the Mediterranean, Italy was the weakest Axis opponent. [18]American ground troops, under General Dwight Eisenhower, joined British tank forces in former French territories of Northern Africa in 1942, in order to gain a foothold in the Mediterranean. [19]By the end of the year, the German army in Northern Africa was defeated at the Battle of El Alamein in Egypt and at Kasserine Pass in Tunisia. [20]Allied forces were now able to launch an attack on southern Italy by the summer of 1943. [21]After taking the Italian island of Sicily, Allied troops moved onto the Italian mainland. [22]Success there demoralized (deprived the spirit and courage) the Italians. [23]In September, their government surrendered and their leader, Benito Mussolini, went into hiding in northern Italy. [24]German troops, however, rushed into Italy to replace the defeated Italians. [25]The Allies would continue to fight Nazis in Italy for the next two years.

U.S. General Dwight Eisenhower (left) rode with the commander of the French forces as they inspected Allied troops in North Africa in 1942.

[26]U.S. farms and factories supplied not only the American military but aided U.S. allies as well. [27]Using many American-made supplies, the Soviet Union was able to stop the German invasion of its country by winning a decisive battle at Stalingrad in 1943. [28]This was a turning point in the war in Europe. [29]Then, as American and British armies moved northward up the Italian peninsula, the Soviet army pushed the Nazis out of the USSR and back into Poland from the east. [30]The Allies were now "closing the ring" on Germany.

## B. War in the Pacific

[31]At the beginning of the U.S. involvement in WWII, the American strategy was to bring only defensive actions in the Pacific Ocean while concentrating on the fight in Europe. [32]However, President Roosevelt felt it was important to boost the American spirit quickly after the attack on Pearl Harbor. [33]Only two weeks after Japan declared war on the United States, President Roosevelt approved a plan to do just that. [34]By April 1942, Doolittle's Raid was implemented (performed, carried out). [35]Sixteen U.S. bombers, under the

© 2016 The Critical Thinking Co.™ • www.CriticalThinking.com • 800-458-4849

Lt. Col. James Doolittle (standing left) with some of his "raiders" in 1942.

A painting by artist John Greaves entitled "Head on at Midway" shows a scene from that 1942 battle.

command of Lieutenant Colonel James Doolittle, launched from aircraft carriers in the Pacific. [36]They dropped bombs on Tokyo and other Japanese cities before landing in western China. [37]Although this attack on the Japanese mainland did relatively little damage, it boosted the morale of the American public, while creating doubt in the minds of the Japanese that they would be able to defend their island nation.

[38]Then, in 1942, three naval battles in the Pacific Ocean (see map, pg. 176) became turning points on the Pacific front in World War II for the Allies. [39]In April, the U.S. Navy defeated Japan at the Battle of Coral Sea in the South Pacific. [40]This action stopped a Japanese invasion of Australia. [41]A month later, the United States won another sea battle near an important military base on Midway Island, west of Hawaii in the Central Pacific. [42]This Battle of Midway wielded a serious blow to Japanese resources and stopped any plans of Japanese expansion toward the west coast of the United States. [43]Later, in early 1943, American sea and air forces won yet another major victory near an island in the South Pacific called Guadalcanal. [44]With these three victories, America could now go on the offensive against Japan.

[45]U.S. military advisors planned a two-pronged (part) advance in the Pacific Ocean. [46]In 1943 and 1944, the U.S. Navy, under the command of Admiral Chester Nimitz, started "island-hopping" across the Pacific Ocean. [47]Forces under Nimitz began leapfrogging over islands heavily defended by Japan to capture islands less fortified, thereby leaving great numbers of Japanese forces isolated; this tactic conserved American resources. [48]The idea was to eventually capture islands within range of Japan in order to launch air attacks against the Japanese mainland. [49]Meanwhile the U.S. Army, led by General Douglas MacArthur, advanced island by island, north of Australia, to recapture the American territory of the Philippines which had been taken by the Japanese early in the war. [50]This was accomplished by the fall of 1944.

[51]Taking back islands as they advanced toward Japan was a slow and brutal process for Allied forces. [52]Although some Japanese soldiers surrendered, most fought to their deaths. [53]Some Japanese pilots, called "kamikaze," attacked Allied warships until out of ammunition, then flew their planes—packed with high explosives—on suicide missions into Allied vessels. [54]The Japanese had been taught from an early age that their emperor was a living god and that war was an act that could purify not only their nation, but the world. [55]Even Japanese civilians resisted capture. [56]As American Marines advanced on the island of Saipan, they witnessed Japanese mothers jumping off cliffs with their children rather than be taken prisoner. [57]A Japanese soldier named Hiroo Onoda was given the following order when shipped to his island base: "Whatever happens, we'll come back for you. [58]Until then, so long as you have one soldier, you are to continue to lead him. You may have to live on coconuts. [59]If that's the case, live on coconuts! Under no circumstances are you to give up your life voluntarily." [60]Even though Japan surrendered one year later, Onoda followed his orders. [61]Alone in a Philippine island jungle and not believing that Japan could lose the war, he continued to hide out for 29 more years until the Japanese government finally sent a military officer who convinced him that the war had ended decades earlier.


© 2016 The Critical Thinking Co.™ • www.CriticalThinking.com • 800-458-4849

## C. Japanese Internment Camps

62Well before the United States entered World War II, FDR became concerned with Japan's rapid military buildup and the number of Japanese Americans living in Hawaii. 63He had contemplated internment (relocation and imprisonment) of Japanese Americans and Japanese nationals living in the United States. 64In addition to FDR's concern and strategy over Japanese Americans, racial prejudice against Asian Americans (mainly for economic reasons), had long been an issue in the United States, even before the war. 65Before the Japanese attack on Pearl Harbor, most Americans did not view Japanese Americans as security risks. 66Following the attack, although no Japanese Americans were found to have aided the Japanese attack on Pearl Harbor, public and military distrust of Japanese Americans and Japanese nationals living in the United States began to shift against them.

67In 1942, FDR issued Executive Order 9066 giving regional military leaders the power to remove and relocate more than 110,000 Japanese immigrants and their families living in the western United States—the majority of them U.S. citizens. 68The internees were sent to so-called "relocation centers" or "internment camps." 69Prior to their removal, Japanese families often had to sell most of their possessions at whatever prices they could obtain.

70These were not "forced labor camps" or "death camps" such as those run by Nazi Germany. 71Internees were allowed to start schools, organize sports teams, and hold social events in the camps, but the camps were not a pleasant experience. 72Hastily built in desolate parts of the interior of the country, the camps were surrounded by barbed wire and guarded by armed soldiers. 73Living quarters in the camps were crudely constructed, did not protect families from the harsh climate, and did not afford privacy. 74Some Japanese Americans were allowed to leave if they took factory jobs, went to college on the East Coast, or joined the U.S. military to fight in Europe. 75Most were interned for the duration of the war.

76In 1944, before the end of the war, the Supreme Court ruled, in *Korematsu v. United States*, that the establishment of the internment camps was constitutional. 77Years later, however, in 1988, Congress passed the Civil Liberties Act—signed into law by President Ronald Reagan—which called the internment camps a "grave injustice." 78The act officially apologized for the internment of Japanese American citizens, admitting that government actions were based on "race prejudice, war hysteria, and a failure of political leadership" and were not justified out of military necessity. 79Eventually federal reparations (payments) were made to many of the camp survivors and their heirs.

Three boys from the internment camp at Manzanar, California, look through a barbed wire fence under the watch of a guard tower.

**Fun Fact Feature**

The 442nd regimental combat team became the most honored unit of the U.S. military during World War II. Their motto was "Go for Broke." In total, about 14,000 men served—mostly in the Italian campaign—earning 9,486 Purple Hearts, 21 Medals of Honor, and seven Presidential Unit Citations. What was unique about the men who served in this regiment?

1. What was America's strategy when it actively joined World War II?
   a. Use almost all of its military resources to fight Japan.
   b. Split U.S. resources evenly to fight on two fronts.
   c. Use most of its military resources to fight in Europe first while controlling Japanese expansion in the Pacific.
   d. Use most of its military resources to fight Japan first while controlling Hitler in Europe.

   Which sentences best support the answer?

   _____ _____

2. Josef Stalin insisted that the Allied Powers open a western front in Europe to relieve the pressure on his country, which was desperately fighting the German army. Stalin ruled which Allied nation?
   a. Poland
   b. Soviet Union
   c. Italy
   d. Great Britain

   Which sentence best supports the answer?

   _____

3. Where did the Allies decide to open a western front against the Axis Powers of Europe in 1942?
   a. the Soviet Union
   b. Northern Africa
   c. across the English Channel
   d. the Pacific Ocean

   Which sentences best support the answer?

   _____ _____

4. Which of the three main Axis Powers nations surrendered first in World War II?
   a. Japan
   b. Germany
   c. Italy

   Which sentence best supports the answer?

   _____

5. Which American military leader led a successful air attack on the Japanese mainland only a few months after Pearl Harbor?
   a. James Doolittle
   b. Dwight Eisenhower
   c. Chester Nimitz
   d. Douglas MacArthur

   Which sentence best supports the answer?

   _____

6. Who used "island hopping" as a battle strategy during World War II?
   a. the United States
   b. Japan
   c. the Soviet Union
   d. the Philippines

   Which sentence best supports the answer?

   _____

7. What were Japanese pilots who carried out suicide missions against Allied naval vessels in World War II called?
   a. korematsu
   b. internees
   c. manzanar
   d. kamikaze

   Which sentence best supports the answer?

   _____

8. What did President Roosevelt's Executive Order 9066 establish?
   a. an attack on the "soft underbelly of Europe" in North Africa
   b. the Doolittle Raid attack on Tokyo, Japan
   c. bombing raids on German cities
   d. internment camps for Japanese Americans

   Which sentences best support the answer?

   _____ _____


© 2016 The Critical Thinking Co.™ • www.CriticalThinking.com • 800-458-4849

9. What occurred in 1988 that was the opposite of *Korematsu v. U.S.* in 1944?
    a. Hiroo Onoda incident
    b. retaking of the Philippines by General Douglas MacArthur
    c. Civil Liberties Act
    d. Executive Order 9066

Which sentence best supports the answer?

_____

### Written Response Question

10. Use complete sentences to name several important battles in World War II and explain why each is considered to be a "turning point" in favor of the Allies.

______________________________________________________________________

______________________________________________________________________

______________________________________________________________________

______________________________________________________________________

______________________________________________________________________

______________________________________________________________________

______________________________________________________________________

______________________________________________________________________

**Fun Fact Finale**

The 442nd regimental combat team, the most honored unit of the U.S. military during World War II, was composed entirely of Japanese American soldiers.

# Bonus Activity
# World War II Map of Europe

Look at the map of World War II at the height of Axis control in 1943 to answer the questions.

World War II European Front in 1943

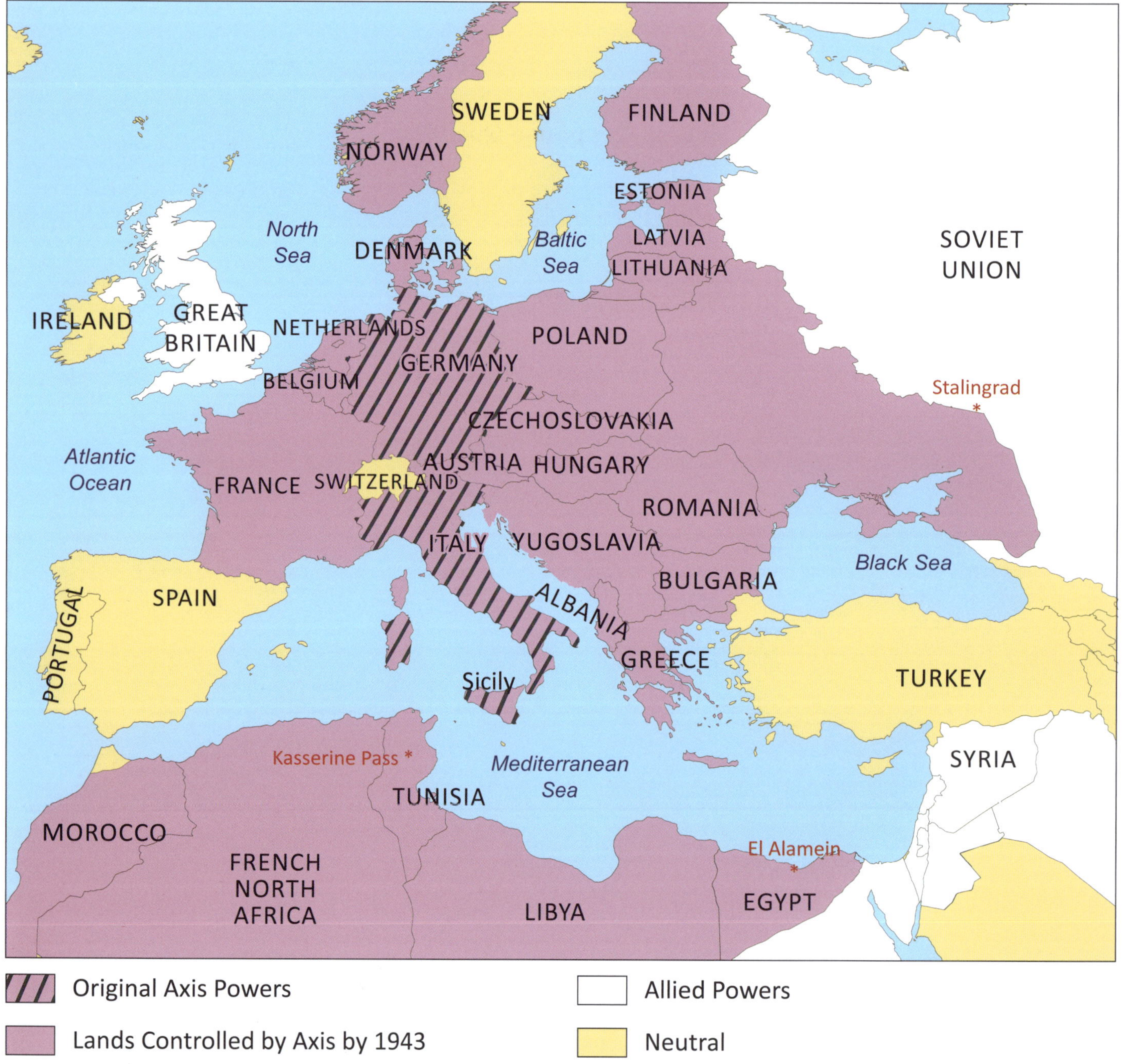




© 2016 The Critical Thinking Co.™ • www.CriticalThinking.com • 800-458-4849

1. Which two nations were the Axis Powers in Europe?

______________________ ______________________

2. Which was the only non-neutral Allied nation in Western Europe that was not under Axis control by 1943?

______________________

3. Which small nation in the center of Western Europe still managed to maintain neutrality during World War II?

______________________

4. Which Allied nation was partly controlled by the Axis until winning the Battle of Stalingrad in 1943?

______________________

5. The Allies decided to blockade the water regions north of Germany in 1942. Which two "seas" were blockaded?

______________________ ______________________

6. What water region separates Northern Africa from the "soft underbelly of Europe"?

______________________

7. The turning point battle of El Alamein was in which country?

______________________

8. Once the Allies won an important battle in Tunisia in 1943, they were able to begin an invasion of Italy at the island of Sicily. What was the name of that Tunisian battle site?

______________________

© 2016 The Critical Thinking Co.™ • www.CriticalThinking.com • 800-458-4849

# Bonus Activity
# World War II Map of the Pacific

Look at the map of World War II at the height of Axis control in the Pacific to answer the questions.

World War II in the Pacific

© 2016 The Critical Thinking Co.™ • www.CriticalThinking.com • 800-458-4849

1. What nation did Japan control prior to the start of World War II in Asia in 1937?

______________________________

2. Japan successfully attacked not only Pearl Harbor, Hawaii, in late 1941, but three other important cities as well. Name them.

__________ __________ __________

3. Japan attacked China in 1937. Did Japan successfully control all of China during World War II? Explain.

______________________________

4. Name three U.S. territories in the Pacific which were attacked or threatened by Japan in World War II.

__________ __________ __________

5. Which Allied nation/continent, south of the Equator, was saved from Japanese control with Allied victories at the Coral Sea and Guadalcanal?

______________________________

6. What Allied victory near Hawaii kept the line showing Japanese control only to the eastern half of the Pacific Ocean?

______________________________

7. What two Allied victories in the spring of 1945 would have threatened the Japanese mainland with launching sites for Allied bombing raids?

__________ __________

© 2016 The Critical Thinking Co.™ • www.CriticalThinking.com • 800-458-4849

Lesson 33

# WW II and American Society

## A. Women and Children During the War

[1]During WWII, the U.S. government encouraged American women, even married women, to work in war production jobs to "release able-bodied men for fighting." [2]In response to the call, more than six million additional women joined the workforce. [3]Before the war, working women were generally young and single. [4]During WWII, however, two-thirds of female workers were over age 35 and three-quarters were married. [5]They took blue-collar (manual labor) jobs that involved heavy lifting, machine work, and large tools, as well as traditional white-collar jobs such as secretarial, nursing, and teaching. [6]Some women used pneumatic (air powered) rivet guns to help manufacture planes and ships, and soon "Rosie the Riveter" became a proud nickname and symbol of females in war production. [7]By war's end, a third of the American workforce was female.

This magazine cover drawn by artist Norman Rockwell in 1943 helped create the symbol of "Rosie the Riveter." Here Rosie takes a lunch break while stepping on a copy of Adolf Hitler's book, *Mein Kamph*.

[8]More than 350,000 women also joined the armed forces in the WAC (Women's Army Corp), WAVES (the Navy's Women Appointed for Volunteer Emergency Services), or WASPs (Women's Airforce Service Pilots). [9]For the first time in U.S. history, women served their country with regular military standing and non-combat jobs other than nursing.

[10]One-third of women working in defense jobs during the war had young children. [11]Families used older siblings or other relatives to watch preschool children, and some companies began to provide day-care services. [12]However, there were many children between the ages of 6 to 17, who had both parents working or in the military, left unsupervised for part of each day. [13]They were nicknamed "latchkey kids," because they carried a key to open the doors of their homes when they returned from school. [14]This additional strain on families showed up in two statistics: The divorce rate nearly doubled, and reports of anti-social or criminal activity among juveniles increased fivefold.

## B. Minorities During the War

[15]Before the war, black Americans had traditionally held only low-paying jobs in agriculture or service industries. [16]As the war began, a campaign called "Double V"—victory over aggression abroad and over racial discrimination at home—was started by some black newspapers. [17]They called for expanded opportunities for African Americans in the workplace and in the military to create a united country that could defeat the Axis Powers. [18]One black leader, A. Philip Randolph, a civil rights activist, union organizer, and socialist, threatened to march 50,000 blacks to the U.S. capital to protest the racial discrimination toward blacks in federal employment and the military. [19]In response, President Roosevelt issued Executive Order 8802, known as the Fair Employment Act, in 1941. [20]This made it illegal for government agencies, unions, or companies that worked on government defense contracts to practice racial discrimination. [21]It was the first time since the 1870s that a presidential directive tried to improve racial employment opportunities. [22]After the executive order, Randolph cancelled the march, but other black leaders felt betrayed since FDR's order did not end segregation in the military.

A. Philip Randolph

[23]More than a half-million African Americans, both men and women, did take new skilled jobs in war production plants or within the federal government in the early 1940s. [24]Many blacks moved out of the South to take these new jobs. [25]As a result of these improved opportunities, the annual wages of black Americans increased fourfold during the war.

[26]More than one million African Americans also joined the military. [27]For the first time in U.S. history, blacks were allowed to join the Marine Corps and the Coast Guard, while the Army and Navy allowed training for black males


© 2016 The Critical Thinking Co.™ • www.CriticalThinking.com • 800-458-4849

in combat positions. [28]The number of African American military officers increased from five in 1940 to more than 7,000 by the end of the war. [29]However, most blacks in the military were still commanded by white officers and served in units separated from their fellow white soldiers. [30]This would be the last war to have a segregated U.S. military. [31]One African American unit that claimed great fame during WWII was known as the Tuskegee Airmen. [32]Trained at a base near the black college of Tuskegee University in Alabama, these men became the first black military pilots in the U.S. Armed Forces. [33]They served with distinction in combat in Africa and Italy during the war.

This WWII poster featured a Tuskegee Airman.

[34]More than 50,000 Native Americans left reservation lands during the war to work in war production jobs, many living in urban areas for the first time. [35]Another 25,000 Native Americans served in the military during the war. [36]One particular group, Navajo "code-talkers," greatly helped the Marines by relaying messages to American commanders using their unique and complex language, which Japanese spies could not decipher (discover the meaning).

[37]Like other minority groups, Mexican Americans often left traditional agricultural jobs for work in factories and shipyards. [38]West Coast cities in particular, such as Los Angeles and San Diego, California, grew very quickly with this new Hispanic population. [39]More than 350,000 Mexican Americans also joined the Armed Forces. [40]Mexican American soldiers were not segregated and were allowed combat roles immediately. [41]Many earned awards for their service, including 17 who were given the elite Medal of Honor.

[42]Overall, WWII helped to shape a new attitude among minorities and whites about social justice. [43]More leaders began urging an end to the "separate but equal" policies established during the Reconstruction era. [44]Also, as more minorities began voting in elections and living in new regions of the country, politicians paid more attention to civil rights issues. [45]Important strides in civil rights for minorities would be made in the decades following the war.

### C. Entertainment During the War

[46]With so many young men joining the military, the loss of male enrollment drove colleges to admit more women than ever before. [47]These educated women helped spur a doubling of book sales during the war. [48]New to the bookshelf were paperbacks—fictional novels, classics, and nonfiction not available in hardcover. [49]Magazine sales also soared. [50]During the war, young people commonly read comic books featuring new superheroes such as Captain America and Captain Marvel.

A comic book hero battled Germany's Adolf Hitler in this WWII edition.

[51]Women and men also used leisure time to attend movies. [52]About half of the U.S. population attended theaters on a weekly basis during the war. [53]Before the feature film, which was often a war drama, audiences usually learned about the progress of the war by watching "newsreels." [54]Walt Disney produced cartoons featuring his animated characters fighting Axis dictators or working for the war effort.

[55]Americans listened to the radio more than ever before—for an average time estimated at 4.5 hours per day during the war. [56]News programing on radio accounted for about a third of broadcasting. [57]Even radio dramas adapted to the war effort. [58]Dick Tracy, a fictional FBI radio character, took on the task of catching Nazi spies. [59]When not listening to war news, listeners loved the sound of musicians such as Glenn Miller, Tommy Dorsey, or Benny Goodman. [60]It was the "Swing Era" of big bands, featuring fast tempo dance music with strong rhythm sections, lots of brass instruments, woodwinds, and noted soloists. [61]One rising star was singer Frank Sinatra. [62]He appealed strongly to an audience that had not been tapped before: teenage girls.

**Fun Fact Feature**

A popular song called "Goodbye Mama, I'm Off to Yokohama" was the biggest hit in early 1942. The lyrics were about a GI shipping off to war. What was a "GI," and where was he going?

1. Compared to times before WWII, what were two things that were different about women in the workforce during the war?

   a. ______________________________

   ______________________________

   b. ______________________________

   ______________________________

2. What was a "latchkey kid" in WWII?
   a. A teenager who worked in a defense industry job.
   b. A black man who was discriminated against because of his race.
   c. A child who was often unsupervised at home while his parents worked.
   d. A child who had keys to the family car so he could learn to drive at a young age.

   Which sentence best supports the answer?

   ______

3. One of the intended "v's" in the Double V campaign of WWII was victory:
   a. over discrimination against women in the workplace.
   b. for African American civil rights.
   c. over communism.
   d. in the 1944 presidential election.

   Which sentence best supports the answer?

   ______

4. Who was an important civil rights leader of the 1940s?
   a. A. Philip Randolph
   b. Frank Sinatra
   c. Benny Goodman
   d. Captain Marvel

   Which sentence best supports the answer?

   ______

5. Which of these was NOT an important minority group that contributed to the American war effort in WWII?
   a. Captain America and Captain Marvel
   b. Navajo code talkers
   c. Rosie the Riveters
   d. Tuskegee Airmen

   Which sentence best supports the answer?

   ______

6. During WWII, which soldiers were segregated into separate combat units?
   a. Hispanics
   b. Native Americans
   c. Southerners
   d. African Americans

   Which sentence best supports the answer?

   ______

7. What is one reason why the U.S. government tried to encourage women to work in defense industry jobs during WWII?

   ______________________________

   ______________________________

8. What did Americans do about 4.5 hours a day, on average, during WWII?
   a. went to a movie
   b. danced to big-band "swing era" music
   c. listened to radio
   d. read comic books

   Which sentence best supports the answer?

   ______

9. Which of the following decreased during the WWII era?
   a. divorce rate
   b. employment for minority groups
   c. book and magazine sales
   d. men attending college

   Which sentence best supports the answer?

   ______


© 2016 The Critical Thinking Co.™ • www.CriticalThinking.com • 800-458-4849

## Written Response Question

10. Use complete sentences to describe ways that the U.S. military had a different makeup during WWII.

______________________________________________________________________

______________________________________________________________________

______________________________________________________________________

______________________________________________________________________

______________________________________________________________________

______________________________________________________________________

______________________________________________________________________

______________________________________________________________________

### Fun Fact Finale

The song "Goodbye Mama, I'm Off to Yokohama" was released shortly after the attack on Pearl Harbor. The lyrics, displaying the racial insensitivity of the times, included these lines:

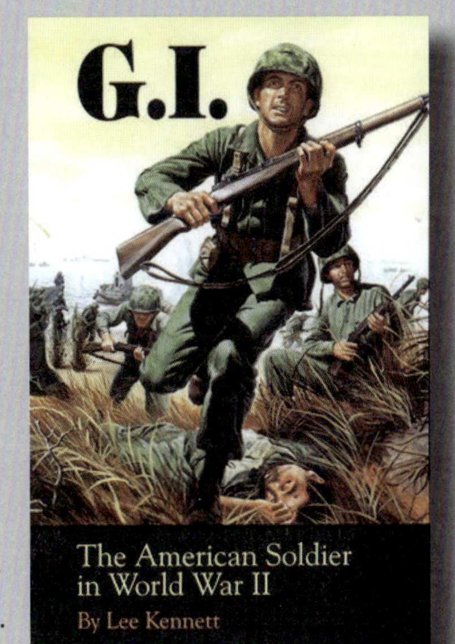


"Goodbye Mama, I'm off to Yokohama,
For the red, white, and blue – My country and you.
Goodbye Mama, I'm off to Yokohama
Just to teach all those Japs, the Yanks are no saps.
A million fightin' sons of Uncle Sam if you please,
Will soon have all those Japs right down on their Japa-knees."

The "sons of Uncle Sam" were American soldiers, nicknamed GI's, (which stood for "government issue"—the standard uniform and military gear he was given). They were heading off to fight Japan in the Pacific. Yokohama is a major city in Japan.

Lesson 34

# WW II Ends in Europe

## A. D-Day

[1]By 1944, the Allied nations had started to close in on the Axis Powers of Europe (Germany and Italy). [2]The Soviet Army had pushed German troops west into Poland. [3]American and British forces had cleared the Nazis out of Africa and were pushing north up the Italian peninsula. [4]By mid-year it was time to launch an attack on a third European front—across the English Channel and into northern France. [5]Under the leadership of U.S. General Dwight Eisenhower, British, Canadian, and American military officials prepared for "Operation Overlord" months in advance. [6]It was important to keep the cross-channel attack as secret as possible so that Hitler could not concentrate his defensive forces. [7]In case spies learned of the invasion, Allied officials never referred to the specific moment the attack would begin. [8]Instead their plans only referred to "D-Day" and "H-hour."

[9]The Allies sent the largest armada (a huge fleet of ships) ever assembled across the English Channel to land on German-controlled shorelines of the Normandy region of northern France on June 6, 1944—a day thereafter known in history as D-Day. [10]More than 5,000 vessels transported nearly 200,000 troops while 11,000 Allied aircraft provided air cover and support. [11]As the battle began on the Normandy beaches, President Roosevelt made a radio address to tell the American people about the invasion. [12]He led a prayer which said in part: "Almighty God: Our sons, pride of our nation, this day have set upon a mighty endeavor, a struggle to preserve our Republic, our religion, and our civilization, and to set free a suffering humanity … Help us, Almighty God, to rededicate ourselves in renewed faith in Thee in this hour of great sacrifice."

D-Day Invasion

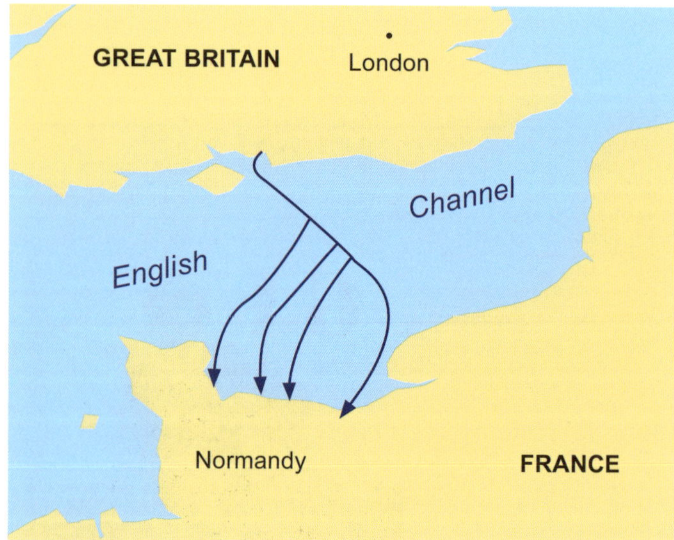


[13]It took a week to fully secure the beaches. More than 4,000 Allied troops lost their lives in the D-Day invasion, with thousands more wounded, captured, or missing. [14]By the end of June, nearly three-quarters of a million Allied troops, thousands of vehicles, and tons of equipment were safely landed. [15]Allied armies started marching inland, liberating (setting free) dozens of French towns that had been controlled by German (Nazi) forces. [16]By late August, the capital of France (Paris) was also released from the grip of the Nazis, after four years of German control.

## B. The Battle of the Bulge

[17]As American, Canadian, British, and French forces moved east in the fall of 1944 to launch a full-scale assault on the Nazis, Hitler ordered a last-ditch counter-offensive (an attack against someone who has already attacked you). [18]In mid-December, the German military succeeded in pushing back a weak point in the American position. [19]A bend in the U.S. frontlines was created that was 80 miles long and 50 miles wide. [20]The so-called "Battle of the Bulge" lasted for a month and was one of the toughest U.S. battles of the war. [21]More than 55,000 U.S. soldiers were killed or wounded in the fight. [22]In one desperate situation, an American unit that was nearly surrounded by German forces and weakened from the snowy winter conditions, was told to surrender by the Germans. [23]U.S. General Anthony C. McAuliffe sent back a one-word reply to the Nazi commander—"Nuts!"—which inspired his troops to continue to fight. [24]Eventually McAuliffe and the Allied forces prevailed (succeeded, won). [25]Germany was now out of manpower and equipment and open to an invasion of Germany itself in the spring of 1945.

U.S. troops fought winter and the Axis Powers at the Battle of the Bulge.


© 2016 The Critical Thinking Co.™ • www.CriticalThinking.com • 800-458-4849

## C. The Holocaust

[26]As early as 1942, Americans had started to hear about atrocities (behavior that is wicked, ruthless, or extremely cruel) in prisoner-of-war camps in areas controlled by the Nazis. [27]As Allied troops moved into Germany and Poland in 1945, and entered the camps, the evidence was overwhelming: the Axis Powers had systematically killed more than six million Jews and several million more gypsies, communists, Polish Catholics, and others deemed unfit to live under Nazi rule. [28]"The things I saw beggar description," wrote General Eisenhower when he entered a death camp. [29]"The visual evidence and the verbal testimony of starvation and cruelty were so overpowering as to leave me a bit sick." [30]He and his troops viewed dead bodies of prisoners stacked like firewood, train cars holding piles of human bones, and huge pits filled with thousands of murdered people. [31]They took photographs and wrote personal descriptions of what they saw so that others would later believe the horrors they had witnessed.

Allied troops and surviving prisoners view a pile of bodies at a Nazi death camp.

[32]About 75 percent of European Jews, a religious group called inferior by the Nazis, had been sent to poison-gas chambers or shot, in a program Nazi rulers called "the Final Solution." [33]Historians have since labeled this event as the "Holocaust." [34]A holocaust is defined as "complete destruction by fire." [35]Many of the dead in Nazi death camps, like Auschwitz or Dachau, had been burned in crematoriums (buildings where bodies were burned into ashes).

## D. V-E Day

[36]Soviet troops raced into the heart of Germany from the east as British and U.S. forces came from the west in the spring of 1945. [37]Just as victory in WWII seemed near, Americans were shocked to learn that their president had died.

[38]Franklin Roosevelt had been reelected to a fourth consecutive term as president in November of 1944. [39]The next February, he traveled to Yalta in the U.S.S.R. to meet with Britain's Winston Churchill and the Soviet leader, Josef Stalin, to discuss how to conclude the war. [40]The trip weakened FDR, and the exhausted president died of a stroke on April 12, 1945, within a month of taking the oath of office for his fourth term. [41]Harry S. Truman had been a U.S. Senator from Missouri until his 1944 selection as Roosevelt's vice president. [42]He felt ill-prepared to take on the responsibility of Commander-in-Chief. [43]"Last night the moon, the stars, and all the planets fell on me," he told reporters on his first day as FDR's successor.

[44]Favorable war news soon reached President Truman and Americans, however. [45]At the end of April, Italy's Benito Mussolini was captured and executed by Italian fighters, and Soviet troops invaded Berlin, Germany, closing in on Hitler's headquarters. [46]As the Allied troops advanced on his headquarters, Adolf Hitler committed suicide on April 30, 1945. [47]Surviving leaders in Germany soon surrendered to the Allies. [48]On May 8, 1945, Americans celebrated V-E Day (Victory in Europe Day).

The funeral procession for FDR in Washington, D.C., in 1945.

[49]But President Truman had little time to enjoy the victory. [50]Japan was still at war in the Pacific, and now communist Soviet Union was in control of most of Eastern Europe. [51]Truman hoped that a new organization, the United Nations, could help resolve some of the thorny issues remaining. [52]As FDR had urged at the Yalta Conference, the United Nations was formed as an international organization for cooperation among nations of the world. [53]Unlike its earlier cousin, the post-WWI League of Nations, the United Nations was fully supported by the U.S. Congress.

**Fun Fact Feature**

Which major world city is the headquarters for the United Nations?

1. Where did D-Day take place?
   a. across the Mediterranean Sea on the Italian peninsula
   b. in the Soviet Union (USSR)
   c. on the deserts of northern Africa
   d. across the English Channel in Normandy, France

   Which sentence best supports the answer?

   ______

2. About how long after "D-Day" was the capitol of France liberated?
   a. two days
   b. two weeks
   c. two months
   d. two years

   Give Evidence:

   ________________________________________

3. What WWII conflict was named for the shape of the battle lines there?
   a. D-Day
   b. Battle of Berlin
   c. Battle of the Bulge
   d. Battle of Paris

   Which sentences best support the answer?

   ______ ______

4. What did President Roosevelt do on D-Day?
   a. lead a national prayer on radio
   b. commanded the invasion over the English Channel
   c. made a famous speech before Congress
   d. nothing, as it was a secret mission.

   Which sentences best support the answer?

   ______ ______

5. When did Franklin Roosevelt die?
   a. just after WWII ended in Europe
   b. just a month after starting his fourth term as president
   c. shortly after the D-Day invasion
   d. just after Britain's Winston Churchill but before the death of USSR's Josef Stalin

   Which sentence best supports the answer?

   ______

6. Which high-level American official viewed the Nazi death camps as the United States invaded Germany at the end of WWII?
   a. President Roosevelt
   b. President Truman
   c. General Anthony C. McAuliffe
   d. General Dwight Eisenhower

   Which sentence best supports the answer?

   ______

7. Explain the term "Holocaust" (with a capital "H").

   ________________________________________

   ________________________________________

   ________________________________________

   ________________________________________

8. Why did Americans celebrate on May 8, 1945?
   a. The D-Day invasion was a success.
   b. Germany surrendered and WWII ended in Europe.
   c. The Axis dictators Adolf Hitler and Benito Mussolini were both captured on that day.
   d. Americans won the Battle of the Bulge.

   Which sentences best support the answer?

   ______ ______

9. What new organization was created at the end of WWII to help foster international cooperation?
   a. League of Nations
   b. Yalta Conference
   c. Auschwitz
   d. United Nations

   Which sentence best supports the answer?

   ______


© 2016 The Critical Thinking Co.™ • www.CriticalThinking.com • 800-458-4849

## Written Response Question

10. Look at the 1944 political cartoon of D-Day to answer the questions.

a. Who is the main person drawn in the cartoon? What evidence from the lesson and cartoon supports your answer?

______________________________

______________________________

______________________________

b. Whose hand might be resting on the shoulder of the person in this cartoon? What evidence from the cartoon leads you to that conclusion?

______________________________

______________________________

c. What is the soldier looking at in this cartoon? What evidence from the lesson and cartoon supports your answer?

______________________________

______________________________

d. Explain the meaning of the phrase written on the man's shoulder?

______________________________

______________________________

**Fun Fact Finale**

The United Nations headquarters is in the United States in New York City.

© 2016 The Critical Thinking Co.™ • www.CriticalThinking.com • 800-458-4849

Lesson 35

# WW II Ends in the Pacific

## A. Soviet Headaches

[1]In February of 1945, before FDR died, he attended an Allied conference in Yalta with Britain's Churchill and USSR's Stalin. [2]FDR asked Stalin for help fighting the Japanese in the Pacific—to speed up an end to the war—and for the USSR's participation in the United Nations. [3]In return, FDR agreed to give the Soviet Union oversight in the creation of a new Polish government and land in Manchuria and China that the USSR had lost in the earlier Russo-Japanese War. [4]It was also agreed that Allied troops would continue to jointly occupy Germany for several years after its defeat in order to be certain that all Nazi elements were eliminated. [5]The Soviet Union demanded to occupy the eastern region of Germany.

Winston Churchill (left), Harry Truman, and Josef Stalin attended the Potsdam Conference in July 1945.

[6]After FDR's death, President Truman attended a meeting in Potsdam, Germany, in July of 1945 (Potsdam Conference), with Britain and the USSR to negotiate the future of war-torn Europe. [7]Although the Soviet Union still had not entered the war against Japan, Stalin now demanded that Poland remain under communist control as a defensive measure against possible future attacks from Western Europe. [8]Truman was more suspicious of Stalin than FDR. [9]He worried that the Soviet Union would try to expand its communist control over much of Eastern Europe. [10]Although he gave into Stalin's demand for communist control of Poland, Truman told Stalin that America was developing "a powerful new weapon" as a warning against future Soviet aggression.

## B. The Manhattan Project

Enrico Fermi

[11]Although President Truman wasn't very specific, he was talking about the atomic bomb. [12]Early in WWII, the United States had learned that Germany was close to creating an explosive device by splitting uranium atoms. [13]Two scientists who had escaped the Nazis, Albert Einstein from Germany and Enrico Fermi from Italy, had warned President Roosevelt that the United States needed to develop its own atomic research. [14]FDR eventually agreed and secretly ordered the start of the Manhattan Project—the building of an atomic weapon. [15]Some of the work was done at Columbia University on the island of Manhattan, in New York City. [16]Other parts of the project were developed in Hanford, Washington. [17]Fermi, sometimes called "the father of the atomic bomb," worked in Chicago, Illinois.

[18]Development of an atomic bomb was top secret; so secret that Vice President Truman was not told of the Manhattan Project until after FDR's death. [19]By the time Truman was at the Potsdam Conference, he knew that American scientists had successfully tested an atomic bomb in the desert near Los Alamos, New Mexico. [20]President Truman, the U.S. Commander-in-Chief, had a very tough decision to make. [21]If Japan did not surrender, American forces would have to either invade the islands of Japan—risking an estimated one million U.S. deaths—or use an amazing new weapon that would certainly cause mass destruction in Japan.

## C. The Atom Bomb

[22]On July 26$^{th}$, Truman issued an ultimatum (a final demand) to the Japanese: "Surrender unconditionally or face prompt and utter destruction." [23]Truman hoped Japan would quit the war, but all indications were that the Japanese would fight to the death. [24]In previous months, as the United States battled to take the small Japanese-controlled islands of Iwo Jima and Okinawa, Americans suffered tens of thousands of deaths. [25]Kamikaze flights continued to hit U.S. warships, Japanese balloon bombs were launched over the Pacific Ocean toward the


© 2016 The Critical Thinking Co.™ • www.CriticalThinking.com • 800-458-4849

The city of Hiroshima, Japan, was destroyed after it was the target of the world's first atomic bomb.

United States, and Japanese military officials vowed never to surrender.

[26]The Secretary of State, James Byrnes, told President Truman that using the bomb would show U.S. strength in the post-war world and "make Russia more manageable." [27]He urged Truman to use the atomic bomb to end the war before the Soviet Union joined the Pacific front to gain even more territory after the war.

[28]Japanese officials continued to refuse to surrender, so President Truman ordered the use of an atomic bomb. [29]Some scientists on the Manhattan Project urged Truman to warn the Japanese about the explosion or to target the bomb at an uninhabited place to demonstrate its power. [30]President Truman only had two working bombs however, and was unsure that either of them would really work if they were detonated (set off) after being dropped out of an airplane. [31]On August 6, 1945, a B-29 U.S. bomber nicknamed *Enola Gay* dropped an atomic bomb on a large city, Hiroshima, on the Japanese mainland. [32]Sixty thousand Japanese civilians died instantly and another seventy-five thousand died within the next few months.

[33]Two days later, American planes dropped leaflets on Japan warning of another attack. [34]The Soviet Union also finally declared war on Japan. [35]Yet, despite the horror of atomic warfare and its desperate military circumstances, the Japanese government again refused to surrender. [36]On August 9th, the United States targeted another large Japanese city, Nagasaki, with a second atomic bomb. [37]Another seventy thousand lives were instantly extinguished. [38]President Truman explained his decision to use the bomb in a speech to the American people shortly after the bombing of Nagasaki. [39]He said in part: "Having found the bomb we have used it. [40]We have used it against those who attacked us without warning at Pearl Harbor, against those who have starved and beaten and executed American prisoners of war, against those who have abandoned all pretense of obeying international laws of warfare. [41]We have used it in order to shorten the agony of war, in order to save the lives of thousands and thousands of young Americans."

[42]"V-J Day" came five days later on August 14, 1945, when Japan finally gave up. [43]U.S. General Douglas MacArthur accepted the Japanese surrender papers two weeks later.

[44]World War II was finally over and the Axis Powers defeated. [45]Four years of war, involving half of the war's population, had resulted in the deaths of fifty million people. [46]Forty percent of those war dead—twenty million—were from the Soviet Union. [47]American deaths totaled more than four hundred thousand.

### Fun Fact Feature

A Japanese film-maker in the 1950s introduced an enormous, violent, prehistoric sea monster who, the film suggested, was awakened and empowered by nuclear radiation from the atomic bomb blasts. (See photo at right.) Can you name this fictitious monster?

1. Which Allied Power gained control over lands in China and Poland at the end of WWII?
   a. Soviet Union
   b. France
   c. Great Britain
   d. United States

   Which sentence best supports the answer?

   ______

2. At the Yalta Conference, Allied Powers agreed to jointly occupy which Axis country after the war in order to be certain that all Nazi elements were eliminated?
   a. Germany
   b. Italy
   c. Japan
   d. Soviet Union

   Which sentence best supports the answer?

   ______

3. At the Potsdam Conference, who became worried that the Soviet Union would continue to expand its communist control over much of Eastern Europe after WWII?
   a. Josef Stalin
   b. Enrico Fermi
   c. General Douglas MacArthur
   d. Harry Truman

   Which sentences best support the answer?

   ______ ______

4. What was the code name for America's top secret development of an atomic weapon?
   a . V-J Day
   b. Enola Gay
   c. Manhattan Project
   d. D-Day

   Which sentence best supports the answer?

   ______

5. Who is sometimes called "the father of the atomic bomb"?
   a. James Byrne
   b. Adolf Hitler
   c. Enrico Fermi
   d. Albert Einstein

   Which sentence best supports the answer?

   ______

6. Who made the ultimate decision to use the atomic bomb against Japan?
   a. General Douglas MacArthur
   b. President Harry Truman
   c. President Franklin Roosevelt
   d. Secretary of State James Byrnes

   Which sentence best supports the answer?

   ______

7. What is ironic (a twist of fate) about the origin of the men who advised America to start development of an atomic weapon?

   ________________________________________

   ________________________________________

8. Why was August 6, 1945, an important day in world history?
   a. the first atomic bomb was used in warfare
   b. World War II in the Pacific ended
   c. World War II in Europe ended
   d. President Truman met USSR's Josef Stalin for the first time

   Which sentence best supports the answer?

   ______

9. Explain the term "V-J Day."

   ________________________________________

   ________________________________________


© 2016 The Critical Thinking Co.™ • www.CriticalThinking.com • 800-458-4849

## Written Response Question

10. Use complete sentences to describe some of the arguments for and against America using the atomic bomb in 1945.

**Fun Fact Finale**

The monster, Godzilla, has “atomic breath”—a nuclear blast that it generates inside of its body and unleashes from its jaws in the form of a blue or red radioactive heat ray.

© 2016 The Critical Thinking Co.™ • www.CriticalThinking.com • 800-458-4849

# Review: Lessons 30-35
## WW II Vocabulary

Write the letter of the definition of each vocabulary word. The number following each vocabulary word is the number of the lesson (30-35) where the word was used. All definitions are used once.

_____ 1. pretext (30)
_____ 2. feeble (30)
_____ 3. refugee (30)
_____ 4. appease (30)
_____ 5. compensation (31)
_____ 6. intelligence (31)
_____ 7. infamy (31)
_____ 8. duration (31)
_____ 9. synthetic (31)
_____ 10. dislodge (32)
_____ 11. demoralize (32)
_____ 12. implement (32)
_____ 13. intern (32)
_____ 14. decipher (33)
_____ 15. armada (34)
_____ 16. liberate (34)
_____ 17. prevail (34)
_____ 18. atrocity (34)
_____ 19. ultimatum (35)
_____ 20. detonate (35)

a. being known for a shameful, criminal act
b. to deprive one's spirit and courage
c. wicked, cruel, ruthless behavior
d. to perform or carry out
e. to satisfy or relieve a demand
f. to confine
g. an excuse, misleading statement
h. to succeed, win out
i. large fleet of military ships
j. remove or force out
k. weak, lacking force
l. making up for damage with a payment
m. secret information on enemies
n. to set off an explosion
o. a man-made substitute product
p. a final demand
q. entire length
r. a person who leaves his country seeking safety
s. to set free
t. to discover the meaning of


© 2016 The Critical Thinking Co.™ • www.CriticalThinking.com • 800-458-4849

Section 7: Introduction

# The 1950s

Soon after World War II ended, a new war erupted—the Cold War. The Cold War was an unusual kind of conflict. It was a competition of global positioning between the communist Soviet Union and the democratic United States to see which kind of government and economic system would dominate the post-war world. Each side gathered allies, developed intensive spy networks, and built up defense systems. Europe was split, and occasionally the Cold War turned hot—such as in Korea in the early 1950s. The competition even moved above the atmosphere as both countries engaged in a space race. Americans' deep fear of the spread of communism around the world developed into the Second Red Scare.

Despite the ever-growing defense budget, the U.S. economy boomed in the 1950s. Veterans received government aid to improve their education and find low-cost housing. Jobs were plentiful. Consumer spending was higher than ever before. Automobiles, home appliances, and televisions—a new popular form of entertainment—dominated the consumer market. After years of depression and war, Americans were happy to settle down, find a home, and start families. As a result, the birth rate increased tremendously and a "Baby Boom" generation made significant changes to American demographics.

Black Americans challenged the tradition of "separate but equal" more strongly than ever before in the 1950s. Martin Luther King led a movement that energized students and adults to take action to improve the treatment of black Americans. Congress, the Supreme Court, and Presidents Truman and Eisenhower each made significant moves in the area of civil rights.

## U.S. Presidents

33. Harry S. Truman
1945-1953

34. Dwight Eisenhower
1953-1961

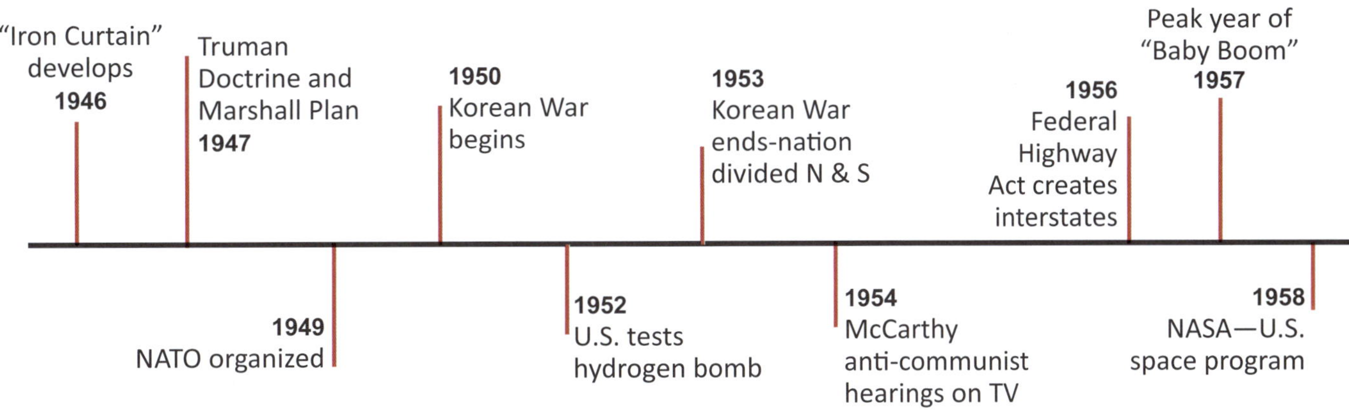

Lesson 36

# The Cold War Begins

## A. Mutual Mistrust

[1]Although the United States and the Soviet Union had been Allies against the Axis Powers (Germany, Japan, and Italy) in the early 1940s, their relationship had not been strong. [2]Americans disliked the communist form of government that had ruled the Union of Soviet Socialist Republics (USSR) ever since the Russian Revolution of 1917. [3]The Red Scare of the early 1920s in America was born out of a fear that communism was a threat to the U.S. capitalist economy and the civil liberties (civil rights and protections) provided by the U.S. constitution. [4]FDR and U.S. military officials had cooperated with Josef Stalin and the Red Army in World War II only because Adolph Hitler's Nazis had seemed an even greater threat. [5]After the war ended, relations were further strained when the United States agreed to accept the USSR's control of Poland, Czechoslovakia, Hungary, Romania, and Bulgaria, along with the eastern half of Germany, in exchange for the Soviet's help fighting the Japanese in the Pacific—something the Soviet's agreed to do, but never did.

[6]From the Soviet Union's point of view, it was upsetting that for the first 16 years after the Russian (Communist) Revolution in 1917, the United States did not send diplomats to its country. [7]Only when WWII threatened did the United States recognize the USSR as a legitimate nation. [8]Then, during the war, Stalin felt betrayed that the United States and Great Britain had taken so long to open a military front in France, forcing his country to fight alone on the Eastern Front. [9]In addition, neither Presidents Roosevelt nor Truman had ever told Stalin (the Soviet leader) about the development of the atomic bomb.

The Soviet Bear and the American Eagle—Symbols of the USSR and the U.S.—Divided After WWII

[10]Whatever shaky relationship held the United States and USSR together during WWII quickly disintegrated (broke apart) right after V-J Day. [11]For the next 45 years, the two countries engaged in an international rivalry that is called the Cold War. [12]During the Cold War, the United States and USSR both built separate alliances with other nations for self-defense, created spy networks, engaged in an arms race, competed for the best military technology,and even pursued a race into outer space. [13]Although there were no direct military campaigns against one another, the two superpowers spent billions of dollars on their national security, which included their military as well as control or influence over countries in many different regions of the world. [14]Occasionally, as in the Korean and Vietnam wars, the two nations came close to direct confrontation, but in both wars, the USSR refrained from sending Soviet troops directly against U.S. troops, but instead sent large amounts of military aid to its communist allies who were fighting U.S. troops and their allies.

## B. Divided Europe

[15]The competition for global or international strategic (important, crucial) positioning began in Eastern Europe in 1945. [16]Soviet troops, who had pushed back Nazi invaders all the way to Berlin, Germany, as WWII ended, continued to occupy Poland, Czechoslovakia, Hungary, Romania, Bulgaria, the former Baltic countries, and Eastern Germany. [17]Stalin noted that his country had been attacked from the west twice in the 20th Century and said the USSR needed to control these Eastern European territories for its own national security. [18]The USSR set up communist-controlled governments in those Eastern European countries to create a buffer (protection) zone, forced those nations to close their doors to trade from Western democracies, and attempted to deny all American influence in that region.

[19]Britain's Winston Churchill, on a visit to the United States in 1946, said the USSR was creating an "iron curtain" separating the Eastern half of Europe from the West. [20]He called upon President Truman and democratic nations to enact a policy of containment—uniting military and economic strategies to curb (control, limit) further Soviet expansion. [21]Truman and the U.S. government responded. [22]In 1947, the president announced


© 2016 The Critical Thinking Co.™ • www.CriticalThinking.com • 800-458-4849

a plan called the Truman Doctrine. [23]Abandoning any earlier policies of U.S. isolationism or neutrality, Truman proclaimed the United States would act as a global policeman. [24]It would provide economic aid to any democratic nation struggling for "freedom and liberty" against the threat of "oppression and

Joseph Stalin and Harry Truman at Potsdam, 1945

terror" posed by communist forces. [25]Specifically, he got the support of Congress to give 400 million dollars in aid to the countries of Turkey and Greece, both of which had rebel forces trying to resist communist takeovers.

[26]That same year, Congress approved an idea put forward by the U.S. Secretary of State called the Marshall Plan. [27]This program eventually spent 17 billion dollars more in U.S. aid to recovering European countries desperate for food, clothing, and shelter for their war-torn citizens. [28]Western European democracies gratefully accepted the help. [29]Within a few years, France, Britain, Ireland, Belgium, Western Germany, Italy, and the Scandinavian economies recovered from the war and remained solid U.S. allies. [30]These nations engaged in vigorous trade with the United States, which greatly strengthened the post-war economies of all of these nations. [31]The Eastern European nations under communist control—the so-called "satellite nations" or "Eastern bloc"—refused this aid, which continued the rejection of any U.S. influence in that region. [32]The USSR created its own aid program for that region called the Council for Mutual Economic Assistance (COMECON).

### C. Military Responses

[33]America responded to the crisis of the "iron curtain" not only economically but also militarily. [34]Within two years of the end of WWII, Congress passed the National Security Act of 1947, which did three important things. [35]First, all U.S. armed forces were united under one agency called the Department of Defense. [36]Each branch of the military—Army, Navy, Marines, Coast Guard, and the new Air Force—designated an officer to serve on the Joint Chiefs of Staff to advise the president on all military matters. [37]Secondly, a new U.S. spy network, called the Central Intelligence Agency (CIA), was formed to secretly gather information in foreign countries about matters regarding U.S. national security. [38]Thirdly, the National Security Council (NSA) was formed. [39]The head of the CIA, the Joint Chiefs, the Secretaries of Defense and State, joined the president and vice president to constantly monitor security issues.

[40]In 1949, the United States led the formation of a military alliance in Western Europe, called the North Atlantic Treaty Organization or NATO. [41]Ten original nations—there would be 28 worldwide by the early 2000s—joined together for mutual defense in response to an attack on any one of them by an external party—the principal threat being the USSR. [42]President Truman convinced Congress to fund the deployment of thousands of U.S. troops, under NATO commanders, to serve at military bases established in Europe. [43]The Soviet Union responded with a spy agency of its own, called the KGB, and its own military alliance. [44]The Eastern bloc governments joined the USSR in the Warsaw Pact in 1955—a military alliance like NATO.

Original NATO Members

[45]The Soviet Union caught up with U.S. nuclear technology by 1949, when it successfully tested its own atomic bomb. [46]Fearful Americans were soon instructed by the new Federal Civil Defense Administration on measures to be taken in case the bomb was ever directed at U.S. targets. [47]Air-raid shelters were set up in most cities and public school children learned how to dive under their desks and shield their eyes from possible atomic blasts during "duck and cover" drills. [48]More than a million U.S. citizens bought or constructed their own nuclear bomb shelters for their homes by the early 1950s.

A 1952 film discussed ways that Americans could protect themselves in the event of a nuclear attack by the USSR.

[49]President Truman authorized the development of a new weapon—the hydrogen bomb (H-bomb)—and it was ready for testing by 1952. [50]The H-bomb was a thousand times more powerful than the atomic bombs dropped on Japan. [51]When publicly detonated (set off) on tiny U.S. controlled test sites in the Pacific, such as Bikini Island, the bomb showed its awesome power. [52]However, it also spread radioactive material for miles that eventually created environmental problems and health issues for U.S. soldiers and Pacific Island natives. [53]Not wanting to fall behind, Soviet physicists developed their nation's own H-bomb by 1953. [54]The "arms race" was on.

**Fun Fact Feature**

After WWII, democratic nations with free market economies led by the United States and Western European countries were one part of the world. A second part of the world was communist nations led by the Soviet Union. What term was used to describe nations—generally poorer and undeveloped—which were not yet aligned with either the U.S. or the USSR?

 © 2016 The Critical Thinking Co.™ • www.CriticalThinking.com • 800-458-4849

1. What are two reasons the U.S. government was upset with the Soviet Union before 1946?

   a. ________________________________

   b. ________________________________

2. What are two reasons the Soviet Union was upset with the U.S. government before 1946?

   a. ________________________________

   b. ________________________________

3. What was the name for the international rivalry that existed for decades between the United States and the Soviet Union after the end of World War II?
   a. Marshall Plan
   b. Cold WAr
   c. Joint Chiefs
   d. Civil Defense

   Which sentence best supports the answer?

   ______

4. The "iron curtain" was a phrase used by Winston Churchill to describe an attempt by the USSR to separate __________ from __________.
   a. the USSR from China
   b. the USSR from the United States
   c. Germany from France
   d. Eastern Europe from Western Europe

   Which sentence best supports the answer?

   _____

5. Which of these promised U.S. aid to nations fighting takeover by communist forces after WWII in order to "contain" communism?
   a. Warsaw Pact
   b. the United Nations
   c. Truman Doctrine
   d. Federal Civil Defense Administration

   Which sentences best support the answer?

   _____ _____

6. What U.S. program gave massive economic aid to European nations trying to recover from World War II?
   a. COMECON
   b. Joint Chiefs of Staff
   c. Marshall Plan
   d. NATO

   Which sentences best support the answer?

   _____ _____

7. What U.S. led effort gave massive military aid to Western European nations trying to insure collective security after World War II?
   a. NSC
   b. CIA
   c. NATO
   d. KGB

   Which sentences best support the answer?

   _____ _____

8. The United States developed the world's first atomic bomb. Which nation first developed the more powerful hydrogen bomb (H-bomb)?

   __________________________

   Which sentence best supports the answer?

   _____

9. Which U.S. law established a U.S. spy agency, a united military command, and a special security advisory group for the president?
   a. National Security Act of 1947
   b. Truman Doctrine
   c. Marshall Plan
   d. Eastern bloc

   Which sentences best support the answer?

   _____ _____ _____ _____

## Written Response Question

10. Look at the political cartoon at the right to answer the questions.

a. Describe three pieces of the device in the cartoon.

______________________________________

______________________________________

______________________________________

______________________________________

b. What is the message of the cartoonist?

______________________________________

______________________________________

______________________________________

______________________________________

**Fun Fact Finale**

After WWII, democratic nations with free market economies led by the United States and Western European countries were one part of the world. A second part of the world was communist nations led by the Soviet Union. Countries that were generally poorer, undeveloped, and not yet aligned with either the United States or the USSR were called "Third World Nations."


© 2016 The Critical Thinking Co.™ • www.CriticalThinking.com • 800-458-4849

Lesson 37

# The Cold War Heats Up

## A. Positioning in the Pacific

[1]After World War II, the United States left occupation forces in Japan under the command of U.S. General Douglas MacArthur. [2]Many Japanese cities and much of the Japanese economy were destroyed during the war, which resulted in food shortages and starvation. [3]MacArthur's first goal was to feed the starving Japanese citizens. [4]His next goal was to demilitarize (weaken the power of the Japanese military) and replace Emperor Hirohito with a democratic leader to strengthen the economy and to avoid Japan embracing communism or becoming a military threat. [5]Even after the formal U.S. occupation ended in 1952, the United States retained military bases in Japan and promised to protect it if attacked by enemy forces.

[6]The American government also helped put down a communist rebellion in the former U.S. territory of the Philippines and supported France in its efforts to reestablish postwar rule in Indochina (now Vietnam). [7]The United States also signed mutual defense deals with Australia and New Zealand.

[8]The USSR countered by making moves in China. [9]During WWII there had been two Chinese leaders, each with different ideas on the future of China, leading the fight against Japanese forces. [10]The United States had backed a nationalist leader named Jiang Jieshi (also known as Chiang Kai-shek), who seemed to favor the idea of a democratic postwar China. [11]After the war, the United States continued to support his forces with three billion dollars in aid. [12]Jiang Jieshi and his nationalists were overtaken in 1949 by Chinese communist forces led by Mao Zedong. [13]Now there were two Chinas: The Republic of China, a nationalist government pushed out to the small island of Taiwan, and the communist People's Republic of China (PRC or Red China) on the mainland of Asia. [14]For the next several decades, the United States refused to recognize the PRC as the legitimate government of China and its one billion people.

## B. Korean War

[15]Between Japan and China lay the peninsula of Korea. [16]The United States and the Soviet Union agreed to jointly occupy Korea after the U.S. victory over Japan. [17]A supposedly "temporary" borderline at the $38^{th}$ parallel of latitude separated the Soviet-backed north from the American-backed south for the first five years of occupation.

[18]But in June of 1950, North Korean troops—supplied by China and the Soviet Union—attacked South Korea, pushing deep down the peninsula. [19]President Truman, who had been stung by the fall of China to the communists the year before and the continued occupation of Eastern Europe by the communists, reacted swiftly. [20]Rather than ask Congress to declare war, the president proposed that United Nations forces, under the command of General Douglas MacArthur, repel the North Korean attack. [21]The UN agreed. Soon troops, mainly U.S. forces that had been based in Japan, were on the counterattack.

[22]In the first year of the Korean War, the North Korean military nearly conquered the entire peninsula (see Korean War map, page 202). [23]However, in September of 1950, MacArthur led a daring UN attack 150 miles north of the front, at the western port city of Inchon, and surprised the communist forces. [24]In a matter of weeks, UN forces regained not only all the land south of 38°, they pushed north all the way to the Korean/Chinese border at the Yalu River. [25]MacArthur hoped to liberate all of Korea from the communists. [26]He even pressed President Truman to allow UN forces to continue into Red China if necessary to gain "total victory" and suggested the possible use of atomic weapons. [27]President Truman refused. [28]Truman and other UN leaders only wanted a "limited war."

[29]In the winter of 1950-1951, more than 300,000 communist Chinese soldiers struck at MacArthur's position in the Yalu River region and drove the UN army all the way out of North Korea in a bloody counterattack. [30]MacArthur blamed Truman, the

© 2016 The Critical Thinking Co.™ • www.CriticalThinking.com • 800-458-4849

commander-in-chief of the U.S. military, for not allowing him to cross the Yalu River. [31]Then, when Truman sought a negotiated peace with the communists for a permanently divided Korea, MacArthur again publicly criticized the president. [32]Despite American public opinion, which largely supported MacArthur's views, the president fired MacArthur for insubordination (putting a commanding officer in an inferior position). [33]"We are trying to prevent a world war," Truman said, "not to start one."

[34]The war became a stalemate at mid-peninsula for the next two years. [35]In July 1953, both sides of the Korean War came together at Panmunjom, just north of the South Korean capital of Seoul. [36]They reached an agreement to end the fighting and establish a permanent border where the war had originally started—the 38th parallel. [37]More than 54,000 Americans died in this so-called "police action" that cost 54 billion dollars. [38]The war had convinced Americans that national defense against communism must now be a priority. [39]By the mid-1950s, America had stockpiled (reserved or cached) about 750 nuclear bombs. [40]Almost 60 percent of the U.S. federal budget was dedicated to defense spending as compared to about 16 percent today.

### C. Second Red Scare

[41]Obsessed with security, many state governments, as well as the federal government, started passing laws requiring government workers to sign loyalty oaths in order to retain their jobs. [42]In 1947, President Truman signed an Executive Order called the Federal Employee Loyalty Program that allowed the Attorney General's office to investigate any federal employee who was found to have associated with any of nearly 90 organizations the government listed as "subversive." [43]The list included various communist groups, Nazi groups, and the Ku Klux Klan. [44]Any federal employees found to be associating in any way with an organization on the list were investigated. [45]Hundreds were fired or denied employment without trial or the ability to face their accusers.

[46]The House Un-American Activities Committee (HUAC) had been started in the WWII era as a way to investigate Nazi activity within the United States. [47]By the late 1940s, that Congressional committee began investigating whether or not communists had infiltrated (penetrated, worked into) the U.S. government. [48]In 1951, communists Klaus Fuch, Julius Rosenberg, and Ethel Rosenberg (Julius's sister)—who had each worked on the Manhattan Project—were found guilty and executed for passing atomic secrets to the USSR. [49]The Soviet possession of atomic weapons, the "fall" of the Republic of China, and spies in the United States were many things that worried Americans in the early 1950s. [50]They feared that their nation could soon be under attack by communists. [51]This wave of anti-communist fears after WWII has been called the Second Red Scare.

A 1947 Comic Book Cover

[52]Hollywood movie producers came under special scrutiny (intense inspection) as HUAC felt certain that communist propaganda films were being made. [53]No threat to America was uncovered in the film industry, but many directors, writers, and actors found it hard to find work when they were put on the "blacklist" (an unofficial record of persons under suspicion).

[54]The Senate side of Congress also had its anti-Red crusaders. [55]Two of the most well-known senators were conservative Republicans Richard Nixon and Joseph McCarthy who gained fame for implicating Alger Hiss, a State Department official who had worked with FDR at the Yalta Conference, in a treason scandal. [56]Joseph McCarthy of Wisconsin, fighting for reelection in 1950, sought the limelight of being an anti-communist crusader.


© 2016 The Critical Thinking Co.™ • www.CriticalThinking.com • 800-458-4849

[57]He claimed he had uncovered "205 cases of individuals who would appear to be card-carrying members, or certainly loyal to, the Communist

Senator Joseph McCarthy

Party, but who nevertheless are still helping to shape our foreign policy" in the State Department. [58]McCarthy never actually found even one person, but this smeared the reputation of many Americans in the process. [59]In 1954, McCarthy used television for the first time to broadcast a Senate hearing investigating his charge that communists ran the U.S. Army, and the American public saw first-hand what he was —a bully and a liar. [60]Embarrassed, the Senate passed a resolution calling McCarthy's accusations "a fraud and a hoax." [61]McCarthy died three years later of alcohol-related causes. [62]The term "McCarthyism" still means using political charges to attack an individual's or group's patriotism and/or character without reasonable evidence.

**Fun Fact Feature**

After reading this lesson, it should be clear which color is connected with communism. Name it.

1. What large Asian nation came under communist control in 1949?
   a. Japan
   b. China
   c. India
   d. Korea

   Which sentence best supports the answer?

   _____

2. Who led the American occupation forces in Japan after WWII and UN forces during the Korean War?
   a. Mao Zedong
   b. Douglas MacArthur
   c. Julius Rosenberg
   d. Joseph McCarthy

   Which sentences best support the answer?

   _____ _____

3. Which part of the Korean peninsula did the United States support?

   ______________________

   Which sentence supports your answer?

   _____

4. The Red Scare in America followed the Great War (WWI). What did the Second Red Scare follow?
   a. the Korean War
   b. the start of the Great Depression
   c. McCarthyism
   d. World War II

   Which sentence supports your answer?

   _____

5. How was the Korean War settled in 1953?

   ____________________________________

   ____________________________________

   ____________________________________

6. General MacArthur was fired because he publicly argued with his superior officer, President Truman, and United Nations leaders over policy in the Korean War. MacArthur wanted “total victory” over the communists. What did the president and the UN want?
   a. atomic warfare
   b. a surrender to North Korea
   c. a limited war and divided Korea
   d. the Second Red Scare

   Which sentences support your answer?

   _____ _____

7. Which of these persons was elected to Congress by using the fear of communism associated with the Second Red Scare?
   a. Joseph McCarthy
   b. Douglas MacArthur
   c. Harry Truman
   d. Alger Hiss

   Which sentence supports your answer?

   _____

8. What was the HUAC?
   a. a subversive communist organization
   b. the nickname for UN forces in the Korean War
   c. a new type of atomic weapon
   d. an anti-communist Congressional committee

   Which sentences support your answer?

   _____ _____

9. How many cases of communists in the U.S. State Department did Senator McCarthy uncover in his investigation in the early 1950s?
   a. zero
   b. only 1
   c. sixteen
   d. more than three dozen

   Which sentence supports your answer?

   _____


© 2016 The Critical Thinking Co.™ • www.CriticalThinking.com • 800-458-4849

## Written Response Question

10. Use complete sentences to describe why "McCarthyism" is used as a negative term.

___

___

___

___

___

___

___

___

### Fun Fact Finale

After reading this lesson, it should be clear that red is the color associated with communism. Do you remember why? If not, review Lesson 20. The symbol at the right, the hammer and sickle, also represents communism.

© 2016 The Critical Thinking Co.™ • www.CriticalThinking.com • 800-458-4849 

# Bonus Activity
# Korean War Geography

Look at the maps below and review lesson 37 to answer questions about the Korean War.

Phases of the Korean War

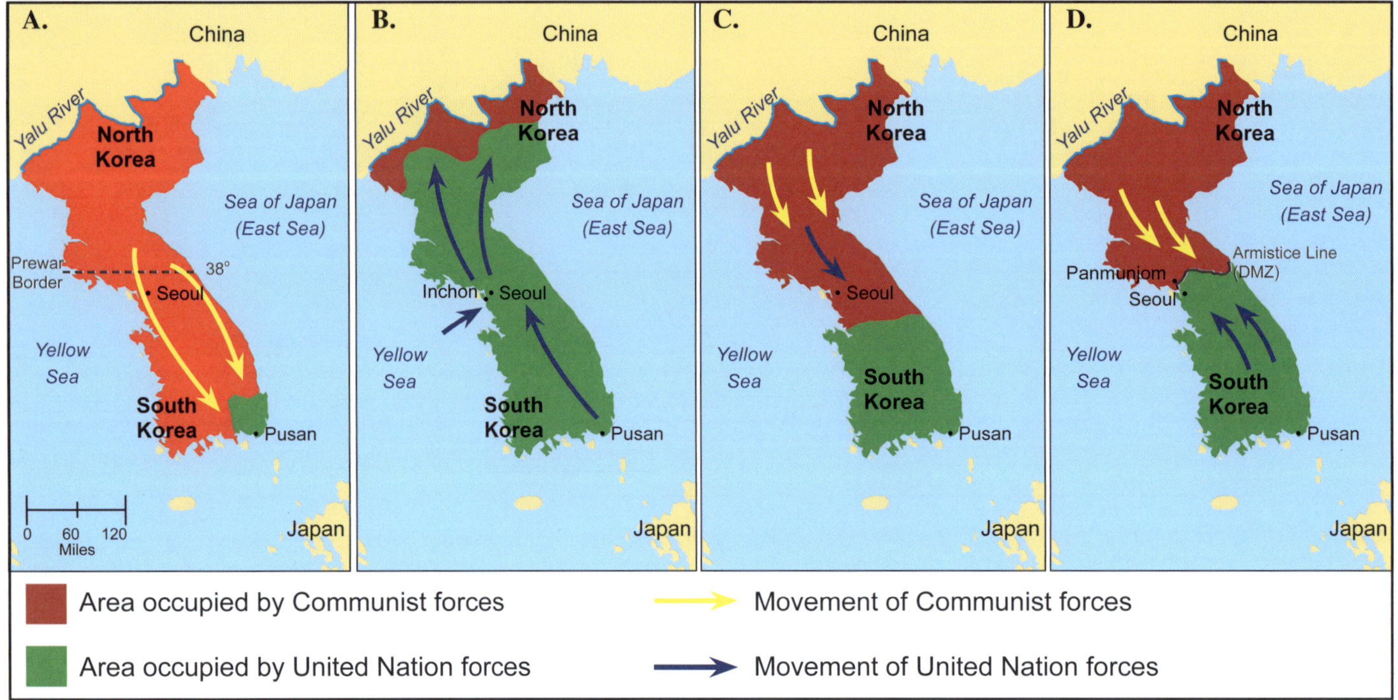


_______________ 1. Which of these panels (A, B, C, or D) represents General MacArthur's surprise attack on communist forces in September of 1950?

_______________ 2. Give a time reference for Panel A.

_______________ 3. Give a time reference for Panel D.

_______________ 4. Name the two seas that are east and west of the peninsula of Korea.

_______________

_______________ 5. What river forms the boundary between North Korea and China?

_______________ 6. Korea was divided before and after the Korean War near which parallel of latitude?

_______________ 7. Using the scale on the map, approximately how many miles separate the Japanese mainland from South Korea?


© 2016 The Critical Thinking Co.™ • www.CriticalThinking.com • 800-458-4849

Lesson 38

# The Baby Boom

## A. Birth Rate Soars After WWII

[1]Between 1946 and 1964, there was a huge increase in the birthrate in America. [2]During the Great Depression and WWII, the birthrate had been low, but during the so-called "Baby Boom" following World War II, the birthrate was higher than ever before in U.S. history. [3]In the year after the war, 1946, the birth rate was up 20 percent. [4]By the peak year of the boom, 1957, about 11,800 babies were born in the United States every day. [5]This meant millions of young children. [6]By 1960, one-third of the U.S. population were "Baby Boomers." [7]The birth rate declined to normal levels by about 1964. [8]This generation has had amazing effects upon U.S. culture throughout its existence.

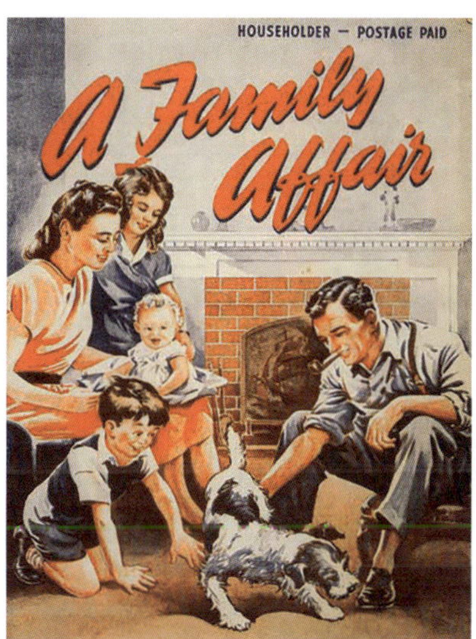

A 1949 Magazine Cover

[9]During WWII, couples had delayed starting their families because women were often working in war production plants while their husbands were off fighting the war. [10]Women saved their money because there were so few consumer goods to purchase in wartime. [11]After the war, men and women wanted to settle down to a more normal, peacetime lifestyle. [12]Women were expected to give up their jobs to returning servicemen and return to the "home." [13]Women were marrying earlier than those of the previous generation, giving them more childbearing years.

[14]With more affordable transportation (cars, trains, and busses) many families decided to move to the suburbs (housing outside the urban downtown) where they could find new, inexpensive housing in quiet, safe, neighborhoods. [15]During WWII, a contractor named William Levitt had perfected techniques to quickly build housing units at military bases. [16]After the war, he understood the desire of families for new suburban housing. [17]Levitt purchased a large plot of land outside of New York City and created 27 different teams of builders—a team for each phase of construction—and began mass production of homes. [18]Each of his homes was simple and the same. [19]Each home was built on a concrete slab with two bedrooms, one bathroom, a small garage, a family room and dining room, and a kitchen at the back of the house, so mothers could watch over their children playing in the backyard. [20]By completing 36 houses a day, Levittown, New York, was soon a large suburban area of more than 6,000 homes. [21]It quickly filled with families as they realized the cost of owning these homes was less than the rent they'd been paying for their inner-city apartments. [22]Other contractors copied Levitt's techniques and soon every city saw a housing growth on its outskirts.

An Ad For a New "Ranch-Style" Home in Levittown in the 1950s

## B. Baby Boom Products

[23]Baby Boom parents read books such as *Baby and Child Care* by Dr. Benjamin Spock, to learn how to raise their ever-growing families. [24]Dads read the new paperback novels that were very popular. [25]Their children eventually read comic books that were cheap and fun.

[26]Businessmen realized that this large number of children created a market for baby-related products. [27]Diapers, baby food, and toys sold in huge quantities. [28]Hula hoops and Davy Crockett coonskin caps became the rage. [29]Many of these products were purchased with new plastic "credit cards" when parents went to newly developed "shopping malls." [30]There were only eight shopping malls in the United States in 1945. [31]By 1960, there were 3,840.

[32]People saw many products while watching a new home gadget called television. [33]Television sets for the home market began selling to the wealthy class after the war. [34]Before long they were more affordable and, by the end of the 1950s, more than 75 percent of all homes had one. [35]Family shows such as *Leave It to Beaver*, *Father Knows*

*Best*, *I Love Lucy*, and *The Mickey Mouse Club* were popular—and filled with advertising. [36]Frozen TV dinners were invented to take advantage of this new situation.

A family watches television in 1958.

[37]When the weather outside was nice, the barbeque on the deck or patio was the place to be. [38]If moms decided to cook their meals indoors, they had all kinds of new kitchen gadgets: electric can openers, refrigerator-freezers, and electric knives. [39]If a family decided to eat out, they wanted inexpensive food that was quickly prepared in a clean, family-oriented environment. [40]Maybe that's why McDonald's hamburger restaurants became so popular by the end of the decade.

[41]As the children grew a little older, they started listening to a new type of music called "rock and roll." [42]Elvis Presley became "the King" of rock and roll. [43]He was heard on radio, seen in movies, and often appeared on TV shows such as *American Bandstand*. [44]Some older, conservative, religious Americans thought that this new music was deviant (perverted, weird). [45]They also questioned the values of the beat generation "beatniks," who embraced jazz music, poetry, and artistic creativity while rejecting what they considered American materialism.

[46]The automobile was more popular than ever before. [47]There had not been any civilian cars made during WWII, so Americans were anxious to purchase new models. [48]The cars were loaded with chrome. [49]"Fins" made them look a little like WWII fighter planes. [50]New highways were developed and Americans had more mobility than ever before. [51]They needed all these new roads so they could take family vacations every summer and commute to work from the suburbs. [52]More dads were going to jobs such as accounting, advertising, sales, and other business-related occupations than in the past.

The 1957 Chevrolet Bel-Air featured fins and chrome.

### C. Baby Boom Culture

[53]Cartoon film maker Walt Disney started Disneyland in Southern California in 1955, as a place for families to have fun. [54]Soon other family theme parks followed suit. [55]Families took their automobiles to the new drive-in theaters, often viewing science-fiction thrillers. [56]On weekends, dads took the kids to see baseball games or to the bowling alley. [57]Baseball and bowling were more popular than ever because they were such family-oriented sports.

[58]All these children created a need for new elementary schools. [59]Schools were constructed rapidly and cheaply following WWII, and they filled up as quickly as they were built. [60]Grade school teachers were in short supply. [61]The PTA (Parent Teacher Association) movement was at its peak. [62]At school, girls wore poodle skirts and their hair in ponytails. [63]Boys had short hair in "crew cut" style. [64]They wore T-shirts more often than button down shirts.

[65]Children were taught "right and wrong" in school and at home. [66]Churches were more popular than ever before. [67]Church membership doubled in the 1950s and, by the end of the decade, more than 90 percent of American families said that they were affiliated with a church. [68]The Reverend Billy Graham became a popular evangelist by not only appearing in large outdoor stadiums but by using the new medium of television. [69]Some historians note that the increased religious activity may have been another Red Scare response. [70]Vladimir Lenin, who had led the Communist Revolution in 1917, had said that religion was a tool used by the ruling classes to give working classes false hope. [71]In the era of Stalin, the Soviet Union was promoting atheism (no belief in God), churches were often closed, religion discouraged, and religious followers often persecuted. [72]Congress reacted by adding the words "In God We Trust" to U.S. coins and currency, and the phrase "under God" to the American Pledge of Allegiance.

© 2016 The Critical Thinking Co.™ • www.CriticalThinking.com • 800-458-4849

**Fun Fact Feature**

Perhaps the most popular U.S. doll ever made was created in 1959. Can you name her?

1. What years do historians give for the "Baby Boom"?

   ___________ to ___________

   Which sentences best support the answer?

   _____ _____

2. According to the chart below, and text in the lesson, what was the peak year of the Baby Boom?

   ___________

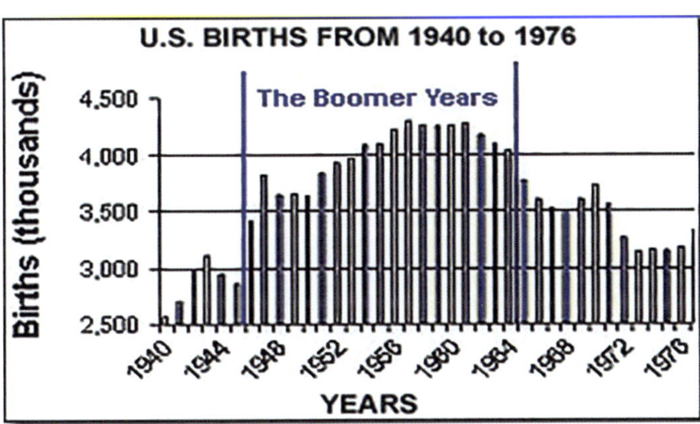


3. What was William Levitt's contribution to the Baby Boom era?
   a. He led a religious revival in America.
   b. He created the fast food industry.
   c. He built the most stylish car of the era.
   d. He mass produced homes in the suburbs.

   Which sentence best supports the answer?

   _____

4. Which of these persons is NOT associated with the American "Baby Boom" era?
   a. Vladimir Lenin
   b. Walt Disney
   c. Benjamin Spock
   d. Reverend Billy Graham

   Which sentence best supports the answer?

   _____

5. Name four products that showed tremendous growth in the 1950s.

   a. ______________________

   b. ______________________

   c. ______________________

   d. ______________________

6. What did Reverend Billy Graham do that helped him become extremely popular in spreading his religious message in the 1950s?
   a. run for political office
   b. appear on television
   c. make radio sermons
   d. travel to the Soviet Union

   Which sentence best supports the answer?

   _____

7. Which of these sports was the most popular in the 1950s?
   a. professional football
   b. baseball
   c. soccer
   d. basketball

   Which sentence best supports the answer?

   _____

8. Elvis Presley became the most popular figure in which area?
   a. modern art
   b. professional sports
   c. religion
   d. rock and roll music

   Which sentence best supports the answer?

   _____

© 2016 The Critical Thinking Co.™ • www.CriticalThinking.com • 800-458-4849 

9. What appeared on U.S. money and in the "Pledge of Allegiance" for the first time during the 1950s?
    a. communism
    b. God
    c. U.S. flag
    d. the word "democracy"

    Which sentence best supports the answer?

    ______

## Written Response Question

10. Use complete sentences to discuss three reasons why the "Baby Boom" occurred.

________________________________________

________________________________________

________________________________________

________________________________________

________________________________________

________________________________________

________________________________________

________________________________________

**Fun Fact Finale**

The Barbie doll was created by Ruth Handler for the Mattel toy company in 1959. Ruth, inspired by dolls she'd seen on a trip to Europe, and from watching her own daughter, Barbara, created an adult doll for children. Twelve inches high and plastic, the new "Barbie" doll and her fashionable and separately-sold clothing were an instant hit.


© 2016 The Critical Thinking Co.™ • www.CriticalThinking.com • 800-458-4849

Lesson 39

# Truman and Eisenhower

## A. Truman Administration

[1]Immediately after the end of World War II, economists, who had helped engineer FDR's New Deal programs, predicted horrific economic problems as government spending slowed and millions of returning soldiers left the military looking for jobs. [2]Government spending did drop nearly 75 percent after the war, yet a booming economy developed. [3]More than four million jobs were created between 1945 and 1947. [4]In spite of the growing economy, President Harry Truman was forced to decide how to deal with dissatisfaction at home and the Cold War abroad. [5]After the war, many unions went on strike (work stoppage), demanding higher wages. [6]The union strikes and the booming economy created shortages of housing and consumer goods. [7]The public blamed the Truman administration, because of the Democratic Party's close ties with large labor unions. [8]This dissatisfaction led to Republican majorities in both houses of Congress in the 1946 mid-term elections.

[9]To help the president with these complex economic issues, Truman urged Congress to pass the Employment Act of 1946. [10]This law created the Council of Economic Advisors to help the president make informed economic policy. [11]The Council recommended, and Truman agreed, to discontinue many New Deal work programs. [12]"The American people have been through a lot of experiments," Truman said, "and they want a rest." [13]Price controls and rationing that had been in place during the war were lifted.

[14]To help returning veterans, Congress passed the Serviceman's Readjustment Act. [15]Commonly called the G.I. Bill, the law gave veterans priority for many jobs, granted government loans to G.I.s who wanted to buy a home or start a business, and provided money to attend school or college to retrain for new jobs. [16]By 1947, more than half of all college students were veterans. [17]The number of college degrees issued doubled between 1940 and 1950. [18]A college education, once generally only an upper-class privilege, was becoming a standard opportunity for the middle class.

[19]As the 1948 election approached, Truman remained unpopular with the American public, which caused many to believe he faced certain defeat in the 1948 presidential election. [20]Liberal Democrats, who were upset that Truman had abandoned many New Deal programs, reformed the Progressive Party and ran Henry Wallace as their candidate. [21]Southern conservative Democrats, concerned with Truman's attempts to advance civil rights for minorities, formed the Dixiecrat Party and ran Strom Thurmond of South Carolina as their candidate.

A Chicago newspaper was so certain Dewey would win the 1948 election, they mistakenly printed the wrong advanced headline, much to President Truman's delight.

[22]"To err is Truman," some joked, using the president's name instead of the word "human" in the famous quote. [23]It looked like the Republican candidate, New York governor Thomas Dewey, would easily win the 1948 election.

[24]Undeterred by the predictions, Truman campaigned hard. [25]He won the union vote by vetoing the Taft-Hartley Act, a Congressional bill that would have limited union activity. [26]He won the votes of minorities by proposing civil rights legislation and becoming the first presidential candidate to openly campaign for black support. [27]He also kept the vote of most moderate Democrats, who thought the Progressive and Dixiecrat parties too extreme. [28]In perhaps the biggest presidential upset in U.S. history, Truman won a second term.

## B. "I Like Ike"

[29]Truman's second term was overwhelmingly burdened with Cold War decisions. [30]The Second Red Scare and the Korean War dogged his presidency. [31]Truman could have run for president again

© 2016 The Critical Thinking Co.™ • www.CriticalThinking.com • 800-458-4849 

in 1952—the 22nd Amendment limiting a president to two terms had just been ratified but it did not apply to Truman—but Truman's approval rating was very low. 32Instead, Democrats nominated Illinois governor Adlai Stevenson. 33Republicans chose self-described "Progressive Republican"—and World War II hero—Dwight Eisenhower as their candidate. 34Eisenhower, to appease more conservative members of the Republican Party, chose Richard Nixon as his running mate. 35"I Like Ike" (Eisenhower's nickname) became their catchy campaign slogan. 36When Eisenhower promised to go to Korea personally to end the war, if elected, the American public responded positively. 37His strong military background was a positive attribute (characteristic or quality) in the Cold War era. 38In 1952, he won 39 of the 48 states and became the first Republican president in 20 years.

39President Eisenhower was a comfortable choice for Americans in the 1950s. 40"Ike" seemed moderate (not extreme left or right wing policies), non-political, and trustworthy. 41He had grown up in a poor Kansas family and worked his way up to the highest ranks of the Army by sharing authority with trusted aides, while never seeking the limelight. 42He had not even sought the presidency in 1952, and said that he only agreed to be a candidate out of a sense of duty to the country.

43As president, Eisenhower caused few controversies and remained popular with the public. 44Even though he experienced a heart attack in 1955, the American public voted to reelect him to a second term the next year.

### C. Domestic Issues of the Eisenhower Years

45Behind the scenes, President Eisenhower worked hard to create his vision of America. 46He called his economic policies "Modern Republicanism." 47He expanded some popular liberal programs such as Social Security and the minimum wage but supported conservative efforts to keep inflation in check and to decrease overall government spending.

48Eisenhower did want to spend tax money on improving roads, however. 49He championed the Federal Highway Act of 1956 that authorized the building of a national interstate system of freeways across the country. 50This was the largest public works project yet in American history. 51Eisenhower signed the bill, however, arguing that the freeways were a national defense project. 52If America was ever attacked by communist forces, cities would have to be evacuated and military equipment moved quickly throughout the nation.

Los Angeles, California, was one major city that depended upon the new interstate highways for transportation in the 1950s.

53President Eisenhower also created a new cabinet level agency, the Department of Health, Education, and Welfare. 54During the 1950s, a tremendous scientific effort was made to prevent some major disease outbreaks. 55Doctors Jonas Salk and Albert Sabin developed vaccines for polio, the disease that paralyzed FDR, by mid-decade. 56A new measles vaccine stopped another frequent childhood disease. 57Penicillin and other anti-bacterial drugs became common ammunition for doctors engaged in the fight against infection.

58By decade's end, a book titled *Affluent Society* by economist John K. Galbraith described an America where two-thirds of families owned homes and three-fourths owned cars. 59The country did indeed seem affluent (having an abundance of wealth or material goods): federal deficit spending was nearly eliminated, unemployment rates averaged only five percent, wages were up thirty-five percent since the end of WWII, electrical consumption tripled, and the United States enjoyed the world's highest standard of living.

### D. Foreign Policy Challenges

60President Eisenhower could not dodge Cold War confrontations, of course. 61After the armistice was signed in Korea in 1953, incidents in the Middle East forced him to issue the Eisenhower Doctrine. 62The president said the United States was prepared to send military and economic aid, as well as U.S. troops, to the Middle East to counter aggression from any country in that region threatened by communism. 63During his administration, Eisenhower sent aid and troops to places such as Jordan, Egypt, and Lebanon and allowed the CIA to help rebels overthrow a


© 2016 The Critical Thinking Co.™ • www.CriticalThinking.com • 800-458-4849

government in Iran that was thought to be an enemy of the United States. [64]Eisenhower also lent U.S. support to the French government, which was holding on to territory in Southeast Asia, in a region later called Vietnam.

A young Siberian Husky named Laika, rescued from the streets of Moscow, USSR, was a passenger aboard Sputnik - the first satellite to orbit Earth - in 1957.

[65]The Cold War also erupted in the skies overhead in the 1950s. [66]In 1957, the USSR was the first nation to successfully launch a satellite into orbit—"Sputnik"—that could send radio messages back to Earth. [67]Soon animals, and even human "cosmonauts," were encircling the planet in Soviet spacecraft. [68]President Eisenhower pushed Congress to enter the "space race" by creating America's National Aeronautics and Space Administration (NASA) in 1958. [69]The National Defense Education Act, also passed in 1958, gave billions of dollars to improve science and technology education in the United States at all levels. [70]An "astronaut" named John Glenn became the first American to orbit Earth in a U.S. made rocket ship in 1962.

**Fun Fact Feature**

This lesson noted that Eisenhower won 39 of 48 states in the presidential election of 1952. In 1959, two more states were added to the Union. What were the country's 49th and 50th states?

1. What law provided housing and education benefits to returning WWII American veterans?
    a. National Defense Education Act
    b. Employment Act of 1946
    c. Federal Highway Act of 1956
    d. G.I. Bill

    Which sentence best supports the answer?

    _____

2. Who was the U.S. president for most of the decade of the 1950s?
    a. Dwight Eisenhower
    b. Harry Truman
    c. Thomas Dewey
    d. Richard Nixon

    Which sentences best support the answer?

    _____ _____

3. Who does the Council of Economic Advisors advise?
    a. Congress
    b. Supreme Court
    c. President
    d. Wall Street

    Which sentence best supports the answer?

    _____

4. Which of these is NOT a good descriptive term for Dwight Eisenhower?
    a. WWII Army hero
    b. Democrat
    c. political moderate
    d. born to a poor Kansas family

    Which sentence best supports the answer?

    _____

5. Look at the political cartoon on page 209.
    a. Who is the man in the cartoon?

    ______________________________

    b. Who might the woman represent?

    ______________________________

    c. Why might the man be welcomed?

    ______________________________

6. Doctors Albert Sabin and Jonas Salk were famous for what in the 1950s?
    a. creating a vaccine against polio
    b. designing the first American rocket to orbit the earth
    c. writing the best seller *Affluent Society*
    d. forming a new political party to challenge Truman in 1948

    Which sentence best supports the answer?

    _____

7. What became the largest federal public works project in U.S. history in the late 1950s?

    ______________________________

    ______________________________

8. In this political cartoon of 1957, what is apparently interrupting President Eisenhower's golf game?
    a. a communist caddy
    b. Soviet satellite
    c. Korean War
    d. heart attack

    Which sentence best supports the answer?

    _____

9. The Eisenhower Doctrine was a policy statement by the president in reaction to communist threats in which region of the world?
    a. Korea
    b. outer space
    c. South America
    d. Middle East

    Which sentence best supports the answer?

    _____


© 2016 The Critical Thinking Co.™ • www.CriticalThinking.com • 800-458-4849

## Written Response Question

10. Use complete sentences to describe why Truman's reelection as president in 1948 was an upset victory.

_______________________________________________
_______________________________________________
_______________________________________________
_______________________________________________
_______________________________________________
_______________________________________________
_______________________________________________
_______________________________________________
_______________________________________________
_______________________________________________
_______________________________________________

**Fun Fact Finale**

Alaska became the 49th state and Hawaii the 50th state in 1959.

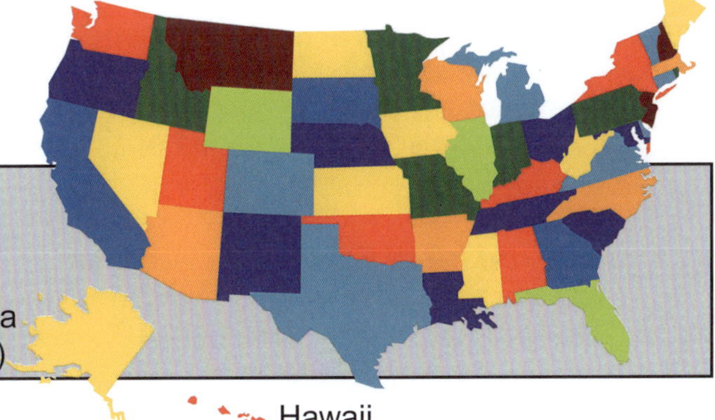

Lesson 40

# Post WWII Civil Rights Movement

## A. Post War Gains

[1]A black veteran returning to his home in South Carolina soon after WWII was attacked and blinded by racist whites for failing to sit in a segregated section of a bus. [2]This was one of many incidents of racial discrimination in the 1940s that horrified President Truman. [3]In 1946, he established the President's Commission on Civil Rights to make recommendations on ways "to ensure the equality of treatment and opportunity" for all Americans. [4]Acting on several proposals of the commission's report, Truman issued executive orders that banned racial discrimination in hiring for federal jobs. [5]He also ordered the desegregation of the military in 1948. [6]The Korean War would be America's first conflict in which whites and blacks fought side by side.

[7]A black veteran, Jackie Robinson, made a huge impact on civil rights when he returned home from his WWII military service. [8]A four-sport athlete in college, Robinson joined a team in the Negro Baseball League soon after the war. [9]His tremendous talent caught the eye of Branch Rickey, the general manager of the Brooklyn Dodgers—a team in the all-white major league. [10]Rickey dared to offer, and Robinson dared to accept, the challenge of an African American ball player breaking the color barrier in professional sports. [11]Enduring insults, rough play, and much discrimination, Robinson earned Rookie of the Year honors in 1947 and was voted the best player in baseball in 1949. [12]By the early 1950s, other teams in professional baseball, basketball, and football started employing black athletes as well.

A 1951 comic book cover featured baseball star Jackie Robinson.

## B. *Brown v. Board of Education of Topeka*

[13]"Separate but equal" was the phrase used to describe the practice of separating blacks and whites in America since the end of the Civil War. [14]The Supreme Court's decision to legally uphold segregation, nicknamed "Jim Crow," in the *Plessy v. Ferguson* case of 1896 (see Lesson 14) had solidified the practice. [15]However, the post-WWII Supreme Court under Chief Justice Earl Warren reversed course. [16]Thurgood Marshall, a black lawyer for the National Association for the Advancement of Colored People (NAACP), argued a case before the court on behalf of the Kansas family of Linda Brown. [17]Brown had wanted to attend a grade school near her home but was denied by the city's school board because she was black. [18]Instead, she was bussed to a school across town. [19]In 1954, the Court ruled unanimously (an agreement by all) in *Brown v. Board of Education of Topeka* that separate schools for blacks and whites was "inherently unequal." [20]Even if each facility was physically the same in every way—which often was not the case—the court ruled that segregation was a violation of the 14th Amendment, which guaranteed equal protection for all citizens under the nation's laws.

Linda Brown

[21]The Supreme Court can make constitutional rulings but has no power of enforcement. [22]It is the Executive Branch of government that has the power to enforce law. [23]In the first few years after the Brown ruling, states in the Deep South refused to allow school integration. [24]President Eisenhower was slow to act to enforce the *Brown* ruling. [25]He finally used his power to uphold the law in 1957 at Little Rock, Arkansas, when the governor of that state used National Guard troops to block nine black students from entering the city's Central High School, when school started in September. [26]The president could not allow his authority to be undermined. [27]Eisenhower ordered federal troops into Little Rock to open the school for the black students and provide security for them during the rest of the school year. [28]It took years, however, for many school districts in the South to end the practice of segregated schools. [29]All across the South, White Citizens' Councils and a revived Ku Klux Klan defended separation of the races and fought civil rights legislation and court rulings wherever possible.


© 2016 The Critical Thinking Co.™ • www.CriticalThinking.com • 800-458-4849

## C. Montgomery Bus Boycott

[30]In 1955, just before Christmas in Montgomery, Alabama, a black seamstress and civil rights activist returning home from work was arrested for refusing to give up her seat on a city bus to a white passenger. [31]Rosa Parks later recalled it wasn't that she was physically tired, just "tired of giving in," when she was ordered to move by the white bus driver. [32]Arrests such as Parks' had been anticipated by local civil rights activists, but still spotlighted the continued discrimination of segregation. [33]The arrest of Parks sparked a movement in Montgomery of other African Americans who were "tired" of segregation.

Rosa Parks

[34]Led by a 27-year-old local church minister named Martin Luther King, Jr., blacks began a boycott of city buses. [35]They walked, rode bikes, or organized carpools in order to put a financial squeeze on the city's bus system. [36]They demanded that seating on buses be allowed on a first-come-first-served basis, not by segregation. [37]A year later the Supreme Court agreed. [38]In a case called *Browder v. Gayle* in 1956, the Court ordered desegregation of public transportation in Montgomery.

[39]The Montgomery bus boycott showed Americans that blacks wanted action against "separate but equal" practices. [40]This put Reverend Martin Luther King into the national spotlight. [41]He had earned a doctorate degree in theology (the study of religion) and used Bible passages and historic speeches from America's founding fathers to inspire both black and liberal white audiences. [42]King admired the tactics of non-violent civil disobedience he had learned from reading the Bible and the writings of Henry David Thoreau and Mahatma Gandhi. [43]Dr. King and other black ministers from the South formed a group in 1957 called the Southern Christian Leadership Conference (SCLC). [44]They encouraged people to actively "carry on nonviolent protests against the evils of second-class citizenship."

Martin Luther King, Jr.

[45]Young black students, in particular, heeded the call of Dr. King and the SCLC. [46]Wherever they found racial discrimination, they protested it—usually in nonviolent ways. [47]In 1960, at a segregated lunch counter in Greensboro, North Carolina, college students organized a "sit-in." [48]Black students simply sat in a white-only section and, when arrested, were continually replaced by hundreds of other students until the city leaders finally gave up and ended restaurant segregation. [49]Thousands of other protesters throughout the South staged "read-ins" at segregated public libraries, "wade-ins" at white only beaches, "sleep-ins" in motel lobbies, and "play-ins" at public parks.

[50]Black students even formed their own organization called SNCC (known as "snick")—the Student Nonviolent Coordinating Committee. [51]This group worked at ways to end segregation, register black voters, and ensure black voting rights. [52]In 1961, many SNCC members participated in "freedom rides." [53]They rode buses to Southern cities to protest segregation at interstate transportation facilities and to register black voters. [54]At Anniston, Birmingham, and Montgomery, Alabama, freedom riders were attacked by racist white mobs.

[55]The publicity surrounding the segregation controversy at educational facilities, and the sit-ins and freedom rides, brought to the national forefront the long overdue need for government and society to change the course of race relations in America.

**Fun Fact Feature**

What person, mentioned in this lesson, was later appointed to the Supreme Court by President Lyndon Johnson, thereby becoming the first African American to serve on the highest court of the land?

© 2016 The Critical Thinking Co.™ • www.CriticalThinking.com • 800-458-4849 

1. Give two examples that show President Truman tried to improve civil rights.

   a. ______________________________

   ______________________________

   b. ______________________________

   ______________________________

2. What did Jackie Robinson want desegregated?
   a. schools
   b. restaurants
   c. professional sports
   d. public transportation

   Which sentence best supports the answer?

   _____

3. What did the family of Linda Brown want desegregated?
   a. schools
   b. restaurants
   c. professional sports
   d. public transportation

   Which sentence best supports the answer?

   _____

4. What did Rosa Parks and other civil rights activists want desegregated?
   a. schools
   b. restaurants
   c. professional sports
   d. public transportation

   Which sentence best supports the answer?

   _____

5. Which Supreme Court case was the first, and unanimous, decision by the court to reverse years of the practice of "separate but equal"?
   a. *Plessy v. Ferguson*
   b. *Brown v. Board of Education of Topeka*
   c. *Browder v. Gayle*
   d. *U.S. v Little Rock Central High*

   Which sentence best supports your answer?

   _____

6. This 1956 cartoon below makes a statement about the slow response of the "Chief" in the face of the civil rights crisis in the country. Who might be the man wearing the fire chief's hat in this cartoon?

   ______________________________

   Which sentence best supports your answer?

   _____

7. Who led the Montgomery Bus Boycott and formed the civil rights organization called SCLC?
   a. Earl Warren
   b. Thurgood Marshall
   c. Branch Rickey
   d. Martin Luther King, Jr.

   Which sentences best support your answer?

   _____ _____

8. Who is associated with the strategy of "nonviolent civil disobedience" in the civil rights movement of the 1950s?
   a. White Citizens' Councils
   b. Thurgood Marshall
   c. Dwight Eisenhower
   d. Martin Luther King, Jr.

   Which sentence best supports your answer?

   _____


© 2016 The Critical Thinking Co.™ • www.CriticalThinking.com • 800-458-4849

9. What was the name of the student led organization in the civil rights movement of the 1950s?
   a. SCLC
   b. White Citizens' Councils
   c. SNCC
   d. KKK

   Which sentence best supports your answer?

   _____

### Written Response Question

10. Put the following civil rights events in chronological order and supply the year of the event:

| Event | Order of Event (by letter) | Year |
|---|---|---|
| a. freedom riders | 1. _____ | ______________ |
| b. *Brown v. Board of Ed* | 2. _____ | ______________ |
| c. desegregation of the military | 3. _____ | ______________ |
| d. President's Commission on Civil Rights | 4. _____ | ______________ |
| e. Rosa Parks arrested | 5. _____ | ______________ |
| f. Jackie Robinson plays for Dodgers | 6. _____ | ______________ |
| g. Greensboro, N.C. sit-in | 7. _____ | ______________ |
| h. Little Rock Central High | 8. _____ | ______________ |
| i. *Browder v. Gayle* | 9. _____ | ______________ |

**Fun Fact Finale**

The lawyer in the *Brown v. Board of Education of Topeka* case, Thurgood Marshall, was the first African American appointed to the Supreme Court, in 1967. He served until 1991.

© 2016 The Critical Thinking Co.™ • www.CriticalThinking.com • 800-458-4849

# Review: Lessons 36–40
# 1950s Vocabulary

Write the letter of the definition of each vocabulary word. The number following each vocabulary word is the number of the lesson (36–40) where the word was used. All definitions are used once.

_____ 1. disintegrate (36)

_____ 2. strategic (36)

_____ 3. buffer (36)

_____ 4. curb (36)

_____ 5. detonate (36)

_____ 6. insubordination (37)

_____ 7. stockpile (37)

_____ 8. infiltrate (37)

_____ 9. scrutiny (37)

_____ 10. blacklist (37)

_____ 11. suburbs (38)

_____ 12. deviant (38)

_____ 13. atheist (38)

_____ 14. attribute (39)

_____ 15. moderate (39)

_____ 16. affluent (39)

_____ 17. astronaut (39)

_____ 18. segregation (40)

_____ 19. unanimous (40)

_____ 20. theology (40)

a. to set off a bomb

b. separation of the races

c. intense inspection

d. the study of religion

e. housing outside the urban area

f. perverted or weird

g. not extreme left or right wing policies

h. a person who does not believe in God

i. a zone of protection

j. to control or limit

k. break apart

l. putting a commanding officer in an inferior position

m. to penetrate or work into

n. a person aboard a rocket to outer space

o. to reserve or cache

p. an agreement by all

q. characteristic or quality of a person

r. important, crucial

s. abundance of wealth or material goods

t. an unofficial record of persons under suspicion


© 2016 The Critical Thinking Co.™ • www.CriticalThinking.com • 800-458-4849

Section 8: Introduction

# The 1960s

John F. Kennedy (JFK) was forty-three years old when he took the oath of office as president at the start of the 1960s. He proclaimed that "the torch has been passed to a new generation of Americans." He urged young Americans to work for civil rights and to serve their country in the Peace Corps. JFK also challenged Americans to land a man on the moon by the end of the decade. Like other post-WWII presidents, Kennedy had to devise Cold War strategies to fight communism. During his term of office, he dealt with events in Cuba and Vietnam that posed threats to U.S. security.

When Kennedy was assassinated in 1963, his vice president, Lyndon B. Johnson (LBJ), assumed the nation's highest office. LBJ tried to establish a number of liberal programs he called the "Great Society," but his escalation of the war in Vietnam took away that focus and sharply divided the nation. A "generation gap" also divided the nation in the 1960s. Young "hippies" led a counterculture movement that produced unrest between the old and young as well as between conservatives and liberals. The Sixties were a volatile time with antiwar protests, violent socialist groups trying to overthrow the government, a women's liberation movement, an environmental movement, a sexual revolution, race riots, and civil rights protests.

When Johnson announced he would not seek reelection in 1968, Republican Richard Nixon won the White House. Nixon started to wind down the Vietnam War, but not before reigniting antiwar protests on college campuses with his plans to drive the communist North Vietnamese government to the bargaining table. Eventually, an end to the Vietnam War came with the Paris Accords. President Nixon also tried to ease Cold War tensions by visiting "Red" China and Moscow, USSR. These actions helped to propel him to reelection in 1972.

## U.S. Presidents

35. John F. Kennedy
1961-1963

36. Lyndon B. Johnson
1963-1968

37. Richard Nixon
1969-1974

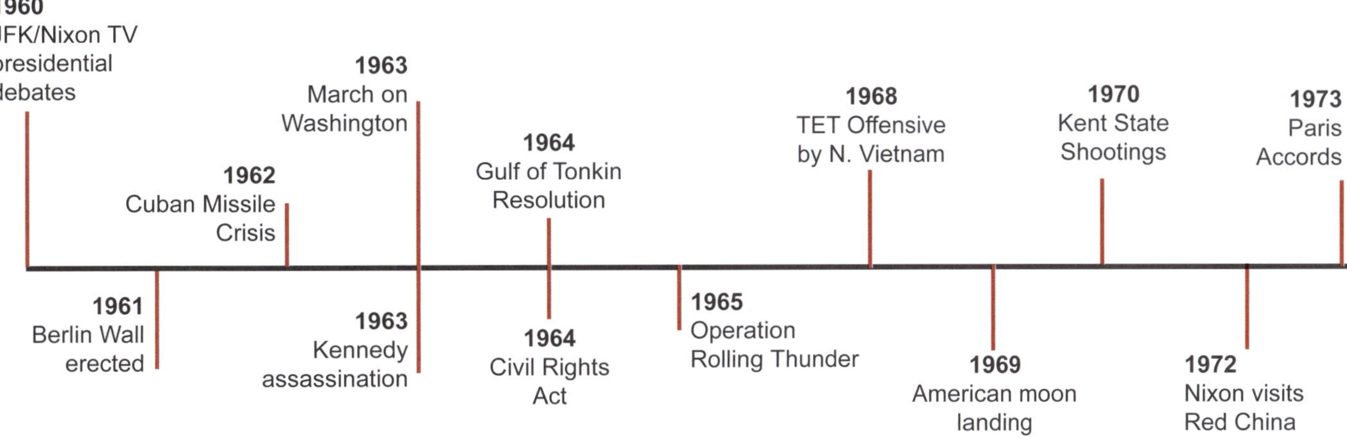


© 2016 The Critical Thinking Co.™ • www.CriticalThinking.com • 800-458-4849 

Lesson 41

# President John F. Kennedy

## A. Election of 1960

[1]In the 1950s, Richard Nixon was Eisenhower's vice president for eight years. [2]A Republican with a strong anti-communist record, Nixon easily won his party's nomination for the presidency in 1960. [3]His Democratic challenger was John F. Kennedy (JFK) of Massachusetts. [4]Kennedy was a Harvard graduate from a wealthy family. [5]He had earned medals for heroism during WWII for saving many crewmen aboard his naval vessel after it was rammed by a Japanese boat in the Pacific Ocean. [6]After the war, Kennedy served as a U.S. Representative and Senator and authored a Pulitzer Prize-winning history book.

[7]Kennedy's ancestors had emigrated from Ireland; the family was Catholic. [8]No Catholic had ever won a U.S. presidential election. [9]Many voters feared that a president who attended the Catholic Church would owe allegiance (loyalty or devotion) to the Pope in Rome over American interests. [10]To counter these fears, Kennedy stressed his belief in the U.S. tradition of separation of church and state. [11]During the campaign, he addressed a gathering of Protestant ministers and chose a Protestant Senator from the Southern state of Texas, Lyndon B. Johnson (LBJ), as his running mate.

The Kennedy-Nixon debate in 1960 was the first ever televised election debate.

[12]News organizations predicted a very close election and it turned out to be one of the narrowest margins of victory ever. [13]Nixon won 49.5 percent of the popular vote, including most of the Western states. [14]Kennedy won 49.7 percent of the vote and most of the Midwestern and Northeastern states. [15]In this extremely close vote, historians point out a critical event that occurred in the campaign. [16]For the first time, presidential candidates conducted a series of public debates, and the four debates were shown on television. [17]In the first debate, Nixon handled himself well on the issues, but his physical appearance was no match for his opponent. [18]Nixon had campaigned up until a few hours before and was recovering from a bacterial infection. [19]In addition, he refused makeup. [20]He appeared tired, sweaty, and pale to viewers. [21]In contrast, Kennedy had rested before the debate, used makeup, and thus appeared healthy, comfortable, and confident. [22]In the next three debates, Nixon was rested, wore makeup, and looked healthier. [23]However, not as many voters watched the last three debates. [24]Kennedy went from slightly behind in the polls (a sampling of opinions on the candidates taken from a random group of persons) before the debates to slightly ahead.

## B. JFK's Domestic Policies

[25]When Kennedy took his oath of office in 1961, young people in particular were excited to have America's first president born in the 20th Century. [26]The youngest-ever elected president at age 43, he proclaimed that "the torch has been passed to a new generation of Americans." [27]He challenged youth to serve their country and many soon responded. [28]Some joined the civil rights movement while others worked on environmental causes. [29]Some young people volunteered with the Peace Corps, a new organization JFK created a few months after his inauguration to promote international service in Third World countries.

[30]Kennedy pledged to balance the budget (avoid deficit spending) and pushed for lower taxes to stimulate more economic growth. [31]He stated in an economic speech that he believed the present U.S. tax system hurt economic growth because it took too large a share of personal and business purchasing power and reduced efforts by businesses and individuals to invest and take

 © 2016 The Critical Thinking Co.™ • www.CriticalThinking.com • 800-458-4849

economic risks. [32]Working with Congress, JFK cut business taxes from 52 percent to 47 percent and the highest personal income taxes from 91 percent to 65 percent. [33]He also raised the minimum wage and extended Social Security benefits.

[34]JFK was also an advocate for civil rights reforms. [35]A young black student named James Meredith was inspired by JFK's inaugural address to work for civil rights. [36]He was denied admission to the University of Mississippi but won an appeal in the Supreme Court to attend the college. [37]When the governor of Mississippi still denied admission to Meredith, President Kennedy ordered National Guard troops to escort Meredith to his classes on the university campus. [38]Kennedy also forced the governor of Alabama to allow black students to attend the University of Alabama. [39]In the summer of 1963, JFK addressed the nation on television and said: "Race has no place in American life or law." [40]He then asked Congress to pass a law outlawing segregation in public facilities.

[41]In 1963, numerous civil rights groups won President Kennedy's approval for the March on Washington. [42]This peaceful assembly for civil rights attracted more than a quarter of a million blacks and whites to the nation's capital. [43]The highlight of the demonstration was a speech given by Martin Luther King, Jr. on the steps of the Lincoln Memorial. [44]In the speech, he repeatedly used the phrase "I have a dream," each time explaining how he envisioned a country with racial harmony. [45]In one of King's most memorable lines, he stated: "I have a dream that my four little children will one day live in a nation where they will not be judged by the color of their skin but by the content of their character."

Martin Luther King, Jr. addressed thousands at the March on Washington in 1963.

### C. Kennedy and the Cold War

[46]Another point President Kennedy made in his inaugural address was his desire for stronger U.S. national security. [47]"We shall pay any price, bear any burden, and meet any hardship," JFK said, "to assure the success of liberty." [48]The Marshall Plan under President Truman had directed American aid toward war-torn Europe. [49]Under the Eisenhower Doctrine, the United States supported nations in the Middle East that wanted help resisting communism. [50]President Kennedy created the Alliance for Progress. [51]Development funds were granted to nations in Latin America that were dedicated to fighting communism.

[52]President Kennedy also persuaded Congress to bolster (reinforce, strengthen) the defense budget to its highest levels of the Cold War. [53]In particular, he asked Congress to provide a larger budget for the National Aeronautics and Space Administration (NASA) space program. [54]He challenged American scientists to land a man on the moon by the end of the decade. [55]He once declared: "We stand today on the edge of a new frontier … a frontier with uncharted areas of science and space, unsolved problems of peace and war, unconquered problems of ignorance and prejudice, unanswered questions of poverty and surplus." [56]As a result, the Kennedy years are sometimes referred to as the "New Frontier."

[57]Revolutionary leader Fidel Castro gained control of Cuba about the time JFK became president, and soon his island country became the first communist nation in the Western Hemisphere.

Fidel Castro (left) and Cuba were soon supported by U.S.S.R. leader, Nikita Khrushchev.

[58]Kennedy responded by ending diplomatic relations with Cuba and imposing a trade embargo (no imports or exports). [59]In 1961, JFK authorized a plan developed to overthrow the communist government of Cuba. [60]However, the plan failed when fifteen hundred Central Intelligence Agency

(CIA ) sponsored anti-Castro Cuban exiles (persons banished from their own country) were killed or captured when they landed at the Bay of Pigs in Cuba, at the start of the failed operation.

[61]To defend his nation against future attacks, Castro installed nuclear weapons from the USSR in Cuba the next year. [62]When the United States learned that major U.S. cities were within range of Cuban nuclear missiles, an event known as the Cuban Missile Crisis occurred. [63]President Kennedy sent the U.S. Navy to form a sea blockade to prevent further missiles from entering Cuba and publicly demanded that the weapons already in Cuba be dismantled and returned to the USSR. [64]He also stationed 250,000 U.S. troops in south Florida in case war erupted. [65]The American public closely followed the news of the two superpowers trying to avoid a nuclear confrontation. [66]After two weeks of intense negotiations, the USSR agreed to take back the nuclear weapons from Cuba in exchange for a United States promise to never again invade Castro's nation. [67]Secretly, JFK also agreed to dismantle U.S. missiles in Turkey and Italy that could have been launched on the Soviet capital of Moscow.

Cuban Missile Crisis

[68]President Kennedy visited a grim symbol of the Cold War when he traveled to Europe in 1963. [69]Two years earlier, the Soviets had constructed the concrete Berlin Wall through and around Germany's capital city. [70]It separated the communist-controlled half of Berlin from the democratically-controlled half. [71]In the first two years of its existence, armed guards from watchtowers shot and killed nearly 200 people who tried to escape over the Berlin Wall to freedom in the West. [72]To show American support to West Germans, JFK made a speech in which he said "Ich bin ein Berliner" ("I am a Berliner"). [73]The divide between the USSR and the USA was deep. [74]Soon the Cold War would play out its next chapter in Southeast Asia.

**Fun Fact Feature**

In August of 1963, the Kennedy administration installed a special telephone system called the "hotline" at the Pentagon to communicate with Nikita Khruschev. It could transmit emergency messages directly and quickly. Which nation was at the other end of the line?


© 2016 The Critical Thinking Co.™ • www.CriticalThinking.com • 800-458-4849

1. Which campaign event did polls show affected John Kennedy's close election victory in 1960?
   a. Cuban Missile Crisis
   b. televised debates
   c. JFK's inaugural address
   d. Bay of Pigs

   Which sentence best supports the answer?

   _____

2. Kennedy's election to the U.S. presidency was the first-ever for a:
   a. Harvard graduate.
   b. member of a wealthy family.
   c. Catholic.
   d. war hero.

   Which sentence best supports the answer?

   _____

3. Kennedy's "New Frontier" speech challenged America to do what?
   a. open up wilderness lands in the West to development
   b. explore the deepest regions of the oceans
   c. create the most powerful atomic weapon yet invented
   d. land a man on the moon by the end of the 1960s

   Which sentence best supports the answer?

   _____

4. Which European city was divided by a physical wall, constructed by the Soviets in 1961, to keep people in the communist half of the city from escaping to the West?
   a. Moscow
   b. Paris
   c. Berlin
   d. Havana

   Which sentences best support your answer?

   _____ _____ _____

5. The political cartoon below appeared in October of 1962. What event does it show?
   a. Berlin Wall creation
   b. Bay of Pigs invasion
   c. Alliance for Progress
   d. Cuban Missile Crisis

   What clues in the cartoon lead you to your answer?

   ______________________________

   ______________________________

6. A phrase in the quote below, from a speech made in Washington, D.C. in 1963, indicates which of the following as the speaker?

   "I have a dream that one day on the red hills of Georgia, the sons of former slaves and the sons of former slave owners will be able to sit down together at the table of brotherhood."

   a. Martin Luther King, Jr.
   b. Richard Nixon
   c. John F. Kennedy
   d. James Meredith

   Which sentence best supports your answer?

   _____

7. Which Latin American country was controlled by communist revolutionary Fidel Castro by the early 1960s?
   a. Germany
   b. Cuba
   c. Brazil
   d. Mexico

   Which sentence best supports your answer?

   _____

© 2016 The Critical Thinking Co.™ • www.CriticalThinking.com • 800-458-4849

8. A black man, James Meredith, was protected by the National Guard when President Kennedy enforced Meredith's rights to:
   a. demonstrate at the March on Washington.
   b. attend the University of Mississippi.
   c. join forces to overthrow communist Fidel Castro.
   d. become an astronaut in the New Frontier.

   Which sentence best supports your answer?

   _____

9. What happened to defense spending under the Kennedy administration?

   ________________________________________

   ________________________________________

## Written Response Question

10. Use complete sentences to show how John Kennedy's age was a factor in his legacy (how he is remembered).

________________________________________________________________________

________________________________________________________________________

________________________________________________________________________

________________________________________________________________________

________________________________________________________________________

________________________________________________________________________

________________________________________________________________________

________________________________________________________________________

**Fun Fact Finale**

In the aftermath of the Cuban Missile Crisis, the "hotline" was new technology that allowed the U.S. president to communicate directly with the premier of the Soviet Union in cases of emergency. A special 10,000 mile long cable connected Washington, D.C. with Moscow.


© 2016 The Critical Thinking Co.™ • www.CriticalThinking.com • 800-458-4849

Lesson 42

# End of the Kennedy Era

## A. Cold War in Vietnam

[1]After World War II, France desperately tried to reestablish its colonial rule of the Vietnam region of Southeast Asia. [2]In 1954, however, the French lost a major battle at Dienbienphu to communist forces. [3]The Communist leader, Ho Chi Minh, took control of Vietnam north of the 17th parallel of latitude and centered his government in the city of Hanoi. [4]While maintaining control of the north, Minh gave military support to South Vietnamese communist rebels called the Vietcong, who fought to unite South Vietnam with communist North Vietnam. The Eisenhower administration used the CIA to help Ngo Dinh Diem establish a democratic government in Saigon, the capital city of South Vietnam. [6]President Eisenhower also sent financial assistance to Diem's government.

[7]Eisenhower, and his successor Kennedy, believed in the "domino theory": if Vietnam fell to the communists, neighboring nations—and perhaps all of Asia—might eventually fall under communist rule. [8]When Kennedy became president, he and his advisors agreed that the United States should support democracy whenever possible in Southeast Asia. [9]JFK sent large shipments of weapons to Diem's government. [10]By 1963, he had also directed 16,000 U.S. special-operations military personnel to operate in South Vietnam—most as advisors to Diem's army. [11]Yet Diem proved unpopular with his own people, and Kennedy began to question the wisdom of further U.S. involvement in the war. [12]He thought that the United States did not have a prayer of staying in Vietnam because the people hated Americans. [13]Kennedy felt that Americans were going to be thrown out of Vietnam at any point. [14]However, Kennedy believed he couldn't give up that territory to the communists and convince the American people to reelect him. [15]Diem was soon killed in a coup (a quick action from forces within a country who take over the government). [16]Americans were learning more and more about Vietnam from news programs, which had increased broadcasting time from 15 minutes to 30 minutes each evening, in 1963.

## B. JFK Assassination

[17]What President Kennedy would have done next in Vietnam is unknown because he was killed on November 22, 1963, just a month after Diem's assassination. [18]Kennedy had been looking ahead to reelection in 1964 and decided to make a political visit to Texas, the home state of Vice President Johnson. [19]The president and his wife Jackie, and the Texas governor and his wife, paraded through Dallas in an open touring car. [20]Suddenly JFK was shot and died within an hour. [21]As the country was gripped in shock about the news, Dallas police arrested the suspected gunman. [22]Lee Harvey Oswald was an ex-Marine rifleman who had joined the communist movement in support of Fidel Castro.

President Kennedy touring Dallas in an open touring car just prior to his assassination.

[23]Only two days after his arrest, as Oswald was being moved to a different jail, Americans watched television in disbelief as Oswald himself was shot by a Dallas man upset about the murder of the president. [24]Oswald died immediately and never went to trial. [25]The government launched an investigation of the Kennedy assassination, led by Supreme Court Chief Justice Earl Warren. [26]Eventually the Warren Commission concluded that Oswald acted as a lone assassin. [27]Controversy, however, surrounded the Warren Commission's efforts. [28]Conspiracy theories dogged the report for decades afterward.

[29]Kennedy's assassination, funeral, and the findings of the Warren Commission were covered on all the major TV networks. [30]Kennedy was laid to rest in a ceremony watched by millions of Americans on television.

## C. Civil Rights in the Mid-1960s

[31]Lyndon B. Johnson, Kennedy's vice president, was in a different vehicle in the Dallas parade at the moment of the JFK assassination. [32]He was whisked immediately to the Dallas airport and sworn in as president prior to his flight back to Washington, D.C. [33]Johnson (LBJ) was a former history teacher who had served many terms in

© 2016 The Critical Thinking Co.™ • www.CriticalThinking.com • 800-458-4849 

Congress. [34]After Kennedy's funeral, LBJ decided that one of the best tributes to the fallen president would be the passage of civil rights legislation that JFK had tried unsuccessfully to pass. [35]Urging

Lyndon B. Johnson took the oath of office on a plane at the Dallas airport soon after JFK's death. Mrs. Johnson (left) and Mrs. Kennedy (right) stood by.

pressure from unions, civil rights groups, and the public at large, Johnson worked hard to get Congressional approval of the most significant civil rights law in U.S. history—the Civil Rights Act of 1964. [36]The law made racial discrimination and segregation in public facilities illegal and created an agency to block job discrimination. [37]Johnson won the presidential election of 1964 after finishing out the final year of JFK's term.

[38]In 1964, the 24th Amendment was added to the Constitution. [39]The 24th Amendment and the Voting Rights Act of 1965, which followed soon after Johnson's election, banned practices that made it hard for blacks to register to vote. [40]Voting by black Americans in the South tripled as a result, between the elections of 1964 and 1968. [41]The number of blacks holding public offices in the South also rose dramatically over the next decade, going from just 24 to more than 1,200 by the early 1970s. [42]For the first time since the Reconstruction days of the late 1800s, blacks were elected to Congress from former Confederate states.

[43]For some minority leaders, the slow pace of civil rights reform seemed to bring few economic gains. [44]Many of the poorest parts of Southern society and the worst sections of Northern and Western cities were still black neighborhoods. [45]Poverty among blacks was often three times as high as among whites, and graduation rates were less than half those of whites. [46]Even though laws were changing to ban segregation, racial discrimination was still prevalent (widespread). [47]Black civil rights activists pushed "Black Pride" and "Black is beautiful." [48]They advocated the importance of blacks learning about and celebrating their own culture.

[49]Some black leaders, such as Malcolm X, argued against Martin Luther King, Jr.'s strategy of non-violent resistance, rejected integration with whites, and called for armed self-defense. [50]"If ballots don't work," Malcolm X once said, "bullets will." [51]The life of Malcolm X ended with a bullet when he was killed by feuding members of the Black Muslim faith. [52]Inspired by Malcolm X and other Black Power organizations, Huey Newton and Bobby Seale formed the Black Panther Party for Self Defense in Berkeley, California. [53]According to its founders, the Black nationalist and socialist organization was formed in 1966 in response to police brutality against blacks. [54]The Black Panthers also rejected King's non-violence philosophy. [55]They wore military-style garb, armed themselves with weapons, and had many clashes with the police. [56]"Political power comes through the barrel of a gun," repeated some Black Panther leaders.

Malcolm X

[57]Militant black leaders preached armed self-protection and armed revolution using the slogan "Black Power." [58]In the summers of the mid-1960s, race riots broke out in several major cities across the United States. [59]Hundreds of people were killed, thousands were injured or arrested, and millions of dollars of property was damaged. [60]The worst rioting came in April 1968, when Martin Luther King, Jr. was shot and killed by a white racist in Tennessee. [61]King had come to the city of Memphis to support a union of black sanitation workers and to start a movement he called the Poor People's Campaign. [62]The civil rights movement was now without its most important leader. [63]Violent protests erupted all over the nation. [64]The U.S. Army was ordered to surround the U.S. Capitol and the White House with machine guns to defend against potential rioters.


© 2016 The Critical Thinking Co.™ • www.CriticalThinking.com • 800-458-4849

**Fun Fact Feature**

An "eternal flame" marks a grave in Arlington National Cemetery in Washington, D.C., in remembrance of one person discussed in this lesson. Can you guess who?

1. After a battle loss at Dienbienphu in 1954, which government lost control of its colonial territory of Vietnam?
   a. United States
   b. USSR
   c. France
   d. China

   Which sentence best supports the answer?

   ______

2. Look at the political cartoon below. Describe what the cartoon's artist has portrayed.

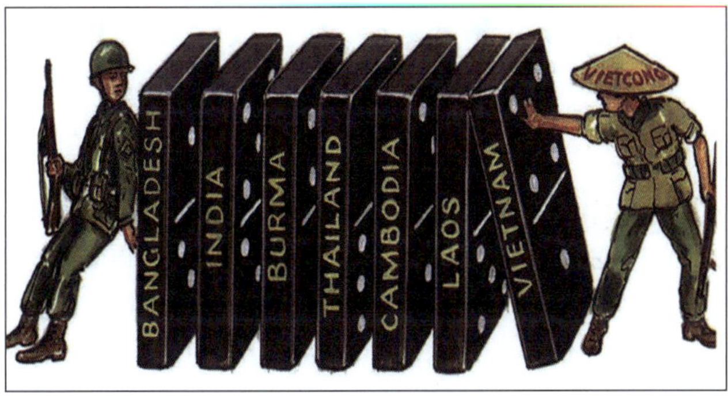


   ______________________________

   ______________________________

   ______________________________

3. President Kennedy was not the first, nor the last, to involve the United States in the affairs of Vietnam. What two actions did JFK take to support South Vietnam?

   a. ______________________________

   ______________________________

   b. ______________________________

   ______________________________

4. Who did the Warren Commission say asassinated President John F. Kennedy?
   a. Earl Warren
   b. Ho Chi Minh
   c. Fidel Castro
   d. Lee Harvey Oswald

   Which sentence best supports your answer?

   ______

5. Who became president immediately after the assassination of John F. Kennedy?
   a. Earl Warren
   b. Lyndon Johnson
   c. Malcolm X
   d. Richard Nixon

   Which sentences best support your answer?

   ______ ______

6. Which piece of legislation provided extra support to voting rights granted in the 24th Amendment to the U. S. Constitution?
   a . Voting Rights Act of 1965
   b. Warren Commission Report
   c. Civil Rights Act of 1964
   d. Black Power movement

   Which sentence best supports your answer?

   ______

7. The actions and strategies of the Black Panther Party and of Malcolm X were in direct contrast to whom?
   a. Martin Luther King, Jr.
   b. Ngo Dinh Diem
   c. Lee Harvey Oswald
   d. Ho Chi Mihn

   Which sentences best support your answer?

   ______ ______

© 2016 The Critical Thinking Co.™ • www.CriticalThinking.com • 800-458-4849

8. Even though improvements were made for civil rights after WWII, race riots were widespread in the mid-1960s. Give two possible reasons why some minority groups rioted.

   a. ______________________________

   b. ______________________________

9. How did Martin Lulther King, Jr. die in 1968?
   a. killed in riots in Washington, D. C.
   b. cancer
   c. murdered by rival members of a religious group
   d. shot by a white racist in Tennessee

   Which sentence best supports your answer? _____

## Written Response Question

10. Use complete sentences to discuss the influence of television on American history in the 1960s.

______________________________________________________________________

______________________________________________________________________

______________________________________________________________________

______________________________________________________________________

______________________________________________________________________

______________________________________________________________________

______________________________________________________________________

______________________________________________________________________

### Fun Fact Finale

President John F. Kennedy's grave is marked by an "eternal flame." Jacqueline Kennedy requested an eternal flame for her husband's grave. She admired the eternal flame at the Tomb of the Unknown Soldier at the Arc de Triomphe in Paris, which she and her husband had seen during a visit to France in 1961.

© 2016 The Critical Thinking Co.™ • www.CriticalThinking.com • 800-458-4849

Lesson 43

# 1960's Culture

## A. Counterculture

[1]In the mid-1960, as Baby Boomers (people born after World War II, between 1946-1964) grew into their teens and early twenties, they continued to have an amazing effect upon American culture. [2]The high percentage of young people in the population helped to create a very energetic and powerful era. [3]The lifestyle of their suburban parents did not appeal to many Boomers. [4]Many rejected what they saw as "American materialism" (the purchase of many consumer goods), called for more love in the world, and embraced long hair and mind-altering drugs. [5]They described themselves as "hip" and the rest of the world as

Hippies or Flower Children of the 1960s

"square." [6]The news media called them "hippies" or "flower children." [7]Timothy Leary, a psychology professor from Harvard, gave youth their slogan of the age: Tune in, turn on, and drop out. [8]Some hippies preferred life in cities, but others chose what they called a more natural life in rural communes, where they sometimes lived together in small groups, sharing possessions, and living non-traditional lifestyles. [9]Historians described hippies as members of the "counterculture." [10]"Counter" means "to go against."

[11]Young people of the 1960s developed new kinds of music to define their distinct culture. [12]Bands such as The Beach Boys seemed innocent enough in the early 60s, as did a dance craze called "The Twist." [13]But after The Beatles hit it big in 1964, a revolution in music occurred. [14]Soon, groups such as The Rolling Stones and The Doors joined in, and rock and roll music got a rougher edge. [15]Folk artists such as Bob Dylan and Janis Joplin used their music to protest against the values and lifestyle of the previous generation and the war in Vietnam. [16]In 1969, hundreds of thousands of young people attended the biggest and most famous outdoor rock concert of the age at Woodstock, New York. [17]Hippies claimed it was the "Age of Aquarius," an astrological reference to an era of love and peace. [18]In the language of the day, the event was "groovy."

[19]However, crime rates increased dramatically in the 1960s, while religion declined. [20]Race riots occurred in several major cities. [21]Church membership fell way off, especially among the newly independent Boomers. [22]"God is dead" was a slogan that was heard from time to time. [23]Illegal drug use, crime rates, rock music, tie-dyed clothing, and a generation that had little interest in the American dream of prosperity offended the Boomers' parents. [24]The conformity of 1950s society had given way to a "do your own thing" culture of the 1960s. [25]A so-called "generation gap" developed between youth and older Americans.

## B. Feminism

[26]The rebellion of youth generated several revolutions. [27]One was the women's liberation movement. [28]In 1963, the publication of *The Feminine Mystique*, by Betty Friedan, highlighted the dissatisfaction of many females with the middle-class lifestyle that often put men's needs above women's. [29]Women pointed out that they were discouraged from entering certain careers and, when they did join the workplace, they were usually paid less than men for the same jobs.

[30]The feminist movement that emerged after Friedan's book produced a number of results. [31]Women's magazines became more popular. [32]Products for women, such as *Virginia Slims* cigarettes, were marketed. [33]Many feminists protested the idea of women wearing bras, the practice of women shaving their legs and underarms, and beauty contests such as the *Miss America* pageant. [34]They argued that if men didn't do it, women shouldn't either. [35]The movement also led to girls wearing pants more often, especially denim. [36]Others wore "mini-skirts." [37]More women than ever before joined the college ranks. [38]The number of women who worked outside the home tripled from the 1960s to the 1980s. [39]Women successfully included language into the Civil Rights Act of 1964 that prohibited discrimination in the

© 2016 The Critical Thinking Co.™ • www.CriticalThinking.com • 800-458-4849

workplace based on gender. [40]Then, in 1966, a civil rights group for women was formed—the National Organization for Women (NOW). [41]NOW was active in bringing gender discrimination cases to the courts. [42]They encouraged women to vote

A women's rights protest on a college campus in the 1960s.

and join the political process. [43]In 1972, women's rights groups won a major victory when Title IX of the Education Amendments Act attempted to enact laws to give equality of opportunity at schools. [44]As a result, many more sports and sports scholarships became available for female athletes in high schools and colleges.

[45]The right to make decisions about child-bearing was another important issue for women. [46]In 1960, an effective oral contraceptive, simply nicknamed "the pill," became available, which allowed women to control when they could conceive children. [47]An equal rights amendment (ERA) to the Constitution was proposed first in 1923 and then again in 1972. [48]The amendment was very controversial—even within women's groups. [49]Proponents, often middle and upper class women, claimed it would guarantee equal rights for women. [50]Opponents, often working-class women, claimed it would harm working women because it would eliminate current legislation on the books specifically protecting women. [51]Thirty eight states were needed to approve the ERA to make it law. [52]Thirty-five states approved it, but later five of those approving states reversed course and removed their approval, leaving the ERA eight states short of the needed approval.

### C. Minority Rights

[53]African Americans and women were not the only groups who campaigned hard for civil rights in the 1960s. [54]Native Americans suffered the highest poverty, disease, and death rates, and the poorest education levels and housing conditions of any other American group after WWII. [55]In 1961, representatives from dozens of tribes came together to protest federal Native American policy and to demand government help. [56]When Lyndon Johnson became president, he urged Congress to put more funding in the federal budget for Native American reservations. [57]Some militant Native Americans felt the pace of reform was too slow. [58]In 1968, they formed a group called the American Indian Movement (AIM) and confronted authorities, sometimes violently, in California, South Dakota, and Washington, D.C. [59]"Red Pride" became a rallying cry for Native Americans. [60]More and more, Native Americans developed their own businesses and actively sought ways to rediscover their heritage and culture.

This AIM badge recalled an earlier battle between the government and Native Americans.

[61]The fastest growing minority of Americans in the 1960s were Hispanics. [62]After the Immigration Act of 1965 abolished the old immigrant quota system of the 1920s, the number of legal and illegal Hispanic immigrants entering the United States for jobs and higher wages more than tripled over the next decade. [63]Just like Native and African Americans, some Hispanics faced discrimination. [64]Legal Hispanics working as farm laborers found their own civil rights activist in Cesar Chavez. [65]Chavez was born in Arizona and worked as a migrant (a person who moves from place to place) farm worker following his service in the U.S. Navy during WWII. [66]Chavez began to devote himself to improving the wages and living conditions for legal Mexican American farm workers in California in the 1960s. [67]Together with co-founder Dolores Huerta, they started the United Farm Workers (UFW) union and led

Cesar Chavez


© 2016 The Critical Thinking Co.™ • www.CriticalThinking.com • 800-458-4849

non-violent actions—such as boycotts of certain crops—to protest low wages, demand better living conditions for farm workers, and to stop the hiring of illegal immigrants. [68]Under UFW leadership, farm workers won the right to form unions and bargain with employers.

## C. Environmentalism

[69]In 1962, author Rachel Carson published a book called *Silent Spring* that sparked another revolution. [70]Her research showed the horrible effects of pesticides on birds and other animals. [71]The environmental movement drew many people from all generations. [72]They led protests about water pollution, acid rain, and what they claimed was a need for wilderness protection. [73]In April of 1970, they started a national day of environmental awareness called Earth Day. [74]That same year the Environmental Protection Agency (EPA) was created by the federal government. [75]It has the responsibility of maintaining and enforcing national environmental standards and laws.

[76]A year later, environmental political action groups protested and fought to stop the international hunting of whales. [77]Then, in 1973, the Endangered Species Act was passed. [78]It was designed to protect critically threatened animals from extinction. [79]Also in 1973, environmentalist action groups led protests against logging operations in the Pacific Northwest, the creation of nuclear power plants, and the Trans-Alaska oil pipeline. [80]The pipeline was designed to bring oil to Valdez, Alaska, where it was loaded aboard tankers headed to U.S. refineries in the lower 48 states.

## D. Other 60's Cultural Notes

[81]High schools and colleges became the focus of the boom in education in the 1960s. [82]College campuses in particular became the gathering places for millions of young people. [83]Often schools were the sites of youth protests about civil rights, women's rights, or the Vietnam War.

[84]When not listening to the music of their generation, young people still liked to watch television. [85]Sit-coms (situation comedies) such as *Gilligan's Island* were popular. [86]The popularity of the space race was reflected in TV shows such as *Star Trek* and in movies such as *2001: A Space Odyssey*. [87]Cold War culture was represented in James Bond movies and in novels such as *The Spy Who Came in From the Cold*.

[88]Football, especially professional football, became the popular sport of the decade. [89]It was a more action-packed sport than baseball and it appealed to youth. [90]The Super Bowl started in 1965 and the Football Hall of Fame was created as well.

[91]Food was faster than ever before. It wasn't just McDonald's anymore. [92]Pizza, chicken, and Mexican fast food franchises sprung up everywhere, even in small towns. [93]Small convenience markets, such as 7-Eleven®, sprung up too. [94]People wanted to quickly shop for candy bars, pop, and snack food.

[95]The automobile was still popular, especially sports cars and "muscle cars." [96]The Ford Mustang was the hot new American car in 1964. [97]The inexpensive Volkswagen Beetle and VW van were popular among young people at college. [98]They were using these cars more and more for drive-through fast food, drive-up banking, and drive-through pharmacies.

**Fun Fact Feature**

This colorful symbol to the right was seen in many places in the 1960s. Do you know what it stands for?

1. Which of these people is associated with an awakening of the environmental movement in the 1960s?
   a. Janis Joplin
   b. Betty Friedan
   c. Timothy Leary
   d. Rachel Carson

   Which sentence best supports the answer?

   ______

2. NOW was a 1960s organization that worked for civil rights for which group of Americans?
   a. Native Americans
   b. women
   c. Hispanic Americans
   d. Asian Americans

   Which sentence best supports the answer?

   ______

3. The terms Woodstock, flower children, Age of Aquarius, and counterculture are all best associated with which of these 1960s groups?
   a. Hispanics
   b. hippies
   c. feminists
   d. football players

   Which sentences best support the answer?

   ______ ______ ______ ______

4. Cesar Chavez is noted for obtaining and organizing civil rights for which group of people?
   a. Hispanic Americans
   b. African Americans
   c. women
   d. Native Americans

   Which sentence best supports the answer?

   ______

5. List two examples of success in the women's liberation movement.

   a. ______________________________

   ______________________________

   b. ______________________________

   ______________________________

6. Which of the following statements is NOT true about social trends of the 1960s?
   a. Football became a more popular sport than baseball.
   b. Rock and roll and folk music were popular with youth.
   c. Church membership reached an all-time high.
   d. Mind-altering illegal drugs became available and openly used.

   Which sentence best supports the answer?

   ______

7. Name two things which show evidence that the environmental movement of the 1960s put pressure on the federal government to act.

   a. ______________________________

   ______________________________

   b. ______________________________

   ______________________________

8. Name four symbols from the image below that show this is a cartoon about the 1960s.

   a. ______________________________

   b. ______________________________

   c. ______________________________

   d. ______________________________


© 2016 The Critical Thinking Co.™ • www.CriticalThinking.com • 800-458-4849

9. Write the letter of the term that describes the 1960s item on the left.

| | | |
|---|---|---|
| 1. food | ______ | a. muscle |
| 2. football | ______ | b. Cold War/space |
| 3. cars | ______ | c. fast |
| 4. film | ______ | d. sit-com |
| 5. tv | ______ | e. most popular |

## Written Response Question

10. Use complete sentences to describe some ways that the energy of the youth rebellion of the 1960s brought some positive changes to American society.

______________________________________________

______________________________________________

______________________________________________

______________________________________________

______________________________________________

______________________________________________

______________________________________________

______________________________________________

### Fun Fact Finale

The symbol is often known as the peace sign or peace symbol. It was designed in 1958 by a British artist who combined two letter symbols used in semaphore (signaling using flags) into one image with a circle around it. The "N" symbol (shown on the left) stood for "nuclear." The "D" symbol (shown on the right) stood for "disarmament." American college students spread buttons with this symbol all over the United States by the mid-1960s.

© 2016 The Critical Thinking Co.™ • www.CriticalThinking.com • 800-458-4849

Lesson 44

# President Johnson and Vietnam

## A. Gulf of Tonkin Resolution

[1]Presidents Truman, Eisenhower, and Kennedy made some commitments of U.S. materials and manpower to prevent communist control of Southeast Asia. [2]President Truman sent military equipment and 120 military advisors to help prevent the communists from seizing control of Vietnam. [3]President Eisenhower raised the number of military advisors to 900. [4]President Kennedy sent more combat equipment, military advisors, and U.S. Special Forces, which became the first U.S. forces to engage in combat in Vietnam. [5]At the time of Kennedy's death, the number of U.S. military personnel in Vietnam had escalated (raised, increased in intensity) to 16,000. [6]After becoming president following Kennedy's assassination, it was Lyndon Johnson's time to deal with the Cold War in that part of the world. [7]On the one hand, Johnson was fearful that an all-out U.S. military effort in Vietnam might lead to another world war. [8]Johnson, like Eisenhower and Kennedy, believed in the "domino theory"—that communist control of Vietnam would lead to other regional countries falling to communism as well. [9]As a result of this fear, Johnson, like Kennedy, decided to continue to commit American support to the Vietnamese civil war, to prevent the spread of communism.

[10]In early August 1964, North Vietnamese gunboats reportedly fired on U.S. Navy ships that were stationed ten miles offshore of communist North Vietnam, in the Gulf of Tonkin. [11]President Johnson, battling for reelection that fall, used this incident to show his aggressive anti-communist nature. [12]He ordered U.S. military attacks on North Vietnamese naval bases and then demanded that Congress also respond with support. [13]With nearly unanimous consent, Congress empowered Johnson to "take all necessary measures" to repel further North Vietnamese aggression and defend democratic South Vietnam. [14]The "Tonkin Gulf Resolution" gave the president a blank check (full power, unrestricted authority) to wage the war in Vietnam as he saw fit.

## B. Vietnam War Escalates

[15]Johnson won the 1964 presidential election and soon flexed his new power. [16]In February 1965, he ordered Operation Rolling Thunder to begin. [17]This was a plan for the U.S. Air Force to drop tons of bombs on North Vietnam and its capital city of Hanoi in order to force communist leader Ho Chi Minh to negotiate a settlement that would give all of Vietnam a democratic government. [18]Between 1965 and 1968, more bombs were dropped on North Vietnam than all the bombs used by both sides during World War II.

President Johnson and General Westmoreland

[19]North Vietnam refused to quit. [20]Its Viet Cong forces continued to attack democratic South Vietnamese targets by supplying its militants via a route known as the Ho Chi Minh Trail. [21]This trail went through the neighboring countries of Laos and Cambodia. [22]Johnson secretly ordered U.S. bombing raids there as well, not telling the American people or Congress about this expansion of the conflict. [23]Often unable to see the enemy through the dense growth of Vietnam's jungles, the U.S. military also dropped chemicals, Agent Orange and Napalm, to defoliate (strip trees of leaves) the jungle in order to flush out the enemy. [24]The Viet Cong continued to use the Ho Chi Minh trail despite these grave risks. [25]They burrowed underground, building 30,000 miles of tunnel networks to keep supply lines open.

[26]Soon it became clear to General William Westmoreland, the U.S. military commander in Vietnam, that combat troops on the ground would be necessary to win a victory. [27]Agreeing with his general's assessment, Johnson ordered thousands of U.S. ground troops to Vietnam starting in the spring of 1965. [28]By 1968, nearly one-half million U.S. soldiers were fighting in Vietnam—more than had been sent to the Korean War. [29]Many of the U.S. soldiers were very young, often below the voting age of 21. [30]Eighty percent of them were often from poor or working-class families, partly because men who were entered in college were allowed a deferment (a temporary exemption from military service).


© 2016 The Critical Thinking Co.™ • www.CriticalThinking.com • 800-458-4849

**C. Quagmire**

[31]By the end of 1967, a word often used to describe the Vietnam War was "quagmire" (an entanglement; being bogged down). [32]It seemed like the U.S. military could make little progress in its objectives. [33]The climate and vegetation of Southeast Asia made fighting difficult. [34]The enemy, nicknamed "VC" or "Charlie," were hard to identify. [35]They fought a hit and run style of combat, often ambushing U.S. troops. [36]A seemingly friendly Vietnamese peasant farmer by day could turn out to be a guerilla fighter by night. [37]Many Americans died on search and destroy missions in the jungles when stepping on land mines or by triggering booby traps. [38]Direct confrontation was rare.

[39]Then, on January 31, 1968—the first day of Tet, the Vietnamese New Year—the North Vietnamese military launched a major, multi-pronged attack deep into South Vietnam. [40]More than 100 towns, including South Vietnam's capital city of Saigon, were struck by the communist forces. [41]Although the Tet Offensive was eventually repulsed by United States and South Vietnamese forces, the scale of the attack convinced the bulk of the American public that the United States would have a very difficult time winning a war in Southeast Asia. [42]The support of "hawks" (Americans who supported the war) fell sharply while the anti-war "doves" gained the support of many newspaper, magazine, and TV reporters and editors.

Tet Offensive January 30 & 31, 1968

[43]TV and newspaper images of wounded American soldiers and burned out Vietnamese villages with dead civilians brought the horror of the war home to Americans. [44]More than one hundred U.S. soldiers were dying each week. [45]Large, anti-Vietnam War protests drew thousands in every region of the United States. [46]College campuses across the country saw massive anti-war rallies. [47]Martin Luther King, Jr. was among dozens of celebrities calling for an end to the war. [48]Eugene McCarthy, an anti-war U.S. Senator from Johnson's own Democratic Party, announced he would challenge the president for the 1968 election nomination. [49]So did Democratic Senator Robert Kennedy, the brother of JFK.

[50]On March 31, 1968, President Johnson made two startling announcements on a televised speech to the nation. [51]First he disclosed that he was ordering an end to the bombing of North Vietnam in an effort to begin peace talks. [52]He then surprised listeners by stating: "I shall not seek, and I will not accept, the nomination of my party for another term as your president."

An Anti-War Protest at the University of California at Berkeley in 1968

**D. End of "The Great Society"**

[53]When he had succeeded JFK, Johnson championed a program he called "The Great Society." [54]This was a collection of liberal ideas involving new laws, agencies, and government spending designed to extend the American Dream to minorities and the poor. [55]To fight racial discrimination in voting, Johnson succeeded in getting the Voting Rights Act through congress. [56]This act outlawed racial discrimination in the voting process. [57]To fight poverty, Johnson declared an "unconditional war on poverty in America" by convincing Congress to pass Medicare (health insurance for the aged) and Medicaid (a health plan for the poor). [58]Johnson also backed the Economic Opportunity Act and created a new cabinet position called the Department of Housing and Urban Development. [59]He was the first president to send a special message to Congress on the environment that produced results such as the Clean Air and Water Act and the Endangered Species Act.

[60]Although Johnson managed to pass nearly all of his Great Society legislation during his presidency, his popularity with the American public continued to fall. [61]The Vietnam War was expensive and had become very unpopular. [62]In addition to fighting and funding an unpopular war, Johnson's Great Society legislation was viewed by many as too costly and overreaching.

**Fun Fact Feature**

The Vietnam War helped bring about an amendment to the U.S. Constitution. It had to do with 18 year olds. Can you guess what the 26th Amendment changed and why it passed?


© 2016 The Critical Thinking Co.™ • www.CriticalThinking.com • 800-458-4849

1. What were Hanoi and Saigon?
    a. nicknames of the two sides in the Vietnam War
    b. capital cities of North Vietnam and South Vietnam
    c. the most famous battles of the Vietnam War
    d. names of the two most important Vietcong military leaders

    Which two sentences best support the answer?

    _____ _____

2. Which act of Congress gave President Johnson the authority to conduct the war in Vietnam in as he saw fit?
    a. Civil Rights Act of 1965
    b. Economic Opportunity Act
    c. Gulf of Tonkin Resolution
    d. Tet Offensive

    Which sentences best support the answer?

    _____ _____

3. True or False? Lyndon Johnson was the first U.S. president to become involved in the Vietnam War.

    ______________

    Which sentence best supports the answer?

    _____

4. Put the following four events from the Vietnam War era in chronological order: Tet Offensive, Gulf of Tonkin incident, 500,000 U.S. ground troops in Vietnam, Operation Rolling Thunder.

    1st ______________________________

    2nd ______________________________

    3rd ______________________________

    4th ______________________________

5. Describe what tactic the U.S. military used to expose the communist forces in the Vietnamese jungles.

    ______________________________

    ______________________________

6. What did President Johnson call his program to expand the American Dream by ending racism and poverty?
    a. Great Society
    b. Operation Rolling Thunder
    c. the Economic Opportunity Act
    d. Medicare

    Which sentences best support the answer?

    _____ _____

7. When Americans debated the war in Vietnam, some were called "hawks" and others "doves." Which of these Americans was against U.S. involvement in Vietnam?

    ____________________

    Which sentence best supports the answer?

    _____

8. In the spring of 1968, who declared an end to the bombing of North Vietnam and announced he would not run in the upcoming presidential election of that year?
    a. Lyndon Johnson
    b. Robert F. Kennedy
    c. William Westmoreland
    d. Eugene McCarthy

    Which sentences best support the answer?

    _____ _____

9. Give two reasons why the Vietnam War was being called a "quagmire" by the late 1960s.

    a. ______________________________

    ______________________________

    b. ______________________________

    ______________________________

© 2016 The Critical Thinking Co.™ • www.CriticalThinking.com • 800-458-4849

## Written Response Question

10. The political cartoon at the right was drawn in 1966. Use complete sentences to describe the cartoon. Who is the person in the cartoon and why do you say so? What is the scar on the chest that he points to? What is the opinion of the cartoonist?

David Levine, *New York Review of Books*, May 12, 1966.

### Fun Fact Finale

The 26th Amendment to the U.S. Constitution was passed in 1971, giving 18-year-old citizens the right to vote. Previously the minimum voting age had been 21. It only seemed fair that 18-, 19-, and 20-year-old citizens, who could be drafted for war, should be able to vote on U.S. policy.


© 2016 The Critical Thinking Co.™ • www.CriticalThinking.com • 800-458-4849

Lesson 45

# Nixon and the Cold War

## A. Nixon Works for Peace in Vietnam

[1]The Republican Party won back the White House in 1968 when former senator and vice president, Richard Nixon, won the presidential election. [2]Nixon's campaign had called for an easing of tensions in the Cold War. [3]To accomplish this, he stressed it would be important to have "peace with honor" in Vietnam, an end to the nuclear arms race with the Russians, and a better relationship between the United States and communist China.

[4]In Nixon's first year of office, he announced the Nixon Doctrine, stating that "the United States would assist in the defense and development of allies and friends," but would not "undertake all the defense of the free nations of the world." [5]This put a new spin on the earlier Truman and Eisenhower Doctrines which had taken the stance that the United States would basically give military aid and/or send U.S. soldiers to help all free people fighting communism. [6]With regards to the war in Southeast Asia, Nixon promoted a plan called Vietnamization—gradually reducing the number of U.S. troops in the war and replacing them with South Vietnamese military personnel to defend their own democracy. [7]President Nixon also sent Secretary of State Henry Kissinger to Paris, France, to negotiate directly for peace with North Vietnamese diplomats.

[8]To put added pressure on the communists to come to a peace agreement, Nixon also resumed massive bombing raids on North Vietnam. [9]Secretly, the president also ordered bombing raids on the Viet Cong targets in the neighboring nations of Laos and Cambodia. [10]When the news leaked out that Nixon had expanded the war into other formerly neutral Southeast Asian countries, student unrest on college campuses reignited and intensified. [11]Some protests turned destructive when protestors burned college and government buildings. [12]Other protests turned violent when anti-war protests were joined by various socialist organizations hoping to take advantage of the protestors' anger at the government. [13]These groups bombed buildings and encouraged violence against the police and firemen who were trying to control the protestors and limit the destruction. [14]In 1970, at Kent State University in Ohio, the governor sent in National Guard troops following threats and violent protests on campus. [15]After some of the protestors threw rocks at National Guardsmen who were trying to disperse them with teargas, some soldiers fired into the crowd of protesters. [16]Four students died and eleven others were wounded.

National Guard troops shot at anti-war protesters at Kent State University in 1970.

[17]Some Americans blamed the shootings on the violent and destructive turn in the protests, while others thought the shootings were an overreaction on the part of the soldiers and police. [18]The war had divided the nation more than ever. [19]More than 400 anti-war protests and demonstrations occurred across the country—many on college campuses.

## B. Vietnam War Ends

[20]Despite Nixon's attempt to end the war, the conflict in Vietnam continued throughout his first term. [21]In April 1972, the North Vietnamese launched their largest attack since the Tet Offensive. [22]It was called the Easter Offensive, and North Vietnamese troops won valuable territory in South Vietnam, which put them in a stronger position at the Paris Peace Talks. [23]Nixon ordered increased bombing of North Vietnam in response.

[24]Nixon's campaign for a second term was bolstered (boosted, supported) a month before the election when news arrived that an agreement on a ceasefire in Vietnam had been reached at the Paris Peace Talks. [25]"Peace is at hand," said Secretary of State Kissinger. [26]America promised to start a complete withdrawal of U.S. troops and North Vietnam agreed to halt further attacks and provide for the return of American POWs (prisoners of war). [27]A signing of the Paris Accords in January 1973 officially stopped hostilities between the United States and North Vietnam, and ended America's longest war.

© 2016 The Critical Thinking Co.™ • www.CriticalThinking.com • 800-458-4849

[28]However, there was no agreement between North and South Vietnam on the future government for that region. [29]After an interlude (a lull in the action) of two years, North Vietnamese troops completely overran South Vietnam and took control of the capital in Saigon in April 1975. [30]In 1976, North and South Vietnam were united under one communist government of Vietnam. [31]America's goal of a democratic government for Vietnam was defeated.

[32]More than 58,000 Americans lost their lives and more than 300,000 were wounded in the Vietnam War. [33]The war cost billions of dollars, hurt U.S. relations with its allies, divided the nation, and demoralized the military. [34]Many returning veterans found it painful to come home to a country where half the citizenship did not honor their military service or considered it immoral.

## C. Détente

[35]With a peace treaty in hand for Vietnam, Richard Nixon won a second term as president and continued his goal of easing Cold War tensions—a course of action called "détente." [36]He became the first U.S. president to travel to Moscow, Russia. [37]There he signed agreements with the Soviets on trade (exports of U.S. wheat to the USSR), technical cooperation (joint space exploration), and a reduction of nuclear weapons. [38]The Strategic Arms Limitation Treaty (SALT) stopped both sides from building more offensive atomic missiles for five years and attempted to create a balance in nuclear firepower between both countries.

President Nixon met the premier of the People's Republic of China, Zhou Enlai (right), in 1972.

[39]President Nixon also was the first U.S. chief executive to travel to China. [40]Ever since WWII, the United States had not recognized the communist government of "Red" China as a legitimate ruler of that region. [41]Since 1949, America had not engaged in any trade with the Chinese. [42]After Nixon's visit to the capital city of Beijing in 1972, both nations made an effort to normalize relations. [43]By the end of the decade, China was allowed to join the United Nations and trade had resumed between the United States and China.

[44]In the Middle East, Israel and neighboring Arab nations battled one another on several occasions. [45]During the so-called Yom Kippur War in 1973, Nixon sent military supplies to support Israel. [46]Seven oil-producing Arab nations, which sold large amounts of oil to the United States, were angered by the military support and stopped shipments of crude oil to the United States and her allies. [47]This caused a huge increase in gasoline prices and provoked some gas rationing in the United States. [48]The energy crisis and the threat of expansion of Soviet influence in the Middle East caused Nixon to react. [49]He sent Secretary of State Kissinger to work for peace in the region. [50]After two years of "shuttle diplomacy," during which Kissinger visited government officials in many nations in the Middle East, a cease-fire and an end to the oil embargo were negotiated. [51]By that time, however, Nixon was no longer president. [52]A dramatic political scandal had forced his resignation.

### Fun Fact Feature

A year before President Nixon's visit to China, some American athletes were allowed to enter the country for a competition in a sport loved by the Chinese. Can you guess the sport?


© 2016 The Critical Thinking Co.™ • www.CriticalThinking.com • 800-458-4849

1. Under President Nixon's plan of Vietnamization, which country would replace U.S. troops in the Vietnam War?
   a. North Vietnam
   b. South Vietnam
   c. China
   d. France

   Which sentence best supports the answer?

   ______

2. In the 1969 political cartoon below, who is probably the "soldier" weighed down in the jungles of Southeast Asia with the weight of Vietnam, and the extra weight of Cambodia and Laos on his back?

   a. Richard Nixon
   b. Henry Kissinger
   c. Zhou Enlai
   d. Lyndon Johnson

   Which sentences best support the answer?

   ______ ______ ______

3. What did the events at Kent State in 1970 show?
   a. student protests over Nixon's plan for détente
   b. American support for the Nixon Doctrine
   c. the unity Americans displayed in the era of the Vietnam War
   d. antiwar unrest over Nixon's secret bombing of more nations in Southeast Asia

   Which sentence best supports the answer?

   ______

4. The Nixon Doctrine suggested the United States would support its allies but:
   a. never send troops to support them in time of war.
   b. only if they needed help fighting communism.
   c. not ever provide economic assistance.
   d. not provide the sole defense of every free nation.

   Which sentence best supports the answer?

   ______

5. What were the Paris Accords of 1973?
   a. an alliance between the United States and France
   b. an end to the nuclear arms race between the USSR and the USA
   c. ended the Vietnam War for the United States
   d. opened up a new diplomatic relationship between the United States and China

   Which sentence best supports the answer?

   ______

6. "Shuttle diplomacy" was an effort by Secretary of State Henry Kissinger to bring peace:
   a. to the Middle East.
   b. to Vietnam.
   c. to Red China.
   d. between the United States and China.

   Which sentences best support the answer?

   ______ ______

7. By 1976, what happened to Vietnam?
   a. It was still divided between communist North and democratic South.
   b. It was taken over by the communist Red Chinese.
   c. It became one country controlled by a communist government.
   d. It was still at war with the United States?

   Which sentence best supports the answer?

   ______

© 2016 The Critical Thinking Co.™ • www.CriticalThinking.com • 800-458-4849

8. The SALT talks produced an agreement between the United States and the Soviet Union to do what?
   a. send American grain to the USSR
   b. end the Cold War
   c. limit their nuclear arms
   d. end an oil embargo against the USA

   Which sentence best supports the answer?

   ______

9. Richard Nixon:
   a. was forced out of office before the end of his first term.
   b. won reelection for a second term as president.
   c. was a senator and vice president but never won a presidential election.
   d. was the first president to visit France.

   Which sentence best supports the answer?

   ______

## Written Response Question

10. Use complete sentences to discuss three areas of the world where President Nixon tried to ease Cold War tensions during his term of office.

______________________________________________________________________

______________________________________________________________________

______________________________________________________________________

______________________________________________________________________

______________________________________________________________________

______________________________________________________________________

______________________________________________________________________

______________________________________________________________________

**Fun Fact Finale**

The U.S. table tennis team was playing matches in Japan when they were invited by the Chinese to become the first Americans to enter Beijing since 1949. The visit became known as "Ping Pong Diplomacy," because it thawed relations between the two countries and paved the way for President Nixon's historic visit the next year.


© 2016 The Critical Thinking Co.™ • www.CriticalThinking.com • 800-458-4849

# Review: Lessons 41-45
## 1960's Vocabulary

Write the letter of the definition of each vocabulary word. The number following each vocabulary word is the number of the lesson (41-45) where the word was used. All definitions are used once.

_____ 1. allegiance (41)

_____ 2. poll (41)

_____ 3. exiles (41)

_____ 4. legacy (41)

_____ 5. balanced budget (41)

_____ 6. coup (42)

_____ 7. disillusioned (42)

_____ 8. prevalent (42)

_____ 9. materialism (43)

_____ 10. counter (43)

_____ 11. migrant (43)

_____ 12. contraceptive (43)

_____ 13. escalate (44)

_____ 14. blank check (44)

_____ 15. defoliate (44)

_____ 16. deferment (44)

_____ 17. quagmire (44)

_____ 18. interlude (45)

_____ 19. détente (45)

_____ 20. bolster (45)

a. widespread

b. lost idealism, disenchanted

c. to strip trees of their leaves

d. a sampling of opinions of random persons

e. to increase in intensity

f. being bogged down in an entanglement

g. a temporary exemption from military service

h. loyalty or devotion

i. an easing of tensions

j. to support, boost

k. how a person is remembered

l. to go against

m. government spending without deficits

n. quick action from forces within a country to take over the government

o. persons banished from their own country

p. a lull in the action

q. full power, unrestricted authority

r. a person who moves from place to place

s. buying many consumer goods

t. any device that prevents the conception of children

© 2016 The Critical Thinking Co.™ • www.CriticalThinking.com • 800-458-4849

Section 9: Introduction

# 1970s-2016

The reelection of Richard Nixon in 1972 was soon tainted by scandal. The Watergate investigation by Congress resulted in the first ever resignation of a U.S. president. Gerald Ford finished out Nixon's second term in office. President Ford presided over the American withdrawal of forces in Vietnam. Jimmy Carter became the next American leader in the late 1970s. With a poor economy and troubles in the Middle East however, voters made him a one-term president.

Ronald Reagan (two terms) and George H.W. Bush (one term) put the Republican Party in charge of the nation from 1980 to 1992. Reagan's economic policies led to the largest peacetime economic growth in U.S. history. The Iran-Contra Scandal that erupted during Reagan's administration had little effect on his wide popularity. A so-called "Cold Warrior," Reagan put much pressure on the Soviet Union, which then helped lead to the fall of the Berlin Wall in 1989 and the collapse of the USSR in 1991, during George H.W. Bush's term in office. Bush also was president during the Persian Gulf War when an American-led coalition fought a dictator in Iraq who threatened United States' allies—Kuwait and Saudi Arabia.

Bill Clinton was the two-term president of the 1990s. America faced global violence in Yugoslavia, North Korea, Africa, and the Middle East during those years. It was also the beginning of the Age of Information, ushered in by a revolution in computer-related technologies. During Clinton's second term, he was impeached by the House of Representatives on charges relating to a sex scandal in the White House but was not convicted by the Senate.

The most controversial election in U.S. history resulted in the presidency of George W. Bush in 2000. Homeland security was the overriding issue of his two terms in office after a major terrorist attack on September 11, 2001, rocked the nation. Bush also presided over a renewed conflict in the Middle East—the Iraq War—and efforts to halt global terrorism by sending troops to Afghanistan.

The first African American president, Barrack Obama, took office in 2009. Military involvement in Iraq and Afghanistan and a reform of the health care system in the United States were the main issues he confronted during his two terms in office.

## U.S. Presidents

38. Gerald Ford 1974-1977

39. Jimmy Carter 1977-1981

40. Ronald Reagan 1981-1989

41. George H. W. Bush 1989-1993

42. Bill Clinton 1993-2001

43. George W. Bush 2001-2009

44. Barack Obama 2009-2017

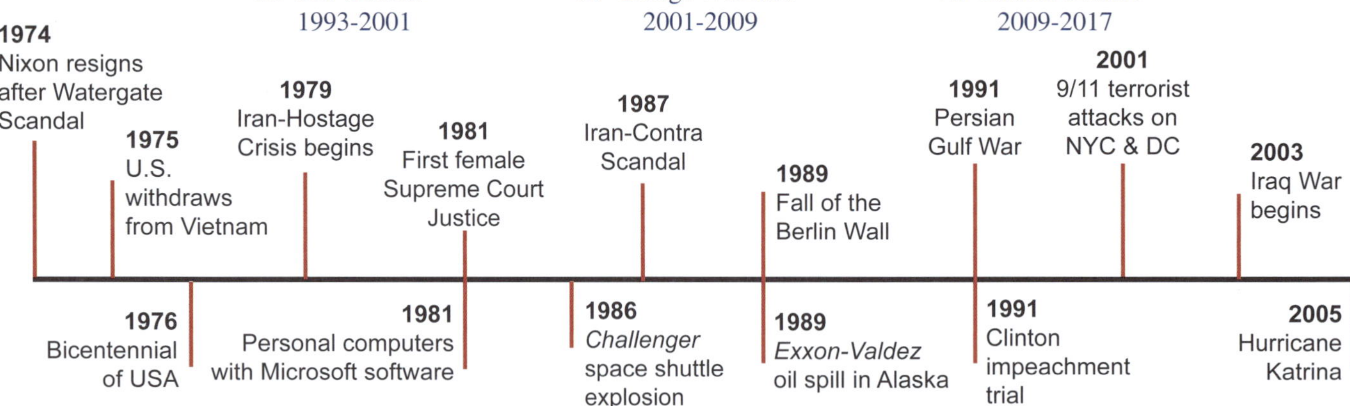



© 2016 The Critical Thinking Co.™ • www.CriticalThinking.com • 800-458-4849

Lesson 46

# Watergate Scandal

## A. Enemies List

[1]On July 21, 1969, when American astronauts Neil Armstrong and Edwin "Buzz" Aldrin landed on the moon, the United States had a reason to celebrate. [2]The country also celebrated President Nixon's foreign policy successes in his first term—

Buzz Aldrin (left) and Neil Armstrong

the SALT talks and his trip to China—but the war in Vietnam dragged on longer than anticipated, and Nixon feared it would hurt his chances for reelection in 1972. [3]In order to help win the vote of what he called "the silent majority" of blue-collar workers and suburban families, he took a strong public stand against protesters, criminals, and drug use.

[4]In 1971, during Nixon's first term in office, the U.S. government suffered political embarrassment when antiwar activist and former military advisor Daniel Ellsberg leaked a U.S. Defense Department study, called the Pentagon Papers, to the press. [5]The study exposed the fact that the United States (Johnson administration) had secretly bombed neighboring countries used by Vietnamese communists to smuggle arms and supplies into Vietnam. [6]It also showed that the Johnson and Nixon White House misled the public and Congress about the progress of the Vietnam War. [7]Embarrassed by these now public facts, the Nixon administration responded by forming a small (five members), secret, White House investigative group called the White House Plumbers. [8]The Plumbers tried to help stop the leaking of classified information. [9]The Plumbers first action was the illegal burglary of Daniel Ellsberg's psychiatrist's office. [10]The burglary was committed without the knowledge or consent of Richard Nixon. [11]The burglars had hoped to find some embarrassing information to use against Ellsberg, but found nothing of value. [12]Ellsberg was later charged with espionage (spying) and the theft of government property. [13]The charges against Ellsberg were thrown out of court after the Plumber's action was discovered.

## B. Dirty Tricks

[14]In the same year that the Nixon administration created the White House Plumbers, it also created a list of political opponents which later became known as the "enemies list." [15]The list was made up of people the administration believed threatened Nixon's reelection and people the president did not like. [16]Members of the Nixon administration used their influence with cooperating members of the FBI (Federal Bureau of Investigation), CIA (Central Intelligence Agency), and IRS (Internal Revenue Service) to target people on the list. [17]The harassment included investigations by the FBI and IRS and secret recordings of private conversations, in an effort to discredit Nixon's enemies. [18]When the IRS commissioner refused to target the people on the enemies list, the Nixon administration tried to have him replaced.

[19]As the 1972 election drew nearer, Nixon asked the head of his Justice Department, Attorney General John Mitchell, to lead the Committee to Reelect the President (CRP). [20]Under Mitchell's direction, the CRP engaged in "dirty tricks" and illegal targeting of several Democratic enemies of Richard Nixon. [21]These "dirty tricks" were paid for by CRP campaign dollars and used to undermine the targets by leaking embarrassing or other damaging information. [22]In June—unknown to Richard Nixon—Mitchell approved a plan to have a paid CRP team secretly wiretap the phones in the offices of the headquarters of the Democratic National Committee. [23]Mitchell hoped that by listening to Democratic election strategies, the Nixon reelection committee (CRP) could thwart (obstruct) them. [24]The Democratic headquarters was in a Washington, D.C. office building called Watergate.

The Watergate Office Building in D.C.

© 2016 The Critical Thinking Co.™ • www.CriticalThinking.com • 800-458-4849

[25]The wiretap effort failed when the CRP agents were discovered and arrested in the act of breaking-in. [26]An investigation connected money found on the burglars to the Committee to Reelect the President. [27]When Nixon later learned of the break in, he did not go to the authorities, but instead tried to cover it up. [28]He told the American public: "I can say categorically that ... no one on the White House staff, no one in this Administration, presently employed, was involved in this very bizarre incident." [29]Nixon also tried unsuccessfully to have the CIA block the FBI's investigation into the source of the burglary to protect national security.

[30]With these tactics, the Watergate story seemed to fade in the mind of the public and Nixon was easily reelected president by a landslide in November of 1972.

## C. The Tapes

[31]After the election, the Watergate cover-up unraveled in a scandal that cost Nixon his job. [32]During the trial of the Watergate burglars, one of the burglars confessed that people in the White House had pressured defendants to commit perjury (to lie in legal court). [33]This statement along with heavy press coverage and investigative reporting by *Washington Post* reporters Carl Bernstein and Bob Woodward put pressure on the U.S. Senate to form a special investigative committee to look into the Watergate matter in the spring of 1973. [34]The Senate committee's hearings revealed a direct connection between the White House and the illegal targeting of people on its enemy's list. [35]President Nixon attempted to save face by firing some of his White House aides who had knowledge of the illegal activities, including Attorney General John Mitchell. [36]This move backfired on Nixon when the new attorney general assigned a special prosecutor to continue the investigation of Watergate.

President Nixon and the White House Tapes

[37]In the fall of 1973, the Senate committee and the special prosecutor were shocked to learn that President Nixon had been secretly tape recording all his conversations in the Oval Office of the White House. [38]Nixon had hoped to preserve a record of all his accomplishments as president. [39]The investigators immediately demanded to listen to the tapes to learn "what the president knew and when he knew it" with regards to Watergate. [40]Nixon refused to turn over the tapes, again citing national security issues. [41]He also ordered the Justice Department to fire the special prosecutor. The department's attorney general and several other officials resigned in protest. [42]Nixon tried to explain his side of the story in a televised speech in November where he declared: "I am not a crook." [43]However, new officials in the Justice Department and Congress filed a case with the Supreme Court demanding that the White House tapes be turned over to investigators.

[44]In July of 1974, the Court ruled in *United States v. Nixon* that the tapes must be turned over to Congress. [45]When Congress and the special prosecutor listened to the tapes, it was clear that Nixon's staff had tried to erase some damaging evidence about Watergate. [46]In spite of their efforts to hide evidence, the tapes still proved that President Nixon had lied to the American public and been deeply involved in the Watergate cover-up. [47]It was clear, for example, that the president had authorized secret payments to the arrested Watergate burglars who were blackmailing (demanding money for their silence) the Nixon Whitehouse. [48]The burglars wanted "hush money" in return for not revealing the Whitehouse's connection to the Watergate break-in.

[49]The House of Representatives started an impeachment process by voting to charge the president with obstruction of justice, abusing the powers of his office, and contempt of Congress. [50]Nixon, certain that the Senate would find him guilty of the charges at his trial, chose to quit. [51]In August of 1974, Nixon became the first U.S. president to resign his office.


© 2016 The Critical Thinking Co.™ • www.CriticalThinking.com • 800-458-4849

## Fun Fact Feature

President Nixon loved a particular sport so much that he had a special facility built into the basement of the White House. Can you guess his favorite sport?

1. Who was Neil Armstrong?
   a. an American astronaut who landed on the moon
   b. U.S. Attorney General for President Nixon
   c. a member of CRP
   d. a reporter for the Washington Post during the Watergate scandal

   Which sentence best supports the answer?

   _____

2. Whose votes did Nixon hope to win during his reelection campaign in 1972?
   a. "the plumbers"
   b. Anti-Vietnam war protesters
   c. African Americans and recent immigrants
   d. the "silent majority"

   Which sentence best supports the answer?

   _____

3. Daniel Ellsberg was on Nixon's "enemies list"; why?
   a. he misled the public about the Vietnam War
   b. he taped Nixon's conversations
   c. he lied to the American public
   d. he leaked the Pentagon Papers to the press

   Which sentence best supports the answer?

   _____

4. What facts did the Pentagon Papers expose to the American public?

   a. ________________________________

   ________________________________

   b. ________________________________

   ________________________________

5. Why did agents of the Committee to Reelect the President (CRP) try to wiretap the Watergate office building in Washington, D.C.?
   a. anti-war protesters were holding a rally there
   b. the Vietnam War peace talks were in session at that location
   c. it was the headquarters of the Democratic election campaign
   d. it was the site office of the Watergate special prosecutor

   Which sentence best supports the answer?

   _____

6. True or False? The Watergate scandal ruined Nixon's chance for reelection as president in 1972.

   ____________________

   Which sentence supports the answer?

   _____

7. The trial of the Watergate burglars and the newspaper reports by the *Washington Post* put pressure on whom to investigate the Watergate incident further in 1973?
   a. Attorney General John Mitchell
   b. the Supreme Court
   c. the Senate
   d. Woodward and Bernstein

   Which sentence best supports the answer?

   _____

8. Nixon was not the first president to be impeached (charged with crimes by the House, leading to a trial in the Senate). Andrew Johnson was impeached in 1868, but Nixon was the first president to:
   a. win his impeachment trial in the Senate.
   b. lose his impeachment trial in the Senate.
   c. resign his office.
   d. die in office.

   Which sentence supports the answer?

   _____

9. Look at this 1974 political cartoon on the right.

   a. Who is the person caught in the web?

   ______________________________

   b. What is the web made of?

   ______________________________

   c. What Supreme Court case may have just occurred prior to the publication of this cartoon?

   ______________________________

## Written Response Question

10. Use complete sentences to show at least three pieces of evidence you see in this lesson that might have led to a guilty verdict on the charges against President Nixon at his impeachment trial.

______________________________

______________________________

______________________________

______________________________

______________________________

______________________________

______________________________

______________________________

### Fun Fact Finale

One of Nixon's favorite pastimes in the White House was bowling. He'd even bowl a few frames dressed in his suit. The president had a one lane bowling alley built in the basement beneath the North Portico entrance to the White House while he was in office.

© 2016 The Critical Thinking Co.™ • www.CriticalThinking.com • 800-458-4849

Lesson 47

# Ford and Carter

### A. A President and Vice President With No Election

[1]As the Watergate scandal was unfolding, the Nixon administration was dealt another blow. [2]His vice president, Spiro Agnew, pleaded "no contest" to charges of bribery and income tax evasion when he was the governor of Maryland and then vice president. [3]After his trial in October 1973, Agnew resigned his office. [4]According to the 25th Amendment, passed only six years before, in 1967, when a vacancy exists in the office of the vice president, the president shall nominate a replacement that Congress approves with a majority vote. [5]Nixon replaced Agnew with Gerald R. Ford, a Michigan Republican who was well respected by both Republicans and Democrats while serving 25 years in the House of Representatives. [6]When Nixon resigned ten months later in August of 1974, Ford became president and he, in turn, had to appoint a new vice president (Nelson Rockefeller). [7]Ford and Rockefeller thereby became the only U.S. president and vice president to ever hold those offices at the same time without having been elected by American voters.

[8]After taking office, President Ford told the country "Our long, national nightmare is over." [9]Rather than have the nation focused on a long criminal trial of the resigned former president,

The New York Times

CITY EDITION

FORD GIVES PARDON TO NIXON, WHO REGRETS 'MY MISTAKES'

U.S.-Bound Plane With 88 Crashes in Sea Off Greece

'PAIN' EXPRESSED

Ex-President Cites His Sorrow at the Way He Handled Watergate

NO CONDITIONS SET

Action Taken to Spare Nation and Ex-Chief, President Says

The Statement by Nixon

Proclamation of Pardon

State Panel Charges City Fails to Pursue Fugitives

he decided to use his presidential powers to try to move beyond the scandal. [10]Ford issued a presidential pardon to Nixon in September 1974, for "any and all crimes" Nixon may have committed while in office. [11]Many Americans who wanted Nixon to stand trial for his actions were upset with Ford's pardon.

[12]Ford also had to deal with a struggling American economy which was feeling the pain of rising foreign oil prices. [13]Inflation (when prices rise quickly) was a major problem, especially for oil and gasoline. [14]Frustrated Americans sat in their cars in long lines to get high-priced gas in the mid-1970s. [15]The president tried to encourage the American public to lower their consumption, thus lowering demand, which would, in turn, lower inflation. [16]He called this program WIN—"Whip Inflation Now." [17]He also proposed raising taxes five percent on corporations and wealthy individuals, but the controlling Democratic Party refused to pass his increase through Congress. [18]Faced with an economy heading for recession, Ford then proposed a tax cut, but inflation became even worse. [19]So did unemployment. [20]Especially hard hit were the traditional automobile manufacturing centers in the upper Midwest and the Northeast. [21]As higher oil prices, old technologies, and foreign competition drove many businesses in those regions to close, that section of the country became known as the "Rust Belt."

[22]Ford ran for reelection, but the Nixon pardon and the poor economy doomed his success. [23]Voters were also discouraged when South Vietnam was taken over by communist forces in April of 1975. [24]Many felt it was time for a change in the federal government.

### B. Jimmy Carter

[25]The bicentennial of the Declaration of Independence was in 1976, and Americans celebrated 200 years of independence. [26]That year Jimmy Carter, a former U.S. Naval officer and the Democratic governor of Georgia, won

Jimmy Carter and his wife Rosalyn walked from the Capitol Building to the White House on inauguration day to show he planned to be a different type of president.

© 2016 The Critical Thinking Co.™ • www.CriticalThinking.com • 800-458-4849

the presidential election. [27]He campaigned as a Washington D.C. outsider and centrist (not too far right or left) who had no connection with the Watergate scandal in the nation's capital. [28]White Southerners, working-class Americans, and black Americans from every region were especially happy to vote for a "Washington outsider."

[29]However, President Carter was such an "outsider" that he didn't get along with Washington, D.C. politicians from either party. [30]His administration made little progress over the next four years on the nation's problems. [31]He upset Democratic liberals by budgeting less money for social programs and removing government price controls on many corporations. [32]Carter created a new cabinet position, the Department of Energy, but it did little to slow rising oil prices, resulting in high gasoline prices. [33]He upset conservative Republicans when his officials negotiated a treaty that transferred full control of the Panama Canal, a U.S. territory since 1903, back to Panama. [34]Republicans also showed little support for Carter's efforts to improve a nuclear arms treaty with the Soviet Union. [35]Both liberals and conservatives were saddened that Carter cancelled U.S. participation in the 1980 Summer Olympics scheduled for Moscow, USSR—a move the president made in protest over the Soviet invasion of Afghanistan.

## C. Middle East Mess

[36]The biggest headache for President Carter came from the Middle East. [37]At first, Carter seemed to win a victory when he arranged for a

Israeli Leader Menachem Begin, President Jimmy Carter, and Egyptian President Anwar Sadat at Camp David, 1978

peace agreement called the Camp David Accords. [38]Camp David is a presidential retreat in Maryland. [39]Carter invited the leaders of Egypt and Israel—former enemies—to the retreat to work out an end to ongoing conflicts in the Middle East. [40]Success came when Egypt agreed to become the first Arab nation to officially recognize the post-WWII Jewish nation of Israel as a true country. [41]In return, Israel withdrew its military from a section of disputed Arab land. [42]However, peace in the Middle East between Arabs and Jews fell apart within a few years.

[43]The U.S. relationship with Iran also fell apart. [44]After WWII, the United States had supported Shah Mohammed Pahlavi as Iran's leader. [45]The shah had been a strong anti-Soviet force in the Middle East. [46]He had also sold oil to the United States even when neighboring Muslim countries stopped selling U.S. oil because of the U.S.'s support for Israel. [47]The shah's close relationship with the United States and his harsh treatment of his own Iranian people led to his removal in early 1979 by a group of Muslims led by Ayatollah Khomeini. [48]The shah fled his country and asked the United States to take him in.

[49]President Carter allowed the shah to receive cancer treatment in the United States in November. [50]Khomeini and his supporters were angered by this move. [51]Iranian militant groups publicly burned American flags and attacked the U.S. embassy in Iran's capital, capturing 66 American workers. [52]For the next year and a half, Carter tried to negotiate the release of the U.S. hostages. [53]When that didn't work, the president ordered a U.S. military strike to rescue them. [54]But Americans were further embarrassed when the rescue attempt failed miserably; the military helicopters crashed, killing eight U.S. airmen.

[55]Jimmy Carter was nominated by the Democratic Party to run for reelection in 1980 but lost by one of the largest electoral margins in U.S. history to the Republican candidate—Ronald Reagan. [56]That meant that no president had completed two terms in office since Dwight Eisenhower in the 1950s. [57]In a bittersweet (both painful and pleasant) move, Iranian authorities released the American hostages the very day that Carter left office—January 21, 1981.


© 2016 The Critical Thinking Co.™ • www.CriticalThinking.com • 800-458-4849

**Fun Fact Feature**

Jimmy Carter was a farmer in Georgia before becoming president. Can you name the crop that he grew? He kept a jar with this product on his White House desk.

1. Why did President Nixon have to appoint a new vice president in 1973?

______________________________________

______________________________________

2. What was unusual about Gerald Ford and Nelson Rockefeller as president and vice president?
   a. They were not of the same political party.
   b. They were not elected for those offices by voters.
   c. They were the first to be voted in from the Independent Party.
   d. They were related to one another.

   Which sentence best supports the answer?

   _____

3. What did President Gerald Ford do about the Watergate scandal when he took office?
   a. He pardoned Nixon.
   b. He ordered the Attorney General to prosecute Nixon.
   c. He proposed a program called "WIN."
   d. He did nothing.

   Which sentence best supports the answer?

   _____

4. What new cabinet position did President Carter create while in office?

______________________________________

______________________________________

5. Jimmy Carter was elected in the same year as:
   a. the Watergate scandal.
   b. the Iran hostage crisis.
   c. Nixon's pardon.
   d. America's bicentennial.

   Which sentences best support the answer?

   _____ _____

6. What does the map below, drawn in the 1970s, probably represent?

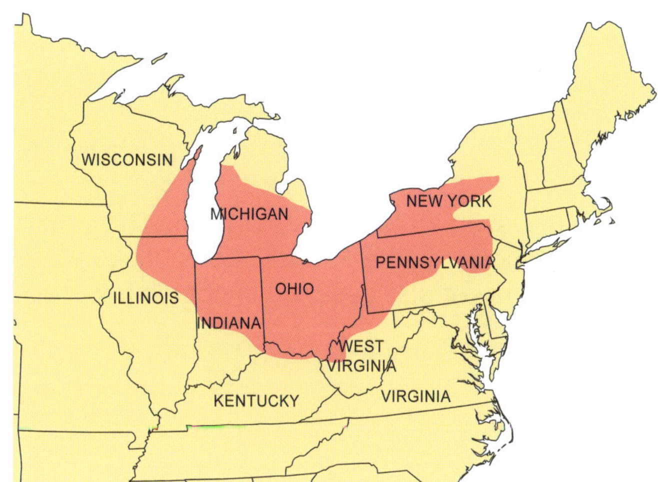


   a. the region of lowest inflation
   b. the Rust Belt
   c. where Jimmy Carter won the most votes for president
   d. the Watergate scandal

   Which sentences best support the answer?

   _____ _____

7. The Iranian hostage crisis erupted when which fallen leader entered the United States upon the invitation of President Carter?
   a. Spiro Agnew
   b. Ayatollah Khomeini
   c. the leader of the Soviet Union
   d. Shah Mohammed Pahlavi

   Which sentences best support the answer?

   _____ _____

8. The Camp David Accords were an attempt by the Carter administration to bring peace to:
   a. Afghanistan.
   b. the Cold War between the U.S. and the USSR.
   c. the Middle East.
   d. Maryland.

   Which sentence best supports the answer?

   _____

9. The Carter administration negotiated a treaty that gave back what American territory?
    a. Iran
    b. Puerto Rico
    c. Panama Canal
    d. Israel

    Which sentence best supports the answer?

    ______

## Written Response Question

10. This lesson states that as of 1980, "No president had completed two terms in office since Dwight Eisenhower in the 1950s." Look back on previous lessons in this book. List the five presidents since Eisenhower and describe in complete sentences why each did not finish a second term.

a. ____________________________________________

____________________________________________

b. ____________________________________________

____________________________________________

c. ____________________________________________

____________________________________________

d. ____________________________________________

____________________________________________

e. ____________________________________________

____________________________________________

**Fun Fact Finale**

Jimmy Carter struggled early in his farming career—he and his wife once lived in public housing—but eventually became a prosperous peanut farmer. A peanut statue now stands near his home town of Plains, Georgia.

© 2016 The Critical Thinking Co.™ • www.CriticalThinking.com • 800-458-4849

Lesson 48

# 1970's Culture

## A. The "Me Generation"

[1]Baby Boomers (people born between WWII and 1964) had been instrumental in the protests and counter-revolution of the 1960s. [2]In the United States and Europe they were the most privileged generation in the history of the world, growing up in a time of huge economic gains and government assistance in housing and education. [3]By the mid-1970s, in spite of their good fortune, many American Baby Boomers had become disillusioned (embittered, disenchanted). [4]The assassinations of Martin Luther King and Robert Kennedy, the political scandals of the Nixon administration, the unsatisfying end of the Vietnam War, the Iranian hostage crisis, and the worsening economy were among many things that cast doubt among Boomers in the future of America. [5]As a result, many Boomers began to look inward to find ways to achieve personal happiness and self-fulfillment rather than try to change the whole of society.

[6]In 1976, the writer Tom Wolfe coined (invented) a new term for Boomers with this attitude—"The Me Generation." [7]He said that many young 1960s radicals had abandoned their ideals to focus on "remaking, remodeling, elevating, and polishing one's very self … and observing, studying, and doting on it (Me!)" [8]Examples of the inward-looking culture of the day showed up in many ways in the 1970s. [9]Yoga, jogging, fad diets, and therapy sessions became popular as many Boomers, now in their thirties, focused on trends to extend their physical and mental health. [10]"Earth Shoes" were designed to promote a natural and healthier way of walking and fit in nicely with the environmental movement. [11]A magazine called *Self* started publication in 1979. [12]Its title highlighted the focus of Boomers in that decade. [13]The editor of that magazine proclaimed in the first issue that, "*Self* will be a guide to the vitality we need to do all the things we want to do."

[14]Fashions of the 1970s reflected an effort to call attention to oneself. [15]Clothing such as designer jeans, with clearly marked manufacturers' labels, were worn. [16]The widening of shirt collars, ties, and lower pant legs ("bell bottoms") called for attention as did tall platform shoes worn by both men and women to boost their height. [17]Shunning the gray business suit of an earlier era, men wore "leisure suits"—polyester outfits consisting of a jacket, vest, and pants in citrus or pastel colors.

[18]Self-expression in hair was important. [19]Men grew mustaches and long, bushy sideburns. [20]Wide chain necklaces drooped into V-neck shirts with exposed chest hair. [21]Many African Americans grew out their hair in a large, ball-shaped style called the "Afro." [22]"Big hair" was also a fashion trend of women, especially long "feathered" hairstyles. [23]In 1979, a musical called *Hair* became a stage play and a movie theater hit.

## B. Music and Fads

[24]Nightclubs with dance floors which flashed lights that kept time to loud music became popular places for Boomers in the 70s. [25]Music played at these nightclubs was labeled "disco" (which came from the shortened French name for the club—discotheque). [26]Disco music emphasized a steady drumbeat, electronic instruments, and strong vocals. [27]A mirrored disco ball overhead reflected light. [28]The music was meant for dancing and "The Hustle" and "The Bump" became favorite dance styles. [29]The Bee Gees, KC and the Sunshine Band, and Donna Summer were examples of popular disco bands. [30]The disco movie *Saturday Night Fever*, released in 1977, was a huge success.

[31]Some music was now produced on tapes, rather than on vinyl records, and was played with devices called eight-track players. [32]This technology was short-lived. [33]By the late 1970s, music was being played on smaller cassette tape players. [34]Some disco listeners may have worn the popular "mood ring." [35]This was a temperature-

© 2016 The Critical Thinking Co.™ • www.CriticalThinking.com • 800-458-4849

sensitive ring that purported (claimed) to indicate a person's inner feelings by changing colors when worn. [36]There were people in the Me Generation who also owned a "pet rock." [37]This was a perfectly normal rock that came with instructions on how to treat it like "the perfect pet"—it wouldn't eat, make noise, or need to be potty trained. [38]This 1975 fad earned the inventor more than four million dollars in sales.

[39]Artists in the 1970s tried to stay away from traditional forms of art. [40]They were highly individualistic and did not want to be lumped together into any one style. [41]Some created "land art"—large pieces of natural material placed on Earth's landscape. [42]Others tried "performance art"—using their own bodies as a canvas or for an artistic expression. [43]"String art" involved arranging colored thread between raised points to form abstract geometric patterns or designs.

[44]Maybe the ultimate fad of the decade was "streaking"—people running naked at public events. [45]It was especially popular on college campuses and at sporting events. [46]The high point of this fad was when a streaker ran across the stage at the televised Academy Awards show in 1974. [47]That year song writer Ray Stevens performed *The Streak*, a novelty song about a man who is "always making the news wearing just his tennis shoes." [48]The song, amazingly, reached number one on the music charts.

## C. Feminism

[49]In 1970, a New York attorney, civil rights activist, and feminist, Bella Abzug, was elected as a U.S. Representative in Congress and famously declared "A woman's place is in the House." [50]A new wave of activity for women's rights was underway. [51]The next year one of the most popular songs was called *I Am Woman*. [52]"I am woman, hear me roar," sang the artist Helen Reddy. [53]In 1972, a new magazine devoted to women's issues, called *Ms.*, was founded by feminist Gloria Steinem. [54]"Ms." was a new title used by women who did not necessarily want to be judged as to whether they were married (Mrs.) or single (Miss). [55]Female American tennis star Billie Jean King defeated a senior male challenger, Bobby Riggs, in a televised "Battle of the Sexes" tennis match in 1973 that did much to popularize women in sport.

[56]In 1971, the New England Free Press published a book by a dozen women who had met to have an open discussion about women's health issues. [57]*Our Bodies, Ourselves* soon became a bestseller. [58]Abortion (the early termination of a pregnancy) was an issue discussed in the book. [59]Two years later, a hugely important case was heard by the Supreme Court. [60]The Court ruled in *Roe v. Wade* (1973) that state laws prohibiting abortion in the first three months of a pregnancy were unconstitutional. [61]Over the next decades, the country would be deeply divided over whether a woman's rights included the right to abort a pregnancy. [62]Those in favor of a woman's right to make this decision called themselves "pro-choice," and those who believed the rights of the unborn fetus trumped (surpassed) the rights of the mother to decide called themselves "pro-life."

This issue of *Ms.* magazine featured a photo of the founder, Gloria Steinem.

[63]More and more, women were standing up for themselves in the workplace, in politics, and in society. [64]The term "sexual harassment" (the pressuring, intimidating, or coercion of someone regarding their gender) became part of the American vocabulary in the early 1970s. [65]Businesses, schools, and other institutions were urged to prevent this form of discrimination. [66]Politicians also created laws to close the "gender pay gap" when it was clearly shown that female workers were often paid less than their male counterparts for the same jobs. [67]In the late 1970s, the phrase "glass ceiling" was being used to describe "the unseen, but too commonly impenetrable barrier that kept many minorities and women from rising to the upper rungs of the corporate ladder, regardless of their qualifications or achievements."

[68]The idea of divorce became less taboo (a topic or practice forbidden by society) in the 1970s. [69]The divorce rate soared during the decade, especially after a 1974 book called *The Courage to Divorce* encouraged individuals to put their own happiness above that of their spouses and children. [70]*Kramer vs. Kramer*, a movie about divorce and its effect on children, was one of the most watched films of 1979.

 © 2016 The Critical Thinking Co.™ • www.CriticalThinking.com • 800-458-4849

**Fun Fact Feature**

In 1979, an era of women's rights, a voting rights activist from the 1800s was honored as the first American woman to be recognized in a special way. How was Susan B. Anthony honored?

1. What was the nickname given to the Baby Boomers living in the 1970s?
    a. The Hustle
    b. Age of Aquarius
    c. Ms.
    d. Me Generation

    Which sentences best support the answer?

    _____ _____

2. What 1970s magazine was a prime example of the focus of Americans in the 1970s?
    a. *The Streak*
    b. *Saturday Night Fever*
    c. *Self*
    d. *Time*

    Which sentences best support the answer?

    _____ _____

3. Which body feature did men and women of the 1970s often use to creatively express themselves?
    a. shoulders
    b. toes
    c. hair
    d. arms

    Which sentence best supports the answer?

    _____

4. What was a popular form of dance music in the 1970s?
    a. swing
    b. disco
    c. rap
    d. mood music

    Which sentences best support the answer?

    _____ _____

5. What were schools of art often called in the 1970s?
    a. Hudson River
    b. Ashcan
    c. Disco
    d. none of the above

    Which sentences best support the answer?

    _____ _____

6. The 1970s political cartoon below is making a point about which issue?

    a. education opportunities
    b. women's employment opportunities
    c. abortion
    d. child care

    Explain the message of the cartoonist.

    ______________________________

    ______________________________

    ______________________________

7. Name three phrases that came into the American lexicon (vocabulary used by a culture) in the 1970s that are related to the women's rights movement.

    a. ______________________________

    ______________________________

    b. ______________________________

    ______________________________

    c. ______________________________

    ______________________________

© 2016 The Critical Thinking Co.™ • www.CriticalThinking.com • 800-458-4849 

8. *Roe v. Wade* (1973) was a Supreme Court decision about what issue?
   a. abortion
   b. education
   c. sports
   d. music

   Which sentence best supports the answer?

   _____

9. Bella Abzug and Gloria Steinem are Americans known as pioneers in which field?
   a. women's rights
   b. art
   c. music
   d. sports

   Which sentences best support the answer?

   _____ _____

## Written Response Question

10. List five ways that the women's rights movement accomplished its goals in the 1970s.

1. ______________________________________________

______________________________________________

2. ______________________________________________

______________________________________________

3. ______________________________________________

______________________________________________

4. ______________________________________________

______________________________________________

5. ______________________________________________

______________________________________________

### Fun Fact Finale

Susan B. Anthony was the first woman to be honored by having her likeness appear on a circulating United States coin. President Jimmy Carter signed the Susan b. Anthony Dollar Coin Act into law.

© 2016 The Critical Thinking Co.™ • www.CriticalThinking.com • 800-458-4849

# Bonus Activity
# Culture of the 1970s

Review Lesson 48, then give a name to each image shown below from the culture of the '70s.

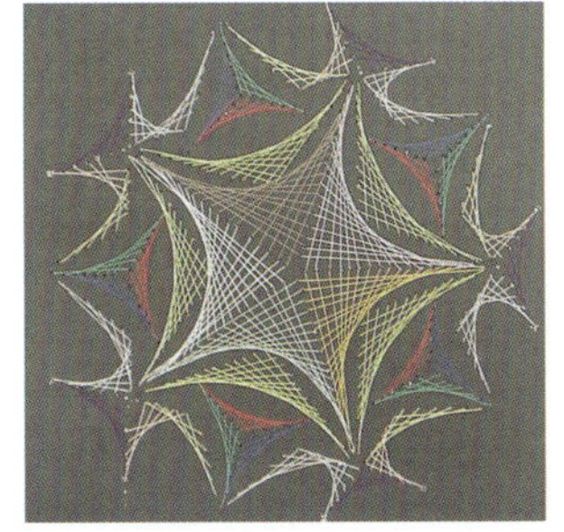

1. ______________________

______________________

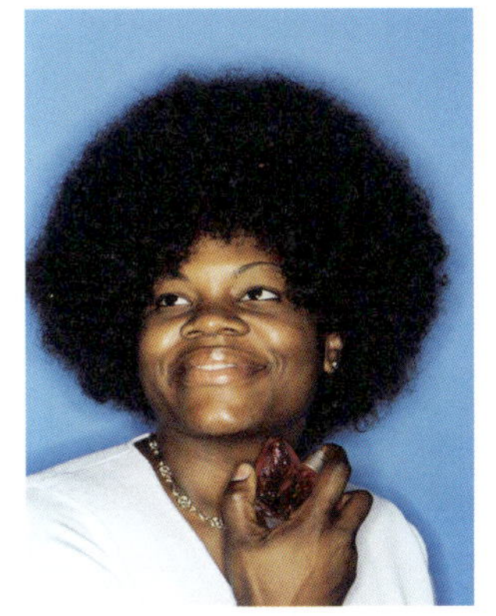

5. ______________________

______________________

2. ______________________

______________________

6. ______________________

______________________

3. ______________________

______________________

7. ______________________

______________________

4. ______________________

______________________

8. ______________________

______________________

# Bonus Activity
# 1960s and 1970s

Review Lessons 41-48. Write the events from the choice box in the Venn diagram according to the times in which they occurred.

| | | | |
|---|---|---|---|
| Watergate | Vietnam War | JFK assassination | disco music |
| Ford pardons Nixon | Great Society | President Nixon | Title IX |
| anti-war protests | Woodstock concert | women's rights movement | |
| U.S. Moon landing | Iran hostage crisis | "I have a dream" speech | |

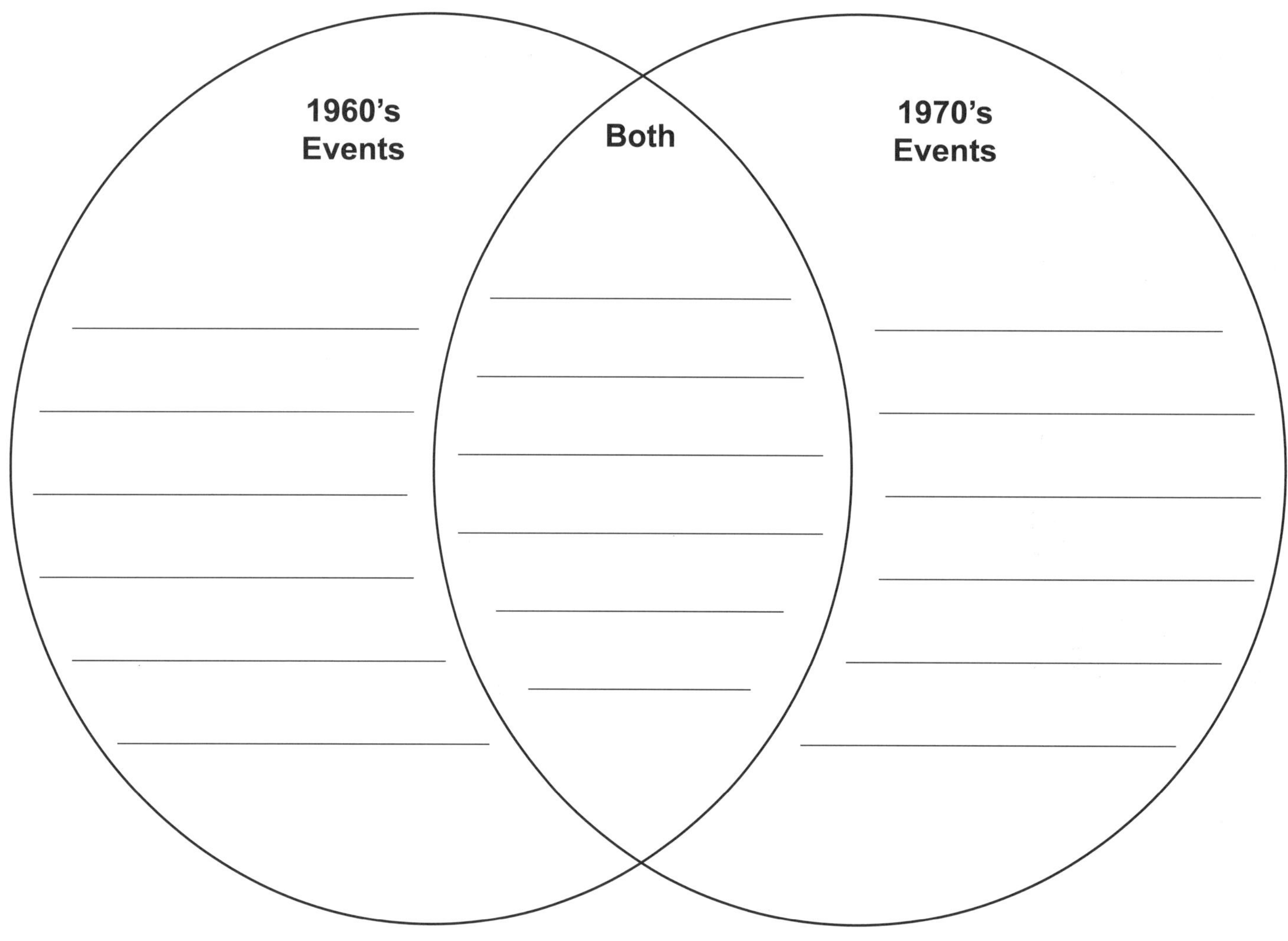



© 2016 The Critical Thinking Co.™ • www.CriticalThinking.com • 800-458-4849

Lesson 49

# Ronald Reagan Takes Office

## A. Background of Ronald Reagan

[1]During the Great Depression, a young man named Ronald Reagan found work as a baseball announcer at a Midwestern radio station. [2]Reagan had come from a poor family and, like his father, was a Democrat who supported the New Deal programs of President Franklin Roosevelt. [3]A strong opponent of racial discrimination even in his youth, Reagan was known to bring black Americans who were refused a room in his small town's hotel to his home, where the Reagan family took them in and let them stay for free. [4]Reagan attended a small Midwestern college, studied economics, and was elected student body president. [5]In 1937, he moved to Southern California and found work as an actor in Hollywood films. [6]Over the next two decades, the increasingly popular Reagan acted in more than fifty movies and eventually became president of the Screen Actors Guild.

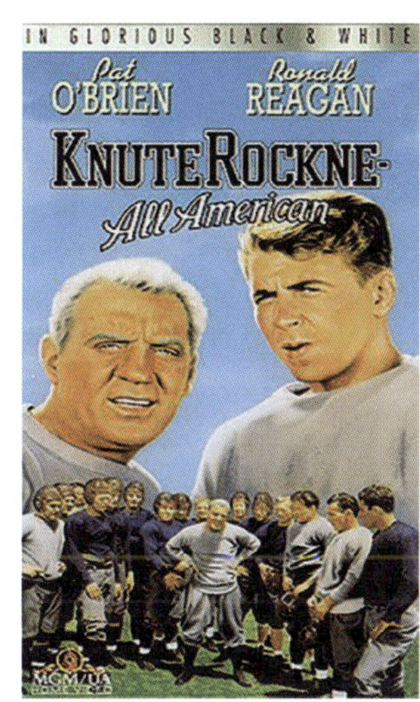


Reagan played a football star in one movie and was often called "The Gipper" for this role afterwards.

[7]A strong anti-communist in the early days of the Cold War, Reagan cooperated with the House Un-American Activities Committee (HUAC) by testifying before Congress and providing the FBI with names of fellow actors who he believed might have been sympathetic to, or cooperating with, Russian communists. [8]Reagan backed the Democrat Truman in 1948 but supported the Republican Eisenhower in the 1950s. [9]Reagan started appearing on television and became widely known for his work as a spokesman for the General Electric Company (GE). [10]Reagan was encouraged by an influential GE executive to educate himself about the working of American democracy and the capitalist economy. [11]This education made Reagan more conservative and in the early 1960s, he decided to become more involved in politics. [12]Reagan switched his allegiance from the Democratic Party to the Republican Party, stating "I didn't leave the Democratic Party, the Party left me." [13]His 1964 speeches in support of the unsuccessful Republican candidate, Barry Goldwater, gained even more fame for Reagan.

[14]Although a supporter of FDR's New Deal programs his entire life, Reagan was a staunch opponent of Lyndon Johnson's Great Society social spending programs. [15]Reagan claimed they created a new class of Americans dependent on government handouts, created massive new government debt, and failed to reduce the number of Americans living in poverty. [16]Although Reagan also wanted to give support to the poor, he didn't want to create a huge governmental agency to do it.

[17]In 1966, he successfully won the election for governor of California by campaigning as a law-and-order politician and a financial conservative. [18]Reagan then successfully ran for president in 1980 when he opposed Democrat Jimmy Carter, who was hindered by a suffering U.S. economy. [19]His overwhelming landslide victory captured forty-four states to Carter's six and also helped elect the first Republican Party majority in the Senate since 1952. [20]In doing so, he became the oldest person to be elected; he was nearly 70 when he took the oath of office.

[21]Reagan's years as a radio announcer and actor had trained him to be comfortable as a speaker. [22]He gained the nickname "The Great Communicator" for his air of confidence, enthusiasm about the future, and patriotism. [23]Only a few months into his presidency, however, a would-be assassin shot Reagan outside of a Washington, D.C. hotel. [24]Reagan survived surgery to remove a bullet and joked with his doctors: "I hope you are all Republicans."

## B. Reaganomics

[25]The 1970s had been a decade of rising prices, climbing unemployment, and economic uncertainty. [26]President Reagan followed a theory called "supply-side economics" as he began his first term. [27]Reagan believed that excessive government regulation, an unfair tax burden, and too much government spending on social problems were choking the economic growth of the United States. [28]He and his economists believed the national economy would experience growth and recovery if the federal government lowered taxes and eased government regulations on American businesses. [29]Reagan argued that taxing less

© 2016 The Critical Thinking Co.™ • www.CriticalThinking.com • 800-458-4849

of the public's income would allow the public to spend and invest more, which would stimulate the economy and create new jobs. [30]The media dubbed his plan "Reaganomics." [31]His liberal critics labeled his economic plan "Trickle-Down Economics," claiming that it was designed to benefit the wealthy and limited benefit would trickle down to the poor.

The president went on national television in 1981 to explain his economic proposal—a plan the media called "Reaganomics."

[32]In July 1981, months after Reagan took office, the United States entered into a recession that had spread throughout most of Western Europe and North America. [33]In August 1981, Reagan managed to get his economic plan through Congress. [34]Although Democrats still controlled the House, they passed most of Reagan's economic proposals, which then passed the Republican controlled Senate and were signed into law by Reagan. [35]A twenty-five percent reduction on federal income taxes was passed along with reductions on business regulations. [36]The yearly growth in spending on social programs was reduced by three percent.

[37]Reaganomics worked and led to the largest peacetime economic growth in U.S. history. [38]The United States climbed out of the recession, and the U.S. economy continued to expand until 1990. [39]Liberal critics of Reaganomics point out that the expanding economy only paid for half of the lost tax revenue while Reagan was in office and thus added to the U.S. debt. [40]Conservative supporters of Reaganomics point out that the economic boom not only pulled the United States out of the 1981 economic recession, it also benefited all parts of the economy (the poor, middleclass, and wealthy). [41]The American public overwhelmingly sided with Reagan, and he remained very popular

### C. Other First Term Actions

[42]Reagan had a strong effect on the Supreme Court during his tenure in office. [43]As Supreme Court vacancies occurred during his first term, he nominated two conservative justices and one moderate justice to fill the openings on the court. [44]All three nominations were approved by the Republican Party controlled senate. [45]His moderate nomination was the first woman Supreme Court justice. [46]In 1981, the Senate confirmed Reagan's choice of Sandra Day O'Connor.

[47]Reagan was known as a Cold Warrior—a strong anti-communist—and once spoke of the Soviet Union as the "evil empire." [48]He pushed for large increases in defense spending by doubling the military budget. [49]He ordered more than 500 nuclear weapons to be placed at NATO bases in Western Europe to counter Soviet missiles in Eastern Europe. [50]This dramatic, expensive increase in U.S. military spending put tremendous pressure on the Soviet economy and leadership, bringing about the historic changes in the Soviet Union covered in the next lesson.

[51]During the same time period, Reagan backed a CIA plan to finance an anti-communist army, called the Contras, in Nicaragua. [52]He sent 2,000 U.S. troops to the Caribbean island of Grenada to oust a communist regime (system of government). [53]The impact of the Reagan administration's handling of the Contra's will be covered further in the next lesson.

[54]The Middle East continued to be an area of conflict with U.S. interests as well. [55]The Reagan administration financed Islamic forces in Afghanistan fighting the Soviet Union and sent 2,000 Marines to Lebanon to keep peace in that country. [56]In 1983, radical Muslim forces reacted to U.S. troops in the region by crashing an explosive-laden truck into the U.S. barracks in Lebanon, killing 239 Marines. [57]Over the next few years, anti-American and anti-Western European terrorist bombings, hijackings, assassinations, and hostage-taking by radical Muslims in the Middle East sharply increased.

[58]Liberal Americans opposed to Reagan's foreign policies held rallies across the nation in protest. [59]They were especially critical of the international buildup of nuclear weapons. [60]In an effort to soften their criticism, the Reagan administration suggested an alternative weapons system to neutralize the communist threat, called

 © 2016 The Critical Thinking Co.™ • www.CriticalThinking.com • 800-458-4849

the Strategic Defense Initiative (SDI). [61]It was a proposal to build a computerized anti-Soviet missile system that used laser beams launched from stations orbiting in space to defend the country. [62]Protesters nicknamed the idea *Star Wars*, after a popular science fiction movie of the era. [63]The SDI faced steep technological challenges and a spiraling budget and was eventually canceled before completion.

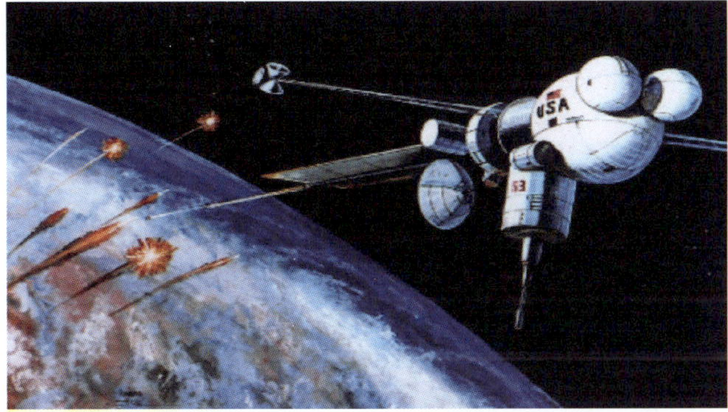

Reagan proposed a plan called the SDI, which involved orbiting U.S. laser stations.

[64]President Reagan and his vice president, George H.W. Bush, ran for reelection in 1984 against the Democratic team of Senator Walter Mondale and Geraldine Ferraro—the first woman from a major party to run for vice president. [65]Despite the foreign policy challenges, Reaganomics (the strong economic growth that began in his first term) and Reagan's call for a strong America carried him to the largest electoral victory of any U.S. president in history (525 of 538 electoral votes). [66]Reagan won 49 of the 50 states, losing only the state of Minnesota to his Democratic Party opponent.

**Fun Fact Feature**

Whereas Carter had a jar of peanuts on his presidential desk in the White House, Reagan had a jar of jellybeans. When the Jelly Belly Company heard of Reagan's fondness for the candy, they invented a new blueberry flavor. Why?

1. What career made Ronald Reagan nationally famous prior to entering politics?
   a. radio
   b. movies
   c. sports
   d. the military

   Which sentence best supports the answer?

   _____

2. What evidence from the 1940s/1950s can you cite showing that Reagan was an avid anti-communist?

   ______________________________

   ______________________________

3. Which of these was Ronald Reagan's first time to hold public office as an elected government official?
   a. student body president
   b. union president
   c. state governor
   d. U.S. President

   Which sentence best supports the answer?

   _____

4. Which political party did Reagan support as a youth? To which political party did Reagan belong by the 1960s?
   a. Democrat, Democrat
   b. Republican, Republican
   c. Republican, Democrat
   d. Democrat, Republican

   Which sentences best support the answer?

   _____ _____

5. "Supply side" and Reaganomics were names for the President Reagan's:
   a. military strategy in the Cold War.
   b. election strategy for the 1980 presidential election.
   c. environmental policy.
   d. economic policy.

   Which sentences best support the answer?

   _____ _____

6. The Strategic Defense Initiative (SDI) was President Reagan's plan to use lasers in space to defend against:
   a. Star Wars.
   b. Soviet nuclear missiles.
   c. Middle East terrorism.
   d. Muslim bomb attacks in Lebanon.

   Which sentences best support the answer?

   _____ _____

7. Who might the woman be on the magazine cover below?

   a. ______________________________

   Name two clues in the image which led you to your conclusion.

   b. ______________________________

   c. ______________________________

8. What was one of the negative consequences of Reaganomics?
   a. a deeper federal budget deficit (debt)
   b. a lowering of inflation
   c. increased numbers of nuclear weapons
   d. increased spending on social programs

   Which sentence best supports the answer?

   _____

9. True or False? Reagan's economic and military policies proved so unpopular that he was defeated in a bid to win a second term as president.

   ____________

   Which sentence best supports the answer?

   _____


© 2016 The Critical Thinking Co.™ • www.CriticalThinking.com • 800-458-4849

## Written Response Question

10. "President Reagan was known as a Cold Warrior—a strong anti-communist." Tell five ways that evidence supports this statement.

a. ______________________________

______________________________

b. ______________________________

______________________________

c. ______________________________

______________________________

d. ______________________________

______________________________

e. ______________________________

______________________________

**Fun Fact Finale**

When the Jelly Belly Company heard of Reagan's fondness for their candy, they invented a new blueberry flavor so that he could have a jar with red, white, and blue (patriotic colors) jelly beans on his desk.

© 2016 The Critical Thinking Co.™ • www.CriticalThinking.com • 800-458-4849

Lesson 50

# Reagan's Second Term

## A. Reagan Reelected

[1]During the 1984 reelection campaign, President Reagan proudly told the American public: "It's morning again in America. [2]Today more men and women will go to work than ever before in our country's history. [3]With interest rates at about half the record highs of 1980, nearly 2,000 families today will buy new homes, more than at any time in the past four years. [4]This afternoon, 6,500 young men and women will be married, and with inflation at less than half of what it was just four years ago, they can look forward with confidence to the future." [5]The expanding economy produced by Reagan's tax cuts, and the public's belief that the country was once again on the right track helped Reagan to be elected for a second term.

## B. Reagan Administration Criticism and Scandals

[6]During Ronald Reagan's two terms in office, nearly one hundred American and Western European hostages were kidnapped by a Middle East Muslim organization called Hezbollah. [7]Hezbollah was controlled by the radical Muslim leader of Iran, Ayatollah Khomeini. [8]Since most of the hostages were Americans, the Reagan administration was actively involved in trying to free them by secretly negotiating with a few moderate leaders in the Iranian government.

[9]At the same time, the Reagan administration had also been providing money and arms to an army in Nicaragua called the Contras, who were fighting the Cuban-backed communist Sandinista army in Nicaragua. [10]During Reagan's first term, Congress became nervous that American support of the Contras could turn into another Vietnam-type quagmire (a situation that is hard to get out of), so Congress banned further military aid to the Contras.

[11]Despite the ban, Oliver North, a high-ranking official in Reagan's National Security Council, devised a plan to try to free American hostages in the Middle East while providing aid to the Contras. [12]His plan was to have Israel sell arms to moderates in Iran in exchange for the release of U.S. hostages. [13]The money Israel collected from the sale of the arms would then be given directly to the Contras by the Israeli government. [14]The Reagan administration would then resupply Israel with the arms it sold to moderates in Iran.

[15]A month before Congress lifted the ban on supplying aid and arms to the Contras, they discovered the Reagan administration's plan to avoid the ban. [16]In early 1987, Congress began an investigation of the so-called Iran-Contra Scandal. [17]The public was upset to learn that weapons had been sold to Muslim factions in Iran—a nation that had held Americans hostage in the Carter years—and that aid to Nicaraguan Contras had continued despite a ban by Congress. [18]Reagan denied having any knowledge of North's plan, and the Congressional investigation found no evidence that he did.

Oliver North testified before Congress about the Iran-Contra Scandal.

[19]Another scandal involving the Reagan White House involved steering federal housing projects to Reagan supporters. [20]The scandal involved Reagan's head of Housing and Urban development, Samuel Pierce. [21]Pierce was never charged, but several of his aides were charged and convicted of influence trading. [22]Reagan was never implicated (connected, shown to be involved) in either of these scandals and the scandals had little effect on his popularity. [23]Some of his frustrated critics started describing Reagan as the "Teflon President" because none of the scandals involving his administration seemed to stick to him.

[24]The Reagan administration was also criticized by liberal opponents for its deregulation of the savings and loan industry. [25]The Reagan administration cut reporting regulations to make it easier for the institutions to make car and home loans to consumers. [26]Months after the deregulation, the Federal Reserve System doubled


© 2016 The Critical Thinking Co.™ • www.CriticalThinking.com • 800-458-4849

the interest rates it charged banks and savings and loan institutions to borrow money. [27]The move was made to help control inflation, but the dramatically higher cost of borrowing money led to many loans held by lending institutions costing more money instead of making money. [28]As a result, more than 740 of the lending institutions were forced to close.

[29]In response to the closures, the federal government was forced to bail out (pay for losses) to protect the American public's savings and loans with the failed institutions. [30]The Reagan administration deregulation did not cause any of the closures, but its deregulation did allow the failed institutions more time before they had to report their financial crises. [31]The additional time added to the cost of the crises eventually was paid by the federal government. [32]Liberal critics pointed at the deregulation while Reagan supporters argued the real problem was the doubling of interest rates by the Federal Reserve without regard for the consequences.

## C. End of the Cold War

[33]When Ronald Reagan ran for the presidency, he promised to limit federal spending and balance the budget, just like Franklin D. Roosevelt (FDR) did. [34]Also like FDR, Reagan did not make good on that promise. [35]FDR increased the U.S. debt with his social programs and defense spending before and during World War II. [36]Reagan increased the U.S. debt with his tax cuts and his defense spending, aimed at keeping the U.S. military superior to the Russian (Soviet Union) military. [37]Because of the economic boom triggered by Reaganomics, Reagan added much less to the debt than FDR, but his massive increase in defense spending had both liberal and economic critics.

Gorbachev (left) and Reagan signed the INF Treaty.

[38]Reagan's military spending was expensive for the United States, but even more expensive for the Soviet Union. [39]The communist leaders of the Soviet Union were intent on having a military superior to or equal with the U.S. military. [40]The capitalist economy of the United States far out-produced the Soviet communist (socialist) economy. [41]Even before Reagan significantly increased U.S. military spending, the Soviet Union was struggling to keep up. [42]After Reagan's increase, Soviet leaders began to realize their goal of military superiority or even parity (equality) with the United States was hopeless. [43]For the first time since the beginning of the Cold War, some Soviet leaders began to question the wisdom of communism and socialism.

[44]One of those leaders was Mikhail Gorbachev who, during Reagan's second term, became the new leader of the Soviet Union. [45]Reagan liked the new communist leader. [46]The economy of the Soviet Union was in deep trouble as Soviet citizens dealt with common shortages of goods and a much lower standard of living under its socialist economy compared to the United States and Western Europe's capitalist economies. [47]Gorbachev introduced a policy of "glasnost" (openness) that allowed ideas and products from capitalist nations into the Soviet Union. [48]Gorbachev also knew he had to lower his government's defense spending to spend more money on Soviet citizens and to help balance the Soviet budget. [49]To help accomplish this goal, Gorbachev knew he had to negotiate arms reduction with the United States.

[50]In June 1987, Ronald Reagan traveled to the Berlin Wall, built by the Soviets to keep citizens of communist controlled East Germany from fleeing to democratically controlled, capitalist West Germany. [51]In a speech there, Reagan challenged Gorbachev to move forward with his commitment to peace and freedom. [52]"We welcome change and openness," the president proclaimed, "for we believe that freedom and security go together, that the advance of human liberty can only strengthen the cause of world peace. [53]There is one sign the Soviets can make that would be unmistakable, that would advance dramatically the cause of freedom and peace. [54]General Secretary Gorbachev, if you seek peace, if you seek prosperity for the Soviet Union and Eastern Europe, if you seek liberalization, come here to this gate. [55]Mr. Gorbachev, open this gate. [56]Mr. Gorbachev, tear down this wall!"

The Berlin Wall started to fall in November 1989, and the Cold War ended soon thereafter.

[57]A few months later, Reagan invited Gorbachev to Washington, D.C, and the two leaders signed the Intermediate-Range Nuclear Forces (INF) Treaty. [58]This agreement removed and destroyed 2,500 U.S. and Soviet missiles from Europe. [59]The next year (his final year in office) Reagan returned the favor and traveled to Moscow and walked through Red Square with the Russian leader.

[60]In 1988, as the Soviet Union underwent historic, political and economic changes, Reagan's vice president, George H.W. Bush, won the presidential election against his liberal Democratic rival George Dukakis. [61]Months later, several Eastern European countries controlled by the Soviet Union erupted and overturned their communist governments. [62]In the fall of 1989, East Germany, no longer under Soviet control, began to tear down the Berlin Wall. [63]The wall had stood as the symbol of the Iron Curtain erected after World War II by the Soviets separating the communist East from the democratic governments of the West. [64]By 1991, the Soviet Union itself broke apart. [65]The inability of the Soviet government's socialist economy to compete with American capitalism dissolved the Soviet empire into 15 separate new independent nations. [66]The Cold War was over.

[67]President Bush declared: "Now we stand triumphant—for a third time this century—in the wake of the end of the Cold War. [68]As in 1919 and 1945, we face no enemy menacing our security." [69]The Cold War had cost thousands of American lives in Korea, Vietnam, and other places, and billions of defense dollars. [70]Unfortunately, even after the break-up of the Soviet Union, new enemies would indeed menace the United States. [71]But in some ways, facing a single superpower may have been simpler than taking on dozens of terrorist groups that would violently challenge the nation over the next decades.

**Fun Fact Feature**

Long before he was president, Ronald Reagan starred in a popular 1951 comedy movie called *Bedtime for Bonzo*. His co-star was an animal to which Reagan's character was trying to teach human behaviors. Can you guess which animal?

 © 2016 The Critical Thinking Co.™ • www.CriticalThinking.com • 800-458-4849

1. What phrase did Ronald Reagan use to describe his philosophy that the 1980s were a time for a fresh start for the United States?

_______________________________________

_______________________________________

2. Why did President Reagan's liberal critics describe Reagan as "the Teflon President"?
    a. The administration scandals did not impact his popularity
    b. The president often liked to cook his own breakfast
    c. He had historic election victories
    d. He ended the Cold War

   Which sentence best supports the answer?

   _____

3. The Iran-Contra Scandal was about profits from U.S. weapons sales to Iran that were used to finance anti-communist forces where?
    a. Sandinista
    b. the Middle East
    c. Berlin
    d. Nicaragua

   Which sentence best supports the answer?

   _____

4. What was accomplished by the The INF Treaty signed by the Soviet Union and the United States in 1987?
    a. The Soviet Union broke up.
    b. It reduced the number of nuclear missiles in Europe.
    c. A "glasnost" was started in Russia.
    d. The Iran-Contra Scandal was exposed.

   Which sentences best support the answer?

   _____ _____

5. What challenge did Ronald Reagan give to the leader of the Soviet Union in a speech in Berlin?
    a. overcome Glasnost
    b. breakup the Soviet Union
    c. feed his starving people
    d. tear down the Berlin Wall

   Which sentence best supports the answer?

   _____

6. Why did Congress ban the Reagan Administration's aid to the Contras during his first term?
    a. Congress faced a budget crisis and could not spare the money.
    b. They wanted to use the money to send weapons to Hezbollah instead.
    c. They feared "another Vietnam" type of conflict.
    d. The Berlin Wall came down.

   Which sentence best supports the answer?

   _____

7. Which U.S. President declared an end to the Cold War?
    a. Ronald Reagan
    b. Jimmy Carter
    c. George H.W. Bush
    d. Bill Clinton

   Which sentence best supports the answer?

   _____

8. What happened to the Soviet Union in 1991?
    a. It no longer remained a united country.
    b. It signed an anti-nuclear missile treaty with the United States.
    c. It was attacked by a radical Muslim group.
    d. It was implicated in the Iran-Contra Scandal.

   Which sentence best supports the answer?

   _____

9. Look at the 1987 political cartoon on the right.

   a. What event is being shown?

   ______________________________

   b. Who is the person in the cartoon?

   ______________________________

   c. What two items are being symbolically destroyed?

   ______________________________

   ______________________________

## Written Response Question

10. Part of the legacy (what is remembered of the past) of President Reagan is his role in ending the Cold War. Use complete sentences to explain Reagan's role in ending the war and what impact his actions had on the Soviet Union after Reagan left office.

______________________________________________________________

______________________________________________________________

______________________________________________________________

______________________________________________________________

______________________________________________________________

______________________________________________________________

______________________________________________________________

______________________________________________________________

### Fun Fact Finale

Long before he was president, Ronald Reagan starred in a 1951 comedy movie called *Bedtime for Bonzo*. His co-star was a chimpanzee to which Reagan's character was trying to teach human behaviors.

© 2016 The Critical Thinking Co.™ • www.CriticalThinking.com • 800-458-4849

# Review: Lessons 46-50
## 1970s-1980s Vocabulary

Write the letter of the definition of each vocabulary word. The number following each vocabulary word is the number of the lesson (46-50) where the word was used. All definitions are used once.

_____ 1. blackmail (46)

_____ 2. perjury (46)

_____ 3. espionage (46)

_____ 4. thwart (46)

_____ 5. inflation (47)

_____ 6. vacancy (47)

_____ 7. bittersweet (47)

_____ 8. bicentennial (47)

_____ 9. purport (48)

_____ 10. streaker (48)

_____ 11. abortion (48)

_____ 12. taboo (48)

_____ 13. lexicon (48)

_____ 14. coined (48)

_____ 15. divorce (49)

_____ 16. recession (49)

_____ 17. regime (49)

_____ 18. parity (50)

_____ 19. implicate (50)

_____ 20. rocked (50)

a. to make a claim

b. to connect, show to be involved

c. to end a marriage

d. a topic or practice forbidden by society

e. rapid price increases

f. to lie in court

g. to obstruct

h. equality

i. vocabulary used by a culture

j. any established system of government

k. an opening, an unfilled office

l. spying

m. invented a word or phrase

n. to demand money for silence on an issue

o. the early termination of a pregnancy

p. someone running naked at a public event

q. shaken, jolted

r. 200th anniversary

s. something both painful and pleasant

t. a slowdown of the economy

© 2016 The Critical Thinking Co.™ • www.CriticalThinking.com • 800-458-4849 

Lesson 51

# The 1980s

## A. 1980s Consumerism

[1]As the Baby Boomers of the '70s moved into the '80s, many were now labeled "yuppies." [2]Yuppie stood for "young, urban, professionals"—people with college educations and well-paying jobs who lived and worked in large cities. [3]With the growing economy and low inflation, American consumerism (increasing purchasing power) reached new levels in the 1980s. [4]Americans in the 1980s were buying more consumer goods than their parents or grandparents had purchased. [5]Credit card usage was higher than ever before.

[6]By the end of the 1980s, two-thirds of American households had cable TV. [7]Americans took advantage of the new 24-hour cable television channels such as *MTV* (music), *ESPN* (sports), *CNN* (news), or *Nickelodeon* (children's programming). [8]A TV show called *Lifestyles of the Rich and Famous* was popular. [9]If a person wanted to watch a TV show again, it could be recorded with a VCR (video cassette recorder) and played back at a more convenient time. [10]Blockbuster movies such as *E.T.: The Extra-Terrestrial*, *Return of the Jedi*, or *Raiders of the Lost Ark* could be rented on videotape and played in the comforts of home.

[11]Female rock star Madonna had a hit song called *Material Girl,* which some critics of the era believed captured the essence of the '80s consumerism. [12]Others saw the 1980s as an era of great innovation as well as artistic and personal expression. [13]Listeners could play Madonna's music, songs by popular Michael Jackson, and many other artists on their new CD (compact disc) players. [14]They also could go mobile with the first portable music players with headphones or carry around a large "boom box"—a CD player with built-in speakers. [15]Music videos also influenced fashion. [16]Fans all over the country copied hairstyles and clothing choices.

[17]If not watching a TV screen, people gathered around a video game monitor. [18]By the mid-1980s, video games became a major entertainment industry. [19]The Nintendo Entertainment System controlled 90 percent of the market by the end of the decade with popular games such as *Donkey Kong* and *Super Mario Bros.*

The graphics were unsophisticated but video games such as *Super Mario Bros.* were new and popular in the 1980s.

## B. Computers

[20]High on the list of things to buy in the 1980s were items in the fast-paced world of new technology. [21]Besides TV screens, many people were now viewing personal computer screens. [22]Computers for the military, government, and business had been around since World War II. [23]They had been built with large vacuum tubes and were big and bulky. [24]With the development of the tiny silicon chip transistor in the 1960s, computers became desk-sized.

An Apple II Computer From the 1980s

[25]In the late 1970s, young Steven Jobs and Stephen Wozniak started a company called Apple that sold computers for personal use. [26]In 1981, a rival company, IBM, also started selling their PC's (personal computers). [27]IBM's new operating software was developed by Bill Gates and Paul Allen, who owned the company Microsoft. [28]In 1984, Apple countered with the MacIntosh personal computer. [29]The tech wars were on. [30]Many new computer hardware and software companies were located just south of San Francisco, California—a region with the nickname "Silicon Valley." [31]By the end of the decade, the


© 2016 The Critical Thinking Co.™ • www.CriticalThinking.com • 800-458-4849

public was able to start searching the Internet (World Wide Web)—an international network of computers that share information—from their homes, offices, or schools. [32]The "Information Age" had begun.

### C. War on Drugs

[33]By the 1980s, it was clear that many drugs used recreationally in the previous decades were, in fact, addictive substances. [34]New drugs, such as crack cocaine, also made the drug problem worse. [35]Shortly after Ronald Reagan became president, he announced a new effort on the "war on drugs" started by previous presidents. [36]"We're taking down the surrender flag that has flown over so many drug efforts," Reagan said. [37]"We're running up a battle flag." [38]The president called for strengthened drug enforcement by creating mandatory minimum sentencing and forfeiture of cash and real estate for drug offenses. [39]The First Lady, Nancy Reagan, used her celebrity status to start a "Just Say No" campaign to educate children about harmful drugs. [40]By the mid-1980s, she had visited numerous drug rehabilitation centers and abuse prevention programs, appeared on television talk shows, and recorded public service announcements about the danger of illegal drugs. [41]Some research shows that the use and abuse of illegal recreational drugs did significantly decline during the Reagan presidency.

### D. Space Shuttle

[42]After a series of successful moon landings in the 1970s, the American space program (NASA), shifted to using a "Space Shuttle" in the 1980s. [43]The shuttle was a winged spacecraft that was launched in a traditional manner and then docked to an International Space Station (ISS) that was orbiting Earth. [44]After a crew of astronauts and scientists carried out various space experiments, some crew members would maneuver the shuttle to re-enter Earth's atmosphere and glide to a landing strip. [45]The shuttle could be reused for other flights with new crew members rotating onto the ISS.

[46]By mid-decade, NASA was feeling confident enough about the program to send non-traditional astronauts into space. [47]Christa McAuliffe, a high school social studies teacher from New Hampshire, was selected from more than 11,000 applicants to become the first teacher in space. [48]McAuliffe planned to conduct experiments and teach two lessons while on the Space Station. [49]Unfortunately, disaster struck when the space shuttle *Challenger* exploded shortly after take-off on January 28, 1986, killing McAuliffe and the six other crew members.

Christa McAuliffe (back row, 2nd from left) died along with the entire crew when the space shuttle *Challenger* exploded in 1986.

**Fun Fact Feature**

When there is a problem with a computer's operation, we often say it has a "bug" in the program. Why do we use that term?

1. In the 1980s, many Baby Boomers were now called “yuppies.” How were they described?
   a. drug using hippies
   b. young, high income, urban professionals
   c. Reagan cabinet members
   d. liberal critics of Reagan defense spending

   Which sentence best supports the answer?

   ______

2. What technology of the 1980s contributed to the times being called the start of the “Information Age?”
   a. video recorders
   b. boom box
   c. personal computers
   d. space shuttles

   Which sentences best support the answer?

   ______ ______

3. Steven Jobs and Bill Gates were two men associated with:
   a. computer technology.
   b. the 1980s music industry.
   c. video games.
   d. NASA's space shuttle program.

   Which sentences best support the answer?

   ______ ______

4. What was different about television in the 1980s?
   a. TV was soon replaced by radio.
   b. There were a variety of cable networks with 24 hour programming.
   c. Shows were broadcast in 3-D.
   d. Television was completely replaced by personal computers and the Internet.

   Which sentences best support the answer?

   ______ ______

5. If not watching a TV screen, people in the 1980s often gathered around monitors to:
   a. listen to compact discs (CDs).
   b. become a yuppie.
   c. play video games or use a computer.
   d. go to college.

   Which sentences best support the answer?

   ______ ______

6. When First Lady Nancy Reagan promoted her “Just Say No” campaign, it was an effort to:
   a. end gun violence.
   b. end domestic violence.
   c. fight communism.
   d. educate youth about drugs.

   Which sentence best supports the answer?

   ______

7. Had Christa McAuliffe been successful, she would have been the first:
   a. woman astronaut.
   b. African American in space.
   c. teacher in space.
   d. inventor of the Internet.

   Which sentence best supports the answer?

   ______

8. One important difference about NASA's space exploration program in the 1980s, compared to earlier decades, is that the space shuttle was designed to:
   a. return to Earth after a mission and be reused.
   b. beat the Russians to be the first to land people on the moon.
   c. travel on an extended mission to Mars.
   d. end the Cold War.

   Which sentences best support the answer?

   ______ ______ ______


© 2016 The Critical Thinking Co.™ • www.CriticalThinking.com • 800-458-4849

9. What was the *Challenger*?
    a. a failed NASA mission that ended with a deadly explosion
    b. the first space shuttle to successfully dock with the International Space Station
    c. the only space mission with more than two crew members
    d. the first space shuttle ever launched

    Which sentence best supports the answer?

    _____

## Written Response Question

10. Use complete sentences to explain why the 1980s were called a decade of American consumerism.

______________________________________________________________________

______________________________________________________________________

______________________________________________________________________

______________________________________________________________________

______________________________________________________________________

______________________________________________________________________

______________________________________________________________________

______________________________________________________________________

### Fun Fact Finale

Operators of one of the first military computers in 1947 traced one early error to the fact that a moth had actually become stuck in the computer and stopped a relay switch. It was an actual "bug" (see the moth taped to the journal record of that day). The term is still used today to describe a computer error.

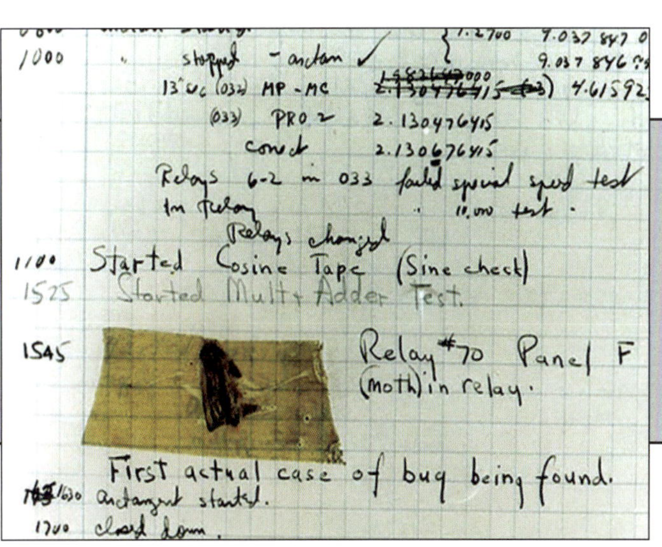

Lesson 52

# President George H. W. Bush

## A. Persian Gulf War

[1]George Herbert Walker Bush postponed his college education after the attack on Pearl Harbor so he could enlist in the U.S. Navy. [2]He became the youngest U.S. Navy pilot of his time. [3]In one World War II battle, Bush's plane caught fire after being shot by Japanese soldiers. [4]In spite of the fire, Bush continued his mission of dropping bombs on targets until he was forced to abandon his plane and parachute into the ocean. [5]After several hours adrift in a lifeboat, Bush was rescued and sent home, but would later return to active duty. [6]After the war, Bush spent many years working in the Texas oil industry and eventually became a millionaire. [7]After becoming interested in politics, he served in Congress, lost a bid to serve in the Senate, and later was named Director of the Central Intelligence Agency (CIA) by President Gerald Ford.

[8]After losing the 1980 Republican nomination for president to Ronald Reagan, Bush accepted Reagan's offer to be his vice president on the Republican ticket. [9]After serving as vice president for two terms, Bush easily won the Republican nomination for president in 1988 and won the national election, carrying 40 of the 50 states. [10]The U.S. Cold War victory during Reagan's second term led to these vast changes in foreign events: the Berlin Wall crumbled, the USSR broke apart, and South Africa saw the end of apartheid (racial separation). [11]Yet soon after the Cold War ended, other conflicts began.

[12]One "war" was the "War on Drugs." [13]Although every president since Richard Nixon made the selling and use of illegal drugs in America a federal effort, it was President Bush who first organized the Office of National Drug Control Policy and appointed a person in charge, who became known as the "Drug Czar." [14]In 1989, as part of that effort, President Bush sent American troops into Panama. [15]He was determined to overthrow the corrupt Central American government of General Manuel Noriega, who had become a dictator and a major cocaine supplier throughout central and North America. [16]Noriega was captured and brought to the United States to stand trial and was convicted for illegal drug trafficking. [17]The conviction led to a truly democratic Panama, but only made a small, high-profile dent in the continuing problem of drug use in America.

[18]The next year, in the Middle East, another dictator—Saddam Hussein of Iraq—ordered the invasion of his oil rich neighboring country, Kuwait. [19]At the time, Iraq had the fourth largest military in the world. [20]Kuwait was a small nation at the western end of the Persian Gulf. [21]The United States did not want Hussein to seize control of Kuwait for a few reasons. [22]Hussein was known as

a sponsor (paid support) of Middle East terrorism groups fighting Israel, a close U.S. ally. [23]Kuwait was a major seller of oil to the United States. [24]If Iraq controlled Kuwait, it would pose a threat to neighboring Saudi Arabia. [25]The Saudis were another major exporter (shipper/seller of goods to one or more foreign countries) of oil and an ally of the United States. [26]If Kuwait and Saudi Arabia fell to Hussein, Iraq would control one-fifth of the world's oil supply.

[27]President Bush convinced the United Nations to impose economic sanctions (punishments designed to cause financial hardship) against Iraq. [28]But Hussein refused to withdraw his military from Kuwait. [29]So President Bush asked Congress, which was controlled by the Democratic Party, to allow him to use military force to protect Kuwait and Saudi Arabia by fighting Iraq. [30]The Democratic leadership opposed the war. [31]They were worried about being on record for supporting a long-lasting, politically unpopular foreign war such as Vietnam going into the next election. [32]In spite of their opposition, Bush won a decisive, bipartisan (both party's) approval of his plan with a vote of 250- 47 in the House and a narrow victory in the Senate, 52-47. [33]Bush convinced a number of other democratic nations to join forces in a coalition


© 2016 The Critical Thinking Co.™ • www.CriticalThinking.com • 800-458-4849

(a temporary combination or alliance) to stop Iraqi aggression. [34]U.S. Army General Norman Schwarzkopf was given command of the coalition. [35]The resulting action was named Operation Desert Storm by the military. [36]Historians often refer to it as the Persian Gulf War.

Gen. Norman Schwarzkopf (left) and President Bush inspect troops in the U.S.

[37]On January 16, 1991, the coalition air force began to drop tons of bombs, targeting the Iraqi Air Force and anti-aircraft facilities. [38]The next target was Iraqi communications facilities. [39]The third and largest bombing was of Iraqi military targets throughout Iraq and Kuwait. [40]A month later, coalition ground troops, including 200,000 Americans, marched through the desert region of Kuwait and into southern Iraq. [41]Western forces soon crushed the Iraqi army. [42]As the Iraqi army retreated, explosives were detonated at many of Kuwait's oil wells, causing environmental damage. [43]The disaster to the environment worsened when Iraqi forces also dumped oil into the Persian Gulf. [44]In a matter of days Saddam Hussein, still in power, directed his government to seek terms for a cease fire. [45]Kuwait was free of the Iraqi invaders and Saudi Arabia was free of the threat of an Iraqi invasion.

[46]President Bush and the victorious coalition governments halted their advance further into Iraq and did not try to overthrow the Iraqi government. [47]They did not want to leave troops in the region for a long occupation, nor did they want to create further tension in the Middle East. [48]One hundred and forty-eight Americans were killed and four hundred sixty-seven were wounded in the short two-month conflict. [49]Tens of thousands of Iraqi soldiers were killed. [50]Coalition forces declared the war a victory.

### B. Economy

[51]While the United States was enjoying the Reagan economic boom of the 1980s, nearly all of the Western world economies were experiencing recession or economic slowdowns. [52]In 1990, the United States entered into a short recession that lasted eight months until March 1991. [53]The U.S. recession was primarily due to the high interest rates established by the U.S. Federal Reserve board, which made it difficult for businesses and consumers to obtain loans after the savings and loan crisis. [54]Another factor was a ten percent down-sizing of the military after the Persian Gulf War. [55]Although the U.S. recession was short lived, job recovery was slow. [56]Despite a campaign promise made by Bush—"Read my lips. No new taxes"—the president agreed to a plan with the Democratic Congress to raise taxes. [57]Bush argued that the deal was good for the country because it would help reduce the budget deficit and lower the growing federal government debt. [58]The dramatic change in tax policy and higher taxes angered many Americans.

### C. Challenges at Home

[59]Environmental challenges occurred during the Bush presidency. [60]In 1989, a large oil tanker, the *Exxon Valdez*, crashed off the coast of Alaska, spilling more than ten million gallons of oil. [61]Tens of thousands of shore birds, nearly 3,000 otters, and an unknown number of fish were killed. [62]President Bush angered some environmental activists when he refused to accept their demands to halt all oil drilling in Alaska. [63]Although saddened by the spill, Bush chose instead to push for safety improvements to the hulls of the tanker ships transporting the oil in order to stop or reduce spills.

Workers attempted to clean the Alaskan shoreline after the huge oil spill in 1989.

© 2016 The Critical Thinking Co.™ • www.CriticalThinking.com • 800-458-4849

[64]Bush justified his decision by pointing to America's energy dependent economy and the economic and military danger of the United States becoming too dependent on foreign oil.

[65]Another environmental challenge came in 1989 when the Environmental Protection Agency found that many U.S. cities had unhealthy levels of air pollution. [66]This led to new amendments of the Clean Air Act in 1990 to help the federal government control growing air pollution in several major U.S. cities. [67]Scientists also started to warn the world that aerosol gas used in hand-held spray cans, and other air pollutants, were depleting the ozone layer over the South Pole. [68]The ozone layer protects Earth from solar radiation, which can cause skin cancer. [69]Since the reduction in aerosol use, the ozone depletion over the South Pole has been shrinking, but has still not reached what many scientists consider normal levels.

[70]During this same time period, many scientists also warned that high levels of carbon dioxide in the air, much of it produced by factories and automobiles, was causing global warming. [71]In response, Bush hosted a conference on climate change in Virginia in 1990, and later signed the United Nations Framework Convention on Climate Change in 1992, making the United States the first industrialized nation to sign the international agreement.

[72]In 1992, the beating of an African American man named Rodney King by policemen became a public concern about police treatment of minorities and an example of the power of the rising use of video cameras by the public. [73]King, who had been drinking and had a violent criminal history, led policemen on a high-speed chase through residential and commercial neighborhoods in Los Angeles, California, to avoid a possible parole violation for a prior robbery conviction. [74]After he was pulled over, police officers recognized King, pulled him out of his car, and beat him brutally. [75]An amateur cameraman caught it on videotape and, after the video surfaced, there was a public outcry to have four L.A.P.D. officers put on trial for charges of assault and excessive use of force. [76]When a jury found the officers not guilty of assault, African Americans rioted in neighborhoods of South Central Los Angeles, targeting mostly white and Asian individuals and businesses. [77]More than 50 people were killed, more than 2,000 were injured, and 9,500 were arrested for rioting, looting, and arson, resulting in one billion dollars in property damage. [78]On the third day of the riots, King himself made a public appearance, making a plea: "Can't we all get along?" [79]Later, two of the police officers were convicted in federal court for violating King's civil rights.

[80]Bush faced a tough battle for reelection in 1992. [81]Not only was unemployment still high, but he faced three opponents. [82]These were a more conservative challenger within his own Republican party, Pat Buchanan, who was a successful independent businessman who ran as a Washington, D.C. outsider; H. Ross Perot; and a young Democratic governor from Arkansas, Bill Clinton. [83]Perot took 19 percent of the vote, mostly from Republican voters. [84]The split vote resulted in a victory for the Democrats. [85]George H.W. Bush became the first elected Republican president since Herbert Hoover in 1932 to not win a second term in office.

**Fun Fact Feature**

George H. W. Bush had been a good college athlete, participating in a sport known as "America's Pastime." Can you guess which sport?


© 2016 The Critical Thinking Co.™ • www.CriticalThinking.com • 800-458-4849

1. Why was George H.W. Bush a well-known candidate in the 1988 presidential election?
   a. He was a former CIA Director and Reagan's vice president.
   b. He had been a famous movie and television actor.
   c. He had served one term as U.S. president and was now running for reelection.
   d. He had brought victory to America in the Persian Gulf War.

   Which sentences best support the answer?

   _____ _____

2. Who was the dictator of Iraq during Operation Desert Storm?
   a. Manuel Noriega
   b. Saddam Hussein
   c. Norman Schwarzkopf
   d. H. Ross Perot

   Which sentence best supports the answer?

   _____

3. During the Persian Gulf War, the United States led a coalition of troops against:
   a. Kuwait.
   b. Saudi Arabia.
   c. Iraq.
   d. Panama.

   Which sentence best supports the answer?

   _____

4. What was/were the imported resource(s) that America was trying to protect in the Persian Gulf War?
   a. gold and silver
   b. illegal drugs
   c. oil
   d. coal

   Which sentence best supports the answer?

   _____

5. True or False? American troops fought alone against the Iraqi invasion of Kuwait in 1991.

   _______________

   Which sentence best supports the answer?

   _____

6. When the Persian Gulf War concluded, what was the situation?
   a. Iraq's military was in ruins, but Sadam Hussein retained control.
   b. U.S. troops took control of the Iraqi capital of Baghdad and ruled the nation.
   c. The war lasted so long that George H.W. Bush was no longer the American president.
   d. America lost the war and Kuwait became a territory of Iraq.

   Which sentences best support the answer?

   _____ _____

7. The *Exxon Valdez* is famous because it was:
   a. a NASA space shuttle.
   b. a battleship attacked in the Persian Gulf in 1991.
   c. an environmental disaster that sparked Congress to create the Clean Air Act of 1990.
   d. a tanker that spilled oil along the Alaskan coastline.

   Which sentence best supports the answer?

   _____

8. To which Central American country did President Bush send U.S. troops to arrest a dictator in 1989?
   a. Panama
   b. Mexico
   c. Nicaragua
   d. Saudi Arabia

   Which sentences best support the answer?

   _____ _____

© 2016 The Critical Thinking Co.™ • www.CriticalThinking.com • 800-458-4849

9. What health issue concerned the Environmental Protection Agency in 1986?
    a. oil pollution
    b. illegal drugs
    c. air pollution
    d. a huge federal debt

    Which sentence best supports the answer?

    ______

## Written Response Question

10. In the political cartoon on the right, the artist is reflecting a negative opinion of George H. W. Bush. Using evidence from this lesson, describe how you can tell this is a negative cartoon.

______________________________

______________________________

______________________________

______________________________

______________________________

______________________________

______________________________

### Fun Fact Finale

George H. W. Bush was captain of the Yale baseball team, which participated in the very first two College World Series games. In the 1948 photo on the right, Bush met Babe Ruth.


© 2016 The Critical Thinking Co.™ • www.CriticalThinking.com • 800-458-4849

Lesson 53

# President Bill Clinton

## A. Background

[1]When William (Bill) Jefferson Clinton won the 1992 presidential election, he became the first person born after World War II to hold that office. [2]Clinton, a member of the Baby Boom generation, was born in Arkansas and attended a segregated high school. [3]He once met President Kennedy at a youth leadership contest, and thereafter decided to seek a career in government service. [4]He attended college in Washington, D.C., at Georgetown University, where he studied international affairs and served as a clerk for a U.S. Senator. [5]He then won a Rhodes scholarship to attend Oxford University in England. [6]When Clinton returned from England, he entered law school at Yale University in Connecticut; there he met and began dating fellow law student Hillary Rodham, whom he married in 1975.

While still in high school, young Bill Clinton (left), met President Kennedy.

[7]After law school, Clinton returned to Arkansas to teach and immerse himself in state politics. [8]In 1979, at the age of 32, Clinton became one of the youngest Americans ever to win an office as a state governor, an office he held for several terms in the 1980s.

[9]In the first two years of the 1990s, George H. W. Bush reversed a pledge not to raise taxes and oversaw an economic recovery that had only a marginal effect on unemployment numbers. [10]These negatives, along with a third party challenge by another conservative, H. Ross Perot, tipped the 1992 presidential election to Bill Clinton.

## B. First Term Scandals

[11]During his first term (1993-1997) in office, Bill Clinton was forced to deal with scandals involving both his personal and public lives. [12]The first major scandal involved a former Arkansas model named Jennifer Flowers. [13]She went public with what she claimed were intimate details of her 12-year relationship with Clinton (a married man) while he held public office in Arkansas. [14]Clinton first denied the adultery charge (a sexual relationship outside of marriage), but later admitted to it when he was forced to testify in a criminal investigation.

[15]The next major scandal to rock the Clinton White House involved an Arkansas Savings and Loan (S&L) company owned by the Clinton's friends and business partners, Jim and Susan McDougal. [16]The S&L went out business, which forced the U.S. government to pay sixty million dollars to cover the money the S&L owed its customers. [17]The collapse of the S&L was traced back to illegal loans involving the McDougals and property owned by the McDougals and Clintons. [18]The potential wrongdoing was called the Whitewater scandal and was first investigated by a Senate committee and then by a special prosecutor. [19]The Clintons denied involvement and were never convicted of wrongdoing, but the investigation led to the conviction of fifteen individuals, including the McDougals and White House council Webster Hubbell. [20]Clinton pardoned Susan McDougal just before leaving office.

[21]In 1994, Paula Jones filed a sexual harassment suit against Bill Clinton. [22]Jones claimed that in 1991, Governor Clinton made unwanted advances. [23]During the case, the judge fined Clinton ninety thousand dollars for not testifying truthfully. [24]Clinton later settled the case with Jones by agreeing to pay her eight hundred and fifty thousand dollars. [25]Prosecutors also looked at the Clinton administration activities involving the replacement of the White House travel office staff with political allies from Arkansas. [26]While neither of these actions ever resulted in convictions of wrongdoing, they still hurt the president's reputation.

## C. First Term Actions

[27]During Clinton's presidential election campaign, a sign over his desk read, "It's the economy, stupid," which he hung as a reminder of the issue he thought was the most important to voters in the 1992 election. [28]Clinton believed that tax increases would improve the economy, so in his first year in office (1993), Clinton and the Democratic controlled Congress passed significant tax increases. [29]As a result of these unpopular tax increases and a pledge from Republicans known as the "Contract with America," Democrats lost congressional seats in the 1994 midterm elections. [30]Fifty-four new Republican U.S. Representatives and eight new Senators gave Republicans control of the House and Senate.

© 2016 The Critical Thinking Co.™ • www.CriticalThinking.com • 800-458-4849 

[31]Known as the "Republican Revolution," the "Contract with America" pledged that Republican's would pass welfare reform, balance the budget, limit political terms, and enact tougher crime laws within the first 100 days of office.

[32]Acting on their "Contract with America" pledge, Republicans passed two welfare reform bills that Clinton vetoed. [33]As the end of Clinton's first term approached, Republicans sent a third version of their welfare reform to Clinton's desk. [34]Although he still opposed the proposal, Clinton worried about the political costs of vetoing a third welfare reform bill brought to his desk, and thus signed the reform into law.

[35]Like his predecessor, George H. W. Bush, Bill Clinton took advantage of the end of the Cold War and the Soviet threat to continue cutting military spending. [36]This savings, along with Clinton's tax increase, savings from the Republican welfare reform bill he had signed, and congressional opposition to new spending, brought the federal budget into balance. [37]The economy gradually improved and, by the end of the 1990s, the federal budget actually showed surpluses (the government received more income than it spent).

[38]In spite of several scandals and accusations of inappropriate behavior involving women, as governor and as president, Bill Clinton made an effort to expand opportunities for women. [39]The first act of Congress he signed was the Family Medical Leave Act of 1993, which allowed parents to take up to twelve weeks of unpaid leave from their jobs to care for a newborn infant or sick relative. [40]He also expanded the budget for a special Supplemental Nutrition Program for Women, Infants, and Children. [41]Clinton appointed several women to high-level governmental positions. [42]His first choice for a vacancy on the Supreme Court was Justice Ruth Ginsberg. [43]He appointed Janet Reno to the position of Attorney General and made Madeleine Albright the first female Secretary of State. [44]He asked his wife, Hillary Rodham Clinton, to lead a task force to propose health care reforms. [45]Her proposal was a large nationalized healthcare system overseen by new government agencies. [46]Physicians groups, hospitals, and insurance companies campaigned against the plan, claiming it was government run healthcare that would be both inefficient, and unaffordable. [47]The public sided with their physicians and the healthcare industry, and the proposals were soundly rejected.

Madeleine Albright

### C. Foreign Affairs

[48]Although the Cold War had ended, serious international issues remained in the 1990s. [49]The break-up of the communist government in Yugoslavia produced a civil war between that nation's Serb, Croat, and Bosnian populations that resulted in a massive death toll. [50]Clinton ordered joint United States and NATO air-strikes to curb the violence and arranged for warring parties to meet in America to create a peace agreement. [51]He committed 20,000 U.S. troops to a NATO operation to enforce the resulting cease-fire.

[52]Earlier, in 1992, President Bush had sent thousands of U.S. troops to Somalia to aid in ending a civil war and famine in that East African nation. [53]Clinton increased United States involvement there, but withdrew the troops in 1994 after dozens of Americans were killed in the conflicts.

[54]North Korea began to develop nuclear weapons and started a missile testing program. [55]In response, the Clinton administration imposed trade sanctions against North Korea.

[56]During his presidency, Clinton also ordered air strikes on a suspected chemical weapons plant in Sudan and on a terrorist training camp in Afghanistan run by Osama Bin Laden. [57]Clinton was also busy dealing with continued conflicts in the Middle East between Israelis and Palestinians.

[58]In February 1993, a bomb set by Islamic extremists exploded in the parking garage under New York City's World Trade Center. [59]Six people were killed and more than 1,000 Americans were injured. [60]A handful of the perpetrators (people who commit criminal or evil acts) were eventually captured and given life prison sentences. [61]Later in the decade, bomb blasts killed Americans in several U.S. embassies in Africa and on a naval ship, the USS Cole, in the Persian Gulf. [62]Secretary of State Albright, commenting upon the terrorist attacks, noted sadly: "We are involved in a long term struggle [that] is, unfortunately, the war of the future."


© 2016 The Critical Thinking Co.™ • www.CriticalThinking.com • 800-458-4849

## D. Second Term Scandals and Impeachment

[63]Clinton won reelection in 1996. [64]However, his second term was marred by more scandals, one of which nearly cost him his office. [65]In testimony from the Paula Jones lawsuit against Bill Clinton for sexual harassment, the Jones legal team provided the name of a White House intern (volunteer seeking job experience) named Monica Lewinsky, as another example of Clinton's sexual harassment. [66]At the time of the alleged affair, Clinton was 49 and Lewinsky was 22. [67]A special government prosecutor investigating the Whitewater scandal was contacted by a coworker of Lewinsky who had recorded conversations between the intern and Clinton.

[68]These conversations showed that Clinton and Lewinsky had lied under oath about the affair.

[69]After the scandal went public, Clinton appeared on TV and claimed: "I did not have sexual relations with that woman." [70]Later, when some strong evidence appeared, Lewinsky admitted to the affair, and then Clinton did as well telling the American people he was ashamed of his "inappropriate behavior."

[71]The special prosecutor in the case recommended that President Clinton be charged with perjury (lying under oath) and obstruction of justice (tampering with a witness). [72]After three months of debate, the Republican controlled House of Representatives voted to impeach (charge) Clinton on those two counts. [73]The only previous president to go through an impeachment trial had been Andrew Johnson in 1868.

[74]Under the guidelines of Article I of the Constitution, a president who has been impeached by the House shall have a trial in the Senate to decide if any of the impeachment offenses qualify as "high crimes and misdemeanors." [75]If a single impeachment offense is judged by two-thirds of the senators to be an offense of this "high" level, then the president is removed from office. [76]The chief justice of the U.S. Supreme Court (William Rehnquist in 1999) was sworn in to preside over the trial and the 100 U.S. senators were sworn in as jurors. [77]The impeachment trial of Bill Clinton began in January 1999 and lasted five weeks. [78]Public opinion polls showed that most people didn't think Clinton's actions reached a level to remove him from office. [79]The Senate agreed. [80]The vote to remove Clinton from office for his perjury was 45 to 55. [81]The vote to remove him for his obstruction of justice was 50-50. [82]Since neither vote reached the two thirds majority needed, the impeached president was allowed to serve out his second term.

[83]Americans had mixed reactions to the trial and Clinton. [84]While much of the public was tired of all the scandals involving the Clintons, they were happy with the healthy economy and the direction of the country. [85]After the Senate trial, Clinton still faced perjury charges from the special prosecutor. [86]Clinton admitted to the perjury charge and was fined twenty-five thousand dollars. [87]After his perjury conviction, the Arkansas Supreme Court stripped him of his license to practice law. [88]In spite of the numerous scandals, Clinton still enjoyed strong popularity with Democrats and some independents. [89]His term of office ended in January 2001.

### Fun Fact Feature

Bill Clinton had a physical trait in common with Presidents George H. W. Bush and Barack Obama and about 10 percent of the American population at large. Don't be "left out"—guess the trait!

© 2016 The Critical Thinking Co.™ • www.CriticalThinking.com • 800-458-4849

1. William (Bill) Clinton was born in, and later became governor of __?__:
   a. New York.
   b. Washington, D.C.
   c. Arkansas.
   d. Connecticut.

   Which sentences best support the answer?

   _____ _____

2. Bill Clinton decided to pursue a career in politics after:
   a. becoming a state governor.
   b. "Internet Day" in 1996.
   c. entering law school at Yale University.
   d. meeting President Kennedy as a youth.

   Which sentence supports the answer?

   _____

3. Clinton was among the __?__ U.S. governors and U.S. presidents in American history.
   a. youngest-ever
   b. richest-ever
   c. tallest-ever
   d. most conservative

   Which sentence best supports the answer?

   _____

4. Who were Madeleine Albright, Janet Reno, and Ruth Ginsberg?
   a. high ranking women appointed to federal offices by Clinton
   b. the first women given U.S. military commissions
   c. feminists in support of the Family Medical Leave Act
   d. influential teachers that Clinton encountered while a college student

   Which sentences best support the answer?

   _____ _____

5. True or False? Bill Clinton was impeached during his second term in office.

   ______________

   Which sentence supports the answer?

   _____

6. In the last 30 years of the 20th Century, three presidents were stung with scandals in their administration. Name those three presidents drawn in the political cartoon below.

   ______________________________________

   ______________________________________

   ______________________________________

7. During the Clinton administration, Osama Bin Laden was identified as a:
   a. leader of North Korea attempting to secure nuclear weapons.
   b. Islamic radical who was training terrorists in Afghanistan
   c. a communist behind the civil war in Yugoslavia.
   d. military commander behind the civil war and famine in Somalia.

   Which sentence supports the answer?

   _____

8. President Clinton failed in his attempt at government run health care reform. Who did he put in charge of that effort during his first term in office?
   a. Monica Lewinsky
   b. Hillary Rodham Clinton
   c. Madeleine Albright
   d. William Rehnquist

   Which sentence supports the answer?

   _____


© 2016 The Critical Thinking Co.™ • www.CriticalThinking.com • 800-458-4849

9. Jennifer Flowers, Paula Jones, and Monica Lewinsky were all:
   a. Clinton White House advisors.
   b. women involved in Clinton scandals.
   c. appointed to public service by Bill Clinton.
   d. White House interns.

   Which sentences best support the answer?

   _____ _____ _____

## Written Response Question

10. Give five examples that prove the statement: "Although the Cold War had ended, serious international issues remained in the 1990s."

1. ______________________________

______________________________

2. ______________________________

______________________________

3. ______________________________

______________________________

4. ______________________________

______________________________

5. ______________________________

______________________________

**Fun Fact Finale**

Bill Clinton had a physical trait in common with Presidents George H. W. Bush and Barack Obama and about 10% of the American population at large: left-handedness.

Lesson 54

# President George W. Bush

## A. A Tight and Highly Contested Election

[1]The presidential election of 2000 was one of the closest in U.S. history, showing a much divided nation. [2]Bill Clinton's vice president, Al Gore, ran as the Democratic candidate. [3]George W. Bush, the governor of Texas and son of former president George H. W. Bush, was the Republican candidate. [4]The Green Party, mainly concerned with environmental and consumer issues, had Ralph Nader as its candidate, but Nader failed to win any states. [5]The election was very close and ballot counting went deep into the night on Election Day in November. [6]When the votes were counted, Gore won more popular votes (48.3% to Bush's 47.8%). [7]However, according to the Constitution, the candidate who wins the most Electoral College votes wins the presidential election. [8]Bush won more states than Gore and in nearly all states the candidate who receives the most votes is awarded all of the states' Electoral College votes. [9]Bush's majority in Florida was in dispute and so close (approximately 2,000 votes) that by Florida law the votes had to be recounted. [10]Democrats and Republicans scrambled to find uncounted votes to increase their totals. [11]When all of the recounts were totaled, Bush's lead had shrunk to 537 votes. [12]Gore appealed the final vote total to a Florida State court, but his appeal was turned down. [13]Gore then appealed this decision to the Florida State Supreme Court—most of whose members were appointed by Democrats—and the justices ordered another recount of 70,000 ballots rejected by machine counters as unreadable. [14]Republicans countered by appealing this decision to the U.S. Supreme Court. [15]In a 7-2 decision, the U.S. Supreme Court declared the Florida Supreme Court's order unconstitutional. [16]The U.S. Supreme Court also ruled the state of Florida's statewide recount could not be completed in a reasonable time and therefore the earlier election results should stand, making Bush the winner of Florida and the next U.S. president. [17]The 2000 election also created an exact 50/50 split between Democrats and Republicans in the U.S. Senate and a narrow majority for Republicans in the House.

Officials in Florida carefully inspected ballots in the 2000 election.

## B. Airline Terror

[18]President Bush was only in office for nine months when an event occurred that dramatically changed the course of U.S. history and dominated the rest of the president's years in office. [19]On September 11, 2001, Muslim terrorists hijacked (seized by force) four U.S. passenger airplanes. [20]Two of the planes were piloted into the twin towers of New York City's World Trade Center. [21]The resulting fires trapped hundreds of people in the towers and eventually caused the towers to collapse, killing more than 2,750 people. [22]A third hijacked plane was flown on a suicide mission into the Pentagon building in Washington, D.C., killing 245 employees. [23]Hundreds more Americans died when the fourth plane, probably headed toward government buildings in the nation's capital, crashed in Pennsylvania after heroic passengers battled with the hijackers. [24]It was the deadliest single attack ever against America. [25]More firefighters (343) and law enforcement officers (72) were killed that day than on any other in the history of the United States. [26]To Americans, the date of the event thereafter served as its name—9/11.

A second hijacked plane heads toward the World Trade Center in New York City on September 11, 2001.


© 2016 The Critical Thinking Co.™ • www.CriticalThinking.com • 800-458-4849

[27]Shocked Americans temporarily put political divisions behind them and rallied around the phrase "United We Stand." [28]President Bush declared the events "an act of war," and Congress agreed, giving the Commander-in-Chief "all necessary and appropriate force" to defend the nation against further attacks. [29]Two weeks after 9/11, President Bush publicly identified the terrorists as members of Al Qaeda, an organization headquartered in Afghanistan and led by Osama bin Laden. [30]Bush also blamed the Taliban, a Muslim extremist group led by Mullah Omar and based in the mountainous region just north of Afghanistan in Pakistan.

[31]By October 2001, a coalition of U.S. forces, NATO troops, and other international military personnel began operations against Al Qaeda and the Taliban in Afghanistan and Pakistan. [32]By the end of the year, United States-led coalition forces had gained control of Kabul, the capital of Afghanistan, and were regularly targeting terrorist training camps in Pakistan. [33]Hundreds of suspected terrorists were captured and sent for interrogation (questioning for information) to the U.S. military base at Guantanamo Bay on the eastern tip of Cuba. [34]Leaders bin Laden and Omar, however, eluded capture.

## C. Homeland Security

[35]A month after the September 11th attacks, Congress passed anti-terrorist legislation called the Patriot Act. [36]It called for a huge expansion of airport security personnel across the nation. [37]It allowed the government the power to monitor telephone calls and email messages sent by suspected terrorists. [38]Based on U.S. intelligence data, hundreds of Middle Easterners in the United States were rounded up and questioned. [39]While some Americans desired even more security safeguards on the part of the government, others protested the Patriot Act as a violation of Constitutional liberties of free speech and privacy.

[40]Congress also created a new cabinet-level agency called the Department of Homeland Security (DHS). [41]While the Department of Defense is in charge of military operations abroad, Homeland Security is in charge of preparing the nation to prevent, and respond to, domestic emergencies, particularly terrorism. [42]DHS has sub-agencies dealing with citizenship issues, border security, immigration and customs enforcement, transportation safety, and the government's response to natural disasters such as earthquakes, tornadoes, and floods. [43]The DHS also manages the Secret Service and the Coast Guard. [44]With about a quarter-million employees, Homeland Security soon became one of the largest of the Cabinet departments.

## D. Iraq War

[45]After 9/11, U.S. anti-terrorism efforts focused on Afghanistan, but President Bush soon pointed to other sponsors of terror who threatened the United States and the Western world. [46]In January 2002, he made a speech naming Iran, Iraq, and North Korea as "the axis of evil." [47]Bush called these countries evil because of their sponsorship of terrorism and pursuit of weapons of mass destruction. [48]A year later, Bush administration officials warned Americans that based on British and U.S. intelligence, Iraq's leader, Saddam Hussein, was developing and stockpiling "weapons of mass destruction." [49]A weapon of mass destruction (WMD) is a chemical, biological, or nuclear device that could cause massive loss of human life. [50]Bush took his concern over Saddam Hussein's and Iraq's potential to develop and use WMD to the public and Congress. [51]He pointed out that Hussein refused to fully cooperate with the world community and in 1988 had used chemical bombs to kill 3,000-5,000 of his own people in northern Iraq. [52]The Iraq resolution easily passed both houses of Congress with Republican and Democratic majorities in the Senate, but only a Republican majority in the House.

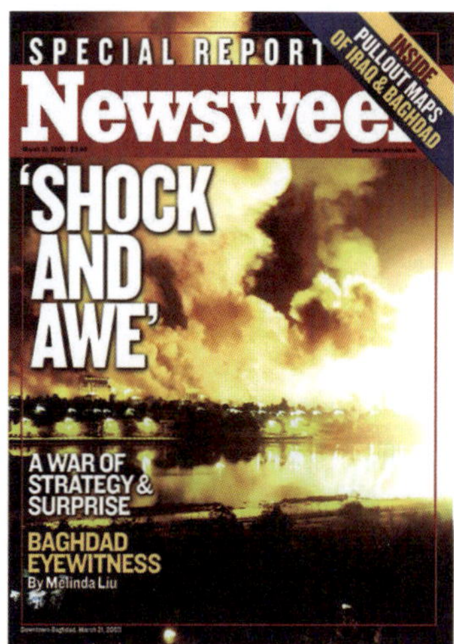


[53]On March 19, 2003, the United States began "Operation Enduring Freedom," with a large air attack on Baghdad, the capital of Iraq. [54]Some called it the beginning of Gulf War II but most refer to it as the Iraq War. [55]The bombing campaign was a tactic called "shock and awe"—the idea being that a massive show of overwhelming power and a spectacular display of U.S. force would paralyze Iraqi forces and destroy their will to fight back. [56]U.S. troops, led by General Tommy Franks, and coalition forces from Britain, Australia, Poland, and other nations, then invaded southern

© 2016 The Critical Thinking Co.™ • www.CriticalThinking.com • 800-458-4849

Iraq. [57]One month later, Hussein fled his capital and his Iraqi government fell. [58]Hussein was eventually captured, put on trial for genocide (the deliberate killing of a racial, political, or cultural group), convicted, and hanged. [59]On May 1, 2003, President Bush made a speech on a U.S. aircraft carrier under a sign that read "Mission Accomplished." [60]He declared: "Major combat operations in Iraq have ended," and Bush was reelected the next year.

[61]Although the U.S. military had soundly defeated the Iraqi military, Iraq proved very difficult to control. [62]Radical Muslim gangs and small regional armies—many supported by neighboring Iran—fought U.S. and U.S.- supported Iraqi troops to remove Western influence from Iraq. [63]Many of these gangs and small armies also fought against each other for territory and influence within the country. [64]Using acts of terror, they kidnapped and assassinated officials of the new government, detonated suicide bombs, and set off homemade bombs on roads throughout the country. [65]American forces still remaining in the country, and Iraqi civilians, were caught in a civil war between two different Muslim factions.

[66]In 2007, in the face of growing U.S. opposition to the Iraq War and public consensus that the United States was losing its grip on the newly won conflict, George Bush ordered the Iraqi Surge, which sent 20,000 more U.S. soldiers into Iraq. [67]Democrats—even many who had supported the war—opposed the Surge. [68]Most Republicans rallied around the president and supported the Surge. [69]Two public polls showed approximately 40 percent favored the surge and 60 percent opposed it. [70]Ignoring the polls, George Bush proceeded with the Surge.

[71]About a year later in early 2008, the public, most news services, and the military thought that the Surge had worked to bring greater stability and control of Iraq. [72]A majority of the U.S. public thought the Surge was successful (52 percent successful to 45 percent unsuccessful) and an even greater percentage of the military (60-30 percent). [73]Nonetheless, the cost of the Iraq War was high. [74]More than 4,000 Americans had died in Iraq and more than 30,000 were injured. [75]Although violence in Iraq had decreased, it never completely stopped. [76]The Iraq war cost the United States 600 billion dollars.

[77]The new Iraqi government was still very unstable and once again, the American public was growing weary of foreign war. [78]The new Democratic majority in Congress claimed the war would never end and the country needed to bring our troops home. [79]They pointed to the fact that no new evidence of WMD's were found after U.S. troops entered Iraq. [80]President Bush and Republicans pointed to the success of the Surge and claimed Iraq would slowly become an important beacon of democratic freedom and prosperity in the Middle East. [81]They also argued that the removal of Saddam Hussein from power, his successful conviction for crimes against humanity, and the end of his sponsorship for terror made the Iraq war worthwhile and a success.

**Fun Fact Feature**

President George W. Bush was not the first son of a U.S. President to also hold that office. Can you name the first?


© 2016 The Critical Thinking Co.™ • www.CriticalThinking.com • 800-458-4849

1. Which state in the 2000 presidential vote was in great dispute over election results?
   a. Florida
   b. Washington, D.C.
   c. Texas
   d. New York

   Which sentence best supports the answer?

   ______

2. The decision of which branch of government ultimately decided the 2000 presidential election?
   a. judicial branch
   b. legislative branch
   c. executive branch
   d. cabinet

   Which sentence best supports the answer?

   ______

3. The event known as "9/11" gets its name from:
   a. the number of terrorists involved in the attacks on the United States.
   b. the number of terrorist attack sites both in the United States and abroad.
   c. a piece of evidence discovered after the terrorist attack.
   d. the date of the event.

   Which sentence best supports the answer?

   ______

4. What phrase best summarized American's feelings soon after the 9/11 attacks?
   a. Mission Accomplished
   b. United We Stand
   c. Shock and Awe
   d. Weapons of Mass Destruction

   Which sentence best supports the answer?

   ______

5. True or False? President Bush was not reelected in 2004.

   ______________

   Which sentence best supports the answer?

   ______

6. Which dictator of Iraq was deposed (removed from high office) by the U.S.-led coalition during the Iraq War?
   a. General Tommy Franks
   b. Al Gore
   c. Saddam Hussein
   d. George W. Bush

   Which sentences best support the answer?

   ______ ______

7. Why was security at U.S. airports particularly expanded after the 9/11 terrorist attacks?

   ______________________________________

   ______________________________________

8. When were the Patriot Act and the creation of the Department of Homeland Security enacted?
   a. just before the Iraq War
   b. soon after 9/11
   c. after the bombing of Al Qaeda and the Taliban in Afghanistan
   d. after the disputed presidential election of 2000

   Which sentences best support the answer?

   ______ ______

9. Why would some people refer to the Iraq War as "Gulf War II"?

   ______________________________________

   ______________________________________

© 2016 The Critical Thinking Co.™ • www.CriticalThinking.com • 800-458-4849

## Written Response Question

10. Use complete sentences to show evidence to support both clauses of the following statement: "At first the Iraq War seemed like a quick victory for the U.S.-led coalition but later proved to be an unpopular and difficult conflict."

**Fun Fact Finale**

Several presidents have family connections. John Quincy Adams (president #6) was the son of John Adams (president #2). Benjamin Harrison (president #23) was the grandson of William Henry Harrison (president #9). Theodore Roosevelt (#26) and Franklin Roosevelt (#32) were distant cousins.


© 2016 The Critical Thinking Co.™ • www.CriticalThinking.com • 800-458-4849

Lesson 55

# Domestic and Foreign Issues Bring Change

## A. Domestic Issues in Bush's Second Term

[1]Problems for the Bush administration went beyond the war weariness of the continuing foreign conflicts in Iraq and Afghanistan. [2]Several issues at home also compounded (increased, added to) President Bush's low approval rating in his second term.

[3]On the education front, President Bush, with bipartisan (liberals and conservatives) support, pushed for major education reforms. [4]The program was labeled "No Child Left Behind." [5]It required public schools to issue standardized tests at many grade levels to mark the progress of students and school programs. [6]Those schools with consistently low test scores faced penalties. [7]Critics attacked the program stating that student performance on the tests put so much pressure on the schools that they spent more time prepping students for the tests and less time teaching. [8]Other critics objected to the federal government taking control of education away from the states.

[9]Illegal immigration reform was another issue widely discussed. [10]In 2006, President Bush sided with Congress who wanted stiffer efforts to solve the illegal immigration problem. [11]He signed Congressional legislation to build a 700-mile barrier along the United States-Mexico border and step up federal efforts to deport (expel from the country) some of the millions of illegal immigrants living in the United States. [12]Some civil rights groups and Hispanic Americans protested the policy's effects on families.

[13]Hurricane Katrina, one of the nation's deadliest natural disasters, hit the United States in late August 2005. [14]The third most severe storm in history to hit the United States caused severe wind damage and flood destruction along the Gulf Coast from Texas to Florida. [15]More than three million people were without electricity in the aftermath of the storm and more than 1,800 people were killed. [16]Approximately 1,400 of these deaths occurred when levees (embankments designed to prevent the flooding of a river) protecting the city of New Orleans from seawater gave way. [17]The levee failure was a result of poor design by the Army Corps of Engineers. [18]Property damage from Hurricane Katrina totaled more than 108 billion dollars. [19]Federal, state, and local emergency officials seemed slow to react to the scale of the crisis. [20]An investigation into the relief effort resulted in the resignation of the director of the Federal Emergency Management Agency (FEMA) appointed by George Bush, as well as criticism of Bush and state and local Democrats including the New Orleans mayor, police superintendent, and the governor of Louisiana. [21]The hurricane drove as many as one million people to leave the Gulf Coast and find new residences—a mass movement that rivaled migrations on the Oregon Trail in the mid-1800s or the Dust Bowl in the 1930s.

A Satellite View of Hurricane Katrina in 2005

[22]During George Bush's last years in office, a U.S. housing bubble (a price cycle characterized by rapid expansion followed by a contraction) caused a deep economic recession (2007-2009) in the United States that led to a world recession, sometimes called the Great Recession. [23]The housing bubble occurred when home buyers,

The Great Recession saw a large drop in the value of homes in America.

© 2016 The Critical Thinking Co.™ • www.CriticalThinking.com • 800-458-4849

builders, and investors pushed the prices of homes beyond a realistic value. [24]When the housing bubble burst, home values came crashing down to reality. [25]Democrats claimed that deregulation of the banking industry by Republicans resulted in risky home loans. [26]Republicans claimed that the bubble was caused by the unwillingness of Democrats to make changes to the management of federally sponsored lending institutions and the pressuring of private lenders to give loans to risky, low income buyers. [27]Both parties blamed the other for causing the bubble, but many lending companies—knowing many of their loans were risky—did not want to keep the loans and thus marketed and sold the risky loans to unsuspecting investors through the stock market. [28]When more and more homeowners could not make their house payments, those stock offerings lost their value. [29]In the fall of 2007, Wall Street suffered its biggest losses since the Great Depression and some of the largest banks in the country were severely weakened. [30]In addition to the damage to banks and other lending institutions, the federal government was forced to bail out (give financial assistance to a failing business to save it from collapse) federally sponsored lending institutions at a cost of more than 300 billion dollars. [31]Lending and credit then slowed, production of goods dropped, and businesses were forced to lay off workers, causing high unemployment.

President Barack Obama

## B. President Barack Obama

[32]Voter discontent with the U.S. economic recession caused by the 2008 housing bubble, and to a lesser extent, U.S. foreign wars, led to a change in executive leadership following the 2008 election. [33]A relatively unknown African American Democratic senator from Illinois, Barack Obama, won his party's nomination, and then the general election, over a Republican Vietnam War hero and long-serving senator, John McCain of Arizona. [34]Obama's campaign often emphasized the words "hope" and "change" which appealed to voters—many of whom blamed George Bush and Republicans for the country's economic recession. [35]The youthful Obama (age 47 upon inauguration) contrasted with the older McCain (72), which helped Obama earn a large percentage of the youth vote. [36]The first-ever major party candidate of African American heritage, Obama had huge support among African Americans and also won two-thirds of the Hispanic vote. [37]When President Obama took the oath of office, he stated that just a generation earlier, black men like his father may have been denied service in Washington, D.C. restaurants because of the color of their skin.

Supreme Court Justice Sonia Sotomayor

[38]Obama filled two Supreme Court vacancies with female appointees. [39]One of them, Sonia Sotomayor, was the first justice of Hispanic background. [40]He also appointed Hillary Clinton to be his Secretary of State. [41]She was one of Obama's Democratic rivals during the election and a former First Lady.

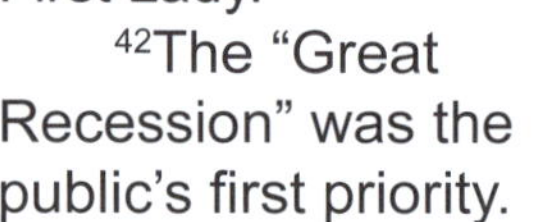

[42]The "Great Recession" was the public's first priority. The American Recovery and Reinvestment Act (ARRA) was passed by both the House and Senate in February of 2009. [43]Like the Keynesian economics of the FDR era, the law was based on the idea that the government should increase public spending during a recession in an effort to try to save jobs and stop a further economic slide. [44]The stimulus (something that quickens action) package combined tax relief for the middle class with government spending on infrastructure projects such as road building, bridge repair, and school building upgrades. [45]The government also made financial loans to two of the major auto manufacturers hit hard during the recession and even seized control of General Motors. [46]The administration also worked for more regulations on lending and investment institutions, claiming they would help prevent future problems. [47]This


© 2016 The Critical Thinking Co.™ • www.CriticalThinking.com • 800-458-4849

increase in federal spending was not without costs. [48]When President Obama entered office, the federal debt was nine trillion dollars. [49]By the end of his first term in office, the federal debt had ballooned to nearly fifteen trillion dollars. [50]Despite the massive government spending, the economic recovery was slow.

[51]In an effort to increase the availability of health insurance, President Obama proposed sweeping health care reforms, which were eventually passed in 2010 by a Democratic Congress. [52]The Affordable Care Act (sometimes called "Obamacare") required all Americans to have health insurance and forced insurance companies to cover all applicants with new minimum standards and offer the same rates, regardless of pre-existing conditions or gender. [53]Critics claimed the program would both increase the cost of healthcare and lower the quality of healthcare while expanding an already bloated federal government.

[54]Meanwhile, in the Middle East, a U.S. Special Forces mission located and killed Al Qaeda leader Osama bin Laden—the mastermind behind the 9/11 terrorist attack in the United States and other terrorist attacks against the U.S. in Pakistan in 2011. [55]However, terrorists still posed a major threat to American security as the twenty-first century progressed.

[56]President Obama withdrew the last U.S. combat troops from Iraq in October of 2011. [57]Critics claimed the withdrawal was rushed and would likely result in the collapse of the new democratic government in Iraq and forfeit (reverse) all the sacrifice and gains made by U.S. forces in the Iraq War. [58]Shortly after the withdrawal, a new Islamic extremist terrorist group, ISIS, seized control of much of Iraq and Syria and threatened the security of the Middle East. [59]Obama also wanted to withdraw all U.S. troops in Afghanistan, but gains made by the Taliban—another radical Islamic group—persuaded Obama to actually increase American military involvement in Afghanistan.

**Fun Fact Feature**

Barack Obama was the first president from America's westernmost, and newest, state in the Union. Can you name that U.S. state?

© 2016 The Critical Thinking Co.™ • www.CriticalThinking.com • 800-458-4849

1. What was President Bush's plan to reform public education called?
   a. No Child Left Behind
   b. American Recovery and Reinvestment Act
   c. the stimulus package
   d. Homeland Security

   Which sentences best support the answer?

   _____ _____

2. What area of the country did Hurricane Katrina greatly impact?
   a. New England
   b. the American Southwest
   c. New Orleans and the Gulf Coast
   d. the Great Lakes region

   Which sentence best supports the answer?

   _____

3. What was constructed along the border between the United States and Mexico during President George W. Bush's years in office?

   ________________________________________

   ________________________________________

4. What was seen as the major cause of the 2008 housing bubble that started in 2007?
   a. "No Child Left Behind"
   b. Hurricane Katrina
   c. the Affordable Care Act
   d. risky home loans and investments

   Which sentences best support the answer?

   _____ _____ _____

5. Which of these phrases is incorrect concerning Barack Obama?
   a. He had little support from African American and Hispanic voters.
   b. He was one of the nation's youngest elected presidents.
   c. He was a Democrat.
   d. He had served as a U.S. Senator before being elected president.

   Which sentence best supports the answer?

   _____

6. Who was appointed by President Obama to be the first Supreme Court justice with a Hispanic background?
   a. Sonia Sotomayor
   b. Hillary Clinton
   c. Michael Brown
   d. John McCain

   Which sentence best supports the answer?

   _____

7. True or False? "President Obama withdrew all U.S. troops from Afghanistan during his presidency."

   _______________

   Which sentence best supports the answer?

   _____

8. What is important to note about President Obama's racial heritage?

   ________________________________________

   ________________________________________

9. The economic philosophy used by President Obama to combat the recession caused by the 2008 housing bubble was similar to that of which president during the Great Depression.
   a. Franklin Roosevelt
   b. Herbert Hoover
   c. George W. Bush
   d. Harry Truman

   Which sentence best supports the answer?

   _____


© 2016 The Critical Thinking Co.™ • www.CriticalThinking.com • 800-458-4849

## Written Response Question

10. Every president is faced with important issues during their term in office. Use complete sentences to list two issues dealt with in President Bush's second term, and two issues dealt with by President Obama.

**Fun Fact Finale**

The future president, Barack Obama, was born and raised in the state of Hawaii.

© 2016 The Critical Thinking Co.™ • www.CriticalThinking.com • 800-458-4849

Lesson 56

# Changes and Challenges

## A. Occupational Changes

[1]From colonial days through the Civil War era, agriculture was the economic backbone of the United States. [2]Farming and farm-related industries were the country's number one occupation and most Americans lived in rural areas. [3]Starting in the late 1800s and into the early 1900s, there was a profound shift to manufacturing and industry. [4]By the 1920s, most Americans were living in urban areas.

[5]As the 20th century progressed into the 21st, the economy evolved again. [6]Professional workers, managers, sales workers, and service workers—generally known as white collar jobs— accounted for about two-thirds of all jobs. [7]There were still farmers and manual labor (blue collar) jobs, of course, but far fewer. [8]With the computer revolution and the Information Age, it became increasingly important for young people to have a strong education. [9]The pace of change at the start of the 21st century was rapid. [10]It seemed as if no job was safe from change as technology quickly advanced. [11]Those who could adapt best had strong skills in reading, writing, math, and science.

[12]Communication is a good example of change. [13]In the decade between 1995 and 2005 alone, the Internet, computer tablets, and "smartphone" technologies dramatically changed the way Americans got their news, listened to music, researched a topic, took photographs, sent mail, kept a calendar, ordered consumer goods, found directions, took classes, chose a place to eat, sleep or visit when traveling ... and talked with one another. [14]These technologies brought the decline of some traditional occupations while creating new ones.

Information at our Fingertips—the Smartphone

[15]In the first hundred years of the nation, the economy grew as the country expanded its geographical size. [16]Resources and markets increased as the nation moved west. [17]But after 1900, the economics of the United States were influenced more and more by events beyond the U.S. borders. [18]As world travel became cheaper and more available, world trade increased. [19]American manufacturers began selling (exporting) goods to foreign markets and American consumers started buying more and more goods from foreign countries. [20]At the same time, foreign manufacturers started selling more goods in the U.S. market. [21]Growing world trade was not always beneficial to every sector of the American economy. [22]Since U.S. wages were some of the highest in the world, some manufacturers moved their manufacturing—especially low-skilled labor manufacturing—to foreign countries with cheaper labor. [23]Many U.S. labor unions fought these moves, but as U.S. manufacturers competed against foreign manufacturers with lower labor costs, U.S. manufacturers claimed the moves were necessary to remain competitive against foreign competition with cheaper labor costs.

[24]Another problem for the United States, as the world economy continued to develop, was a growing U.S. trade deficit. [25]Since the United States and Western Europe had some of the highest wages and standards of living in the world, American consumers had a lot of money with which to buy goods. [26]As the world market continued to grow, more and more of these consumers bought lower-priced goods produced outside the United States instead of more expensive goods produced in the United States. [27]This drop in U.S. sales also lowered the number of workers needed to fill U.S. manufacturing jobs and increased the need for labor in foreign countries manufacturing and selling goods to American consumers. [28]In a market system, the cost of labor will eventually level out, but this can take years, decades, or even longer. [29]Lower labor costs benefit poorer countries by taking jobs away from wealthier countries, until labor costs in the poorer countries rise to a level equal to costs in the wealthier countries. [30]The decline in U.S. manufacturing jobs has resulted in a drop in U.S. manufacturing—especially low-skilled manufacturing. [31]The term used to describe


© 2016 The Critical Thinking Co.™ • www.CriticalThinking.com • 800-458-4849

these trends of national economic influences from international or world markets is called “globalization.”

## B. Population Changes

[32]In the first half of U.S. history, almost all households consisted of two married heterosexual parents with several children. [33]By 1960, three-fourths of American households could still be described that way. [34]But by 2005, only half of U.S. households could be said to be “traditional families.” [35]Single-parent families were more common. [36]Famiies were smaller in size, and, as a result of higher divorce and remarriage rates, often “blended”—consisting of children whose biological parents were not necessarily living in their home.

[37]America has always been a nation of immigrants. [38]Immigration showed vast changes from the late 1800s to the late 1900s. [39]In 1880, census records showed that the top five countries for foreign-born U.S. residents were Germany, Ireland, Great Britain, Canada, and Sweden—in other words, Northern European nations. [40]In the last quarter of the 1900s and the first quarter of the 2000s, illegal immigration dramatically increased in the United States. [41]Most illegal immigrants entering the United States were low-skilled workers. [42]Illegal immigration has also had an impact on the types of ethnicities coming to the United States for a better life. [43]Counting both legal and illegal immigrants who have entered the United States in the last 50 years, the top five regions from which foreign-born U.S. residents have come are Mexico, China, the Pacific islands, India, and Central America—in other words Asia and Latin America. [44]Demographers (people who study population patterns) predict that by 2050, 25 percent of Americans will have Hispanic heritage. [45]Non-Hispanic whites, once the majority of the U.S. population, will account for only half of Americans by mid-century.

**Figure 1. Number and Percent of Immigrants in the U.S., 1900-2010; Plus Census Bureau Projections to 2060**

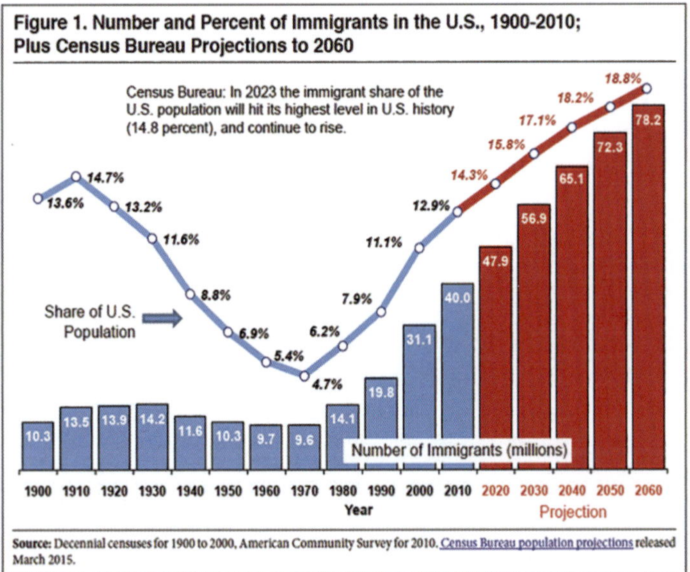


**Source:** Decennial censuses for 1900 to 2000, American Community Survey for 2010. Census Bureau population projections released March 2015.

[46]America is also aging. [47]Baby Boomers are living longer lives than earlier generations, and it is predicted that by mid-21st century, one of every five Americans will be 65 or older. [48]This will put increased pressure on our health care system, Social Security, and housing.

## C. Challenges

[49]In an age of great change, there will be great challenges. [50]As Americans, how will our politics, our education, and our occupations look in the future? [51]How will we conserve our way of life and high standard of living? [52]How will we conserve our resources and take care of our environment for future generations? [53]What is America’s role in the world? [54]How will Americans adapt to changes in the nation’s population?

[55]Some answers to questions like these can be found by studying American history. [56]Every American generation has faced great challenges. [57]Although we use different technologies today, Americans living in the 21st century will still need to approach solutions in a democratic and free society using principles established by our founders in 1787. [58]We must remember our history and learn from it in order to make wise decisions for the future. [59]Every citizen must be responsible for insuring that the goals listed by our early leaders are still valued and maintained. [60]The Preamble of the U.S. Constitution still speaks to us and acts as our guide:

> *We the People of the United States, in Order to form a more perfect Union, establish Justice, insure domestic Tranquility, provide for the common defense, promote the general Welfare, and secure the Blessings of Liberty to ourselves and our Posterity, do ordain and establish this Constitution for the United States of America.*

**Fun Fact Feature**

In 2015, the magazine with the highest circulation in America was one published by an organization called AARP. What does the RP in the acronym stand for (hint: it reflects our aging population)?

1. In the 21st century, two-thirds of Americans held which kind of job?
    a. white collar
    b. farming
    c. blue collar
    d. manufacturing

    Which sentences best support the answer?

    ______ ______

2. Most Americans lived in cities by:
    a. the 1880s.
    b. the 1920s.
    c. the 1960s.
    d. the 21st century.

    Which sentence best supports the answer?

    ______

3. What have computers and smartphones revolutionized?

    ______________________________

4. What is globalization?
    a. the problems of the environment
    b. the U.S. space program (NASA)
    c. a new kind of computer mapping program (GPS)
    d. how American markets are tied to world markets

    Which sentence best supports the answer?

    ______

5. By 2005, what percentage of American households looked like the "traditional family" of the 1800s?
    a. 90 percent
    b. 75 percent
    c. 50 percent
    d. 25 percent

    Which sentence best supports the answer?

    ______

6. What is a person who studies population patterns in society called?
    a. a preamble
    b. part of a blended family
    c. a demographer
    d. a white collar worker

    Which sentence best supports the answer?

    ______

7. What is one of the fastest growing population groups in the United States in the 21st century?
    a. Germans
    b. Scandinavians
    c. Non-Hispanic whites
    d. Hispanics

    Which sentence best supports the answer?

    ______

8. It is predicted that what percentage of Americans will be over age 65 by mid-21st century?
    a. 10%
    b. 20%
    c. 30%
    d. 50%

    Which sentence best supports the answer?

    ______

9. According to the Constitution, who is responsible to improve the Union, establish justice in the U.S., search for peace within our country, defend the nation, improve our economic well-being, and make sure that future generations also enjoy liberty and freedom?

    ______________________________

    ______________________________


© 2016 The Critical Thinking Co.™ • www.CriticalThinking.com • 800-458-4849

## Written Response Question

10. Look at the immigration graph in this lesson and use complete sentences to explain the information contained on the graph.

________________________________________________________________

________________________________________________________________

________________________________________________________________

________________________________________________________________

________________________________________________________________

________________________________________________________________

________________________________________________________________

________________________________________________________________

**Fun Fact Finale**

In 2015, the magazine with the highest circulation in America was one published by the American Association of Retired Persons. (AARP).

# Review: Lessons 51-56
# 1980s-21st Century Vocabulary

Write the letter of the definition of each vocabulary word. The number following each vocabulary word is the number of the lesson (51-56) where the word was used. All definitions are used once.

_____ 1. consumerism (51)

_____ 2. Internet (51)

_____ 3. yuppie (51)

_____ 4. apartheid (52)

_____ 5. sanctions (52)

_____ 6. coalition (52)

_____ 7. sponsor (52)

_____ 8. surplus (53)

_____ 9. perpetrator (53)

_____ 10. adultery (53)

_____ 11. intern (53)

_____ 12. hijack (54)

_____ 13. interrogate (54)

_____ 14. genocide (54)

_____ 15. compound (55)

_____ 16. bubble (55)

_____ 17. bipartisan (55)

_____ 18. deport (55)

_____ 19. levee (55)

_____ 20. globalization (56)

a. to increase, add to

b. international influences on world markets

c. to expel from the country

d. a relationship outside of marriage

e. punishments designed to cause economic hardship on an enemy country

f. a trainee or apprentice

g. to seize a vehicle by force

h. to question a prisoner for information

i. a temporary alliance or combination

j. increased purchasing of material goods

k. nickname for young, urban professionals

l. support from both liberals and conservatives

m. to support; a paid supporter

n. a price cycle characterized by rapid expansion followed by a contraction

o. a designed embankment to control river flooding

p. racial separation

q. more money gained than spent

r. a person who commits a criminal or evil act

s. the killing of racial, political, or cultural groups

t. an international network of computers sharing information


© 2016 The Critical Thinking Co.™ • www.CriticalThinking.com • 800-458-4849

# Answers

**Lesson 1** (p. 4)

1. (any seven) 1) California 2) Nevada 3) Montana 4) Colorado 5) Idaho 6) Arizona 7) South Dakota 8) Alaska
2. d, sentence 8
3. c, sentence 13
4. b, sentences 9, 10
5. a, sentence 24
6. a, sentence 27
7. c, sentences 36, 40
8. b, sentences 40, 44
9. b, sentences 11, 12
10. Key points:
    There were exaggerated stories about lawmen, cattle rustlers, and stage coach robbers; and tales about hunters and scouts. Native Americans were portrayed as villains, women as weak, and the western United States as an area that needed to be conquered. There were also stories about the fantastic geography of the West.

    Easterners learned about the West by reading popular dime novels from writers such as Edward Judson, seeing a Buffalo Bill Wild West show, viewing art pieces by Western artists such as Frederic Remington or Charles Russell, or by reading books such as Theodore Roosevelt's *How the West Was Won*.

**Lesson 2** (p. 9)

1. b, sentences 8, 9
2. d, sentence 14
3. Immense profits could be made.
4. a, sentence 18
5. (any three) 1) increase of railroads 2) settlers plow up prairie grasses 3) barbed wire fences 4) buffalo hunted for profit 5) government encouraged slaughter to eliminate Native American food supply
6. d, sentences 43, 44
7. c, sentences 51, 52
8. As Native American culture faded in the American West, the Ghost Dance told of a day when there would be a peaceful end to white expansion in the West, and the buffalo herds and dead relatives of Native Americans would return.
9. b and c, sentence 65
10. Key points:
    Many things in the mid to late 1800s interfered with the buffalo herds upon which the Natives were so dependent: cattle drives, settlement by whites on the Great Plains as a result of the Homestead Act, demand for buffalo products by Eastern markets, and the construction of railroads. New diseases brought in by the settlers killed many Native Americans. Efforts by the government to put Native Americans on reservations and assimilate them into white culture also caused problems for the tribes. Tribal use of the Ghost Dance brought fear to the government and conflict as well.

**Bonus Activity** (p. 11)

| | | | |
|---|---|---|---|
| 1. WA | 4. N | 7. WA | 10. WA |
| 2. C | 5. WA | 8. WA | |
| 3. C | 6. N | 9. C | |

**Bonus Activity** (p.12)

1. 1850
2. 1850-1870
3. 1870-1890
4. Oklahoma
5. Opened up for settlement
6. Desert (poor land)
7. Texas
8. South Dakota
9. Oregon Trail and transcontinental railroad
10. Dry, desert lands discouraged white settlement there.

**Lesson 3** (p. 16)

1. b, sentences 14, 15
2. America in the late 1800s looked successful but there were problems beneath the surface.
3. b, sentences 25, 26
4. a, sentences 36, 37
5. a, sentence 48
6. d, sentence 27
7. c, sentence 52
8. d, sentences 53, 57
9. c, sentences 6, 9, 10
10. Key points:
    The discovery of many mineral resources, the development of better transportation networks, such as railroads, new sources of power for industry such as electricity, immigration brought cheap labor, and no income tax for entrepreneurs.

**Lesson 4** (p. 20)

1. The American Dream was the idea that in this country one could rise above the social class one was born into and be prosperous and own property.
2. c, sentence 40
3. a, sentence 5
4. a, sentence 4
5. c, sentence 24
6. a, sentence 38
7. b, sentences 44, 45
8. c, sentences 38, 39
9. d, sentence 6
10. Key points:
    Labor unions worked to change long hours for low pay; unsafe working conditions; no health insurance, sick leave, or paid vacation leave; no laws against child labor; unequal pay for African Americans and women; violence against unions and striking workers.

**Lesson 5** (p. 24)

1. b, sentence 1
2. d, sentence 13
3. a, sentences 29, 30, 32
4. The harbor at the mouth of the Hudson River was the gateway into the U.S. for immigrants in the late 1800s.

5. a, sentences 15, 19, 26, 27
6. d, sentence 48
7. b, sentence 3
8. The Statue of Liberty symbolically lights the path toward opportunity in America.
9. c, sentence 52
10. Key points:
Hardships for immigrants from new parts of Europe include: difficult to assimilate their culture into American culture, discrimination from Native-born Americans, often lived in poor slum neighborhoods of cities, taken advantage of for political purposes from groups such as Tammany Hall.

**Bonus Activity** (p. 26)
1. Southern Europe
2. Europe
3. Asia
4. Central Europe
5. 1900-1910
6. Southern Europe
7. Chinese Exclusion Act
8. No
9. Higher in 1900-1910
10. Central Europe, 1900-1910

**Lesson 6** (p. 30)
1. c, sentences 12, 13
2. c, sentence 2
3. d, sentences 34, 35
4. Rates of tuberculosis, typhoid fever and other communicable diseases, as well as death rates of young children, dropped dramatically after 1900.
5. a, sentence 7
6. b, sentence 42
7. d, sentence 14
8. c, sentence 41
9. a, sentence 18
10. Key points:
Women were important in the reform movements of the late 1800s. They formed the YWCA, volunteered at the Salvation Army, were strongly behind the settlement house movement to help immigrants, and started the Women's Christian Temperance Union. Women such as Frances Willard believed that females had special virtues of compassion and nurturing that could help make important improvements to society within the home and outside of it as well.

**Lesson 7** (p. 34)
1. c, sentence 12
2. Unlike the portrait artists of the day who depicted the nice lives of the rich or idealized country life, Ashcan artists were painters and photographers who wanted to portray the realities of modern city living: poor immigrant workers, street kids, unsanitary urban conditions, or crime.
3. b, sentence 7
4. d, sentences 23, 27
5. c, sentence 44
6. a, sentence 33
7. b, sentences 30, 31
8. (any four) 1) singers 2) comedians 3) dancers 4) magicians 5) acrobats 6) animal trainers
9. d, sentence 37
10. Key points:
Wealthy people were more likely to attend operas or fancy parties and own pieces of portrait art. Lower class families were more likely to pay for the more affordable vaudeville shows or amusement parks for recreation. If they owned art it might have been from the Ashcan School of Art. Amusement parks such as Coney Island were places where a lower income person could go on a carnival ride, view strange people or animals in sideshows, and eat different foods. Lower class families could also afford cheap seats at baseball games or boxing matches.

**Lesson 8** (p. 38)
1. d, sentence 20
2. motion picture camera, escalator
3. c, sentence 24
4. c, sentence 38
5. a, sentence 53
6. Edison's inventions directly touched the lives of average Americans.
7. Edison's inventions were not random. He established a laboratory ("invention factory") that employed university trained scientists to regularly produce new technologies.
8. b, sentence 42
9. d, sentences 15, 27
10. Key points:
Students can choose any invention mentioned in the lesson, and must defend their argument about why it was the most important invention of that era.

**Review: Lessons 1-8** (p. 40)

| | | | |
|---|---|---|---|
| 1. g | 6. l | 11. c | 16. b |
| 2. p | 7. k | 12. f | 17. m |
| 3. n | 8. s | 13. q | 18. a |
| 4. h | 9. o | 14. r | 19. d |
| 5. j | 10. e | 15. t | 20. i |

**Lesson 9** (p. 44)
1. b, sentence 3
2. a, sentences 11, 14
3. d, sentence 17
4. b, sentences 25, 26
5. c, sentences 37, 43
6. Americans thought the government's purchase of Alaska was a worthless piece of property.
7. b, sentence 9
8. fertilizer and gunpowder
9. d, sentences 48, 49
10. Key points:
1) the desire for America to keep up with other imperialistic nations 2) the need for more raw materials for manufacturing 3) guano for fertilizer and gunpowder 4) the desire for new markets for goods, to bring western style culture and religion to foreign lands 5) to strengthen America's navy by having good harbors for coal stations

**Lesson 10** (p. 48)
1. c, sentence 4
2. b, sentences 14, 16, 17
3. c, sentences 28, 33, 34
4. a, sentence 43


© 2016 The Critical Thinking Co.™ • www.CriticalThinking.com • 800-458-4849

5. The war was short (only a few months), relatively few Americans were killed, and the USA gained several valuable Spanish territories with the victory.
6. d, sentence 48
7. b, sentence 63
8. a, sentence 61
9. a, sentence 52
10. Key points:
Symbols: newspapermen Pulitzer and Hearst, blocks of newspaper type, clothing represents "yellow journalism" with their words encouraging war, the word "war" is large—headline news

Message: The cartoonist makes these influential newspapermen look like children playing with blocks as if "war" is a game. They are arguing over who gets to "play" with this event.

**Lesson 11** (p. 52)
1. c, sentence 4
2. Roosevelt's wife died in childbirth and his mother died of a disease on the same day (February 14th) in the same house.
3. a, sentence 23
4. d, sentence 10
5. b, sentences 32, 33
6. c, sentences 51, 52
7. c, sentences 58, 59
8. d, sentence 41
9. b, sentence 29
10. Key points:
As a young politician fighting for New York state reforms, Roosevelt upset older politicians. As Civil Service Commissioner, NYC police commissioner, and Asst. Secretary of the Navy, Roosevelt was an aggressive, take-charge, administrator. Later as NY governor, he created a number of reforms which upset some powerful politicians who had previously held control of New York State and city affairs, such as those in Tammany Hall, as well as some big business owners.

**Bonus Activity** (p. 54)
a. 1, 3, 2
b. 3, 2, 1
c. 3, 1, 2
d. 2, 1, 3
e. 1, 3, 2
f. 2, 3, 1

**Lesson 12** (P. 58)
1. a, sentence 4
2. c, sentences 15, 16
3. c, sentence 24
4. d, sentence 33
5. a, sentences 35, 36
6. (any one) 1) supported unions 2) busted up monopolies 3) Pure Food & Drug Act
7. b, sentence 27
8. Symbols: (any two) 1) TR is the central figure dressed with weapons in his Spanish American War uniform (a powerful force) 2) the bears represent trusts or monopolies 3) a "White House" tent in the background symbolizes the presidency

Message: TR will control "good" trusts (such as the one on the leash), but will hunt down and eliminate "bad trusts" (such as the ones he has shot).
9. d, sentence 61
10. (any five) 1) National Child Labor Committee 2) direct primaries 3) women's suffrage 4) direct election of U.S. Senators 5) recall elections 6) referendum 7) initiative 8) secret ballot 9) the Elkins and Hepburn Acts 10) Mann Act 11) Federal Reserve Act 12) Harrison Act 13) 16th, 17th, and 18th Amendments 14) Pure Food and Drug Act 15) the Meat Inspection Act

**Bonus Activity** (p. 60)
1. f
2. d
3. a
4. h
5. g
6. j
7. e
8. c
9. b
10. i

**Bonus Activity** (p. 61)
1. Midwestern/Great Plains farm family
2. A dull, boring lifestyle (or) the hardships of rural farm life
3. Populist Party; Born in rural farming areas with promises to make life better for farmers
4. Wicked Witch
5. Yellow brick road (gold) and silver slippers (silver coinage)
6. Farmers; Working alone all day
7. Eastern factory worker; Not treated like a human being
8. Panic of 1893
9. Politicians or political candidates
10. Coxey's Army
11. Native Americans
12. President; A powerful executive leader who rules the land
13. American Dream

**Lesson 13** (p. 66)
1. b, sentence 3
2. a, sentence 9
3. When the *USS Oregon* took so long to travel from the Pacific Ocean to help out with the Spanish American War in the Caribbean, it showed the need for a quicker route between the two oceans for the American Navy.
4. a, sentence 22
5. d, sentence 31
6. d, sentence 41
7. c, sentences 29, 34
8. c, sentence 44
9. a, sentence 49
10. (any three) TR: 1) created the U.S. Forest Service to protect the wilderness 2) created national parks, national monuments, and wildlife preserves 3) acquired the Panama Canal Zone 4) sent the Great White Fleet on a world tour 5) believed in a "Big Stick" policy

**Bonus Activity** (p. 68)
1. North and South America
2. Atlantic Ocean & Pacific Ocean
3. north-south
4. railroad
5. Gaillard Cut
6. 80-90 miles
7. Gatun Lake
8. rainfall
9. Gatun Locks
10. Miraflores Locks

11. locks
12. raise and lower ships
13. gates
14. water

**Lesson 14** (p. 72)

1. b, sentence 8
2. Although all Americans were declared "equal," it was a method of keeping the races apart (segregated).
3. a, sentences 21, 22
4. c, sentences 28, 31
5. b, sentence 14
6. d, sentence 43
7. (any one) 1) White Progressives—and even a few prominent black Progressives—generally supported the idea of using "eugenics." 2) Many books were written on the subject and hundreds of colleges had courses on eugenics. 3) The theory of eugenics was popular in the United States and Europe in the early and mid-1900s.
8. d, sentence 42
9. a. concept of separate but equal (Jim Crow)
   b. (any one) 1) that the two types of fountains do not appear to be equal 2) ironic that both fountains are using the same water source yet are separated; the signs appear to be mixed up; a black man is drinking from the faucet labeled "WHITE."
10. Key points:
    Booker T. Washington urged black men to be patient about equality. He did not challenge segregation He urged accommodation (to "fit in") with white culture. He thought blacks should focus on vocational skills and occupations.

    W.E.B. DuBois argued against accommodation, was very critical of the Plessy decision, and said blacks should demand an immediate end to segregation. He felt that blacks could seek a classical education (training the mind) and develop leadership skills in law, politics, business, and other professions.

**Review: Lesson 14** (p. 74)

| Washington | Dubois |
|---|---|
| Tuskegee University | *Souls of Black Folk* |
| once a slave | 1st black Harvard PhD |
| Atlanta Compromise | civil rights immediately |
| focus on vocational skills | NAACP |
| *Up From Slavery* | *The Crisis* editor |
| accomodation | |

Both
improve conditions for blacks
highly educated
black leader

**Lesson 15** (p. 77)

1. c, sentence 12
2. b and c, sentence 50
3. a, sentence 15
4. He hoped that African lions might survive Roosevelt's hunt and even eliminate Roosevelt.
5. True, sentence 24
6. d, sentence 26
7. c, sentence 30
8. glasses on the moose and a toothy smile
9. b, sentence 44
10. Key points:
    a. Symbols: The elephant (an upset Republican Party, the Bull Moose or Progressive Party with glasses to represent Teddy Roosevelt, and the donkey (Democratic Party) ridden by Woodrow Wilson are symbols.
    b. Message: The equation shows that Roosevelt's Bull Moose Party is dividing the Republican Party vote resulting in Democrats winning the presidential election victory in 1912.

**Bonus Activity** (p. 79)

1. a. Theodore Roosevelt
   b. Navy boat; Big Stick
   c. U.S. assisting the Panamanian Revolution
   d. to exaggerate their power and influence
2. a. United States
   b. Northern Securities Company; Theodore Roosevelt
   c. President Roosevelt is shown as a trustbuster
3. a. William Taft and Theodore Roosevelt
   b. Roosevelt's initial support of Taft for president (1908) and later TR's attempt to win his own reelection (1912)
   c. TR had just come back from a big game hunt in Africa, (or) TR had been a cowboy and a soldier.
4. a. United States
   b. immigrants coming to the USA
   c. large amount of immigrants wanting to come to the USA
   d. set quotas and only allow a small percent into the country
5. a. to show power of big business/trusts
   b. child laborer
   c. They work long days and give profits to the trusts.
   d. Progressive Movement (or) trustbusting
6. a. Theodore Roosevelt
   b. muckraker
   c. scandal/concern caused by publication of *The Jungle*

**Review: Lessons 9-15** (p. 82)

| | | | |
|---|---|---|---|
| 1. i | 6. b | 11. a | 16. n |
| 2. j | 7. e or l | 12. l or e | 17. q |
| 3. o | 8. m | 13. t | 18. k |
| 4. r | 9. s | 14. d | 19. p |
| 5. f | 10. c | 15. h | 20. g |

**Lesson 16** (P. 86)

1. b, sentences 1, 2
2. Triple Alliance = France, Britain, Russia
3. c
4. d, sentence 42
5. d, sentences 49, 50
6. a, sentence 56
7. Wilson was reelected President
8. a, sentence 51
9. c, sentence 57
10. Key points:
    a. Wilson wanted to follow Washington's advice of not having the U.S. entangled in European wars. Also, we were a nation of immigrants and Wilson thought it would be difficult for the U.S. to choose a "side" in a European war.


© 2016 The Critical Thinking Co.™ • www.CriticalThinking.com • 800-458-4849

b. Americans eventually rejected neutrality because it created economic hardship in the U.S. and because German U-boats sank ships in neutral waters, which killed Americans.

**Bonus Activity** (p. 88)
1. The countries were located in central Europe between enemy countries.
2. French territories
3. Central Powers needed to divide the military forces and were "surrounded"; Allied Powers were separated from each other, making it hard to coordinate battle plans.
4. Lusitania
5. Belgium
6. United States

**Lesson 17** (p. 91)
1. d, sentence 6
2. b, sentence 12
3. Rankin was the first elected female U.S. senator
4. a, "Hun" was the unflattering nickname Americans gave to the Germans.
5. b, sentences 31, 32
6. c, sentences 40, 41
7. Uncle Sam (U.S. government)
8. c, sentences 41, 44
9. a, sentence 47
10. Key points:
Under the Alien and Sedition Acts anti-war protesters and immigrants were unfairly targeted for punishment by U.S government officials. Free speech was severely curtailed. People were jailed unfairly. The Red Cross would not allow volunteers with German last names to serve. Even some vocabulary words linked to German changed to more "American" versions.

**Bonus Activity** (p. 93)
1. a. U.S. government
   b. Eyes and finger follow the viewer.
   c. same colors as the US flag (red, white, blue)
2. a. enemy (Central Powers)
   b. Europe; he's coming across the ocean and we see war ravaged cities in the background
   c. join the military to fight the enemy
3. a. Statue of Liberty; She's a women dressed like the statue, especially the crown on her head
   b. Boy Scouts
   c. Buy a USA Bond to support the war effort
4. a. an American woman (or liberty, or patriotism); She's dressed in the U.S. flag
   b. Food Administration; create a Victory Garden
   c. Victory Gardens release other energies directed at the war effort.

**Lesson 18** (p. 97)
1. c, sentence 14
2. a, sentence 3
3. a, sentences 30, 32
4. d, sentence 42
5. The land between opposing trenches, "No Man's Land," became a difficult place to advance on the enemy. Both sides relied on new weapons to break the stalemate.
6. c, sentences 28, 29
7. c, sentences 47, 48
8. b, sentence 54
9. c, sentence 51
10. (any ten) 1) airplanes 2) machine guns 3) aircraft carriers 4) automobiles 5) tanks 6) U-boats (subs) 7) sonar 8) depth charges 9) radio 10) poison gas 11) gas masks 12) flame throwers

**Lesson 19** (p. 101)
1. a, sentence 3
2. American Expeditionary Forces (AEF)/Doughboys or Yanks
3. d, sentence 9
4. d, sentence 14
5. c, sentences 44, 46
6. The Russian Revolution of 1917 occurred and the Russian government took its country out of the war.
7. c, sentence 28
8. b, sentence 43
9. b, sentence 33
10. Key points:
The troops of the A.E.F. were fresh and eager to fight. French and British troops were worn out by long years of battle. U.S. troops helped to break the stalemate on the Western Front. Also, the collapse of one ally, Russia, left France and Great Britain with fewer troops and Americans filled that void.

**Lesson 20** (p. 105)
1. d, sentence 3 (or 18)
2. d, sentence 9
3. (any six) 1) Austria 2) Hungary 3) Yugoslavia 4) Czechoslovakia 5) Estonia 6) Latvia 7) Lithuania 8) Finland 9) USSR 10) Turkey
4. c, sentences 44, 48, 53
5. b, sentences 24, 25
6. d, sentence 28
7. After President Wilson's stroke, Edith Wilson tried to shield her husband from more stress. She screened all of Wilson's paperwork and allowed very few visitors—even the vice president—to meet with him. In some cases, it is thought that Edith even signed Wilson's name to documents without consulting him.
8. b, sentence 47
9. a, sentence 51
10. Key points:
The bridge in the cartoon represents the League of Nations or the Treaty of Versailles. U.S. President Wilson was key in designing the post-WW I agreements with his 14 Point Plan (on the sign). However the United States (Uncle Sam in the cartoon) did not want to be a part of the League. The Senate rejected the plan. The cartoonist suggests that without the United States, a key part of the structure (the League) would not succeed.

**Review: Lessons 16-20** (p. 108)

| | | | |
|---|---|---|---|
| 1. m | 6. q | 11. d | 16. l |
| 2. r | 7. a | 12. p | 17. t |
| 3. e | 8. o | 13. s | 18. b |
| 4. k | 9. c | 14. j | 19. g |
| 5. i | 10. n | 15. h | 20. f |

**Lesson 21** (p. 112)
1. b, sentence 4
2. d, sentence 16
3. If voting "wet," business and financial institutions prosper. If voting "dry," women, children, and families prosper.
4. c, sentence 19
5. c, sentence 53
6. a, sentences 25, 26
7. a, sentence 42
8. b, sentence 44
9. Harding's vice president was Coolidge, who succeeded him when Harding died in office.
10. Key points:
    Symbols: A teapot (representing the Teapot Dome Scandal) is running down governmental officials. A road sign shows these officials are connected with Harding's White House administration.

    Message: Teapot Dome is an oil scandal that will destroy White House officials.

**Lesson 22** (p. 116)
1. d, sentence 7
2. d, sentence 9
3. c, sentence 23
4. b, sentence 35
5. c, sentence 6
6. c, sentence 36
7. (any two) 1) Band-Aids® 2) insulin 3) antibiotics
8. a, sentence 53
9. b, sentence 32
10. Key points:
    Positives: 1) families could take vacations 2) new businesses such as diners, gas stations, fast food restaurants, and motels 3) can live outside the city and commute to work 4) more independence for women and teens 5) less isolation for farmers

    Negatives: (any five) 1) tractors increase production but keep prices low 2) passenger rail traffic declines 3) traffic jams 4) air pollution 5) traffic fatalities 6) decline in some businesses such as blacksmiths and ironworks 7) easier to skirt Prohibition laws

**Lesson 23** (p. 121)
1. b, sentences 5, 6
2. a, sentences 8, 9
3. (any three) 1) crossword puzzles 2) goldfish swallowing 3) Mah Jongg 4) flagpole sitting
4. b, sentences 20, 26, 33
5. sound and animation
6. b, sentence 36
7. d, sentences 38, 39
8. c, sentence 39
9. c, sentences 44, 45, 48
10. Key points:
    a. an old, poor black musician
    b. he sang and played a tune on a piano
    c. in a city on Lenox Avenue
    d. (any six) 1) melancholy 2) weary 3) drowsy 4) mellow 5) pale 6) dull 7) lazy 8) sad 9) raggy 10) rickety

**Bonus Activity** (p. 123)

| | | | |
|---|---|---|---|
| 1. k | 7. g | 13. r (or) s | 19. n |
| 2. s (or) r | 8. m | 14. b | 20. q |
| 3. t | 9. p | 15. f | 21. d |
| 4. i | 10. c | 16. v | 22. j |
| 5. e | 11. a | 17. u | |
| 6. l | 12. h | 18. o | |

**Lesson 24** (p. 127)
1. c, sentences 1, 2
2. a, sentences 3, 4, 10
3. c, sentences 12, 13
4. d, sentences 19, 20
5. b, sentence 35
6. b, sentence 27
7. a, sentence 40
8. d, sentences 44, 45
9. c, examples: Hemingway, Lewis, Fitzgerald
10. Key points:
    The tensions during the Twenties included: quickened pace of life, Prohibition, fear of foreign immigration, anti-Semitism, rebirth of the Ku Klux Klan, theory of evolution vs. fundamentalism, memories of the horrors of WW I, and a seeming loss of morality.

**Lesson 25** (p. 132)
1. a, sentences 4, 5
2. d, sentences 6, 7
3. a, sentences 24, 25, 26
4. c, sentences 28, 29
5. c, sentence 32
6. sentence 83
7. Americans will become even more prosperous with more spending ability.
8. a, sentences 52, 53
9. b, sentences 38, 40, 44
10. Key points:
    The triggers that put the Great Depression in motion were: 1) high import tariffs 2) debt accumulated from over use of consumer credit 3) poor farm prices 4) a long drought 5) a crisis in the banking industry 6) huge drop in stock market values after some people had over-invested.

**Review: Lessons 21-25** (p. 134)

| | | | |
|---|---|---|---|
| 1. h | 6. c | 11. t | 16. i |
| 2. k | 7. q | 12. e | 17. g |
| 3. f | 8. a | 13. d | 18. m |
| 4. r | 9. p | 14. j | 19. o |
| 5. l | 10. n | 15. s | 20. b |

**Lesson 26** (p. 139)
1. (any four) 1) Bonus Army march 2) business failures 3) bank closures 4) farmers losing their land 5) stock values down by 85% 6) one out of four Americans unemployed
2. b, sentence 9
3. c, sentences 15, 16
4. a, sentence 33
5. a, sentence 19
6. "fear itself"
7. d, sentence 20
8. b, sentence 51
9. c, sentence 36


© 2016 The Critical Thinking Co.™ • www.CriticalThinking.com • 800-458-4849

10. Key points:
    The "3 R's" of the New Deal were Relief (examples: bank holiday, Federal Emergency Relief Act, Home Owners Loan Corporation); Recovery (examples: Civilian Conservation Corps, Tennessee Valley Authority, National Recovery Administration, the Agricultural Adjustment Act); Reform (examples: Emergency Banking Act, Federal Securities Act, FDIC, an end to child labor).

**Lesson 27** (p. 144)
1. d, sentence 35
2. false, sentence 7
3. c, sentence 13
4. a, sentence 25
5. d, sentence 38
6. a. patient: Uncle Sam (USA) or U.S. economy b. doctor: President Roosevelt c. medicine: New Deal legislation; "new governmental agencies" or "alphabet soup."
7. a, sentence 54
8. c, sentence 42
9. b, sentence 49
10. Key points:
    (any three) 1) FDR's programs resembled socialism 2) higher taxes 3) more government regulation of businesses 4) growing national debt 5) growing size of government (bureaucracy) 6) New Deal did not do enough for the poor or elderly 7) Supreme Court declared some programs unconstitutional.

**Lesson 28** (p. 148)
1. d, sentence 5
2. a, sentences 19, 20
3. b, sentence 17 or 18
4. a, sentences 24, 25
5. radio
6. c, sentence 52
7. c, sentence 50
8. d, sentence 22
9. b, sentences 57, 58
10. Key points:
    The movie industry thrived during the Great Depression because: (any five) 1) color, animation, and sound improved movies 2) cheap entertainment as ticket prices were low 3) double-features available 4) drive-in theaters 5) themes of 1930s appealed to audiences 6) musicals 7) movie industry rating system.

**Lesson 29** (p. 153)
1. Democratic Party, sentence 9
2. d, sentence 15
3. FDR won by the largest margin since 1820 and his opponent did not even win over his home state
4. b, sentence 22
5. d, sentences 24, 25
6. b, sentence 52
7. d, sentence 53
8. The public thought it was a political move—the opportunity for the president to appoint more justices in an effort to control the court.
9. a, sentence 69
10. Key points:
    Eleanor was the "eyes, ears, and legs" of the president, she traveled all over the country to inspect New Deal projects and the living conditions of Americans and reported her observations to FDR upon her return to Washington, D.C. She wrote a daily newspaper column and relayed important information to FDR from the hundreds of letters she received daily at the White House.

**Review: Lessons 26-29** (p. 155)

| | | | |
|---|---|---|---|
| 1. k | 6. q | 11. a | 16. e |
| 2. n | 7. h | 12. s | 17. f |
| 3. l | 8. o | 13. t | 18. j |
| 4. p | 9. r | 14. d | 19. c |
| 5. b | 10. g | 15. i | 20. m |

**Bonus Activity** (P. 156)
1. a. President F. Roosevelt
   b. government spending
   c. FDR was criticized for always using government spending as the primary way to end the Great Depression
2. a. Congressmen
   b. Congressional bills or laws suggested by President Roosevelt
   c. FDR is making Congress work very hard.
3. a. President F. Roosevelt
   b. Democratic Party (and/or) FDR's critics
   c. FDR's proposal to add Supreme Court justices (or) "Packing the Court."
   d. FDR did not expect so much criticism of his plan.
4. a. President F. Roosevelt
   b. New Deal programs
   c. "Alphabet Soup"
5. a. President F. Roosevelt
   b. Older generation founding patriots (or) "Miss Democracy" and Uncle Sam
   c. an old horse-drawn cart vs. a new modern automobile
   d. The New Deal is modernizing the old Constitution, or the old guard is making way for the new.
6. FDR is never shown by the cartoonists to be handicapped by his polio.

**Bonus Activity** (p. 162)
1. America First Committee
2. Nazis, Hitler, or Germany; the Nazi symbol, the swastika is on his shirt.
3. It seems strange that Democratic Americans would join a dictator such as Hitler.

**Lesson 30** (p. 163)
1. a. Italy - Benito Mussolini b. Japan - Emperor Hirohito c. Germany - Adolf Hitler
2. c, sentences 5, 10
3. c, sentences 7, 8
4. Despite attempts at appeasement, Japan invaded China and Germany invaded Czechoslovakia and Poland.
5. a, sentence 23
6. d, sentences 31, 33
7. a, sentences 35, 36
8. (any three) 1) by creating alliances with Latin American nations 2) FDR asked for a larger military budget 3) increased production of military

planes, tanks, and weapons 4) a peacetime military draft (Selective Service and Training Act) 5) arming of merchant ships 6) Lend-Lease Act
9. b, sentence 52 or 61
10. Key points:
FDR was occupied by the crisis of the Great Depression. The American public was in an isolationist mood, not willing to involve their country in another disastrous war such as the Great War. The America First Committee was very strong and active; hope that a policy of appeasement would avoid war.

**Lesson 31** (p. 167)
1. d, sentence 4
2. a, sentences 11, 12
3. (any two) 1) U.S. demanded compensation for Panay incident. 2) FDR ordered that all Japanese bank deposits in the United States be frozen 3) All U.S. trade with Japan was suspended.
4. c, sentences 25, 26, 27
5. to avoid loss of American lives at sea
6. a, sentence 34
7. b, sentence 33
8. Henry Kaiser constructed a ship building plant in Portland, Oregon, that could turn out a cargo ship every day by the end of the war.
9. d, sentences 35, 36
10. Key points:
A year after Pearl Harbor, one-third of all U.S. factories were manufacturing military goods for the country and her allies. Two years after Pearl Harbor, the United States alone was making more war equipment than all Axis partners combined. By 1944, the United States was producing two-thirds of all the military gear used by the Allies. American businesses built more than 80,000 tanks and 300,000 planes in the war. Henry Kaiser's factories could turn out a cargo ship every day. The U.S. became the world's largest exporter of synthetic rubber. American scientists improved devices for detecting planes (radar) and submarines (sonar), built America's first rockets and produced new drugs, such as penicillin, to stop the spread of disease. They also constructed the first computer to calculate equations for the military.

**Lesson 32** (p. 172)
1. c, sentences 7, 9
2. b, sentence 12
3. b, sentences 16, 18
4. c, sentence 23
5. a, sentence 34 or 35
6. a, sentence 46
7. d, sentence 53
8. d, sentences 67, 68
9. c, sentence 77
10. Key points:
1) Battle of El Alamein (which secured Northern Africa for the Allies) 2) Battle of Sicily (which allowed the Allies to invade Italy) 3) Battle of Stalingrad in 1943 (stopped the Axis invasion of USSR) 4) Doolittle Raid (which boosted the morale of the American public about fighting Japan) 5) Battle of Coral Sea (which stopped a Japanese invasion of Australia) 6) Battle of Midway (wielded a serious blow to Japanese resources and stopped any plans of Japanese expansion toward the west coast of the U.S.) 7) Guadalcanal (America could now go on the offensive against Japan)

**Bonus Activity** (p. 175)
1. Germany and Italy
2. Great Britain
3. Switzerland
4. Soviet Union
5. North Sea and Baltic Sea
6. Mediterranean Sea
7. Egypt
8. Kasserine Pass

**Bonus Activity** (p. 177)
1. Korea
2. Manilla, Hong Kong, Singapore
3. no, only eastern China
4. Alaska, Hawaii, Philippines, Guam
5. Australia
6. Midway
7. Iwo Jima and Okinawa

**Lesson 33** (p. 180)
1. (any two) 1) two-thirds of female workers were over age 35 2) three-quarters were married 3) women took blue-collar (manual labor) jobs traditionally held by men 4) mothers left their children in the care of others
2. c, sentence 13
3. b, sentence 16
4. a, sentence 18
5. a, sentence 50
6. d, sentence 29
7. to release able-bodied men for fighting
8. c, sentence 55
9. d, sentence 46
10. Key points:
1) 350,000 women joined the armed forces
2) more than one million African Americans joined the military for the first time in U.S. history
4) African Americans were allowed to join the Marine Corps and the Coast Guard while the Army and Navy allowed training for African American males in combat positions 5) the number of African American military officers increased from five in 1940 to more than 7,000 by the end of the war
6) 25,000 Native Americans served in the military
7) more than 350,000 Mexican Americans also joined the Armed Forces

**Lesson 34** (p. 184)
1. d, sentence 9
2. c, D-Day, June 6; Paris, late August
3. c, sentences 19, 20
4. a, sentences 11, 12
5. b, sentence 40
6. d, sentence 28
7. German officials had systematically killed more than six million Jews and several million more gypsies, communists, Polish Catholics, and others deemed unfit to live under Hitler's rule in a program called the "Final Solution."
8. b, sentences 47, 48


© 2016 The Critical Thinking Co.™ • www.CriticalThinking.com • 800-458-4849

9. d, sentence 52
10. Key points:
    a. General Eisenhower; Lesson points out he was in charge of the D-Day invasion.
    b. Uncle Sam (symbol of the USA); His cuff has stars.
    c. Eisenhower is looking at the shores of Europe, which are on fire from the war and controlled by the Axis (evidence: flames and Nazi flag)
    d. "The Great Responsibility" reflects the importance of winning the upcoming battle and the fact that Eisenhower is responsible for so many lives of Allied soldiers under his command.

**Lesson 35** (p. 188)

1. a, sentence 3
2. a, sentence 4
3. d, sentences 8, 9
4. c, sentence 14
5. c, sentence 17
6. b, sentence 28
7. They were refugee Jewish scientists from the enemy Axis Powers.
8. a, sentence 31
9. "Victory Over Japan" Day, August 14, 1945
10. Key points:
    For: 1) Axis Powers countries might develop an atomic bomb before the U.S. if Japan did not surrender. 2) American forces would have to either invade the islands of Japan and risk an estimated one million U.S. deaths, or use the bomb and cause mass destruction in Japan. 3) Kamikaze flights indicated the Japanese would not surrender in conventional warfare. 4) To show U.S. strength in the post-war world and "make Russia more manageable." 5) To end the war before the Soviet Union joined the Pacific front to gain even more territory after the war.

    Against: 1) It would certainly cause mass destruction and death in Japan. 2) It was unfair to not truly warn the Japanese. 3) The U.S. should target the bomb at an uninhabited place to demonstrate its power. 4) The bomb was untested in war and might not work.

**Review: Lessons 30-35** (p. 190)

| | | | |
|---|---|---|---|
| 1. g | 6. m | 11. b | 16. s |
| 2. k | 7. a | 12. d | 17. h |
| 3. r | 8. q | 13. f | 18. c |
| 4. e | 9. o | 14. t | 19. p |
| 5. l | 10. j | 15. i | 20. n |

**Lesson 36** (p. 195)

1. (any two) 1) Americans disliked the communist form of government that ruled the USSR. 2) Communism was a threat to the U.S. capitalist economy and civil liberties 3) The USSR did not help the U.S. fight the Japanese in the Pacific. 4) The USSR controlled governments in Eastern Europe.
2. (any two) 1) United States did not send diplomats to the USSR after the revolution. 2) The Allies had taken too long to open a military front in France to relieve Nazi pressure on the Eastern Front. 3) Neither Presidents FDR nor Truman had ever told the Soviet Union about the development of the atomic bomb.
3. b, sentence 11
4. d, sentence 19
5. c, sentences 22, 24
6. c, sentences 26, 27
7. c, sentences 40, 41
8. United States, sentence 49
9. a, sentences 34, 35, 37, 38
10. Key points:
    a. atomic bombs, world, and a vise or clamp
    b. The world is being pressured and endangered because of the development of atomic weapons by the USA and the USSR. The screw is tightening.

**Lesson 37** (p. 200)

1. b, sentence 12 or 13
2. b, sentences 1, 20
3. South Korea, sentence 17
4. d, sentence 51
5. Korea remained divided with a permanent border at the 38th parallel.
6. c, sentences 31, 33
7. a, sentence 56
8. d, sentences 46, 47
9. a, sentence 58
10. Key points:
    "McCarthyism" still means using scare tactics, wild charges, and unconfirmed claims to personally attack people. It was a time of fear, bullying, and intimidation when freedoms and civil liberties were at risk.

**Bonus Activity** (p. 202)

1. b 2. June 1950 3. July 1953
4. Sea of Japan (East Sea) and Yellow Sea
5. Yalu River 6. 38° N 7. 100-125 mi

**Lesson 38** (p. 205)

1. 1946 to 1964, sentences 1, 2
2. 1957
3. d, sentence 15 or 17
4. a, sentence 70
5. (any four) 1) childcare books or paperback novels 2) comic books 3) baby products such as diapers, baby food, and toys 4) television 5) kitchen gadgets 6) fast food 7) automobiles
6. b, sentence 68
7. b, sentence 57
8. d, sentence 42
9. b, sentence 72
10. Key points:
    (any three) 1) Women were working in war production during WW II. 2) Men had enlisted or been drafted for war; after the war, men wanted to get married and settle down to a more normal, peacetime lifestyle. 3) Women were expected to give up their war jobs to returning servicemen and return to the "home." 4) Women married earlier than the previous generation, giving them more childbearing years.

**Lesson 39** (p. 210)
1. d, sentence 15
2. a, sentences 38, 44
3. c, sentence 10
4. b, sentence 33 or 38 or 46
5. a. Eisenhower
   b. USA, Britain, or the Free World
   c. Ike was a popular WW II hero with a strong military background. He was seen as moderate, non-political, and trustworthy.
6. a, sentence 55
7. the interstate freeway system
8. b, sentence 66
9. d, sentence 61
10. Key points:
    Truman was unpopular with the American public. Liberal Democrats who were upset that Truman had abandoned many New Deal programs reformed the Progressive Party and ran Henry Wallace as their candidate. Southern conservative Democrats, concerned with Truman's attempts to advance civil rights for minorities, formed the Dixiecrat Party. People made jokes about the president such as "To err is Truman." Many newspapers predicted that the Republican candidate would easily win the 1948 election.

**Lesson 40** (p. 214)
1. (any two) 1) Truman established the President's Commission on Civil Rights. 2) He issued executive orders that banned racial discrimination in hiring for federal jobs. 3) He ordered the desegregation of the military in 1948.
2. c, sentence 10
3. a, sentence 17
4. d, sentence 36
5. b, sentence 19
6. President Eisenhower, sentence 24
7. d, sentences 34, 43
8. d, sentence 42
9. c, sentence 50
10.

| | | |
|---|---|---|
| 1. d | 4. b | 7. h |
| 2. f | 5. e | 8. g |
| 3. c | 6. i | 9. a |
| | | |
| a. 1961 | d. 1946 | g. 1960 |
| b. 1954 | e. 1955 | h. 1957 |
| c. 1948 | f. 1947 | i. 1956 |

**Review: Lessons 36-40** (p. 216)

| | | | |
|---|---|---|---|
| 1. k | 6. l | 11. e | 16. s |
| 2. r | 7. o | 12. f | 17. n |
| 3. i | 8. m | 13. h | 18. b |
| 4. j | 9. c | 14. q | 19. p |
| 5. a | 10. t | 15. g | 20. d |

**Lesson 41** (p. 221)
1. b, sentence 24
2. c, sentence 8
3. d, sentence 54
4. c, sentences 69, 70, 71
5. d, The Soviet and U.S. leaders are both wrestling for power while "sitting on" nuclear weapons.
6. a, sentence 44
7. b, sentence 57
8. b, sentence 37
9. defense budget was at its highest levels of the Cold War
10. Key points:
    JFK was the youngest U.S. president ever elected. He said "the torch has been passed to a new generation of Americans." He challenged youth to serve their country and many worked for civil rights. JFK started the Peace Corps.

**Lesson 42** (p. 225)
1. c, sentence 2
2. The domino theory: If Vietnam fell to communism, other Asian nations would also become communist
3. a, JFK sent large shipments of weapons to Diem's government.
   b, By 1963, he had also directed U.S. special-operations military personnel to operate in South Vietnam as advisors.
4. d, sentence 26
5. b, sentences 31, 32
6. a, sentence 39
7. a, sentences 49,54
8. a, The slow pace of civil rights reform seemed to bring few economic gains (poverty rates were high among blacks). b, Graduation rates were low. c, Racial discrimination was still prevalent. d, Police brutality.
9. d, sentence 60
10. Key points:
    Television carried the Nixon-Kennedy debate, which influenced the 1960 election. TV brought home the Vietnam War to Americans. The JFK assassination and funeral events were televised. Much of the civil rights movement was shown on TV.

**Lesson 43** (p. 230)
1. d, sentence 69
2. b, sentence 40
3. b, sentences 6, 9, 16, 17
4. a, sentence 64
5. (any two) 1) Products for women were marketed. 2) Women's clothing styles changed. 3) More women than ever before joined the college ranks. 4) The number of women who worked outside the home tripled. 5) The Civil Rights Act of 1964 prohibited discrimination in the workplace based on gender. 6) In 1966, the National Organization for Women (NOW) was formed. 7) Title IX of the Education Amendments Act attempted to enact laws to give equality of opportunity at schools. 8) The pill became available, which allowed women to control when they could conceive children.
6. c, sentence 21
7. (any two) 1) A national day of environmental awareness called Earth Day was established. 2) The Environmental Protection Agency (EPA) was created by the federal government. 3) In 1973, the Endangered Species Act was passed.
8. (any four) 1) title "Woodstock Museum" 2) VW wagon 3) flowers painted on vehicle 4) 60's words like "groovy," "far out," and "right on" 5) statue of hippies 6) peace signs
9. 1. c 2. e 3. a 4. b 5. d
10. Key points:
    The hippie movement rejected materialism. The youth rebellion supported a strong environmental


© 2016 The Critical Thinking Co.™ • www.CriticalThinking.com • 800-458-4849

movement, women's rights movement, and civil rights for Hispanics and Native Americans. College campuses were vibrant places for protests and peace demonstrations. Youth influenced music, sports, and entertainment.

**Lesson 44** (p. 235)
1. b, sentences 17, 40
2. c, sentences 13, 14
3. False, sentence 1
4. 1st: Gulf of Tonkin Incident 3rd: 500,000 troops
   2nd: Operation Rolling Thunder 4th: Tet Offensive
5. U.S. military dropped chemicals, Agent Orange and Napalm, to defoliate the jungle
6. a, sentences 53, 54
7. doves, sentence 42
8. a, sentences 51, 52
9. (any two) 1) The U.S. military was making little progress. 2) Climate and vegetation of Southeast Asia made fighting difficult. 3) The enemy was hard to identify. 4) The enemy fought a hit and run style of fighting. 5) Troops died on search and destroy missions in the jungles when stepping on land mines or by triggering booby traps. 6) Direct confrontation with enemy was rare.
10. Key points:
    The person in the cartoon is President Lyndon Johnson as seen when comparing the cartoon with the photo in the lesson and noticing the date of 1966. The scar on his chest is in the shape of a map of Vietnam as seen when comparing it with the map in the lesson. The cartoonist is saying that the war in Vietnam has left a scar on an injured president.

**Lesson 45** (p. 239)
1. b, sentence 6
2. a, sentences 8, 9, 10
3. d, sentence 14
4. d, sentence 4
5. c, sentence 24 or 27
6. a, sentences 49, 50
7. c, sentence 30
8. c, sentence 38
9. b, sentence 35
10. (any three) 1) The end the war in Vietnam with plan called Vietnamization. 2) Bomb the nations of Laos and Cambodia to end Vietnam War. 3) Ease tensions with USSR with trade agreements and SALT talks. 4) Resume diplomacy and trade with China. 5) Support of China and end the oil embargo in the Middle East.

**Review: Lessons 41-45** (p. 241)

| | | | |
|---|---|---|---|
| 1. h | 6. n | 11. r | 16. g |
| 2. d | 7. b | 12. t | 17. f |
| 3. o | 8. a | 13. e | 18. p |
| 4. k | 9. s | 14. q | 19. i |
| 5. m | 10. l | 15. c | 20. j |

**Lesson 46** (p. 245)
1. a, sentence 1
2. d, sentence 3
3. d, sentence 4
4. a. The study exposed the fact that the U.S. had secretly bombed neighboring countries used by Vietnamese communists to smuggle arms and supplies into Vietnam.
   b. Both the Johnson and Nixon White Houses misled the public and Congress about the progress of the Vietnam War.
5. c, sentences 23, 24
6. False, sentence 30
7. c, sentence 33
8. c, sentence 51
9. a. Richard Nixon
   b. secret White House tapes
   c. *U.S. v. Nixon*
10. (any three) 1) Nixon administration used its influence with members of the FBI, CIA, and IRS to target people on an "enemies list." 2) Nixon tried to cover up the Watergate break-in by using federal agencies and witness bribery. 3) Nixon's staff had tried to erase some damaging evidence on the White House tapes. 4) Nixon had lied to the American public.

**Lesson 47** (p. 249)
1. Nixon's vice president, Spiro Agnew, had resigned over a bribery scandal.
2. b, sentence 7
3. a, sentence 10
4. Department of Energy
5. d, sentences 25, 26
6. b, sentences 20, 21
7. d, sentences 49, 51
8. c, sentence 39
9. c, sentence 33
10. a. Kennedy; assassinated
    b. Johnson; did not run for re-election
    c. Nixon; resigned over Watergate
    d. Ford; filled in for Nixon, Nixon pardon and bad economy—not reelected
    e. Carter; economy and Iran hostage crisis thwarts his reelection

**Lesson 48** (p. 253)
1. d, sentences 6, 7
2. c, sentences 11, 12
3. c, sentence 18
4. b, sentences 24, 25
5. d, sentences 39, 40
6. b, The really good careers tended to go to men, not women, and women with children did not fit the desired profile at all, despite the law.
7. (any three) 1) feminism 2) *Ms* 3) pro-choice/pro-life 4) sexual harassment 5) gender pay gap 6) glass ceiling
8. a, sentence 60
9. a, sentences 49, 53
10. (any five) 1) women elected to Congress 2) songs and magazines for women 3) the title "Ms" 4) women in professional sports 5) books on women's issues 6) *Roe v. Wade* 7) laws created to close the "gender pay gap" and sexual harassment 8) the idea of divorce became less taboo

**Bonus Activity** (p. 255)

1. String Art
2. Jogging
3. Disco Ball
4. Streaking
5. Afro
6. Bell Bottoms/Leisure Suit
7. Mood Ring
8. Pet Rock

**Bonus Activity** (p. 256)

| 1960's Events | 1970's Events |
|---|---|
| JFK assassination | Watergate |
| Great Society | Title IX |
| Woodstock concert | Ford pardons Nixon |
| 1st U.S. Moon landing | Disco music |
| "I have a dream" speech | Iran hostage crisis |

Both
Vietnam War
President Nixon
Anti-war protests
women's rights movement

**Lesson 49** (p. 260)

1. b, sentence 6
2. Reagan cooperated with the House Un-American Activities Committee by testifying before Congress and providing the FBI with names of fellow actors who he believed might have been communists.
3. c, sentence 17
4. d, sentences 2, 12
5. d, sentences 26, 30
6. b, sentences 60, 61
7. a. Sandra Day O'Connor b/c. (any two) 1) female in a judge's robe 2) law books 3) title with "Justice"
8. a, sentence 39
9. False, sentence 65 or 66
10. (any five) 1) 1950s testimony to HUAC 2) spoke of USSR as the "evil empire" 3) pushed large increases in defense spending, doubling the military budget to increase NATO power 4) backed a plan to finance an anti-communist army, called the Contras, in Nicaragua 5) sent 2,000 U.S. troops to the Caribbean island of Grenada to oust a communist regime 6) started SDI (*Star Wars*) defense system

**Lesson 50** (p. 265)

1. "It's morning in America."
2. a, sentence 23
3. d, sentence 9 or 17
4. b, sentences 57, 58
5. d, sentence 55
6. c, sentence 10
7. c, sentence 67
8. a, sentence 64
9. a. Iran-Contra Scandal
   b. Oliver North
   c. the American flag and the Constitution
10. Key points:
    Reagan increased defense spending to keep the U.S. military superior to the Russian (Soviet Union) military. As the U.S. capitalistic system outpaced communism in the USSR, some Soviet leaders questioned their type of government. Reagan called for the USSR to tear down the Berlin Wall. Reagan negotiated an arms limitation treaty. Reagan's actions brought the Berlin Wall down and the Soviet Union broke apart during the next administration.

**Review: Lessons 46-50** (p. 267)

| | | | |
|---|---|---|---|
| 1. n | 6. k | 11. o | 16. t |
| 2. f | 7. s | 12. d | 17. j |
| 3. l | 8. r | 13. i | 18. h |
| 4. g | 9. a | 14. m | 19. b |
| 5. e | 10. p | 15. c | 20. q |

**Lesson 51** (p. 270)

1. b, sentence 2
2. c, sentences 31, 32
3. a, sentences 25, 27
4. b, sentences 6, 7
5. c, sentences 17, 21
6. d, sentence 39
7. c, sentence 47
8. a, sentences 43, 44, 45
9. a, sentence 49
10. Key points:
    Surveys of yuppies showed that they were more concerned with making money and buying consumer goods than their parents and grandparents had been. American consumerism reached new levels in the 1980s—credit card usage was higher than ever before, *Material Girl* was a hit song, and many new items in technology provided ways to spend money.

**Lesson 52** (p. 275)

1. a, sentences 7, (8 or 9)
2. b, sentence 18
3. c, sentence 33
4. c, sentence 23 or 26
5. False, sentence 33
6. a, sentences 41, 44
7. d, sentence 60
8. a, sentences 14, 15
9. c, sentence 65
10. Key points:
    Bush looks hysterical and is making claims that were not accurate. The cartoonist is making fun of Bush's earlier "Read my lips…" statement on taxes. The president appears to be wearing a purse. The little bird in the lower right hand corner mocks the president.

**Lesson 53** (p. 280)

1. c, sentences 2, 8
2. d, sentence 3
3. a, sentence 8
4. a, sentences 42, 43
5. True, sentence 72
6. Nixon, Reagan, and Clinton
7. b, sentence 56
8. b, sentence 44
9. b, sentences 12, 21, 65
10. Key points:
    (any five) 1) U.S. involved in the civil war in Yugoslavia 2) more U.S. troops sent to Somalia 3) U.S. trade sanctions against North Korea which was building nuclear missiles 4) air strikes on a suspected chemical weapons plant in Sudan and on a terrorist training camp in Afghanistan run


© 2016 The Critical Thinking Co.™ • www.CriticalThinking.com • 800-458-4849

by Osama Bin Laden 5) conflicts in the Middle East between Israelis and Palestinians 6) Islamic extremists exploded a bomb under New York City's World Trade Center 7) bomb blasts killed Americans in several U.S. embassies in Africa and on a naval ship, the USS Cole, in the Persian Gulf

**Lesson 54** (p. 285)

1. a, sentence 9
2. a, sentence 16
3. d, sentence 26
4. b, sentence 27
5. False, sentence 60
6. c, sentences 57, 58
7. The 9/11 terrorist attacks had used hijacked American airplanes.
8. b, sentences 35, 40
9. U.S. troops were again fighting against Iraq and Saddam Hussein.
10. Key points:
    Shock and awe tactics forced the Iraqi government to fall. Saddam Hussein fled within one month of the start of the war and was eventually captured and hanged. However, radical Muslim groups who still supported Hussein continued to commit violence. They kidnapped and assassinated officials of the new government, detonated suicide bombs, and set off homemade bombs on roads throughout the country. Both American forces still remaining in the country and Iraqi civilians were caught in a civil war between two different Muslim factions. By 2008, more than 4,000 Americans had died in the Iraq War and more than 30,000 were injured. The war had cost 600 billion dollars to that point, with no end in sight.

**Lesson 55** (p. 290)

1. a, sentences 3, 4
2. c, sentence 14
3. a 700 mile barrier between Mexico and the United States
4. d, sentences 25, 26, 27
5. a, sentence 36
6. a, sentence 39
7. False, sentence 59
8. Obama was the first-ever president of African American heritage.
9. a, sentence 43
10. Key points:
    President Bush: (any two) 1) Foreign wars 2) education reform 3) immigration reform 4) Hurricane Katrina 5) the Great Recession
    President Obama: (any two) 1) the Great Recession 2) health care reform 3) foreign wars

**Lesson 56** (p. 294)

1. a, sentences 5, 6
2. b, sentence 4
3. communication (and/or the economy)
4. d, sentence 31
5. c, sentence 34
6. c, sentence 44
7. d, sentence 44
8. b, sentence 47
9. We the people (citizens) of this country.
10. Key points:
    The graph shows the number of immigrants coming to the United States since 1900 and projections about immigration up to 2060. It also shows, for those same years, the percentage of the American population who are immigrants. In the 20th century, immigration numbers held steady but the percentage of immigrants in the country generally declined. Since the 1990s, immigration has been on the rise and is predicted to continue to rise through the middle of the 21st century. By 2023, the U.S. is predicted to have its highest percentage of immigrant population in the nation's history.

**Review: Lessons 51-56** (p. 296)

| | | | |
|---|---|---|---|
| 1. j | 6. i | 11. f | 16. n |
| 2. t | 7. m | 12. g | 17. l |
| 3. k | 8. q | 13. h | 18. c |
| 4. p | 9. r | 14. s | 19. o |
| 5. e | 10. d | 15. a | 20. b |

# U.S. History Detective® Book 1

Sample
U.S. History Detective
Book 1
For Grades 8-12+

**Awards:** Creative Child Magazine Book of the Year Award
★Tillywig Brain Child

In this book, students will:

- Supply supporting evidence for many of their answers
- Supply essay evidence to support their conclusions by drawing on specific information from the lesson
- Draw inferences and conclusions based on their evaluation of the evidence
- Distinguish between facts and opinions
- Analyze historical chronology to see history as a series of interrelated events
- Acquire new vocabulary
- Learn to interpret and draw information from geographical maps, political cartoons, and charts

*U.S. History Detective®* can be used as a stand-alone textbook, a resource of supplemental activities to enrich another textbook, or as a review course for older students. The vocabulary and content skills are based on common state social studies standards for Grade 8.

What makes *U.S. History Detective®* different from other American history books is the integration of critical thinking into the content lessons. The questions in this book require deeper analysis and frequently ask for supporting evidence from the lesson. This in-depth analysis produces greater understanding, which results in better grades and higher test scores. Over time, students who practice critical thinking learn to apply it throughout their education and lives. This book also develops reading comprehension and writing skills, and challenges students to learn new vocabulary.

This textbook has both primary and secondary source information. Each lesson provides a passage students must read, followed by multiple choice, short answer, or short essay questions. Sample answers are provided which identify key points for the essays. In addition there are section review activities and some bonus activities.

Lesson 55

## Civil War Turning Point: July 1863

**A. Gettysburg**

[1]General Joseph Hooker, the general Abraham Lincoln appointed to lead the Union's military after General Burnside, did not last long following the Union's defeat at Fredericksburg in December 1862. [2]By the spring of 1863, Lincoln again had to find a new Union general to lead the Army of the Potomac after Hooker suffered a huge defeat at Chancellorsville, Virginia. [3]Robert E. Lee and Stonewall Jackson humiliated (loss of pride or dignity) the North despite having half as many soldiers in the battle. [4]Unfortunately for the Confederate States of America, Jackson was accidentally shot and killed by his own sentries as he returned from the victorious field of battle.

[5]General Lee then decided the South needed to take advantage of its momentum. [6]He marched his 75,000 troops out of Virginia and crossed into the northern state of Pennsylvania in June of 1863. [7]If the South could capture Washington, D.C. or Philadelphia, perhaps they could negotiate for independence for the Confederate States of America. [8]Heading into Pennsylvania along the western hills of the Appalachian Mountains, Lee targeted a small, but critical, transportation junction called Gettysburg. [9]Lee's rebel army needed supplies. [10]Gettysburg had a shoe factory and Lee was desperate to supply his men with new boots.

Gen. Robert E. Lee

[11]As Lee invaded the North, Lincoln replaced Hooker with General George Meade. [12]With 90,000 men, Meade met the Confederate troops at Gettysburg and engaged in a critical three-day battle. [13]Luckily for Meade, the Union was able to dig in on a high point of land called Cemetery Ridge which gave them an edge in battle. [14]On the first day of the fight, the Union was able to defend attacks at the north end of the ridge. [15]On the second day, Lieutenant Joshua Chamberlain defended the south end of the ridge on a hill called Little Round Top. [16]On the third day, Lee sent 15,000 rebel troops under the command of General George Pickett right at the center of the Union defenses. [17]Pickett's Charge was a disaster for the South. [18]Union troops killed, wounded, or captured over half of the rebels who charged up to attack Cemetery Ridge.

[19]On July 4th, a defeated Lee retreated south back into Virginia and never again tried to invade the North. [20]More than one-third (25,000) of his army had been lost at Gettysburg. [21]Seventeen of his generals had been killed. [22]Meade's army, too, had taken a toll. [23]In fact, between the two armies, over 51,000 men had been killed or wounded in the fight. [24]If Meade had pursued and defeated Lee on the 4th, the war may have ended that day, but Meade, only recently promoted, was cautious and also reeling from the battle. [25]Almost one quarter of his army suffered casualties. [26]Meade did not chase Lee's army and remained on Cemetery Ridge.

Battle of Gettysburg, Pennsylvania

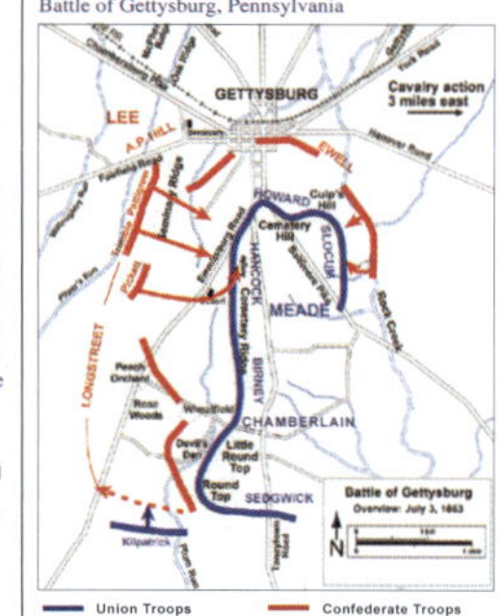


Union Troops — Confederate Troops

**B. Vicksburg**

[27]Just as Lee was retreating from Gettysburg, the South lost another crucial battle on the Mississippi River. [28]Vicksburg, Mississippi, was a town on a high bluff overlooking the river. [29]Southern artillery placed on the bluffs controlled all water traffic below. [30]In May of 1863, Union General Ulysses Grant surrounded the town for six weeks, preventing supplies from reaching Vicksburg. [31]Southern soldiers and citizens there nearly starved and were forced to eat mules, shoe leather, and even rats. [32]By July 4th, the rebels had suffered enough. [33]The 30,000 surviving soldiers surrendered to Grant on the nation's birthday.

[34]This victory at Vicksburg was critical to the North. [35]Vicksburg was the last remaining block to Union control of the entire Mississippi River. [36]Union troops and supplies could now be transported along the entire length of the river from Memphis to New Orleans. [37]In addition, the North had driven a wedge through the Confederacy. [38]Arkansas, Louisiana, and Texas were now cut off from the eastern part of the Confederate States of America. [39]Together, the Union victories at Gettysburg and Vicksburg on July 4, 1863, are considered the turning points of the war in the Union's favor.

Union troops siege Vicksburg on the Mississippi River.

**C. Gettysburg Address**

[40]It took some time to bury the thousands of soldiers who had died at Gettysburg. [41]The old burial ground on Cemetery Ridge had to be greatly expanded. [42]Many of the soldiers were unidentifiable. [43]Long rows of tombs marked "unknown" lined the new graveyard. [44]Local townspeople wanted the place to be dedicated as a national cemetery and, in the fall of 1863, invited the most popular speaker of the day, Edward Everett, to give the main speech. [45]About two weeks before the cemetery dedication, organizers also decided to invite President Abraham Lincoln to the ceremony. [46]They asked him to give "a few appropriate remarks." [47]On November 19th, 1863, Everett, a former senator and president of Harvard, spoke for over two hours. [48]Lincoln followed with a two-minute speech of only ten sentences now known as the Gettysburg Address.

[49]Lincoln understood the significance of the fact that Gettysburg had been secured on July 4. [50]He started the address with a reminder that 87 years earlier the Declaration of Independence said that "all men are created equal." [51]The battle of Gettysburg, he said, was "a new birth of freedom." [52]The Civil War was really a fight for human equality. [53]It was also, Lincoln said, a fight to see whether or not people could rule themselves in a democracy.

[54]Lincoln's speech was so short that many people in the audience did not realize he had even given it. [55]There was little applause. [56]Lincoln thought it a failure, but after the speech was printed in newspapers, people realized how great it was. [57]Edward Everett himself told the president, "I wish that I could flatter myself that I had come as near to the central idea of the occasion in two hours as you did in two minutes." [58]Lincoln's speech helped inspire Union soldiers to continue to fight and to win the war.

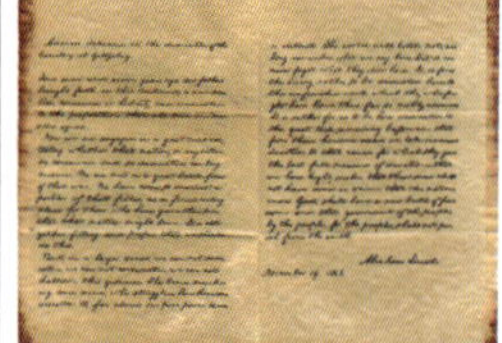

A Draft of Lincoln's Gettysburg Address

**Fun Fact Feature**

Besides the thousands of Confederate and Union soldiers who died at the Battle of Gettysburg, there were an estimated 3,000 to 5,000 of this kind of animal which died in the three-day fight. Can you name the animal?

1. After the Union defeat at Chancellorsville, Virginia, in December, 1862, who did President Lincoln choose as a general to replace Joseph Hooker?
   a. Ulysses S. Grant
   b. George Meade
   c. Robert E. Lee
   d. Edward Everett

   Which sentence best supports the answer?

   ____

2. Which important Confederate general was accidentally shot by his own men at the Battle of Chancellorsville?
   a. George Pickett
   b. Thomas "Stonewall" Jackson
   c. George Meade
   d. Joseph Hooker

   Which sentence best supports the answer?

   ____

3. What was General Robert E. Lee's strategy after winning the Battle of Chancellorsville?

   ______________________________

   ______________________________

4. What was the major reason the Confederate States of America was unable to defeat the United States at the Battle of Gettysburg?
   a. The North had better generals.
   b. The South had more men in uniform.
   c. The North had better momentum after the Battle of Chancellorsville.
   d. The North held the high ground at Gettysburg.

   Which sentence best supports the answer?

   ____

5. What could Union forces have done after the Battle of Gettysburg that might have ended the Civil War earlier?
   a. chase and defeat the retreating CSA army
   b. force the captured Lee to sign a surrender document
   c. defeated Pickett's Charge
   d. marched back to defend Washington, D.C.

   Which sentence best supports the answer?

   ____

6. Who was the victorious Union general at the Battle of Vicksburg?
   a. Ulysses S. Grant
   b. George Meade
   c. Edward Everett
   d. George Pickett

   Which sentence best supports the answer?

   ____

7. After the Battle of Vicksburg in 1863, what important piece of geography did the Union now control?
   a. the Confederate capital
   b. the Appalachian Mountains
   c. Chesapeake Bay
   d. Mississippi River

   Which sentence best supports the answer?

   ____

8. Who was invited to be the main speaker at the dedication of the Gettysburg National Cemetery?
   a. George Meade
   b. President Abraham Lincoln
   c. Edward Everett
   d. Ulysses S. Grant

   Which sentence best supports the answer?

   ____

### Book 1 Contents





© 2016 The Critical Thinking Co.™ • www.CriticalThinking.com • 800-458-4849